⧟ CATO ⧟
SUPREME COURT
REVIEW

2021—2022

CATO SUPREME COURT REVIEW

2021—2022

ROBERT A. LEVY
CENTER FOR CONSTITUTIONAL STUDIES

INSTITUTE
Washington, D.C.

THE CATO SUPREME COURT REVIEW (ISBN 978-1-952223-52-5) is published annually at the close of each Supreme Court term by the Cato Institute, 1000 Massachusetts Ave., N.W., Washington, D.C. 20001-5403.

CORRESPONDENCE. Correspondence regarding subscriptions, changes of address, procurement of back issues, advertising and marketing matters, and so forth, should be addressed to:

Publications Department
The Cato Institute
1000 Massachusetts Ave., N.W.
Washington, D.C. 20001

All other correspondence, including requests to quote or reproduce material, should be addressed to the editor.

CITATIONS: Citation to this volume of the Review should conform to the following style: 2021-2022 Cato Sup. Ct. Rev. (2022).

DISCLAIMER. The views expressed by the authors of the articles are their own and are not attributable to the editor, the editorial board, or the Cato Institute.

INTERNET ADDRESS. Articles from past editions are available to the general public, free of charge, at www.cato.org/pubs/scr.

978-1-952223-52-5 (print)
978-1-952223-53-2 (digital)

Printed in the United States of America.

Cato Institute
1000 Massachusetts Ave., N.W.
Washington, D.C. 20001
www.cato.org

Published through the generosity of George M. Yeager

Contents

FOREWORD

Can Originalism Work?

*Trevor Burrus**

The Cato Institute's Robert A. Levy Center for Constitutional Studies is pleased to publish this 21st volume of the *Cato Supreme Court Review*, an annual critique of the Court's most important decisions from the term just ended plus a look at the term ahead. We are the first such journal to be released, and the only one that approaches its task from a classical liberal, Madisonian perspective, grounded in the nation's first principles: liberty through constitutionally limited government. We release this volume each year at Cato's annual Constitution Day symposium on September 17th or thereabouts.

After 12 years of working on the *Review* in some capacity—first as an intern who laboriously (and, admittedly, often incorrectly) cite checked hundreds of pages, then a managing editor who kept the trains running on time, and then editor in chief for the last four years—this is the first time I am writing the foreword. I'm taking over from Ilya Shapiro, who edited 11 volumes of the *Review*, and who departed the Cato Institute in early 2022 for what we hope are greener pastures. Before Ilya, Roger Pilon, the man who saved me from a life of quiet desperation in corporate law, penned this foreword. I've turned over the task of writing the introduction to my colleague and the *Review*'s managing editor Tommy Berry, who also began as an intern working in the cite-checking mines. Now I get to write about the interesting theme(s) that emerged in the Court's most recent term.

At some point during every year that I work on the *Review*, I think about how quixotic the project is. "Writing and publishing a law

* Research fellow, Robert A. Levy Center for Constitutional Studies, Cato Institute, and editor in chief, *Cato Supreme Court Review*.

review in three months is a crazy undertaking," is a thought that will usually run through my head as I'm editing an article at 3:00 a.m., wondering whether I'm still on track with my deadlines. Only with the able assistance of my interns and colleagues—and of course our (usually) diligent contributors who actually write the articles on very short deadlines—would publishing the *Review* be possible.

While editing the *Review*, it can be easy to miss the forest for the trees and thus hard to find a theme for the term that underlies the decisions. Each article is an in-depth look at an often-monumental case that affects the lives of millions of Americans. Some of those decisions are blockbusters—front-page news—and some fly under the radar but are nonetheless momentous. Those who aren't dedicated Court watchers are often wondering what's going on within the black box of the imposing building at 1 First Street. Are the justices a super-legislature, our life-appointed lords and masters, wielding immense, unelected power?

During a single week in late June 2022, three decisions seemed to confirm to many that the Supreme Court had gone rogue. First, the Court decided that the Second Amendment protects an individual right to carry a firearm outside the home without second-guessing by government bureaucrats. The next day, the Court handed down *Dobbs*, overturning *Roe v. Wade*. Then, before the ink could dry on the jeremiads castigating the Court's audacity, the Court held that the EPA lacked the power to issue sweeping rules intended to counteract climate change.

Guns, abortion, climate change—it was a perfect nightmare for some. Four years of President Donald Trump and three controversial nominations to the Court had produced what many feared: a real-life *Handmaid's Tale* where women are incubators protected by brandished assault weapons while slowly melting from out-of-control climate change.

Originalists—who subscribe to the theory that the Constitution should be interpreted according to the original public meaning of the document's words when they were written and ratified—mostly had a different interpretation. Upholding the right to bear arms was adhering to the explicit words of the Second Amendment, and Constitutions are designed and intended to put some questions outside of the democratic process. Overturning *Roe* was a pro-democracy move, returning the question of abortion to the voters. And limiting the EPA's ability to pass sweeping rules to address climate change was also a pro-democracy move, ensuring that such "major questions" would be answered by a democratically elected Congress rather than bureaucrats. For originalists—at least in theory—the cases had little to do with whether carrying guns is good, abortion is bad, or climate change is a problem.

Thus, conservatives and (some) libertarians celebrated. Progressives recoiled. Conservatives felt their decades-long project of rescuing the Constitution from exile was finally coming to fruition. Progressives thought the Court had become essentially a right-wing dictator and seriously considered, and are considering, severe actions such as Court packing.

Originalists had hoped for a different reaction. They hoped that a concerted movement to rescue the Constitution and return the Court to its proper role would be seen as a restoration, not a revolution or coup. They hoped that, after the constitutional missteps from, roughly, 1930–1980, a Court that took the Constitution seriously would be seen as more legitimate and worthy of respect. They hoped that people would stop demanding that the Court and the Constitution give them everything they want and be an agent for fundamental social change.[1]

Now, more than ever, it's worth asking whether such hopes were ever realistic. Will the originalist project to rescue the Constitution ever be regarded as legitimate by a majority of the people? Do people want an originalist Constitution? Does it matter what they want?

I'm skeptical that the hopes of originalists were realistic, as I think anyone paying attention should be. Many people, on both the left and right, don't seem to want justices who strive to interpret the Constitution impartially. In the wake of the *Dobbs* decision, some of my progressive friends asked me what I thought. I'm not an expert on the Fourteenth Amendment, so I'm still ruminating on *Dobbs*, but, I told them, it is possible to be anti-*Roe*, pro-choice, and pro-life. They were confused. I explained that it is possible to believe that *Roe* was bad constitutional law, that every state should pass pro-choice legislation, and to be generally against abortion. "How?" they asked. "Well, in the same way I think the federal drug war is unconstitutional,

---

[1] Some originalists will argue that I'm mischaracterizing their position as overly Pollyannaish, which is fair, but I think many will agree that such hopes were at least in the back of their minds.

every state should legalize all drugs, and you generally shouldn't take heroin," I responded. They were still confused.

For too many, if they like a policy, it's constitutional; if they don't, it's not. That's true for both sides, of course, as conservatives also tend to find in the Constitution—or not find—those things they like. It's hard to imagine how the hopes of originalism can be realized if more people don't realize that the Constitution, whatever it means and however it is interpreted, does not and should not perfectly align with our policy preferences.

During that consequential week in June when many progressives felt that the world was coming down around them, I found myself wishing for more constitutional literacy, as people in my profession so often do. Do people really understand what the Court does, its role in our constitutional republic? Or, for that matter, do they know what the Constitution says, such as, for example, that Congress has limited and enumerated powers? Civic literacy has been in the doldrums for some time, so I'm not optimistic about public knowledge on these questions.[2]

For many people, the Republican-appointed justices issued those fateful opinions for very simple reasons: they love guns, hate abortion, and are skeptical of climate change. I'm not a mind reader, but I'm confident that, in the minds of the Republican-appointed justices, they were doing their jobs as described and ordained by the Constitution. They are charged with interpreting and applying the law, not with making policy decisions. Through ratification, the Constitution and its amendments placed certain questions outside the democratic process, ensuring that populist waves of voter ire could not upset the cherished rights of a liberal democracy, such as the rights of free speech, religion, self-defense, and due process for the accused.

To those justices, policy-based arguments are usually unhelpful and/or irrelevant. Perhaps carrying guns causes social harms that outweigh the benefits, but if the Constitution, properly interpreted, protects the right to carry guns, then the relevant policy decision

---

[2] I couldn't find polling on these specific questions, but for a discussion of the problem of American civic illiteracy in general, see Judge Don. R. Willett, Flunking the Founding: Civic Illiteracy and the Rule of Law, 2020–2021 Cato Sup. Ct. Rev. 13 (2021).

was made when the amendment was ratified. Until the Constitution is amended, that right is protected despite the social harms.

Some people value certain constitutional rights more than others, and thus the right carries more weight for them against perceived social costs. Gun-rights advocates understand that guns can have large social costs, but they believe the costs are worth the benefits. Similarly, some people place great value on the rights of the accused, which also carry social costs. The right to be free from unreasonable searches and seizures can prevent police from solving crimes and even let accused criminals go free. And the right to freedom of speech allows people to spew hateful rhetoric, to disseminate misinformation, and to flood the airwaves with misleading political ads.

Under one theory of judging, the judge is supposed to ignore such value judgments when interpreting the Constitution. Are misleading political ads bad? Maybe, but the question is whether they are an example of "speech" protected by the First Amendment.[3] Should more power be given to executive agencies to use their expertise to craft specialized regulations? Perhaps, but does the Constitution allow Congress to delegate its legislative power in that way?

Originalism is a theory partially intended to keep value judgments out of judges' reasoning. In the wake of perceived missteps by the Warren and Burger Courts—including *Roe v. Wade*—the first wave of modern originalists believed that the Court had strayed too far from the original meaning of the Constitution. From the massive government programs created by the New Deal and eventually approved by the Supreme Court, to the perceived extra-constitutional expansion of the rights of the accused in cases like *Miranda v. Arizona*, the justices of those eras were thought to be behaving more like a super-legislature than a court—if they liked a law they voted to uphold it, and if not they didn't.

Originalists don't like that theory of judging, and they think something should be done about it. A Supreme Court that doesn't behave like a court is deeply damaging to the country. People keep asking the Court to decide questions that are properly left to the legislature or other political processes. Increasingly, it is a common belief that all Good Things, however defined, can be found in the Constitution.

---

[3] Political speech protected by the First Amendment still undergoes a balancing test, but even under strict scrutiny, the restrictions usually lose.

The only problem is finding enough justices who understand what the Good Things are and can "find" them in the Constitution.

But originalists are often criticized, with good reason, for masking their own preferences in a theory of "impartial judging." Not coincidentally, it is argued, "impartially" interpreting the Constitution according to the original public meaning often yields results that originalists normatively want. Originalists tend to think that the expansive welfare programs of the New Deal are not just bad ideas but also unconstitutional according to the original public meaning. An originalist interpretation of the religion clauses of the First Amendment does not prohibit crosses on public land nor the funding of religious private schools through a tax-credit system, two things that conservatives generally favor as policies. And, of course, an originalist interpretation of the Fourteenth Amendment, it was claimed (and eventually held), does not contain a right to an abortion. Critics wonder whether it is really a theory of impartial judging that is being articulated or just a convenient way for conservatives to get what they want through "impartial" judging.

To be sure, many self-proclaimed originalists often seem to set aside their theories when it comes to criminal justice issues. In *Gonzales v. Raich*, for example, Justice Antonin Scalia voted to uphold the federal prohibition on cultivating medical marijuana, despite that cultivation being legal under state law. The issue concerned the breadth of Congress's commerce power, something Scalia had recently twice voted to limit. When it came to the drug war, however, it seemed something was different. Did Scalia's presumably anti-marijuana views win out over his vaunted hard-line originalism?

And originalists seem to spend more time complaining about the size of federal programs and cases like *Roe* and *Lawrence v. Texas*, which found a right to same-sex intimacy in the Fourteenth Amendment, than they do about mass incarceration and undercutting the rights of criminal defendants. In 1978, in *Bordenkircher v. Hayes*, the Court upheld essentially unlimited coercion of defendants through plea bargaining, allowing prosecutors to threaten the accused with extreme sentences for having the temerity to ask for a trial. The Framers and ratifiers of the Constitution, who viewed the jury trial as one of the most important safeguards of liberty and protected it with numerous clauses in both the original Constitution and the Bill of Rights, would have a huge problem with *Bordenkircher*. But law-and-order conservatives who are self-styled originalists seem to rarely bring up criminal justice cases. Can the originalism project work if it is perceived to be half-hearted and selectively applied?

Some conservative legal scholars have decided that originalism is never going to work, and that it was only useful because it met "the political and rhetorical needs of legal conservatives struggling against an overwhelmingly left-liberal legal culture."[4] Those are the words of Harvard law professor Adrian Vermeule, who is probably the most prominent advocate of so-called "common-good constitutionalism." Common-good constitutionalism calls on conservatives to stop pretending that the Constitution should be interpreted impartially, or even that it can be. The "starting point" is to interpret the "majestic generalities and ambiguities of the written Constitution" in light of "substantive moral principles that conduce to the common good." For Vermeule, that means old conservative values centered around family, traditional hierarchies, and "a candid willingness to 'legislate morality.'"

Vermeule's views fit well with the politics of Donald Trump. For many of his supporters, Trump was refreshing because he took off the gloves and went straight to fighting the culture wars. Many on the American right were tired of being "civil" to the left, and Trump was, and is, a hurricane of incivility. Common-good constitutionalism is a theory designed to allow some conservatives to get what they want out of the Constitution by ignoring it. They think that's what progressives did to get what they wanted, and if you can't beat them with purported "impartial" theories of judging, you might as well join them.

But that approach turns a constitutional order into a Hobbesian battle, and it asks judges to be warriors in that battle. For a judge fighting that battle, why even issue a long-winded, citation-heavy written opinion? Just write, "I like this" and be done with it.

Originalism strives for more, as do other theories of impartial judging. And although judgments often don't come from pure impartiality, a liberal constitutional order demands a theory of impartial judging. But will an increasingly partial populace be able to recognize impartial judging when it occurs? On that question, I'm pessimistic.

[4]Adrian Vermeule, Beyond Originalism, The Atlantic (Mar. 31, 2020), https://bit.ly/3QsrNah.

Introduction

*Thomas A. Berry**

This is the 21st volume of the *Cato Supreme Court Review*, the nation's first in-depth critique of the Supreme Court term just ended, plus a look at the term ahead. This is also my second year as managing editor of the *Review*. With Trevor Burrus assuming the duties of writing this year's foreword, it falls to me for the first time to write this introduction.

While the personnel behind the *Review* may change, its core purpose and unique speed remain the same. We release the *Review* every year in conjunction with our annual Constitution Day symposium, less than three months after the previous term ends and two weeks before the next term begins. It would be almost impossible to publish a journal any faster, and credit for that goes first and foremost to our authors, who year after year meet our unreasonable but necessary demands and deadlines.

This isn't a typical law review. We want you to read this, even if you're not a lawyer. We don't want to scare you off with lots of weird Latin phrases, page-long footnotes, or legalistic jargon. And we don't want to publish articles that are on niche topics, of interest only to the three other academics who write on the same topic. Instead, we publish digestible articles that help Americans understand the decisions of their highest court and why they matter, in plain English.

And as both Trevor and Ilya Shapiro were wont to note in the introductions to previous volumes, we freely confess our biases. We start from the first principles: We have a federal government of limited powers, those powers are divided among the several branches, and individuals have rights that act as shields against those powers. We take seriously those liberty-protective parts of

* Research fellow, Robert A. Levy Center for Constitutional Studies, Cato Institute, and managing editor, *Cato Supreme Court Review*.

the Constitution that have been too often neglected, including the affirmation of unenumerated rights in the Ninth Amendment and the reservation of legislative power to only the *legislature* (not the president) in Article I.

We also reject the tired dichotomy of judicial "restraint" versus "activism." We urge judges to engage with and follow the law, which includes most importantly the Constitution. If that means invalidating a statute or regulation, it is the judiciary's duty to do so, without putting a "deferential" thumb on the scale in favor of the elected branches. At the same time, judges should not be outcome oriented. Some decisions may lead to a bad *policy* outcome, but that's not an argument that the decision was *legally* wrong. Indeed, any honest legal philosophy must sometimes lead to policy outcomes a judge doesn't prefer, or else it is not really a *legal* methodology.

Our articles this year exemplify several of those themes. One author, Jonathan Adler, believes that addressing climate change is "one of the most pressing policy concerns of the 21st century." Yet, as he explains in his contribution to this volume, such a *policy* argument does not answer the *legal* question of whether an EPA regulation addressing climate change was authorized by the Clean Air Act. Respect for the separation of powers sometimes requires saying that an action is good policy, but bad law.

In a similar vein, as Jennifer Mascott and Trent McCotter note in their article on *Egbert v. Boule*, there is a strong policy argument in favor of allowing suits for damages against government agents for violations of constitutional rights. But, they explain, that does not necessarily mean the Constitution authorizes the *courts*, rather than Congress, to make that policy.

Those authors also demonstrate another core value of the *Review*: We acknowledge that many cases are hard and that people of good faith can disagree on both outcomes and reasoning. We don't want the *Review* to simply echo every Cato position on every case; if we did, we could just reprint the amicus briefs we filed throughout the year. Rather, we gather a stellar group of authors we respect and give them the freedom to write what they believe. Sometimes, as in the case of Mascott and McCotter's article, our authors take a position on the opposite side of a Cato amicus brief. Sometimes, as in the case of Evan Bernick's article on *Dobbs*—the monumental case that overturned *Roe v. Wade*—our author takes a strong position in a case where Cato chose not to file a brief at all.[1]

We fully acknowledge that lawyers applying originalism, textualism, and a presumption of liberty can reach differing conclusions on the same cases. We believe that the differing views of authors who broadly share our judicial philosophies are evidence of the strengths and nuances of these theories, not of their weakness or under-determinacy.

* * *

This term the Court's operations approached something closer to normalcy, without getting all the way there. After instituting remote telephonic oral arguments in 2020 in response to the pandemic, the Court finally returned to its marble home for in-person arguments in October 2021. But while the Court, the lawyers, and credentialed reporters got to be in the room where it happened, the general public was still excluded on public-health grounds. Given that we are not likely to have televised hearings any time soon, the continued exclusion of the general public from even the few limited in-person seats is a blow to transparency.[2] In normal times, it is at least theoretically possible for anyone on any given day to see what the Court looks like as it ponders its cases. This year, in a highly contentious term, we had to rely on a few Supreme Court reporters for first-hand accounts of the justices' alleged shrugs and eye rolls from the bench. We can only hope that in the upcoming term the Court will allow some members of the general public back inside its walls.

This term was also unusual for the historically early retirement announcement (relative to the end of the term) of Justice Stephen Breyer. With Judge Ketanji Brown Jackson's swift confirmation to his seat, Breyer spent the latter months of the term in the unusual posture of a lame-duck justice, knowing that his days on the Court were numbered and that his confirmed successor was waiting in the wings. Fortunately, there is no evidence that this knowledge put

---

[1] For a thorough explanation of the reasons why Cato did not file a brief in that case, see Clark Neily & Jay Schweikert, The Hard Problem of Abortion Rights, Cato at Liberty (blog) (June 24, 2022), https://bit.ly/3QsQdjZ.

[2] To give credit where it is due, the Court continued its welcome practice from last term of live-streaming the audio of oral arguments.

Breyer in a funk, as his questions from the bench remained cheerful and whimsical to the last day. And rather than enjoy a well-earned retirement, Justice Breyer has instead jumped right back into the academic career that he had to (mostly) leave behind when elevated to the high court. Now again on the faculty at Harvard Law School, Breyer will hopefully have the chance to bat around long-winded hypotheticals with many lucky students in the seminar room for many years to come. We congratulate Justice Breyer on a long and distinguished judicial career, and congratulations are also warranted for Justice Jackson, the first female African-American justice, who will stake out her own role on the Court in the terms ahead.

Finally, this term was of course extremely unusual for the shocking leak of a draft of Justice Samuel Alito's majority opinion in *Dobbs*. With the leaker still not publicly identified as of this writing, it remains to be seen how this breach of the Court's confidences will affect its work going forward. Perhaps surprisingly, the Court met its customary end-of-June deadline for issuing opinions even as the leak investigation continued. But it seems certain that internal procedures and security will have to change in some ways in terms to come. Court watchers will be looking closely for any signs that the Court's output might also change as a result.

As for the statistics from this past term, just one speaks volumes for the current balance of the Court: each justice's percentage of cases voting in the majority. A glance at the relative rankings reveals three distinct tiers of success, which (roughly) map onto the Court's ideological wings.[3] In the center, and dominating the success rates, are Chief Justice John Roberts (95 percent in the majority), Justice Brett Kavanaugh (95 percent), and Justice Amy Coney Barrett (90 percent). In the next tier, what might be called the "right" tier, are Justices Alito (85 percent), Clarence Thomas (80 percent), and Neil Gorsuch (75 percent). And finally, at the low end of the success-rate curve is the "left" tier, consisting of Justices Elena Kagan (69 percent), Breyer (68 percent), and Sonia Sotomayor (58 percent). Sotomayor's record of being in the majority in only 58 percent of cases is particularly notable as the lowest mark for any of the currently sitting justices in at least the last 10 years (the next closest was Justice Thomas at 61 percent in the 2014–2015 term).

---

[3] All statistics come from Angie Gou, Ellena Erskine, & James Romoser, STAT PACK for the Supreme Court's 2021–2022 Term, SCOTUSblog (July 1, 2022), https://bit.ly/3C7KsEi.

Still, while "left, right, and center" might work as a rough general heuristic to describe these three tiers, the reality in individual cases is often more complicated. The prime example from this term is *Concepcion v. United States*, the only case to have Chief Justice Roberts, Justice Kavanaugh, and Justice Barrett all in dissent. Justices Thomas and Gorsuch joined the three "liberal" justices in interpreting the First Step Act to provide defendants with greater opportunities for arguments at resentencing, demonstrating that their textualist methodology can sometimes lead to more "liberal" results if that's where the statutory text lies. It is thus not strictly true that you have to win at least one justice from the "center" bloc to win a case at this Court, but it certainly helps.

* * *

Turning to this year's *Review*, we begin as always with last year's annual B. Kenneth Simon Lecture. Professor Rachel Barkow of NYU Law School offers a sweeping critique of the Supreme Court's "almost complete abdication to the government in criminal proceedings—in spite of clear constitutional language to the contrary." Barkow identifies several key Supreme Court decisions that have led to the rise of mass incarceration in the United States since the early 1970s. These include decisions giving the green light to coercive plea bargaining, pretrial detention, and excessively long sentences. Barkow identifies the lack of justices with any criminal defense experience as one explanation for these consistently pro-prosecution rulings. Barkow urges that more judges with defense experience be appointed to the bench, to lend their critical perspective.

Barkow's advice has been followed in the year since she delivered the lecture, with Ketanji Brown Jackson becoming the first Supreme Court justice with criminal defense experience since Thurgood Marshall. It remains to be seen whether that new perspective on the Court will temper the reflexive deference toward police and prosecutors that Barkow describes.

Next, Jonathan Adler of Case Western Reserve University School of Law writes on *West Virginia v. EPA*. Adler explains the significance of the Court "invoking the 'major questions doctrine' for the first time in a majority opinion." By doing so, the Court "bolstered the argument that delegations of broad regulatory authority should not be lightly presumed." Nonetheless, Adler finds that the Court provided "little clarity on how the invigorated major questions doctrine should inform statutory interpretation." The decision thus "represents a missed opportunity to clarify and ground the major questions doctrine." To fill this gap, Adler proposes a fleshed-out version of the major questions inquiry, under which courts should ask whether the evidence of an asserted delegation of authority "is commensurate with the nature of the authority asserted."

Ilya Somin of George Mason's Scalia Law School tackles the Court's two vaccine mandate cases, *NFIB v. OSHA* and *Biden v. Missouri*. Given that one decision struck down a mandate and the other upheld a mandate, Somin notes that he is perhaps "one of the relatively few observers who believe the Court got both cases right." Nonetheless, Somin finds that "there are notable flaws and omissions in the majority's reasoning in both cases," and that the opinion striking down OSHA's mandate in particular "got the right result in part for the wrong reasons." Somin explains why the polarized and partisan reactions to the two rulings have been shortsighted and why "Americans across the political spectrum have much to gain from judicial enforcement of limits on executive power." And Somin concludes by noting that "the significant missteps in the reasoning of both cases—especially *NFIB*—reinforce arguments for reform of the shadow docket."

Cato's own Will Yeatman tackles two administrative law cases that both concern regulations issued by the Department of Health and Human Services, and thus both carry the name of the secretary, Xavier Becerra. In the two cases, the Court surprisingly declined to even mention the doctrine of *Chevron* deference, under which courts defer to an agency's reasonable interpretation of an ambiguous law. Yeatman explores the potential meaning behind this silence and questions the "conventional wisdom" that the Court was sending a signal to lower courts "to pay closer attention to the text." Instead, Yeatman suggests that two other factors were at play and contributed to *Chevron*'s absence: a risk-averse litigation strategy by the federal government and deep-seated disagreement within the Court on the continuing wisdom of *Chevron*. Yeatman concludes by noting that if a majority of the Court wishes to rein in the deference often shown by lower courts, "this muted strategy is unlikely to succeed."

Jennifer Mascott and Trent McCotter, also of George Mason's Scalia Law School, write on *Egbert v. Boule*, a case about remedies for constitutional wrongs. They recount a case with perhaps the most colorful background facts of any this term, centering on a hotel at the U.S.-Canada border called the "Smuggler's Inn." After the inn's owner alleged that a border patrol agent assaulted him, the case eventually reached the Court on the question whether the owner could sue for money damages for this alleged constitutional violation. Continuing a consistent trend in its decisions stemming from the 1971 case of *Bivens v. Six Unknown Named Agents of Federal Bureau of Narcotics*, the Court held that he could not. Mascott and McCotter defend this decision, arguing that under the original understanding of the Constitution, it is Congress, not the courts, that should create a cause of action to recover damages for constitutional wrongs.

Enrique Armijo of Elon University School of Law writes on the term's First Amendment signage case, *City of Austin v. Reagan National Advertising*. Armijo criticizes *Austin* for its "partial unwinding" of another signage decision from just seven years earlier, *Reed v. Town of Gilbert*. *Reed* had seemingly set a simple and bright-line rule for determining whether a speech regulation is "content based" and thus subject to strict First Amendment scrutiny. But, as Armijo explains, that line is now less bright after *Austin*. Armijo suggests that the Court may have feared that a strict application of *Reed* would result in "casting tens of thousands of ordinances into constitutional doubt," a fear that was perhaps unfounded. Whatever the cause, the result is that it will now unfortunately be easier for cities and states to discriminate against certain messages based on what they say.

Michael Bindas of the Institute for Justice writes on this term's school-choice case, *Carson v. Makin*. Bindas, who successfully argued *Carson* on behalf of two Maine families, explains how the decision "removed the most significant legal cloud that remained over educational-choice programs." *Carson* held that Maine could not discriminate against sectarian private schools in administering the state's school-choice program for rural students. And while prior Supreme Court cases had already held that states may not discriminate on the basis of a school's religious *status*, *Carson* clarified that states also may not discriminate on the basis of whether funds will go to religious classroom *education*. Bindas concludes that, after *Carson*, "opponents of educational choice can no longer argue that religious use-based exclusions in educational-choice programs are permissible."

Next, Elizabeth Goitein of the Brennan Center for Justice at NYU School of Law writes on the term's two state secrets cases. Goitein explains that in both *United States v. Husayn, aka Zubaydah* and *FBI v. Fazaga*, the Supreme Court "took pains to avoid the primary questions" about the state secrets doctrine "that have occupied courts and commentators." Moreover, the Court in *Zubaydah* "exhibited an unwarranted degree of deference to the government's national security claims." In holding that the "government may assert the state secrets privilege over matters that are well-known to the public," *Zubaydah* "created a dangerous new precedent." Goitein concludes with a call for Congress to step in and institute reforms to ensure "that judicial deference does not turn into judicial abdication" when the government asserts a state secrets privilege.

Next, Evan Bernick of Northern Illinois University College of Law, and a former Cato intern, writes on *Dobbs v. Jackson Women's Health Organization*. Bernick writes that *Dobbs* "lands some justified blows on *Roe* but falls well short of demonstrating that it was 'egregiously wrong.'" Bernick argues that although the majority opinion's "historical critique of *Roe* is compelling," its "other critiques are not." Bernick explains the most important reason why the opinion falls short of making a compelling originalist case for overruling *Roe*: "Originalists generally agree that the Fourteenth Amendment imposes some kind of anti-discrimination requirement on the states," and there is a strong argument that abortion restrictions discriminate on the basis of sex. Because *Dobbs* dismisses these anti-discrimination arguments in a single paragraph, Bernick concludes that "*Dobbs* isn't originalism and gives almost no sense of an obligation to try to be."

Kelly Dineen Gillespie of Creighton University tackles *Ruan v. United States*. Gillespie writes that *Ruan* is an important decision that "constrains federal law enforcement's ability to invade medical care under the Controlled Substances Act." *Ruan* held that to convict a doctor under the act for wrongly prescribing opioids, "the government must prove not only that the doctor acted outside the limits of their federal authorization to prescribe controlled substances, but also that they did so knowingly or intentionally." As Gillespie explains, that means doctors no longer need fear risking felony prosecution under the act "for innovative, mistaken, negligent, or less-than-careful prescribing." Through examples from her own nursing career, Gillespie illustrates why this is a welcome result and why it will hopefully allow practitioners to be "more willing to provide care that they believe is in their patient's interest."

David Kopel of the Independence Institute and University of Denver, Sturm College of Law writes on *New York State Rifle & Pistol Association v. Bruen*. Kopel explains that the opinion is a landmark not only because it "vindicates the right of law-abiding Americans to carry handguns for lawful protection." In addition, *Bruen* "announces a judicial standard of review that applies to all gun control laws throughout the United States," one based on a law's consistency with history, text, and tradition. Kopel describes how *Bruen* will set the standard for future legal battles over other types of gun restrictions, such as red flag laws, handgun bans, and under-21 restrictions. Thanks to *Bruen*, when courts evaluate these laws in the future, "the personal views of judges on gun policy will matter less. Instead, judicial decisions will be based on analysis of the historical facts of the American right to keep and bear arms."

Finally, our former colleague Ilya Shapiro, now of the Manhattan Institute, makes his triumphant return to these pages as author of our annual "Looking Ahead" article. Ilya identifies several major cases to watch next term, on topics ranging from the Clean Water Act to personal jurisdiction over corporations to the dormant Commerce Clause. The Court will also consider whether universities may consider race in admissions decisions and whether a state may compel a website designer to work for same-sex weddings. Add in cases on the constitutionality of the Indian Child Welfare Act, state legislative control of election procedures, and federal immigration policy, and next term has the makings of another high-profile year for the Court.

* * *

This is my second year as managing editor of the *Review*. Cato has been a huge part of my professional life since I first interned here in my second year of law school seven years ago. Reading through the introductions of past volumes of the *Review* offers snapshots of some of my own professional milestones, as I win mention for helping out as an intern, then legal associate, then contributor, then managing editor. Now, as I author my own introduction for the first time, I'm filled with immense gratitude to both Ilya Shapiro and Trevor Burrus, who were there on my first day as an intern and who have both been invaluable mentors in getting me to this point.

Trevor now shoulders the lion's share of work in the Herculean task of getting the *Review* published. I'm grateful to him for showing me the ropes, teaching best editorial practices by example, and playing the bad cop to my good cop in keeping the authors on schedule. And by the transitive property of mentorship, I also owe Roger Pilon a great deal for creating Cato's Robert A. Levy Center for Constitutional Studies and for mentoring Ilya and Trevor, who in turn mentored me.

Trevor and I also had help from many other people. Most important, of course, are the authors themselves, without whose work there would be no *Review*. Our authors this year produced excellent, polished articles under tremendous time pressure and for that I thank them all sincerely. Thanks also go to our Cato Institute colleagues Will Yeatman, Clark Neily, and Jay Schweikert for help in editing the articles. Legal associates Nicole Saad Bembridge, Gregory Mill, and Isaiah McKinney performed the difficult (believe me, I remember) and vital task of cite checking and proofreading. Legal intern Christopher Condon also provided essential help in these tasks. And special thanks to Laura Bondank, who this year replaced Sam Spiegelman (off to greener pastures as a new attorney at Pacific Legal Foundation) as the legal associate tasked with the nuts and bolts of publishing the review. Laura learned a complex process on the fly like a pro, and this volume couldn't have happened without her.

We hope that you enjoy this 21st volume of the *Cato Supreme Court Review*.

The Court of Mass Incarceration

*Rachel E. Barkow**

It's an honor for me to deliver the Simon Lecture today and to celebrate the drafting of the Constitution with all of you on Constitution Day. I'm especially happy to spend this day at Cato because of all the great work Cato does defending constitutional rights.

I primarily write about criminal law, and Cato's work in this space in particular has been nothing short of outstanding. Unfortunately, the contrast between Cato's commitment to constitutional guarantees in criminal cases and the Supreme Court's is stark. And it's the Court's almost complete abdication to the government in criminal proceedings—in spite of clear constitutional language to the contrary—that is going to be the topic of my lecture today.

There is plenty of blame to go around for America's turn to mass incarceration, but today I want to explain the Supreme Court's role. The justices may not have designed our world of mass incarceration, but they have made sure its foundation stays firmly in place.

I. Sweep of Criminal Law

Let me start by getting everyone up to speed on just how nuts America's commitment to incarceration and criminalization is before I turn to the Supreme Court's role in its evolution. America used to look like most of the rest of the world and certainly other Western democracies when it came to incarceration. Until the 1970s, we had a stable incarceration rate on par with other countries.[1] But then our

* Vice dean and Charles Seligson Professor of Law and faculty director, Center on the Administration of Criminal Law, New York University Law School. I owe thanks to Cato for the invitation to give this lecture and to Brooks Weinberger for research assistance.

[1] See Joshua Aiken & Peter Wagner, State Policy Drives Mass Incarceration, Prison Pol'y Initiative (2017) https://bit.ly/3ydMK0S (depicting U.S. incarceration rates from 1925 to 2015); Franklin E. Zimring, The Insidious Momentum of American Mass Incarceration 3–6 (2020).

incarceration rate started to explode. We now lead the world in both the total number of people incarcerated—nearly 2.3 million[2]—and the rate of incarceration per capita.[3] The U.S. incarceration rate is more than five times what it was in 1972, when it began its record climb upward, and is a rate 5 to 10 times higher than that of other industrialized countries.[4] America has less than five percent of the world's population but almost a quarter of the world's prisoners.[5]

As shocking as the incarceration numbers are, they are the tip of an even bigger iceberg of state control. One out of every 52 people in the United States is under some form of criminal justice supervision (such as probation or parole).[6] In some states and communities, the rates are even higher. In Georgia, for example, one out of every 18 people is on probation or parole.[7] We are now living in a country where one out of every three adults in America has a criminal record.[8] For every 15 people born in 2001, one is expected to go to prison at some point in his or her life.[9]

---

[2] Wendy Sawyer & Peter Wagner, Mass Incarceration: The Whole Pie 2020, Prison Pol'y Initiative (Mar. 24, 2020), https://bit.ly/3ur73XA.

[3] See Highest-to-Lowest Prison Population Rate, World Prison Brief, https://bit .ly/3ur7jG2 (last visited Nov. 1, 2021).

[4] See Danielle Kaeble & Mary Cowhig, U.S. Dep't of Just., Bureau of Just. Stat., Pub. No. NCJ 251211, Correctional Populations in the United States, 2016 4 tbl.4 (2018), https://bit.ly/3yJEjvR; Equal Just. Initiative, United States Still Has Highest Incarceration Rate in the World (Apr. 26, 2019), https://bit.ly/3bQvS8S.

[5] See Peter Wagner & Wanda Bertram, "What Percent of the U.S. Is Incarcerated?" (And Other Ways to Measure Mass Incarceration), Prison Pol'y Initiative (Jan. 16, 2020), https://bit.ly/3ONVFgH.

[6] See U.S. Census Bureau, Quick Facts (July 2019), https://bit.ly/3RcZKfJ (estimating the U.S. population in July 2019 to be 328,239,523); Todd D. Minton, Lauren G. Beaty & Zhen Zeng, U.S. Dep't of Just., Bureau of Just. Stat., Pub. No. NCJ 300655, Correctional Populations in the United States, 2019—Statistical Tables 5 tbl.1 (2021), https://bit.ly/3nH1Ln4 (estimating the correctional population of the U.S. to be 6,344,000).

[7] See Alexi Jones, Correctional Control 2018: Incarceration and Supervision by State, Prison Pol'y Initiative (2018), https://bit.ly/2EgcwY4 (finding Georgia had a correctional control rate of 5,143 per 100,000).

[8] Exec. Office of the Pres., Economic Perspectives on Incarceration and the Criminal Justice System 45 (2016), https://bit.ly/2Uff7FN.

[9] Thomas P. Bonczar, U.S. Dep't of Just., Bureau of Just., Stat., Pub. No. NJC197976, Prevalence of Imprisonment in the U.S. Population, 1974–2001 1 (2003), https://bit.ly/3R8Tbei. Broken down by race and gender, the numbers are even starker among men: 1 in 3 Black men, 1 in 6 Hispanic men, and 1 in 17 white men will spend time

This extraordinary amount of state deprivation of liberty does not fall equally on the population. Black people in America bear a disproportionate share of the brunt. African Americans make up about a third of the people incarcerated, even though they are 13.4 percent of the U.S. population.[10] One third of Black men have at least one felony conviction.[11] Black adults are more than five times more likely to be incarcerated than white adults.[12] And here, too, the national averages, as shocking as they are, are smoothing out even more alarming statistics in some communities. In the District of Columbia, for example, more than 75 percent of Black men can expect to be incarcerated at some point during their lives.[13] 75 percent! At our current pace, almost one out of three Black men in the country can expect to be incarcerated during his lifetime compared to six percent of white men.[14]

I could easily fill my time today with numbers as shocking as these that show the sweep of government overreach in criminal matters, whether by detailing the literally thousands upon thousands of collateral consequences of convictions that deprive people of rights and access to governmental benefits or by detailing inhumane conditions in prisons and jails or abuses by police and prosecutors that go unpunished. But instead of detailing the sweep of the governmental excess in all its tragic glory, I want to discuss an overarching question that applies to all of this: How can this happen under our Constitution?

---

in prison. *Id.* These estimates were made assuming that "incarceration rates [would] remain unchanged." *Id.* A more recent study taking new trends into account largely confirms Bonczar's projections. William Rhodes et al., Abt Associates, Estimating Incidence and Cumulative Incidence of Incarceration Using NCRP Data (2021), https://bit.ly/3R62pbj.

10 See U.S. Census Bureau, *supra* note 6; John Gramlich, The Gap between the Number of Blacks and Whites in Prison Is Shrinking, Pew Research Ctr. (Apr. 30, 2019), https://pewrsr.ch/3bQAT1c.

11 Alan Flurry, Study Estimates U.S. Population with Felony Convictions, UGA Today (Oct. 1, 2017), https://bit.ly/3NlT2Lx.

12 John Gramlich, Black Imprisonment Rate in the U.S. Has Fallen by a Third Since 2006, Pew Research Ctr. (May 6, 2020), https://pewrsr.ch/3agMPc9.

13 Jeremy Travis, But They All Come Back: Facing the Challenges of Prisoner Reentry 122 (2005).

14 Bonczar, *supra* note 9, at 1.

II. The Framers' Constitution

You might be thinking that the problem is that the Framers didn't anticipate that the government might be excessively punitive and abuse its coercive powers, so the Constitution doesn't speak to this. If that were the case—if the Constitution were silent on the relevant issues—that would mean we would be stuck with the whims of the democratic process to fix any problems, and the Supreme Court would not bear any of the blame because the justices cannot put things in the Constitution that are not there. But as it turns out, the Constitution is not silent on government overreach in criminal cases. The Framers didn't let state power in the criminal context slip through the constitutional cracks. Quite the opposite, the Framers of our Constitution were well aware of the state's use and abuse of the criminal laws.[15] They knew of the excesses of the Bloody Code in England.[16] They feared majorities that would seek to oppress opponents through the use of criminal law and punishment. They worried about a police state that would deprive people of liberty.

Far from being silent on checking the government's power in criminal matters, the Constitution is obsessed with it.[17] In fact, one of the animating features of the Constitution is its preoccupation with the regulation of the government's criminal powers. Even before the adoption of the Bill of Rights, the Constitution provided protection for the rights of those accused of crimes through its structural provisions. The Framers worried that Congress might single out political enemies and other disfavored individuals through criminal laws that applied only to the targets. Alexander Hamilton observed that "[t]he creation of crimes after the commission of the fact . . . and the practice of arbitrary imprisonments, have been, in all ages, the favorite and most formidable instruments of tyranny."[18] So Article I prohibits bills of attainder and *ex post facto* laws. Article I also limits Congress's authority to suspend the writ of habeas corpus, which is a key protection for individuals against unlawful detention.

---

[15] See, e.g., Federalist No. 74, at 376 (Alexander Hamilton) (Ian Shapiro ed., 2009).

[16] See Steven Wilf, Law's Imagined Republic 140 (2010) ("Criticism of the Bloody Code became commonplace in American writings of the 1780s and 1790s.").

[17] For a more detailed discussion of these issues, see generally Rachel E. Barkow, Separation of Powers and the Criminal Law, 58 Stan. L. Rev. 989 (2006).

[18] Federalist No. 84, at 432 (Alexander Hamilton) (Ian Shapiro ed., 2009).

Article II vests the president with the power to grant pardons for all federal offenses except in cases of impeachment. As the Supreme Court has explained, this power "exists to afford relief from undue harshness or evident mistake in the operation or enforcement of the criminal law."[19] It is, in other words, a way for the president to check excessive punishments and prosecutions.

What happens if the legislature works with the executive branch to single out disfavored minorities for prosecution or to engage in excessive overreach? The Constitution recognizes this danger and relies on the judiciary to be a key check on the political branches.[20] Before people can be convicted, they are entitled to judicial process. The federal scheme, with life-tenured judges who have salary protections, gives the judiciary the kind of independence that, at least in theory, would seem well suited to check both the legislature and the executive and to assure fair and impartial decisionmaking in each case.[21]

But—and this is critical—the Framers did not trust judges alone. Although Article III judges are relatively more independent than Congress and the executive branch, they are still part of the government. They are appointed through a process that favors governmental connections and sympathy to the party in power.[22] The Framers thus did not think judges would be sufficient protection against the possibility of state abuse in criminal cases because of their potential partiality toward the government.[23]

---

[19] Ex parte Grossman, 267 U.S. 87, 120 (1925).

[20] See, e.g., U.S. Const. amends. IV, V, VI.

[21] See Commodity Future Trading Comm'n v. Schor, 478 U.S. 833, 860 (1986) ("The Framers also understood that a principal benefit of the separation of judicial power from the legislative and executive powers would be the protection of individual litigants from decisionmakers susceptible to majoritarian pressures.") (Brennan, J., dissenting).

[22] Cf. Daryl Levinson, Foreword: Looking for Power in Public Law, 130 Harv. L. Rev. 1, 60–61 (2015) ("Owing to some combination of political selection of judicial appointments and ongoing mechanisms of control . . . the empirical reality appears to be that the Court will rarely drift very far from the agenda of a dominant national political coalition."). See also Lee Epstein, William M. Landes & Richard A. Posner, The Behavior of Federal Judges 85–88 (2013); Barry Friedman, The Politics of Judicial Review, 84 Tex. L. Rev. 257, 308–20 (2005).

[23] "For the revolutionary and founding generations, the criminal jury reliably stood between the individual and government, protecting the accused against overzealous prosecutions, corrupt judges, and even tyrannical laws." Jeffrey Abramson, We, The Jury 87 (1994).

The Constitution therefore provides in Article III—the article establishing the judicial role in government—that the trial of all crimes must be by jury. The jury was no afterthought for the Framers. They did not want anyone to be subject to governmental punishment without agreement from ordinary citizens.[24] Under the Constitution's structure, the jury's unreviewable power to acquit would check both the legislative and executive branches. The jury was the key gatekeeping check before criminal punishment of any kind could be imposed.

So even before the adoption of the Bill of Rights, we see the Framers' concern with expansive state criminal powers. The Bill of Rights then brings this home even more. Four of the first 10 amendments deal explicitly with criminal process. The Fourth Amendment regulates the state's policing and investigative powers. The Fifth Amendment acts as a check on the state's executive powers by providing for the right to a grand jury and prohibiting the state from prosecuting individuals twice for the same offense. And, of course, the Fifth Amendment's Due Process Clause (and later, the Fourteenth Amendment's Due Process Clause) requires the government to follow proper process before depriving an individual of life, liberty, or property. The Sixth Amendment reiterates the centrality of the jury's role in adjudicating criminal cases, making clear that the jury will be drawn from the community in which a crime occurs. In addition, the Sixth Amendment provides a host of additional rights to defendants: the right to a speedy and public trial, the right to notice of criminal charges, the right to confrontation, and the right to assistance of counsel. And the Eighth Amendment regulates the government's legislative judgments by putting a cap on punishment and prohibiting cruel and unusual punishments and excessive fines.

It is hard to imagine a constitution more concerned with state overreach in criminal matters. We see constitutional regulation of all aspects of the government's criminal power, from investigation

---

[24] See Rachel E. Barkow, Recharging the Jury: The Criminal Jury's Constitutional Role in an Era of Mandatory Sentencing, 152 U. Pa. L. Rev. 33, 55 (2003) ("Only by interposing the people directly between the state and the individual charged with a crime could the people guarantee that the new government would not mimic the tyranny of its predecessor."). Sources contemporary to ratification called the jury the "Voice of the People" and the "democratic branch of the judiciary power." *Id.* at 56 (quoting both Federalist and Anti-Federalist sources arguing for the jury's necessity).

to prosecution, from adjudication to the legislation defining punishment. So it is plainly not the case that the Constitution fails to protect against government excess in criminal matters.

What I want to persuade you of today is that it is not a failure of the Constitution but of its guardians: the Supreme Court justices. The Court has failed to protect against government excess in criminal matters through a host of decisions that do not bear scrutiny if one cares about the Constitution's text, original meaning, or good government design. These decisions only make sense if the animating principle is an almost pathological deference to the government.

III. The Court's Role in the Rise of Mass Incarceration

I won't go through all the examples of the Court failing to adhere to constitutional protections against government overreach in criminal matters, but I do want to highlight some of the key areas of doctrine that have a direct relationship to the rise of mass incarceration. Keep in mind that two key factors drive incarceration rates: (1) admissions into jails and prisons and (2) the length of sentences. Obviously, the more people who are charged and convicted, the more admissions. And the longer the sentence, the longer people will wait to be released, which also means more people incarcerated on any given day. The Supreme Court has been a critical player in opening the floodgates on admissions and permitting lengthy sentences.

A. Opening the Floodgates of Admissions

Let's start with the Court's role in fostering more people going into prisons and jails. The Court has done two things to accelerate admissions. It has condoned coercive plea bargaining and permitted widespread pretrial detention.

1. Plea Bargaining

The meteoric rise in incarceration in America begins in the early 1970s.[25] That coincides with the Supreme Court's giving its official imprimatur to coercive bargaining tactics by prosecutors that allow them to threaten defendants with punishments orders of magnitude greater if they exercise their jury trial rights. Colloquially known

---

[25] See Aiken & Wagner, *supra* note 1.

as plea bargaining, it is anything but a bargain for defendants or, frankly, for society overall. I cannot prove causation nor am I suggesting plea bargaining is the only cause of mass incarceration, but it is an absolutely critical condition for it. You cannot get mass incarceration without mass case processing, and the only way you can get mass case processing is to do away with jury trials.

Why would a defendant give up the benefit of having a jury of peers make sure the government can prove its case? Why give up the gold standard of the Constitution that the Framers took pains to include? Defendants are not giving trials up willingly. They are coerced. Prosecutors threaten them with longer punishments if they go to trial. And as more and more laws include mandatory minimums, prosecutors fully control the sentencing outcome with the charge. If a defendant is convicted, that minimum will kick in no matter what the judge thinks.

Instead of condemning this coercive regime as placing an unconstitutional condition on the right to a jury trial, in 1971, the Supreme Court gave not only official recognition, but praise to plea bargaining in *Santobello v. New York*.[26] The Court said: "If every criminal charge were subjected to a full-scale trial, the States and the Federal Government would need to multiply by many times the number of judges and court facilities."[27]

I guess they should get points for candor. They all but admit that they do not want life to become too difficult for judges. More than 200 years ago, William Blackstone warned us about this very thing. He told us that we must protect the criminal jury not from "open attacks" but from "secret machinations" that on their face seem convenient and benign.[28] He reminded us that the delays and "inconveniences" of the criminal jury were a fair price for free nations to "pay for their liberty," and that inroads on the jury are fundamentally opposite to the spirit of the constitution.[29] The Framers fully agreed with Blackstone's view of the criminal jury. That is why it was embedded in Article III and again in the Bill of Rights. But the

---

[26] 404 U.S. 257 (1971).

[27] *Id.* at 260.

[28] 4 William Blackstone, Commentaries *350.

[29] *Id.*

Supreme Court focused on its "inconveniences" and not remotely on the reason it is so important.

Maybe you could forgive the Court in *Santobello* for not raising the alarm about plea negotiations because the Court was not yet aware of how coercive they were. *Santobello* involved a situation in which the defendant took the prosecutor's offer and then the prosecutor failed to keep a promise about a sentencing recommendation, so it did not really queue up the fundamental problem of a prosecutor's threat.

But *Bordenkircher v. Hayes* did.[30] Hayes was charged with forging a check for $88.30, a charge that carried a punishment of two to 10 years. During plea negotiations, the prosecutor offered to recommend a sentence of five years to the judge if Hayes pleaded guilty. If Hayes instead opted to exercise his constitutional jury right, the prosecutor threatened to amend the charges to include a violation of the Kentucky Habitual Criminal Act, which would have subjected Hayes to a mandatory sentence of life imprisonment because Hayes had two prior felony convictions. Hayes would have had to risk a mandatory life sentence to exercise his jury trial right—in a case where the prosecutor admitted a sentence of five years was actually the appropriate one. So the life sentence was for the audacity of the defendant exercising his constitutional right. Can you imagine anything more coercive than this?

Shockingly, in a 5-4 decision, the Court refused to say this violated the Constitution. The Court claimed that "defendants advised by competent counsel" are "presumptively capable of intelligent choice in response to prosecutorial persuasion and unlikely to be driven to false self-condemnation."[31]

Let's unpack that. First, can "competent counsel" do anything to help with the coercion? Al Alschuler has colorfully pointed out that "the presence of counsel has little relevance to the question of voluntariness. A guilty plea entered at gunpoint is no less involuntary because an attorney is present to explain how the gun works."[32] Second, how could the Court characterize this dynamic as one of

---

[30] 434 U.S. 357 (1978).

[31] *Id.* at 363.

[32] Albert Alschuler, The Supreme Court, the Defense Attorney, and the Guilty Plea, 47 U. Colo. L. Rev. 1, 55 (1975).

"prosecutorial persuasion"? The threat was of a mandatory life sentence. True enough, that is persuasive, but it is persuasive in the same way a robber is persuasive in getting cash after telling someone "your money or your life." Finally, the Court, without any evidence, thought this regime would not lead to "false self-condemnation." It is hard to know what to make of that statement. Pure naiveté or duplicity? Either way, it is demonstrably false. If we look at exonerations with DNA evidence—themselves only the tip of the iceberg of wrongful convictions because so many cannot be disproven with DNA—we know 15 percent were the result of guilty pleas.[33] These were all innocent people who pleaded guilty because the prosecutor was threatening too much additional punishment if defendants exercised their jury right.

We have an entire doctrine of unconstitutional conditions that says the government cannot force people into giving up their rights by coercively withholding benefits from those who exercise them.[34] So you would think the Court would have said that *Bordenkircher* was a textbook example of that. Except it didn't. It instead said this is just the give and take of plea bargaining.

Since *Santobello* and *Bordenkircher* were decided in the 1970s, guilty plea rates have skyrocketed. For example, 82 percent of federal convictions in 1979 were the product of guilty pleas—now that figure is 98 percent.[35] State court data are tougher to come by, but what we

[33] Nat'l Registry of Exonerations, Innocents Who Plead Guilty 1 (2015), https://bit .ly/3NLijEX.

[34] See Frost & Frost Trucking Co. v. R.R. Comm'n, 271 U.S. 583, 594 (1926) ("If the state may compel the surrender of one constitutional right as a condition of its favor, it may, in like manner, compel a surrender of all. It is inconceivable that guaranties embedded in the Constitution of the United States may thus be manipulated out of existence."). See also Koontz v. St. Johns River Water Mgmt. Dist., 570 U.S. 595, 606 (2013) ("[R]egardless of whether the government ultimately succeeds in pressuring someone into forfeiting a constitutional right, the unconstitutional conditions doctrine forbids burdening the Constitution's enumerated rights by coercively withholding benefits from those who exercise them.").

[35] Compare U.S. Dep't of Just., Bureau of Just. Stat., Sourcebook of Criminal Justice Statistics—1980 428 tbl.5.22 (1981) (27,295 out of 32,913 convictions were by plea bargain) with Ram Subramanian, et. al, In the Shadows: A Review of the Evidence on Plea Bargaining, Vera Inst. of Justice (Sept. 2020) ("Only 2 percent of federal criminal cases—and a similar number of state cases—are brought to trial.").

have show the same pattern.[36] And the difference between sentences after a plea and sentences after a trial is stark. Defendants face sentences three times greater in federal cases if they go to trial.[37] We have similar numbers at the state level.[38] How can prosecutors credibly threaten sentences that are three times longer if a person just wants their right to a jury trial? How can that be anything other than an unconstitutional trial penalty?

Because of the trial penalty, we're losing jury trials and all the protection they bring against government overreach. First, as Judge Learned Hand observed, juries are outside the government, so they are not allied with the government in the same way as judges and prosecutors.[39] The Framers worried that judges were "always ready to protect the officers of government against the weak and helpless citizen."[40] Sadly, the judiciary's track record in criminal cases bears this out. Judges all too often side with the government of which they are a part. Juries by design provide protection that is not affiliated with the government.

Juries act as a check against government excess in a second respect. Because the Double Jeopardy Clause shields a jury's general verdict of acquittal from any review, the jury has the power to prevent punishment either because it thinks the facts do not merit it or because it disagrees that the law should apply in a particular case.[41] This is an important part of the history of the jury in America.

[36] See Sean Rosenmerkel, Matthew Durose & Donald Farole, Jr., U.S. Dep't of Just., Bureau of Just. Stat., Pub. No. NCJ 226846, Felony Sentences in State Courts, 2006—Statistical Tables (2009), https://bit.ly/3OKo9b5 ("Most (94%) felony offenders sentenced in 2006 pleaded guilty.").

[37] See Jackie Gardina, Compromising Liberty: A Structural Critique of the Sentencing Guidelines, 38 U. Mich. J.L. Reform 345, 347–48 (2005) (noting that under the then-current sentencing guidelines, defendants who pled guilty "can be assured, on average, a sentence that is 300 percent lower than similarly situated defendants" who went to trial).

[38] See Rachel Elise Barkow, Prisoners of Politics: Breaking the Cycle of Mass Incarceration 200 (2019).

[39] See United States ex rel. McCann v. Adams, 126 F.2d 774, 775–76 (2d Cir. 1942).

[40] Essay of a Democratic Federalist, Pa. Herald, Oct. 17, 1787, reprinted in 3 The Complete Anti-Federalist 58, 61 (Herbert J. Storing ed., 1981).

[41] See Barkow, *supra* note 24, at 38–49 (noting that the Double Jeopardy Clause means that the jury has "necessarily been given the power to decide the law as well as the facts in criminal cases").

The colonists were well aware of this power because colonial juries acquitted even in the face of applicable law to resist overreach by the Crown. Criminal grand juries refused to indict persons accused either of political offenses such as rioting or of violating imperial statutes such as the revenue laws.[42] John Adams praised the fact that "No Man can be condemned of Life, or Limb, or Property or Reputation, without the Concurrence of the Voice of the People."[43] Crown attempts to interfere with the jury right were among the events leading to the American Revolution. Although we all learn about colonist opposition to the Stamp Act as an instance of taxation without representation, colonists were also outraged that violators of the act were to be tried in admiralty courts in London, thereby depriving them of a local jury.[44] In 1775, the Second Continental Congress listed England's interference with the right to trial by jury among its grievances in the Declaration of the Causes and Necessity of Taking Up Arms.[45] The Declaration of Independence likewise listed deprivation of the jury among its grievances.[46]

As my colleague and noted historian Bill Nelson has observed, "[f]or Americans after the Revolution, as well as before, the right to trial by jury was probably the most valued of all civil rights."[47] Each state guaranteed the right to trial by jury in a criminal case, as had the Articles of Confederation.[48] So when the Framers wrote the Constitution, this was so fundamental as to require no debate. It was the rare area where Federalists and Anti-Federalists agreed. Alexander Hamilton noted in Federalist No. 83 that "[t]he friends and adversaries of the plan of the convention, if they agree in nothing else, concur

[42] See Matthew P. Harrington, The Law-Finding Function of the American Jury, 1999 Wis. L. Rev. 377, 382 (describing grand juries' refusal to convict in *Bushell's Case* and *Seven Bishops' Case* in the 17th and 18th centuries as landmarks for the independence of juries under English rule).

[43] John Adams, Diary Notes on the Right of Juries (Feb. 12, 1771), in 1 Legal Papers of John Adams 228, 229 (L. Kinvin Wroth & Hiller B. Zobel eds., 1965).

[44] See Andrew Joseph Gildea, The Right to Trial by Jury, 26 Am. Crim. L. Rev. 1507, 1508 n.17 (1989).

[45] Harrington, *supra* note 42, at 395.

[46] The Declaration of Independence para. 20 (U.S. 1776).

[47] William E. Nelson, Americanization of the Common Law: The Impact of Legal Change on Massachusetts Society, 1760–1830, 96 (1994).

[48] Id.; Harrington, *supra* note 42, at 396.

at least in the value they set upon the trial by jury."[49] As he put it, the distinction is, at most, between the Federalist view that it is "a valuable safeguard to liberty" and the Anti-Federalist view that it is "the very palladium of free government."[50] As a result, guaranteeing a jury in criminal cases drew no objection at the Federal Convention or in the state ratification debates.[51] The Maryland Farmer, an Anti-Federalist, described the jury as *"the democratic branch of the judiciary power*—more necessary than representatives in the legislature."[52] Thomas Jefferson felt the jury was so critical that he claimed, "[w]ere I called upon to decide whether the people had best be omitted in the Legislative or Judiciary department, I would say it is better to leave them out of the Legislative."

The jury is no constitutional sideshow but one of the key checks on governmental excess. At least that was how it was supposed to work, until the Supreme Court allowed it to be relegated to almost a non-entity. To be sure, even without its approval of plea bargaining, the death knell of juries, the Court significantly undercut the jury's checking role by limiting what the jury is told about the punishment consequences in a given case.[53] This is another mistaken line of Supreme Court authority. Think of the insanity in having a regime in which citizens are supposed to know punishment consequences because that is supposed to incentivize us to obey the law, but, when citizens become jurors, they are not supposed to know those same punishments and cannot be told what the consequences of a guilty verdict are.

Even without that information in a trial, jurors often have an idea what a punishment will be, and when they think it is too much, they acquit. We have seen that in many communities in the few jury trials that remain. When a large proportion of the community knows the going rate for crimes, and when they think that is too high in a particular case, they acquit. In communities like D.C., Detroit, and the Bronx, acquittal rates are higher. Prosecutors have lamented this as nullification, but it is precisely the role the

[49] Federalist No. 83, at 421 (Alexander Hamilton) (Ian Shapiro ed., 2009).

[50] *Id.*

[51] Gildea, *supra* note 44.

[52] Essays by a Farmer (IV), Md. Gazette, Mar. 21, 1788, reprinted in 5 The Complete Anti-Federalist 36, 38 (Herbert J. Storing ed., 1981) (emphasis added).

[53] See Shannon v. United States, 512 U.S. 573, 579 (1994) ("[J]urors are not to be informed of the consequences of their verdicts.").

jury was designed to play.[54] Jurors may be voting as they are in those communities because of greater skepticism of police, closer scrutiny of the government's case, or their increased awareness of the punishments at stake. Coercive plea negotiation tactics allow prosecutors to eviscerate this fundamental jury check because defendants cannot take the risk when so much more punishment is at stake.

Juries act as a check on the government in a third way: a jury trial takes time. That is the reason the Court gave for protecting plea negotiations. But the inefficiency of jury trials is actually one of its virtues. The government has to *earn* that conviction, to invest resources, to prove each element beyond a reasonable doubt. That means the government has to think about which cases are worth it and be sure it has what it takes to win given all the effort that will be expended.

But in a world of mass convictions and pleas, prosecutors do not need to give much thought to cases at all. And, sadly, they don't. They just churn them through—all too often impersonally and without much care. The Framers knew they were setting up an architecture that was not an efficient one conducive to mass processing. That was the point: it is supposed to be hard for the government to put people into cages and stigmatize them with the label of criminal. But all it took was five justices to decide that governmental efficiency was more important than the Constitution's commitment to the jury.

Even worse, when the Supreme Court allowed this protection to be dismantled, it did not insist on anything else in its place. There is effectively no oversight to this regime of prosecutorial pressure. Judges accept pleas reflexively with little thought. George Fisher has documented that judges go along to ease the burden of their dockets—the same reason the Supreme Court allowed the entire enterprise to move forward.[55] They are focused on their own professional self-interest.

---

[54] See Paul Butler, Race-Based Jury Nullification: Case-in-Chief, 30 John Marshall L. Rev. 911, 916–17 (1997); Carissa Byrne Hessick, Punishment without Trial 180–81 (2021).

[55] George Fisher, Plea Bargaining's Triumph: A History of Plea Bargaining in America (2004).

Defendants do not get oversight within prosecutors' offices, either.[56] They have no right to an internal appeal up the chain of command even if they are dealing with a prosecutor who is making outrageous demands. The prosecutor is not obligated to allow defendants to present evidence in their defense.

While the formal trial process is heavily regulated by constitutional provisions, the plea-bargaining process—the real site of decisionmaking for all but a small percentage of cases—is left entirely to the prosecutor's discretion. During plea negotiations, prosecutors can engage in *ex parte* contacts with the police or other investigators and witnesses, and they do not need to share with the defendant information on which they are relying—even information that is exculpatory.[57] Prosecutors never need to explain why they offered a particular sentence to one defendant but refused to do so for another similarly situated defendant. Transparency is woefully lacking in prosecutors' offices, so most defendants usually do not even know what other similarly situated defendants have been offered or if prosecutors are diverging from office policies.[58]

I teach administrative law as well as criminal law, and one of the driving forces of my scholarly inquiries has been understanding how we can possibly live in a legal world where there are far more checks on agencies that regulate industries than on the agencies (prosecutor's offices) that take away liberty.

This world can only exist if you have a Supreme Court that turns a blind eye to the reality of the coercion and deprivation of the jury right. And make no mistake, other institutional actors have adjusted to this new unconstitutional normal. Congress and state legislatures now promulgate criminal statutes for a world in which plea bargaining is the overwhelming default mode of operation.[59] Prosecutors ask

---

[56] See Gerard E. Lynch, Our Administrative System of Criminal Justice, 66 Fordham L. Rev. 2117, 2124 (1998) ("Because our governing ideology does not admit that prosecutors adjudicate guilt and set punishments, the procedures by which they do so are neither formally regulated nor invariably followed.").

[57] *Id.* at 2128–29.

[58] *Id.* at 2132.

[59] Rachel E. Barkow, Administering Crime, 52 UCLA L. Rev. 715, 728 n.25 (2005) (citing examples of Department of Justice requests for more stringent sentences because it would make defendants more likely to cooperate with prosecutors); William J. Stuntz, The Pathological Politics of Criminal Law, 100 Mich. L. Rev. 505, 529–31 (2001).

for and receive from legislators laws with high mandatory minimums to give prosecutors the leverage they need to induce guilty pleas.

They are blatant about it, too. They say on the record they need these laws to get pleas and cooperation.[60] For example, when Congress was considering reducing mandatory minimums for certain drug offenders with no history of violence, the National Association of Assistant U.S. Attorneys—a group representing federal prosecutors—opposed the reduction because the change would make their job harder. It would "prevent[] the government from obtaining benefits gained through concessions during bargaining."[61] They are not saying they need these laws because they believe those penalties should be the actual punishments imposed. They want coercive leverage and do not even see anything wrong in asking for it explicitly. And why should they, given the Court's imprimatur?

2. Pretrial Detention

Coercive plea negotiations are one key way in which the Court paved the way for more jail and prison admissions: it made the job of convicting exponentially easier for prosecutors. But that is not the only way the Court facilitated more admissions. We have about half a million people in America locked in cages without having been convicted of anything and without having pleaded guilty.[62]

That is a direct result of six members of the Supreme Court giving their blessing to pretrial detention on the basis of future dangerousness in *United States v. Salerno*.[63] The Court decided that caging someone under the Bail Reform Act—in the exact same facility where people serve sentences after convictions—is constitutional even before conviction because the detention pretrial is regulatory in nature and not, in the Court's view, punitive.[64] *Salerno* was decided in the

[60] See, e.g., Drug Mandatory Minimums: Are They Working?: Hearing before the Subcomm. on Criminal Justice, Drug Policy, and Human Resources of the House Comm. on Government Reform, 106th Cong. 144–53 (2000) (statement of John Roth, Chief, Narcotic and Dangerous Drug Section, Criminal Division, Dep't of Justice) (arguing in favor of mandatory minimum drug laws because they "provide an indispensable tool for prosecutors" by creating an incentive for defendants to cooperate).

[61] Letter from Dennis Boyd, Exec. Dir., Nat'l Ass'n of Assistant U.S. Attorneys, to Patti B. Saris, Chair, U.S. Sentencing Comm'n (July 2, 2014), https://bit.ly/3ussBD4.

[62] Minton et al., *supra* note 6, at 2 (noting a jail population of 734,500 in 2019).

[63] 481 U.S. 739 (1987).

[64] *Id.* at 746.

middle of the 1980s and the peak frenzy of the War on Drugs and concern with rising crime. The Court bought into the idea of broad pretrial detention because it said the government's interest in preventing crime outweighed the individual's liberty interests.[65]

I have to pause for a moment here to make sure you know that the entire regime of pretrial detention is actually terrible if your goal is preventing crime. We have empirical studies documenting that people detained pretrial are more likely to commit crimes when released than those who are released pretrial—even after controlling for the crimes they have committed, their criminal history, and whatever else you can think to control for.[66] It is the detention itself that increases the risk of crime. And that makes sense when you stop to think about it, because when people are detained, they lose their jobs; they lose their housing because they get evicted for failing to pay rent; they lose custody of their kids. Their lives are in shambles, so it is that much harder to stay on a law-abiding path on release. So as a public-policy matter, pretrial detension is just awful.

Even more egregious is that the Court would think liberty could be stripped away just because the government thought it was a good idea. I cannot do any better than Justice Thurgood Marshall in describing what is wrong here:

> Throughout the world today there are men, women, and children interned indefinitely, awaiting trials which may never come or which may be a mockery of the word, because their governments believe them to be "dangerous." Our Constitution, whose construction began two centuries ago, can shelter us forever from the evils of such unchecked power. Over 200 years it has slowly, through our efforts, grown more durable, more expansive, and more just. But it cannot protect us if we lack the courage, and the self-restraint, to protect ourselves. Today a majority of the Court applies itself to an ominous exercise in demolition. Theirs is truly a decision which will go forth without authority, and come back without respect.[67]

[65] *Id.* at 748 (offering a comparison to detention during times of war or insurrection).

[66] See, e.g., Paul Heaton, Sandra Mayson & Megan Stevenson, The Downstream Consequences of Misdemeanor Pretrial Detention, 69 Stan. L. Rev. 711 (2017) (finding a likely causal relationship between pretrial detention and future criminal activity, even after controlling for initial bail amount, offense, demographic information, and criminal history characteristics).

[67] Salerno, 481 U.S. at 767 (Marshall, J., dissenting).

Amen to that, Justice Marshall. Truly one of the worst decisions issued by the Court.

The result: over half a million people detained pretrial—35 percent of our incarcerated population—who pose no risk at all.[68] They languish in jails because the Supreme Court failed to protect their liberty interests.

And the threat of the detention becomes a bargaining chip that prosecutors use to extract pleas, particularly in misdemeanor cases. Prosecutors get defendants detained pretrial and then say in plea negotiations that they can get sentenced to time served if they plead guilty. Are you surprised that we have an enormous number of people pleading guilty even if innocent, just to get out jail?[69]

Coercive plea bargaining and pretrial detention should not be permitted under our Constitution, but the Court has said otherwise. And admissions have skyrocketed as a result.

B. Keeping the Floodgates Closed with Longer Sentences

The Court also plays a vital role in the second driver of incarceration rates: length of sentences. The Court has utterly failed to police sentence length, again in complete derogation of its duty under the Constitution, which has an entire amendment devoted to cruel and unusual punishments. A majority of justices have agreed that the Eighth Amendment prohibits excessively long sentences.[70] Frighteningly and in contradiction of the language and history of the Eighth Amendment, we have had at least four justices—William Rehnquist, Antonin Scalia, Clarence Thomas, and Samuel Alito—who think no sentence of incarceration can be disproportionate.[71] But the other justices have at least all agreed that a particular sentence could be so long as to be cruel and unusual.

---

[68] See Minton et al., *supra* note 6, at 5 tbl.1.

[69] See generally Jed S. Rakoff, Why Innocent People Plead Guilty, N.Y. Rev. Books, Nov. 20, 2014.

[70] See Ewing v. California, 538 U.S. 11, 20 (2003) (O'Connor, J., joined by Rehnquist, C.J., Kennedy, J.) (noting the narrow proportionality analysis against grossly disproportionate sentences, but finding that "recidivist statutes" serve a "legitimate goal of deterring offenders" and survive such scrutiny).

[71] See Harmelin v. Michigan, 501 U.S. 957, 994 (1991) (Scalia, J., joined by Rehnquist, C.J.) (arguing that proportionality review applies only in capital cases); Graham v. Florida, 560 U.S. 48, 99 (2010) (Thomas, J., dissenting, joined by Scalia, Alito, JJ.) (arguing that proscribing "grossly disproportionate" sentences is an interpretation of the Eight Amendment that's "entirely the Court's creation").

The test the Court now uses to determine if a sentence meets that standard, however, is effectively impossible to satisfy—and in fact, no sentence has been invalidated on that test. The Court uses a test from a concurring opinion of Justice Anthony Kennedy in *Harmelin v. Michigan* that recognizes only a "narrow" proportionality principle in noncapital cases.[72] Under that test, an individual challenging a particular sentence on Eighth Amendment grounds has to make a threshold showing that the sentence is grossly disproportionate to the crime, which in the Court's view means that the defendant has to show that the state has no "reasonable basis for believing" that the sentence will serve any penological goal.[73] But the state's penological goals can be deterrence, retribution, rehabilitation, or—and this one is usually the kicker for dooming any successful claim under this test—incapacitation.

So if the state says it needs to detain someone for stealing a slice of pizza for 25 years to life to incapacitate that person from stealing more pizza because he has a prior record of other thefts, the Court will say okay. (That's a real case, by the way, not some crazy hypothetical I'm using to make my point.[74])

Here are some other real cases in which the Supreme Court said the sentences did not violate its Eight Amendment test:

- a mandatory life sentence for a defendant who committed three separate low-level theft offenses that cumulatively totaled less than $230;[75]
- a mandatory life sentence without parole for a defendant who did not have any prior record and whose only offense was possessing 672 grams of cocaine;[76]
- a sentence of 25-years-to-life for an individual whose third strike under California's three-strikes law was the theft of three golf clubs worth roughly $1,200, because the defendant had a record of prior offenses, including burglaries and a robbery;[77]

[72] 501 U.S. at 996 (Kennedy, J., concurring in part and in judgment).

[73] *Id.* at 957.

[74] Associated Press, 25 Years for a Slice of Pizza, N.Y. Times (Mar. 5, 1995), (§ 1), at 21.

[75] Rummel v. Estelle, 445 U.S. 263 (1980).

[76] Harmelin, 501 U.S. at 961.

[77] Ewing, 538 U.S. at 17–18.

- a 50-years-to-life sentence for an individual whose criminal history contained no violence and whose three strikes consisted of a petty misdemeanor theft and two separate incidents where he stole a total of nine videotapes worth $150 from K-Mart.[78]

All these cases came before the Supreme Court, and the Court ruled that all of them passed constitutional muster. They were clearly not reading the same Eighth Amendment I am when they upheld these sentences. The Court has effectively taken the judiciary out of the business of checking the state when it seeks to impose outrageously long punishments.

The Court knows how to give sentences greater scrutiny for proportionality because it has done so in its capital cases.[79] Its utter failure to do the same in noncapital cases—where the Constitution is no less relevant— is one of the worst judicial abrogations of constitutional rights in the country's history. And there is no doubt it is a key ingredient of mass incarceration because there are effectively no limits on the sentence lengths jurisdictions can pursue.

C. Other Court Decisions Driving Mass Incarceration and the Expansion of Criminal Law

The Court has played a critical role in the expansion of criminal law and punishment in America in many other ways. It has created immunity doctrines that prevent prosecutors and police officers from being accountable for gross abuses of their authority, which has allowed these actors to be overly aggressive without fear of reprisal.[80] The Court has failed to recognize any substantive limits on what can be criminalized, allowing punishment in cases of no blame, whether through strict-liability offenses or most recently by allowing a state to do away with any defense of insanity.[81] Its approach to the egregious disparate impact we see all over criminal law enforcement—from police stops on the basis of race to

[78] Lockyer v. Andrade, 538 U.S. 63 (2003).

[79] See Rachel E. Barkow, The Court of Life and Death: The Two Tracks of Constitutional Sentencing Law and the Case for Uniformity, 107 Mich. L. Rev. 1145 (2009).

[80] See Imbler v. Pachtman, 424 U.S. 409 (1976) (prosecutors); Harlow v. Fitzgerald, 457 U.S. 800 (1982) (police).

[81] Kahler v. Kansas, 240 S. Ct. 1021 (2020).

prosecutorial charging that disfavors Black people to sentencing disparities in noncapital and capital cases—runs counter to the way it views equal protection challenges in other contexts; it ignores the implicit biases and stereotypes that permeate every aspect of criminal law and effectively turns the Equal Protection Clause into a dead letter.[82]

In the interest of time, I will not go into detail in all these areas. But they are all areas in which the Court has been divided and, but for a few votes, the world would look very different.

IV. Reforming the Court

In many of the doctrinal areas I've discussed, the outcome is particularly puzzling because they should be spaces of agreement between more liberal justices and conservative justices who are committed to originalism. Cases involving the jury right, the Eighth Amendment, and pretrial detention, for example, should come out in favor of defendants under an originalist interpretation. At the same time, these areas should appeal to more liberal justices who otherwise have shown an interest in the poor and communities of color who have borne the brunt of excessive criminalization.

So what's particularly odd at first glance is the absence of a coalition to protect these constitutional rights. But the result is only odd if you tend to think of the Court as divided along conservative and liberal lines. Focusing on that division might make you miss that the

---

[82] See Radley Balko, There's Overwhelming Evidence That the Criminal Justice System Is Racist. Here's the Proof., Wash. Post (June 10, 2020), https://wapo.st/3Ax5VWa (cataloging studies of racial profiling and disparities in police stops); Pamela S. Karlan, Race, Rights, and Remedies in Criminal Adjudication, 96 Mich. L. Rev. 2001, 2023–24 (1998) (arguing that *United States v. Armstrong* placed a heightened pleading standard for selective prosecution that has the effect of "immuniz[ing] from full-scale litigation, at least in the context of a criminal trial, a claim to which the government would be required to respond more fully if it involved any state function other than criminal prosecution"); McCleskey v. Kemp, 481 U.S. 279, 339 (1987) (Brennan, J., dissenting) ("The Court next states that its unwillingness to regard petitioner's evidence as sufficient is based in part on the fear that recognition of McCleskey's claim would open the door to widespread challenges to all aspects of criminal sentencing. Taken on its face, such a statement seems to suggest a fear of too much justice.") (citation omitted). See also Karlan, *supra*, at 2005 ("*Armstrong* and *McCleskey* deploy what the Court calls 'traditional equal protection principles' essentially to strip the concept of selective prosecution of virtually any real-world effect: they define away the right and the remedy simultaneously.").

Court is united along one very important dimension when it comes to criminal law: deference to prosecutors and police. There always seems to be an overwhelming majority on the Court for that position regardless of the justice's ideological background or theory of jurisprudence.

One reason for that bias is that the Supreme Court bench is drawn overwhelmingly from a pool of government lawyers. These are people who have spent their careers defending and representing the government—as prosecutors, at the solicitor general's office, in other positions at the Department of Justice, or in state government. Rarely have we had justices who have represented regular individuals, who have seen their stories up close and witnessed the toll of government abuse and misconduct. Rarer still are justices who have defended those accused of crimes. So they have a skewed perspective. They see themselves in these government lawyers and these government cases, and they are too quick to defer, to assume regularity, to trust the government's position.

The Framers knew better. That is why they wanted to put regular people between the government and decisions about punishment by having jury trials. But the Court has erased that boundary protection and so many others, and it has allowed the complete dominance of the government over individual liberty.

We see this reflected in the lower courts as well. They might not be shaping doctrine in the same way as the Supreme Court, but they have enormous power through their discretionary decisions. Judges decide a host of important issues that affect the criminal justice landscape, from sentences to evidentiary rulings to calling out prosecutorial misconduct. And for the most part, what you see around the country are judges exercising discretion in deference to whatever the government wants, from pretrial detention, to sentencing recommendations, to the inability to call out prosecutors and police who engage in misconduct.[83]

There are no easy answers to any of this, but I would like to emphasize one place to start. We should diversify the professional background of those who serve as judges. Currently the bench is dominated by former prosecutors and lawyers who represented the government. No one has done better research on this than Cato.

---

[83] See Barkow, *supra* note 38, at 69–70, 155–56, 200–01.

A May 2021 report by Clark Neily looked at the background of federal judges and found that 44 percent were former government advocates compared to just over six percent who were advocates for individuals against the government.[84] That is a seven-to-one imbalance. If we look at just those with criminal law experience, the ratio of prosecutors to defense attorneys on the bench today is almost exactly four to one.[85] Andrew Crespo notes that, since the early 1970s, the Supreme Court has seen a threefold increase in the number of its justices with experience working as criminal prosecutors before their ascension to the bench.[86]

But it is not just the rise of prosecutors that is disturbing. It is the lack of justices who have represented people who have been stopped, frisked, arrested, and subject to governmental coercion. Justice Thurgood Marshall brought that experience to the Court and could share with his colleagues his perspective representing indigent criminal defendants. But, as Crespo notes, until this year, "no justice, serving now or since Marshall's retirement, has spent any significant time working as a criminal defense attorney prior to joining the Court."[87] Instead, we have a Court whose only direct experience with criminal law enforcement is "advocating 'with earnestness and vigor' on behalf of the interests of law enforcement, in the always challenging struggle to contain and combat crime."[88] It is wholly missing the perspective of those who, in Tony Amsterdam's words, have repeatedly "seen policemen from the nightstick end."[89]

I join and applaud Cato in calling out the need to get more criminal-defense lawyers and public-interest lawyers who defend civil liberties on the bench. We cannot have a bench dominated by former government lawyers and expect the results to be any different than what we have seen.

[84] Clark Neily, Are a Disproportionate Number of Federal Judges Former Government Advocates?, Cato Inst. (May 27, 2021), https://bit.ly/3RpoB0j.

[85] See Barkow, *supra* note 38, at 200.

[86] Andrew Manuel Crespo, Regaining Perspective: Constitutional Criminal Adjudication in the U.S. Supreme Court, 100 Minn. L. Rev. 1985, 1992 (2016).

[87] *Id.* at 1990. This changed with the confirmation of Justice Ketanji Brown Jackson, who spent part of her career working in public defense.

[88] *Id.* at 2000 (quoting Berger v. United States, 295 U.S. 78, 88 (1935)).

[89] Anthony G. Amsterdam, Perspectives on the Fourth Amendment, 58 Minn. L. Rev. 349, 409 (1974).

In the past few months, we have seen that's just starting to change. Many of the federal vacancies filled by President Joe Biden have been with people with civil liberties and criminal defense backgrounds.[90] That push needs to continue, and it cannot just be at the federal level. State courts and state judges matter, too.

Many of you may be aware that there is a big push right now to get prosecutors elected who understand the excesses of punishment and who are committed to achieving real public safety results instead of tough-on-crime rhetoric and approaches that are not actually effective at combatting crime. Many in this new wave of prosecutors support important reforms such as alternatives to incarceration, the elimination or curtailment of cash bail, shorter sentences, and more reentry opportunities for those coming out of prisons and jails.[91] Those interested in criminal law reform need to focus on the bench as another area for this kind of fundamental personnel and outlook change. That means paying attention to local judicial elections in the same way as prosecutor elections to unseat those local and state judges who have poor track records in protecting individual rights and who reflexively side with the government in criminal matters no matter what the facts or issue.

We know other interest groups pay close attention to the judiciary and make sure their issues are addressed. Labor groups know how important the D.C. Circuit is to their issues, and abortion rights groups pay attention to Supreme Court appointments.[92] Those interested in criminal justice reform should be just as vigilant, particularly with Supreme Court nominations, but with other judicial appointments as well.

And reformers should not assume that liberal appointees will be in favor of their positions or that conservative appointees will not. These are issues that often transcend traditional left/right splits. We frequently see judges appointed by Democratic presidents

---

[90] See Nate Raymond, U.S. Senate Confirms Voting Rights Advocate Perez to 2nd Circuit, Reuters (Oct. 25, 2021), https://reut.rs/3AB9ASN; Sahil Kapur, With Public Defenders as Judges, Biden Quietly Makes History on the Courts, NBCNews (Oct. 18, 2021), https://nbcnews.to/3IgfR8e.

[91] Angela J. Davis, Reimagining Prosecution: A Growing Progressive Movement, 3 UCLA Crim. Just. Rev. 1, 6–14 (2019).

[92] See Barkow, supra note 38, at 200 (describing organized opposition to various judicial appointments).

representing a hard line on criminal justice issues. And sometimes we see Republican presidents appointing judges who, because of their originalist and textual methodologies, end up favoring certain criminal justice positions in ways that other Republican appointees, who speak in terms of strong law enforcement or have pro-government leanings in criminal cases, often do not.

It is possible in either a Republican or a Democratic administration to seek judges who are committed to protecting constitutional rights and do not reflexively side with the government. But one key to that is to make sure we are getting criminal-defense lawyers and those who have dedicated themselves to representing individuals and protecting civil liberties. We cannot just draw from a pool of former government lawyers. Forty-one percent of President Barack Obama's judges had prosecution experience, and only 14 percent had public-defense experience.[93] And that is from a president who claimed to be committed to criminal justice reform. (He even wrote a law review article about it.[94]) I mention the Obama track record to highlight that reformers cannot be complacent and assume that even someone who claims to be interested in criminal justice reform will reflect that concern in judicial appointments. This issue did not receive attention in the Obama administration, and that was a lost opportunity.

We are seeing a different pattern now from President Biden, and it is precisely because reformers have been clamoring for just this kind of professional diversity on the bench. It is not taking place evenly across the country, though, because there is still deference to home state senators in judicial selection.[95] And not all the senators are doing a good job on this front. So if you care about these issues, I urge you to follow what your senators are doing and encourage them to put forth judicial nominations of people who have represented individual clients and protected civil liberties instead of spending their lives siding with the government.

[93] See Casey Tolan, Why Public Defenders Are Less Likely to Become Judges—And Why That Matters, Splinter (Mar. 18, 2016), https://bit.ly/2XeZFLm.

[94] Barack Obama, The President's Role in Advancing Criminal Justice Reform, 130 Harv. L. Rev. 811 (2017).

[95] See generally Denis Steven Rutkus, Role of Home State Senators in the Selection of Lower Federal Court Judges, Cong. Research. Serv., Pub. No. RL34405 (2013).

There is room for both on the bench, but given the gross imbalance we have now, it is going to take a concerted effort to bring in more criminal-defense lawyers and those with civil-liberties experience to come anywhere close to achieving balance. And I think that balance is going to be critical to turn back the tide of mass incarceration. It won't happen overnight and it won't be easy, but it is a necessary first step. The courts have been key players in creating mass incarceration, and they are going to have to be key players in taking it down.

West Virginia v. EPA: Some Answers about Major Questions

Jonathan H. Adler*

Introduction

The Supreme Court's decision to grant certiorari in *West Virginia v. Environmental Protection Agency* (*West Virginia*) was a surprise. The Court rarely grants cases involving challenges to regulations the executive branch no longer wishes to enforce. Once granted, however, the outcome was not surprising at all. Twice before the Court had shown skepticism of broad regulatory authority over greenhouse gas (GHG) emissions. There was no reason to think this time would be different. The EPA would retain its authority to regulate GHGs, but it would not be allowed to redesign the scope of its own regulatory authority for that purpose.

In *West Virginia*, Chief Justice John Roberts wrote the opinion for a 6-3 Court, rejecting claims that the case was nonjusticiable and concluding that the EPA lacks broad authority to limit GHG emissions from power plants under the Clean Air Act (CAA).[1] The chief justice's opinion was joined by the Court's conservatives. Justice Neil Gorsuch wrote a concurring opinion, joined by Justice Samuel Alito. Justice Elena Kagan dissented on behalf of herself and the other liberal justices.

Expressly invoking the "major questions doctrine" for the first time in a majority opinion, the chief justice explained that Section 7411

* Johan Verheij Memorial Professor of Law and director, Coleman P. Burke Center for Environmental Law, Case Western Reserve University School of Law; senior fellow, Property & Environment Research Center. I would like to thank Kristin Hickman, Thomas Merrill, and Christopher Walker for comments on earlier drafts, and Casey Lindstrom and Alexandra Mendez-Diaz for their research assistance. Any errors or inanities are mine alone.

[1] 142 S. Ct. 2587 (2022).

of the CAA does not allow the EPA to require generation shifting (the replacement of coal with natural gas or renewable energy) to reduce GHG emissions.[2] In so doing, the Court rejected the expansive view of EPA's regulatory authority favored by the Obama and Biden administrations and endorsed by the U.S. Court of Appeals for the D.C. Circuit.

West Virginia v. EPA rested on the longstanding and fundamental constitutional principle that agencies only have the regulatory authority Congress delegated to them. The Court further bolstered the argument that delegations of broad regulatory authority should not be lightly presumed. Extraordinary assertions of regulatory authority, such as the EPA's claim that CAA provisions authorizing emission controls on stationary sources could be used to decarbonize the electricity grid, required a clear delegation from Congress.

The case's outcome was foreshadowed in the Court's decisions rejecting emergency pandemic measures barring evictions and mandating vaccination or testing of employees in large companies. Those decisions, arising from the Court's "shadow docket," had signaled the Court's wariness of executive branch efforts to utilize long-extant statutory authority as the basis for novel and far-reaching regulatory initiatives.[3]

While *West Virginia v. EPA* reaffirmed that courts should be wary of allowing agencies to pour new wine out of old bottles, it left substantial questions about the major questions doctrine unanswered. By skimping on statutory analysis and front-loading consideration of whether a case presents a major question, Chief Justice Roberts's opinion failed to provide much guidance for lower courts. It may be clear that statutory ambiguity cannot justify broad assertions of regulatory authority, but *West Virginia v. EPA* provides little clarity

---

[2] *Id.* at 2610 ("this is a major questions case"). In prior cases the Court had relied upon the "major questions" concept without using that specific phrase.

[3] See Ala. Ass'n of Realtors v. Dep't of Health & Human Serv., 141 S. Ct. 2485 (2021) (finding the Centers for Disease Control and Prevention lacked authority to impose an eviction moratorium to prevent the interstate spread of covid-19); NFIB v. Dep't of Labor, OSHA, 142 S. Ct. 661 (2022) (finding the Occupational Safety and Health Administration lacked the authority to impose a universal vaccine-or-test requirement on all firms with more than 100 employees). For a discussion of these cases, see, in this volume, Ilya Somin, A Major Question of Power: The Vaccine Mandate Cases and the Limits of Executive Authority, 2021–2022 Cato Sup. Ct. Rev. 69 (2022).

on how the invigorated major questions doctrine should inform statutory interpretation.

The chief justice's failure to bring clarity to the major questions doctrine is particularly disappointing given that the seeds of a broader doctrine can be found in his own prior opinions, including *King v. Burwell*[4] and his *Arlington v. Federal Communications Commission* dissent.[5] If federal agencies are "creatures of Congress" with only that power Congress has delegated,[6] it would seem to follow that the burden should be on the agency to demonstrate that the power it wishes to exercise has been delegated to it. And when confronted with broad, unprecedented, and unusual assertions of agency power, some degree of judicial skepticism would be warranted—skepticism that can be overcome by a clear statement delegating the power at issue. Such a holding would not satisfy those hoping for a revival of the nondelegation doctrine, but it would ensure that agencies only exercise those powers actually delegated to them.

While *West Virginia v. EPA* represents a missed opportunity to clarify and ground the major questions doctrine, it remains a tremendously important decision. It will be cited routinely in legal challenges to new regulatory initiatives. It also hampers regulatory efforts to address climate change, one of the most pressing policy concerns of the 21st century.[7] The Court denied the most expansive interpretations of EPA's authority under Section 7411 of the CAA but did nothing to curtail the EPA's traditional air pollution control authorities. Nor did it preclude the EPA from using such authorities to regulate GHGs. It did, however, make it more challenging for the EPA or other agencies to develop new climate change policies relying on pre-existing statutory authority directed at other problems.

---

[4] King v. Burwell, 576 U.S. 473 (2015). I have been quite critical of the chief justice's *King* opinion in these very pages, but that criticism focused on his statutory interpretation, not his understanding of the nature of agency power. See Jonathan H. Adler & Michael F. Cannon, King v. Burwell and the Triumph of Selective Contextualism, 2014–2015 Cato Sup. Ct. Rev. 35 (2015). As will become clear in this essay, the chief justice's statutory interpretation in *West Virginia v. EPA* was not exemplary either.

[5] See City of Arlington v. FCC, 569 U.S. 290 (2013).

[6] *Id.* at 371 (Roberts, C.J., dissenting).

[7] For my argument as to why libertarians should care about climate change, see Jonathan H. Adler, Taking Property Rights Seriously: The Case of Climate Change, 26 Social Phil. & Pol'y 296 (2009); see also Jonathan H. Adler, Without Constraint, Times Lit. Supp. (Nov. 13, 2015), https://bit.ly/3oLDBbx.

If there are to be additional tools in the EPA's climate-policy tool-kit, Congress must provide them. The CAA was not written with climate change in mind, and there is only so much the EPA can do to constrain GHG emissions within existing statutory constraints. *West Virginia v. EPA* put Congress in the policy driver's seat. Whether Congress has a direction in mind is yet to be determined.

From *Massachusetts* to *West Virginia*

Because *West Virginia v. EPA* concerns the scope of the EPA's authority to regulate GHG emissions, it is worth placing the decision in the broader context of federal GHG regulation. Controversy over the scope of the EPA's authority to regulate GHG emissions has simmered for decades. Congress has never enacted legislation expressly granting EPA the authority to regulate GHGs as such.[8] Rather, the EPA has relied on various provisions of the CAA to control GHG emissions.

The CAA was enacted in 1970 primarily to control traditional air pollutants, such as lead, soot, and smog. Congress last updated the act in 1990, providing explicit authority to control those pollutants that cause stratospheric ozone depletion and acid rain. Somewhat conspicuously, no equivalent authority was adopted to help mitigate global warming, and subsequent efforts to enact such authority repeatedly failed.[9] It was therefore unclear whether the EPA had the authority to regulate carbon dioxide and other GHGs due to their greenhouse-forcing potential.[10]

In 1999, several environmental organizations petitioned the EPA to regulate GHG emissions from new motor vehicles under

---

[8] Insofar as GHGs have other pollutant characteristics, Congress has enacted provisions that would enable EPA to regulate those substances due to factors other than their potential to contribute to climate change.

[9] See Arnold W. Reitze, Jr., Federal Control of Carbon Dioxide Emissions: What Are the Options?, 36 B.C. Envt. Aff. L. Rev. 1, 1 (2009) ("From 1999 to [2007], more than 200 bills were introduced in Congress to regulate [greenhouse gases], but none were enacted."); see also Daniel J. Weiss, Anatomy of a Senate Climate Bill Death, Ctr. for Am. Progress (Oct. 12, 2010), https://bit.ly/3QdBMzT (discussing failure of climate legislation in 2010).

[10] See Richard Lazarus, Environmental Law without Congress, 30 J. Land Use & Envt. L. 15, 30 (2014) ("Climate change is perhaps the quintessential example of a new environmental problem that the Clean Air Act did not contemplate.").

the CAA.[11] The EPA's general counsel had concluded the GHGs could be regulated as air pollutants under the act. Based on this judgment, the groups argued the EPA was required to do something, but the EPA initially ignored the petition. After a change in administrations, however, the EPA formally denied the petition, maintaining that the agency lacked the authority to regulate GHGs and that regulation of such pollutants under the CAA would not constitute an effective means to address the threat of climate change.[12]

A coalition of environmental groups and state governments sued, ultimately prevailing in the Supreme Court. In *Massachusetts v. EPA*, a 5-4 Court concluded that GHGs were "air pollutants" subject to regulation under the CAA, and that the EPA failed to offer an adequate justification for failing to regulate such emissions from motor vehicles.[13] While the Court did not command the EPA to begin regulating GHGs, that was the practical effect of the Court's holding. Under the act, the EPA must regulate motor vehicle emissions of any "air pollutant" that, in the "judgment" of the administrator, "cause, or contribute to, air pollution which may reasonably be anticipated to endanger public health or welfare."[14] As the EPA was long on record acknowledging the threat posed by climate change, recognizing GHGs as pollutants subject to regulation under the act made their eventual regulation inevitable.[15]

The EPA made its first formal "endangerment" finding in December 2009, concluding that GHG emissions from motor vehicles "cause, or contribute to, air pollution which may reasonably be

---

[11] For the full history of the effort to compel the EPA to regulate GHG emissions under the CAA, see Richard Lazarus, The Rule of Five: Making Climate History at the Supreme Court (2020). For a critique of this account, see Lisa Heinzerling, The Rule of Five Guys, 119 Mich. L. Rev. 1137 (2021).

[12] See Control of Emissions from New Highway Vehicles and Engines, 68 Fed. Reg. 52,922 (Sept. 8, 2003).

[13] 549 U.S. 497 (2007). Of note, the Court did not defer to the EPA's interpretation of the CAA on these questions. The Court also held, 5-4, that the petitioners had standing to challenge the EPA's petition denial.

[14] See 42 U.S.C. § 7521(a)(1).

[15] Indeed, in rejecting the environmentalist petition that led to *Massachusetts v. EPA*, the EPA accepted that the federal government "must address" climate change. See Control of Emissions from New Highway Vehicles and Engines, 68 Fed. Reg. at 52,929–31.

anticipated to endanger public health or welfare."[16] The agency's first regulations governing GHG regulations from new motor vehicles followed soon thereafter.[17] This, in turn, set the stage for the regulation of GHG emissions from stationary sources and the beginning of the EPA's troubles trying to control GHGs under the CAA.[18]

The Court in *Massachusetts v. EPA* paid little attention to the difficulty of applying the CAA's provisions to GHGs. Had they done so, they may have discovered that the CAA "is not especially well designed for controlling GHG pollution."[19] Yet the justices are far from CAA experts and the question at hand—whether the EPA could regulate emissions from cars and trucks—did not create much administrative difficulty.[20] By contrast, meaningful regulation of GHGs from stationary sources under the CAA would force the agency "to engage in interpretive jujitsu."[21]

Under Section 165 of the act, "major" stationary sources are required to adopt emission controls for "each pollutant subject to regulation" when built or modified.[22] Title V of the act further requires major sources to file permits demonstrating their regulatory compliance. Both define "major" sources to be those with the potential to emit more than 100 or 250 tons per year of pollutants, depending

[16] See Endangerment and Cause or Contribute Findings for GHGs under Section 202(a) of the CAA, 74 Fed. Reg. 66,496 (Dec. 15, 2009).

[17] See Light-Duty Vehicle GHG Emission Standards and Corporate Average Fuel Economy Standards, Final Rule, 75 Fed. Reg. 25,324 (May 7, 2010).

[18] For a discussion of how the EPA's initial endangerment finding under Section 202 of the CAA paved the way for subsequent GHG regulation, see Jonathan H. Adler, Heat Expands All Things: The Proliferation of Greenhouse Gas Regulation under the Obama Administration, 34 Harv. J.L. & Pub. Pol'y 421 (2011).

[19] Jody Freeman & David B. Spence, Old Statutes, New Problems, 163 U. Pa. L. Rev. 1, 20 (2014).

[20] One issue raised in *Massachusetts* was whether setting GHG emission standards for automobiles would conflict with fuel economy regulations administered by the National Highway Transportation and Safety Administration, but the Court concluded the two agencies could coordinate their efforts to address any potential problems. See Massachusetts, 549 U.S. at 532 ("The two obligations may overlap, but there is no reason to think the two agencies cannot both administer their obligations and yet avoid inconsistency.").

[21] See Freeman & Spence, *supra* note 19, at 21.

[22] See 42 U.S.C. § 7475. These provisions are commonly referred to as "PSD" for "Prevention of Significant Deterioration."

on the type of facility involved.[23] For traditional air pollutants, such as sulfur dioxide or nitrogen oxides, these thresholds only reach the biggest and dirtiest facilities—a total of several thousand facilities nationwide. Applied to GHGs, however, these same numerical thresholds would require the regulation of millions of facilities, including many commercial and residential buildings.[24]

Lest application of the CAA's express terms to GHGs unleash a regulatory tsunami, the EPA proposed to "tailor" the law's application and enforcement so as to reduce the number of regulated facilities.[25] Specifically, the agency decided it would redefine the definition of what constitutes a major source to only reach facilities that emit over 100,000 tons per year.[26] The EPA acknowledged the relevant statutory provisions were "clear on their face,"[27] but defended the new regulation as a "common sense" approach[28] necessary to prevent the CAA's permitting programs from becoming "unrecognizable to the Congress that designed" them.[29]

However much the EPA thought this effort to "tailor" the act's requirements made "common sense," the Supreme Court concluded otherwise. In *Utility Air Regulatory Group v. EPA* (*UARG*), the Court rejected the EPA's claim that it was required to treat GHGs

---

[23] See 42 U.S.C. § 7479(1) (defining emission thresholds for Section 165); 42 U.S.C. § 7661(2) adopts the definition provided in 42 U.S.C. § 7602(j), defining a "major" source as "any stationary facility or source of air pollutants which directly emits, or has the potential to emit, one hundred tons per year or more of any air pollutant." For regulation of hazardous air pollutants, 42 U.S.C. § 7661(2) incorporates the even more stringent definition contained in 42 U.S.C. § 7412.

[24] See Prevention of Significant Deterioration and Title V GHG Tailoring Rule, 74 Fed. Reg. 55,292, 55,294, 55,302 (Oct. 27, 2009); see also Freeman & Spence, *supra* note 19, at 24 (noting the "burden would have overwhelmed the agency and the states, frustrated small business, and led to accusations that the Obama Administration was over-regulating"). For a fuller discussion of the impact of applying the statutory thresholds for major stationary sources to GHGs, see Adler, Heat Expands, *supra* note 18, at 432–35.

[25] Prevention of Significant Deterioration and Title V GHG Tailoring Rule, 74 Fed. Reg. 55,292 (Oct. 27, 2009).

[26] Prevention of Significant Deterioration and Title V GHG Tailoring Rule, 75 Fed. Reg. 31,514 (June 3, 2010).

[27] 74 Fed. Reg. at 55,306.

[28] Akis Psygkas, New EPA Rule Will Require Use of Best Technologies to Reduce GHGs from Large Facilities, Comp. Admin. L. (Blog) (Oct. 1, 2009).

[29] 75 Fed. Reg. at 31,562.

as "air pollutants" for all provisions of the CAA, particularly where doing so would "bring about an enormous and transformative expansion in EPA's regulatory authority without clear congressional authorization."[30] Not only would the EPA's interpretation greatly expand the universe of regulated entities, the Court concluded it would also necessitate granting the agency the authority to rewrite clear statutory thresholds so as to ensure the act's regulatory structure remained operational. In language foreshadowing its decision in *West Virginia v. EPA*, the Court explained: "When an agency claims to discover in a long-extant statute an unheralded power to regulate 'a significant portion of the American economy,' we typically greet its announcement with a measure of skepticism. We expect Congress to speak clearly if it wishes to assign to an agency decisions of vast 'economic and political significance.'"[31] Here, Congress had indicated neither that it wanted the EPA to regulate the millions of facilities that emit modest amounts of greenhouse gases nor that the EPA could revise numerical statutory thresholds.

While *UARG* was working its way through the courts, the agency was also beginning work on regulations governing GHG emissions from new and existing power plants.[32] This was a priority for the Obama administration because electricity generation is responsible for approximately one quarter of annual greenhouse gas emissions.[33]

Under CAA Section 7411, the EPA is instructed to establish federal "standards of performance" for categories of stationary sources that "cause[], or contribute[] significantly to, air pollution which may reasonably be anticipated to endanger public health or welfare."[34] The "standard of performance" is defined as that standard "which reflects the degree of emission limitation achievable through the

---

[30] 573 U.S. 302, 324 (2014).

[31] *Id.* (quoting FDA v. Brown & Williamson Tobacco Corp., 529 U.S. 120, 159 (2000)).

[32] This rulemaking was the result of a settlement agreement the EPA entered into in 2010 under which it committed to proposing such regulations no later than July 2011 and promulgating final rules no later than May 2012. That timeline slipped.

[33] In 2020, the electricity sector was responsible for 25 percent of U.S. greenhouse gas emissions. By comparison, transportation was responsible for 27 percent. See Inventory of U.S. Greenhouse Gas Emissions and Sinks: 1990–2020, EPA (April 2022), https://bit.ly/3vAzDq9.

[34] 42 U.S.C. § 7411(b)(1).

application of the best system of emission reduction," accounting for cost and other factors, that has been "adequately demonstrated."[35] Once such a standard is set for new sources, the EPA promulgates guidelines identifying the standard of performance for existing sources.[36] The EPA does not impose such standards on existing sources directly, however. Rather, Section 7411(d) instructs the agency to issue regulations providing for states to submit plans imposing the appropriate standard of performance on existing sources.[37] Section 111(d) also requires EPA to permit states to "take into consideration . . . the remaining useful life of the existing source" when applying and enforcing the standard of performance to a particular source.[38]

[35] 42 U.S.C. § 7411(a)(1).

[36] 42 U.S.C. § 7411(d)(1). Under this provision, the EPA is not to set standards of performance for emissions from existing sources that are regulated under the CAA's National Ambient Air Quality Standards (NAAQS) or Hazardous Air Pollutant (HAP) provisions. Before the U.S. Court of Appeals for the D.C. Circuit, some petitioners argued that Section 7411 precludes the regulation of emissions from new sources if the *sources* are subject to regulation under Section 112. As power plant emissions of mercury are regulated under Section 112, this would have barred the adoption of any GHG standards for existing power plants under Section 7411. The D.C. Circuit rejected this argument. See Am. Lung Ass'n v. EPA, 985 F.3d 914, 932 (D.C. Cir. 2021). The Supreme Court did not grant certiorari on this question, and the Court's *West Virginia* opinion appears to adopt the D.C. Circuit's interpretation of this provision. See West Virginia, 142 S. Ct. at 2601.

[37] *Id.* A straightforward reading of the statutory language would suggest the EPA lacks the authority to set standards of performance for existing sources, let alone something as ambitious as the Clean Power Plan, but this argument was not raised in *West Virginia v. EPA*. See Tom Merrill, West Virginia v. EPA: Was "Major Questions" Necessary?, Volokh Conspiracy (July 26, 2022), https://bit.ly/3vHp848.

[38] 42 U.S.C. § 7411(d)(1). It is common in environmental law to set different standards for new and existing sources, reflecting both the fact that it is often easier or less costly to install or include pollution control technologies when designing a facility than to retrofit an old one, as well as the fact that owners and employees of existing sources tend to have more political clout than owners and employees of new, not-yet-built sources. See Jonathan R. Nash & Richard L. Revesz, Grandfather and Environmental Regulation: The Law and Economics of New Source Review, 101 Nw. U.L. Rev. 1677, 1733 (2007) ("grandfathering may be appropriate in environmental regulation to the extent that installing and upgrading pollution control equipment in existing plants may be both logistically difficult and expensive"); E. Donald Elliot, A Critical Assessment of the EPA's Air Program at Fifty and a Suggestion for How It Might Do Even Better, 70 Case W. Res. L. Rev. 895, 915–16 (2020) ("Regulating future polluters more stringently than those already operating often happens because it is less difficult politically to impose costs on speculative future projects than on existing industries

After years of development, the EPA finalized a set of regulations governing emissions from new and existing power plants, the latter of which were called the Clean Power Plan (CPP). Under the CPP, the EPA determined that the "best system of emission reduction" (BSER) for existing coal-fired power plants would not be based exclusively on emission reductions that could be achieved at individual plants, such as by the adoption of heat-rate improvements that would result in more efficient fuel consumption. Rather, the EPA set the BSER based on the additional emission reductions that could be achieved by shifting power generation from existing coal-fired power plants to lower-emitting facilities, such as natural gas-fired plants, as well as "new low- or zero-carbon generating capacity," such as wind and solar.

The CPP anticipated that existing coal-fired power plants would reduce their emissions by curtailing their own electricity generation; increasing reliance on new natural gas, wind, or solar facilities; or purchasing emission allowances from lower-emitting sources. As described by the Court in *West Virginia v. EPA*, the BSER for existing coal-fired power plants was "one that would reduce carbon pollution by moving production to cleaner sources," not one that would reduce the emissions from existing sources themselves.[39] Indeed, the ultimate emission limit adopted in the CPP was "so strict" that no existing coal plant could meet the standard without engaging in some form of generation shifting.[40] Under the CPP, states were required to submit their implementation plans in 2018 for how the power sector would achieve the necessary emission reductions by 2030.

Even supporters of the CPP recognized it rested on a "novel and far-reaching" interpretation of the relevant statutory provisions.[41] The CPP, however, would never take effect. States and coal companies immediately filed legal challenges against it. In February 2016, a majority of the Court voted to stay the CPP, pending resolution

---

that are organized and have political clout. . . . [It] seemed intuitively obvious to the drafters that it would be less expensive to design pollution-control equipment for a new plant than to retrofit an existing plant.").

[39] West Virginia, 142 S. Ct. at 2603.

[40] *Id.* at 2604.

[41] See Freeman & Spence, *supra* note 19, at 37.

of the legal challenges, thereby preventing it from ever going into effect.[42]

The election of Donald Trump prompted a dramatic reversal in the EPA's approach to GHG regulation under the CAA. In March 2017, President Trump issued an executive order instructing the EPA to review and consider rescinding the CPP and other EPA regulations affecting the energy industry.[43] Pursuant to this order, the EPA developed an alternative to the CPP, known as the Affordable Clean Energy (ACE) rule.[44] This rule, promulgated in July 2019, was based on a much narrower interpretation of the EPA's regulatory authority under the CAA—an interpretation the agency now claimed was compelled by the plain text of the statute. The EPA also argued that a narrow interpretation was necessary to avoid adopting a broad rule that would trigger the major questions doctrine. Citing the *UARG* decision, the agency noted that "the major question doctrine instructs that an agency may issue a major rule only if Congress has clearly authorized the agency to do so."[45]

Specifically, the EPA now concluded that standards of performance under Section 7411 could only be based on emission-control measures that could be adopted at each regulated source—so-called "inside the fenceline" measures—and this could not include generation shifting. Accordingly, the EPA decided the CPP was unlawful, and the EPA could not impose emission reductions on existing coal-fired power plants beyond that which could be achieved through heat-rate improvements at individual plants. The narrow scope of the rule meant narrow climate benefits. The emission reductions from the ACE rule were estimated to be as little as 1 percent by 2030.[46] Just as red states and coal companies challenged the CPP, blue states and

---

[42] Chamber of Commerce v. EPA, 136 S. Ct. 999 (Mem) (Feb. 9, 2016); see also Jonathan H. Adler, Supreme Court Puts the Brakes on the EPA's Clean Power Plan, Wash. Post (Feb. 9, 2016), https://wapo.st/3zOobK2.

[43] See Promoting Energy Independence and Economic Growth, Exec. Order No. 13783, 82 Fed. Reg. 16,093 (Mar. 28, 2017).

[44] See Repeal of the Clean Power Plan; Emission Guidelines for Greenhouse Gas Emissions from Existing Electric Utility Generating Units; Revisions to Emission Guidelines Implementing Regulations, 84 Fed. Reg. 32,520 (July 8, 2019).

[45] *Id.* at 32,529.

[46] See Kate C. Shouse, Linda Tsang, & Jonathan Ramseur, EPA's Affordable Clean Energy Rule: In Brief, CRS Report R465468, at 7 (2020).

environmental organizations immediately challenged the ACE rule, joined by some electric utilities.

On January 19, 2021, the day before Joseph Biden was to be sworn in as the 46th president of the United States, a divided panel of the U.S. Court of Appeals for the D.C. Circuit concluded that the repeal of the CPP and promulgation of the ACE rule were unlawful.[47] Specifically, the court held that both actions were based on "a fundamental misconstruction" of the EPA's statutory authority.[48] Whereas the Trump EPA believed that standards of performance for existing sources had to be based on measures that could be adopted at each source, the D.C. Circuit concluded that Section 7411 "imposed no limits on the types of measures the EPA may consider" beyond requiring the agency to consider cost, non–air quality health and environmental impacts, and energy requirements.[49] And because the ACE rule rested "squarely" on an "erroneous" reading of the act, it was vacated and remanded to the agency.[50]

One month later, at the Biden administration's request, the D.C. Circuit issued a partial stay of the mandate in the case to prevent imposition of the CPP.[51] While the Biden administration preferred the Obama administration's interpretation of the CAA over that of the Trump administration, the CPP's deadline for state plan submission had passed, and the relevant emission reduction targets had been met or surpassed in much of the country. Despite the stay, a coalition of states and coal companies filed petitions for certiorari, and, somewhat surprisingly, the Court took the case.

Questions about Jurisdiction

From the moment the justices agreed to hear *West Virginia v. EPA*, there were questions about whether the case was properly before the Court. Article III jurisdiction extends only to "cases or controversies." Among other things, this means that those seeking to invoke

[47] Although the three judges disagreed on the rationale, they were unanimous in rejecting the Trump regulation. See Am. Lung Ass'n, 985 F.3d 914.

[48] ALA, 985 F.3d at 930 ("[T]he central operative terms of the ACE Rule and the repeal of its predecessor rule, the Clean Power Plan . . . hinged on a fundamental misconstruction of Section 7411(d) of the Clean Air Act.").

[49] *Id.* at 946.

[50] *Id.* at 995.

[51] See West Virginia, 142 S. Ct. at 2606 (noting stay).

a court's jurisdiction must have standing and the case must present a live controversy that has not been mooted by subsequent events. Given the EPA wanted neither to enforce the CPP nor to defend the ACE rule, it was fair to ask whether there was Article III jurisdiction to hear the case.

Although it had not pressed this issue in its brief opposing certiorari,[52] the solicitor general (SG) argued that the Court lacked Article III standing to hear the petitioners' challenge to the D.C. Circuit's decision.[53] Specifically, the SG maintained that none of the petitioners could demonstrate an actual or imminent injury from the D.C. Circuit decision to vacate the ACE rule and CPP repeal, rendering any Supreme Court decision an "impermissible advisory opinion."[54] Accordingly, the government argued, the Court should either dismiss the case for lack of standing or merely vacate the D.C. Circuit's decision and remand the case back to the EPA. The standing argument was also picked up by the nongovernmental organization and trade association respondents, but not the other parties that intervened on behalf of the EPA.[55]

It became clear at oral argument that there was little support for the SG's jurisdictional arguments, and the dissenting justices did not meaningfully challenge the chief justice's conclusion that the Court had jurisdiction over the case. While some justices suggested there might be prudential reasons to avoid a decision, none pushed hard on the Article III claim—and for good reason. While the decision to grant certiorari in *West Virginia v. EPA* may have been unusually aggressive, the Court had jurisdiction to hear the case.

Standing is necessary both when a plaintiff first files a suit in federal court as well as when a party pursues an appeal.[56] In the latter

---

[52] Of note, neither "standing" nor "case or controversy" appears in the SG's brief opposing certiorari. See Br. for the Federal Respondents in Opposition, West Virginia v. EPA, 142 S. Ct. 2587 (2022) (Nos. 20-1530 et seq.). The brief did, however, suggest that the petitioners' claims would become moot, but only if the EPA adopted a new regulation more akin to the ACE rule than to the CPP. *Id.* at 20.

[53] See Br. for the Federal Respondents at 15–23, West Virginia v. EPA, 142 S. Ct. 2587 (2022) (Nos. 20-1530, et seq.).

[54] *Id.* at 18.

[55] See Br. of Non-Governmental Org. & Trade Ass'n Respondents at 23–32, West Virginia v. EPA, 142 S. Ct. 2587 (2022) (Nos. 20-1530 et seq.).

[56] See Hollingsworth v. Perry, 570 U.S. 693, 705 (2013) (noting "Article III demands that an 'actual controversy' persist throughout all stages of litigation.").

context, the standing inquiry focuses on whether the petitioners experience an injury that is "fairly traceable to the judgment below" and whether a favorable ruling would provide redress for that injury.[57] There was no question the petitioning states met this standard. The D.C. Circuit's judgment invalidated *both* "the ACE rule *and* its embedded repeal of the Clean Power Plan."[58] Thus, as the chief justice explained, insofar as the CPP injured the petitioning states by obligating them to adopt regulations of the power sector, there was "little question" they were injured by the lower court's judgment.[59] Tellingly, the dissent did not contest this point.

While framing the government's argument in terms of standing, the SG also suggested that the D.C. Circuit's decision to stay the mandate until the EPA adopted new regulations under Section 7411 mooted the prior dispute.[60] While intervening events may deprive a litigant of a sufficient stake in the outcome of a lawsuit to deprive a court of jurisdiction, it takes more than a stay of a lower court order to moot a case.[61] Courts are reluctant to allow a party's voluntary cessation of challenged conduct to render a case moot. As the chief justice explained, "voluntary cessation does not moot a case unless it is absolutely clear that the allegedly wrongful behavior could not reasonably be expected to recur."[62] The government offered no assurance it would not rely on generation shifting or the D.C. Circuit's broad conception of the EPA's regulatory authority in a future rule, nor could it. Thus, neither the D.C. Circuit's stay, which could be lifted, nor the potential of new regulatory standards could moot the case. Again, the dissent did not argue the point, even if only because the standard for mootness is "notoriously strict."[63]

While conceding the Court *could* hear the case, Justice Kagan would not concede that Court *should* have heard it. In a rush to "pronounce

[57] Food Marketing Inst. v. Argus Leader Media, 139 S. Ct. 2356, 2362 (2019).

[58] ALA, 985 F.3d at 995 (emphasis added).

[59] West Virginia, 142 S. Ct. at 2606.

[60] See Br. for the Federal Respondents, *supra* note 53, at 17.

[61] At oral argument, Justice Alito asked the SG whether the Court had "ever held that the issuance of a stay can moot a case." The SG conceded she was "not aware of a precedent" to that effect. Tr. of Oral Arg. at 86–87, West Virginia v. EPA, 142 S. Ct. 2587 (2022) (Nos. 20-1530 et seq.).

[62] West Virginia, 142 S. Ct. at 2607 (cleaned up).

[63] *Id.* at 2628 (Kagan, J., dissenting).

on the legality" of an "old rule," Justice Kagan complained, the Court issued "what is really an advisory opinion on the proper scope of the new rule EPA is considering."[64] Whatever the merits of the legal arguments against the CPP, she suggested, the EPA no longer sought to administer it and was well at work on a replacement, so the Court was effectively telling the EPA what it could or could not do in the future.

Justice Sonia Sotomayor pressed a similar point at oral argument, citing the Supreme Court's disposition of *EPA v. Brown*.[65] That case presented a quite different question, however, which may explain why it was not cited in Justice Kagan's dissent. In *Brown*, the Court had accepted certiorari at the government's behest to review multiple lower court decisions striking down EPA regulations that purported to commandeer state governments to implement particular air pollution control measures.[66] Although the government had sought certiorari, it then conceded that the regulations could not be defended as written. Accordingly, the Court declined "the federal parties' invitation to pass upon the EPA regulations" at issue because "the ones before us are admitted to be in need of certain essential modifications."[67] Because the EPA would be revising its rules to cure their legal defects, any decision by the Court "would amount to rendering an advisory opinion."[68] Accordingly, the Court vacated the lower court decisions and remanded the regulations back to the EPA.[69]

Unlike in *Brown*, the EPA did not concede there was any legal problem with the CPP or with the legal theory it was based on. The EPA sought to update and modernize its rules, not reconsider whether it

---

[64] *Id.*

[65] Tr. of Oral Arg., *supra* note 61, at 22 (citing EPA v. Brown, 431 U.S. 101 (1977)).

[66] For a brief discussion of this litigation, see Jonathan H. Adler & Nathaniel Stewart, Is the Clean Air Act Unconstitutional? Coercion, Cooperative Federalism, and Conditional Spending after NFIB v. Sebelius, 43 Ecol. L.Q. 671, 685–86 (2016).

[67] EPA v. Brown, 431 U.S. at 103–04.

[68] *Id.* at 104.

[69] Of note, Justice John Paul Stevens dissented on the ground that the litigation would not be moot unless and until the EPA actually rescinded the regulations at issue, and "an apparent admission that those regulations are invalid unless modified is not a proper reason for vacating the Court of Appeals judgments which invalidated the regulations." *Id.* at 104 (Stevens, J., dissenting).

had the statutory authority to issue them in the first place. Nonetheless, the government's merits brief did suggest a similar disposition: vacating the D.C. Circuit's judgment and remanding the case to the agency.[70] Such a move would have redressed the petitioning states' injuries without requiring the Court to assess the scope of the EPA's authority in the absence of a rule to be enforced and might have appealed to the chief justice's minimalist instincts. Curiously, this possibility was only raised in the SG's merits brief and had not been suggested at the certiorari stage.

Choosing to Answer a Major Question

The Court's decision to grant certiorari and schedule *West Virginia v. EPA* for oral argument was an ominous sign for the EPA. There was no reason to hear the case if a majority of the Court were inclined to rubber-stamp the D.C. Circuit's broad construction of the EPA's regulatory authority. But the breadth of the issues presented—and the various questions presented in the four cert petitions the Court accepted—gave the Court a wide range of options.

At one end of the range of possibilities was a surgical, text-based holding, limiting the "best system of emission reduction" (again, the BSER) to those measures that can be applied at or to a given stationary source subject to regulation. At the other end was an attack on broad delegations of regulatory authority, rejecting even the possibility that Congress could have so casually delegated power to the EPA to decide how to remake the electricity sector. The most likely result, however, was a middle course, echoing *UARG* in relying on the major questions doctrine and the notion that extraordinary assertions of regulatory authority require extraordinarily clear congressional delegations. All four of the cert petitions granted pointed in this direction, and the Court's two covid decisions indicated it was primed to go in this direction.

As expected, Chief Justice Roberts's opinion spent little time focused on the intricacies of statutory text and made scant mention of constitutional concerns about delegation. Instead, after engaging in a bit of traditional interpretive throat-clearing about how to conduct statutory interpretation in an "ordinary case," the chief noted that "these are 'extraordinary cases' that call for a

---

[70] See Br. for the Federal Respondents, *supra* note 53, at 21.

different approach[.]"[71] *West Virginia v. EPA*, the chief announced, was one such "major questions case."[72] The EPA was asserting the authority "to substantially restructure the American energy market" based on an "ancillary" statutory provision that had never before been used for such a purpose.[73] Whether the EPA could define the BSER as generation shifting was not treated as a routine question of statutory interpretation for which a "plausible textual basis for the agency action" would be sufficient.[74] More would be required to justify upholding the EPA's authority to "restructur[e] the Nation's overall mix of electricity generation" under the guise of setting performance standards for stationary sources of air pollution.[75]

In deploying the major questions doctrine, the Court still faced a choice: It could invoke the doctrine as a canon of construction favoring more modest interpretations of agency authority insofar as the scope of delegation is in doubt; or it could use the doctrine to drive a presumption against the agency's claimed authority. These two potential approaches to major questions were illustrated in the Court's decisions rejecting emergency measures during the coronavirus pandemic.

As a canon of construction, the doctrine would help resolve any lingering uncertainty or statutory ambiguity left after directly engaging with the relevant statutory text. That is how the Court deployed the major questions doctrine in the eviction moratorium case.[76] Only after identifying reasons to reject the claim of the Centers for Disease Control and Prevention (CDC) that it had authority to forestall evictions did the Court note that "if the text were ambiguous, the sheer scope of the CDC's claimed authority . . . would counsel against the Government's interpretation."[77] The Court could not see textual or historical support for the CDC's claimed authority, and the major questions doctrine merely confirmed this conclusion. Major questions was icing on the Court's interpretive cake.

---

[71] West Virginia, 142 S. Ct. at 2608.

[72] *Id.* at 2610.

[73] *Id.*

[74] *Id.* at 2609.

[75] *Id.* at 2607.

[76] Ala. Ass'n of Realtors, 141 S. Ct. at 2489.

[77] *Id.*

The approach in *Alabama Association of Realtors* contrasts with that in the Occupational Safety and Health Administration's (OSHA) vaccinate-or-test mandate.[78] In *NFIB v. OSHA*, the Court announced that it expects a clear statement from Congress when "authorizing an agency to exercise powers of vast economic and political significance," and that the OSHA mandate would qualify before even beginning to analyze the relevant statutory text.[79] Here a concern for "major questions," and a skepticism of the government's authority, was baked into the interpretive cake from the beginning. Rather than reject the OSHA policy based on a close reading of OSHA's statutory authority and the agency's historical practice in applying that authority, the Court deployed the major questions doctrine to drive the ultimate outcome.[80]

In *West Virginia*, the chief justice adopted the latter approach. Despite the availability of textual arguments that would have precluded the expansive construction of EPA authority that underlay the CPP, the chief justice opted to deploy the major questions concern at the front end of his analysis. This no doubt allowed for a shorter and less technical opinion and avoided any need to consider whether the EPA's interpretation of Section 7411 could qualify for *Chevron* deference, but it also left the Court majority vulnerable to the criticism that it had abandoned textualism in favor of a result-oriented, purposivist analysis.

Under this approach, even if one might conclude that the EPA's preferred interpretation of Section 7411 were reasonable, the nature of the power the EPA was asserting, and its lack of precedent, counseled a narrower construction. That the EPA's interpretation of its authority to define BSER might be plausible "as a matter of 'definitional possibilities'" was insufficient to justify the breadth of authority the EPA sought to assert.[81] That the word "system"—and the phrase "best system of emission reduction"—could be interpreted broadly when "shorn of all context" was "not close to the sort of clear

---

[78] Nat'l Fed'n Indep. Bus. (NFIB) v. Dep't of Labor, OSHA, 142 S. Ct. 661 (2022).

[79] *Id.* at 665.

[80] For reasons why the OSHA standard was legally vulnerable even without resort to the major questions doctrine, see Jonathan H. Adler, OSHA (Finally) Issues Emergency Standard Mandating Large Employers Require Vaccination or Testing (Updated), Volokh Conspiracy (Nov. 4, 2011), https://bit.ly/3QfVRW2.

[81] West Virginia, 142 S. Ct. at 2614.

authorization required by our precedents."[82] Such a cursory argument may have sufficed given this was a "major questions case," but it was hardly a compelling statutory interpretation.

Justice Kagan did not pass up the opportunity to point out the weakness of the Court's statutory analysis, which relied more on the history of EPA past practices and congressional inaction than on a meaningful engagement with the text. She wrote a forceful dissent, harping on the majority's failure to provide a convincing explanation for why generation shifting could not be a "system" of emission reduction.[83] While her analysis is superficially powerful, Justice Kagan did not grapple with the full statutory text either, nor did she delve much into the CAA's structure and operation. Instead, she hammered away at the pliable nature of the word "system" and the majority's rush to embrace the major questions doctrine. There were textual counterarguments to be made.[84] The majority did not make them. Justice Gorsuch's concurrence responded to the dissent to defend the provenance and utility of the major questions doctrine, but it too failed to square off with Kagan on the statutory text.

What Makes a Question Major?

Once Chief Justice Roberts declared *West Virginia v. EPA* a major questions case, his task became easier. No longer did he need to find that the EPA's desired interpretation of the relevant statutory provisions was out of bounds (with or without *Chevron* deference). Invoking the doctrine enabled him to flip the presumption and demand that those defending the D.C. Circuit's interpretation of the CAA find "clear congressional authorization" for that position.[85] But what made *West Virginia v. EPA* a "major questions case"?

---

[82] *Id.*

[83] *Id.* at 2641 (Kagan, J., dissenting) ("Some years ago, I remarked that '[w]e're all textualists now.' . . . It seems I was wrong. The current Court is textualist only when being so suits it.").

[84] See Nathan Richardson, Trading Unmoored: The Uncertain Legal Foundation for Emissions Trading under § 111 of the Clean Air Act, 120 Penn St. L. Rev. 181 (2015) (identifying reasons why the EPA may not be able to require or utilize emissions trading as the BSER); see also Lisa Heinzerling & Rena I. Steinzor, A Perfect Storm: Mercury and the Bush Administration, 34 Envt. L. Rep. 10297, 10309 (2004) (arguing Section 7411 "clearly contemplates individualized, performance-based standards for sources").

[85] West Virginia, 142 S. Ct. at 2609.

Chief Justice Roberts identified several factors indicative of "major questions" cases under the Court's precedents. These include that an agency is seeking to exercise broad regulatory power over a substantial portion of the economy, that this power is "unheralded" or had not been previously discovered or utilized, and that Congress has "conspicuously and repeatedly declined to enact" express authorization for what the agency wants to do.[86] If these criteria sound somewhat fuzzy, that is because they are. Even before *West Virginia v. EPA*, scholars complained that the doctrine did not produce an administrable line between which cases should be considered major and which should not.[87] Even though *West Virginia v. EPA* was more obviously a "major questions" case than some others, the chief justice did little to delineate a set of clear legal criteria that could resolve closer cases.[88]

In cases such as *FDA v. Brown & Williamson* and *NFIB v. OSHA*, the agencies sought to use long extant power in a new way that was likely unanticipated by the Congress that enacted the statute, or Congresses since. Insofar as an agency's delegated power derives its legitimacy from a deliberate choice by the legislature to authorize such power, finding new powers in old statutes is a problem.[89] If an agency can go decades before discovering broad authority within its authorizing legislation, that is "telling" evidence that such power was not delegated.[90]

The age of the statute and the novelty of the agency's asserted authority played a significant role in the chief justice's analysis. Citing Justice Felix Frankfurter, the chief justice placed substantial

---

[86] *Id.* at 2610.

[87] See Nathan D. Richardson, Keeping Big Cases from Making Bad Law: The Resurgent "Major Questions" Doctrine, 49 Conn. L. Rev. 355, 406 (2016) (noting "it is hard to determine what divides major questions from minor or interstitial ones"); Cass R. Sunstein, Beyond Marbury: The Executive's Power to Say What the Law Is, 115 Yale L.J. 2580, 2607 (2006) (noting there is "no metric . . . for making the necessary distinctions"); Jacob Loshin & Aaron Nielson, Hiding Delegation in Mouseholes, 62 Admin. L. Rev. 19, 23 (2010) ("One judge's mouse is another judge's elephant, and it ever will be so.").

[88] See Richardson, *supra* note 87, at 388–89 (explaining why a challenge to the CPP would almost certainly be considered a "major questions" case).

[89] See generally Jonathan H. Adler & Christopher J. Walker, Delegation and Time, 105 Iowa L. Rev. 1931 (2020).

[90] West Virginia, 142 S. Ct. at 2609.

weight on history and agency practice in the major questions analysis:

> [J]ust as established practice may shed light on the extent of power conveyed by general statutory language, so the want of assertion of power by those who presumably would be alert to exercise it, is equally significant in determining whether such power was actually conferred.[91]

This is a reasonable inference to draw. Yet as discussed below, it is not clear why this inference should only be drawn in the context of "major questions." If the question before the Court is whether an agency is exercising delegated power, and agency practice and historical understandings are probative of statutory meaning, this would seem to be true for major and minor questions alike. Further, suggesting that once litigants are able to convince a court that a given case presents a "major question" they can discard traditional methods of statutory interpretation is not conducive to consistent and principled decisionmaking.

Justice Gorsuch wrote a separate concurrence, stressing his view that the major questions doctrine is properly understood as a clear statement rule that prevents Congress from delegating broad legislative power to agencies. There is much to this intuition, even if one does not ground the major questions doctrine in a concern for excessive delegation, as Justice Gorsuch would wish to do. It does not, however, solve the problem of identifying which cases are major and which are not. If anything, it suggests that whether a case presents a "major question" should not be a threshold inquiry.

A Step (Zero) beyond Major Questions

Rather than focus on whether a given case presents a "major question" that would justify loading the interpretive deck, the Court should have instead started at the beginning, what we might call "delegation step zero."[92]

---

[91] FTC v. Bunte Bros., Inc., 312 U.S. 349, 352 (1941).

[92] See Jonathan H. Adler, A 'Step Zero' for Delegations, in The Administrative State before the Supreme Court: Perspectives on the Nondelegation Doctrine (Peter Wallison & John Yoo eds., 2022), from which this portion of this article draws. For the origins of the "step zero" concept, see Thomas W. Merrill & Kristin E. Hickman, Chevron's Domain, 89 Geo. L.J. 873 (2001).

All legislative powers are vested in Congress. Although such powers may be delegated to the executive branch, there is no question where they begin. Put another way, the constitutional allocation of powers embodies a nondelegation baseline: Absent legislative action, all legislative power is in the legislature's hands, and none is in the hands of any administrative agency or part of the executive branch. This is not a nondelegation doctrine, so much as a *delegation* doctrine; a doctrine that recognizes that delegations are necessary for agencies to have regulatory power.

As the Supreme Court has noted repeatedly, "an agency literally has no power to act . . . unless and until Congress confers power upon it."[93] This is (or should be) "axiomatic."[94] As the Court further explained in *Chrysler Corp. v. Brown*:

> The legislative power of the United States is vested in the Congress, and the exercise of quasi-legislative authority by governmental departments and agencies must be rooted in a grant of such power by the Congress and subject to limitations which that body imposes.[95]

Thus, a delegation of power is necessary for administrative agencies to act. Without a delegation, the agency has no regulatory power.

Chief Justice Roberts reiterated this point in *West Virginia v. EPA*, as he has in other opinions.[96] In his *City of Arlington* dissent, for instance, the chief justice noted that *Chevron* deference is premised on legislative delegation of interpretive authority to a federal agency.[97] Without such a delegation, no deference is due. And because it is for courts to resolve questions of law, "whether Congress has delegated to an agency the authority to provide an interpretation that carries

[93] La. Pub. Serv. Comm'n v. FCC, 476 U.S. 355, 374 (1986).

[94] Bowen v. Georgetown Univ. Hosp., 488 U.S. 204, 208 (1988) ("It is axiomatic that an administrative agency's power to promulgate legislative regulation is limited to the authority delegated by Congress.").

[95] 441 U.S. 281, 302 (1979).

[96] West Virginia, 142 S. Ct. at 2609 ("Agencies have only those powers given to them by Congress.").

[97] City of Arlington, 569 U.S. at 317 (Roberts, C.J., dissenting). According to Tom Merrill, this dissent "deserves to enter the annals as a classic statement of the principles of administrative law." Thomas W. Merrill, The Chevron Doctrine: Its Rise and Fall and the Future of the Administrative State 226 (2022).

the force of law is for the judge to answer independently."[98] Further, such delegations are not dispersed wholesale. Rather, such authority is delegated with regard to "particular" statutory provisions or purposes.[99]

As then-Judge Stephen Breyer noted in a 1985 lecture, "Congress is more likely to have focused upon, and answered, major questions, while leaving interstitial matters to answer themselves in the course of [a] statute's daily administration."[100] While Breyer was focused on the question of *Chevron* deference, he was making a point about when it is reasonable to presume that a delegation of authority has occurred absent a clear statement in the statutory text. This approach simply reflects "common sense as to the manner in which Congress [is] likely to delegate" power to federal agencies.[101]

Statutory language may be ambiguous or creatively interpreted to justify a particular assertion of regulatory power. But ambiguity is not enough to establish that a delegation has taken place. In *Chevron* cases, courts recognize that statutory ambiguity is not enough to justify deference to an agency's interpretation. There must also be reason to believe that Congress delegated authority to resolve the ambiguity to the agency. Thus, in *King v. Burwell*, the Court refused to grant *Chevron* deference to the Internal Revenue Service even though it found the relevant statutory language to be ambiguous (and ultimately agreed with the agency's interpretation on the merits).[102] Likewise, the U.S. Court of Appeals for the D.C. Circuit has recognized that "mere ambiguity in a statute is not evidence of congressional delegation of authority."[103] Ambiguity is necessary but not sufficient.

There is no reason to confine this inquiry to *Chevron* cases. If the *Chevron* step-zero inquiry is necessary because courts must first

[98] City of Arlington, 569 U.S. at 317.

[99] *Id*. at 320.

[100] Stephen Breyer, Judicial Review of Questions of Law and Policy, 38 Admin. L. Rev., 363, 370 (1986). See also Robert A. Anthony, Which Agency Interpretations Should Bind Citizens and the Courts?, 7 Yale J. on Reg. 1, 11–12 (1990) (noting courts were less likely to defer to agencies when a "major question" is at issue).

[101] West Virginia, 142 S. Ct. at 2609 (quoting FDA v. Brown & Williamson, 529 U.S. at 133).

[102] King, 576 U.S. at 485–86.

[103] Am. Bar Assoc. v. FTC, 430 F.3d 457 (D.C. Cir. 2005).

determine whether Congress has delegated interpretive authority before deferring to an agency, then a similar inquiry should be
required before a court upholds an agency's assertion of regulatory authority. And, as with *Chevron*, such authority must be demonstrated. As the Court held in *Interstate Commerce Commission v.
Cincinnati, New Orleans & Texas Pacific Railway Co.*, known as the
Queen and Crescent case, in 1897, the power to issue rules mandating or prohibiting private conduct (in this case, rates for rail transport) "is not to be presumed or implied from any doubtful and uncertain language."[104] The Supreme Court has not always adhered to
this approach (which is why Chief Justice Roberts found himself in
dissent in *City of Arlington*), but it has never been repudiated.[105]

In place of a threshold inquiry into whether the economic or political stakes of a case are sufficiently "major" or "extraordinary," courts
would be better off focusing on the root question of whether Congress delegated the asserted authority to the agency and whether
the evidence of such a delegation is commensurate with the nature
of the authority asserted. In this way, the major-ness of the question
at issue would be less of a threshold to be crossed than a continuum
to be incorporated into the statutory analysis. The weight of evidence
necessary to support an asserted delegation should be proportional
to the breadth, scope, and novelty of the delegated power claimed.

The specific inquiry contemplated here would consider several
factors, all of which center on whether a prior delegation authorizes
the agency action in question. The delegation of authority must be
explicit in the plain language of the authorizing statute, as it would

---

[104] See Interstate Com. Comm'n v. Cincinnati, New Orleans, & Tx. Pacific Ry. Co.,
167 U.S. 497, 505 (1897). The case is referred to as the Queen and Crescent case because
the rail line went between the Queen City (Cincinnati) and the Crescent City (New
Orleans).

[105] The D.C. Circuit has also recognized this doctrine in numerous cases going back
decades. See, for example, Atlantic City Elec. Co. v. FERC, 295 F.3d 1, 9 (D.C. Cir. 2002)
("Agency authority may not be lightly presumed. 'Were courts to presume a delegation of power absent an express withholding of such power, agencies would enjoy
virtually limitless hegemony.'") (cleaned up); Am. Bus. Ass'n v. Slater, 231 F.3d 1, 9
(D.C. Cir. 2000) (Sentelle, J., concurring) ("Agencies have no inherent powers. They .
. . are creatures of statute . . . [that] may act only because, and only to the extent that,
Congress affirmatively has delegated them the power to act."); Ry. Labor Execs. Ass'n
v. Nat'l Mediation Bd., 29 F.3d 655, 659 (D.C. Cir. 1994) ("[T]he Board would have us
presume a delegation of power from Congress absent an express withholding of such
power.") (emphasis is removed).

have been understood at the time of enactment. It must be plausible that the delegation of power is supported by the statute's original public meaning. In addition, the agency must be able to demonstrate that the problem it seeks to address is that which the legislature had in mind when the authority was delegated—or was at least of the sort that the legislative enactment was designed to address. That a contemporary reading of previously enacted statutory language would seem to encompass a previously unknown problem would not be sufficient. Relatedly, insofar as the authorizing legislation embodies an "intelligible principle," this principle should be understood as it would have been at the time of enactment. Accordingly, any such delegation must be understood to address then-contemporary problems and not as an open-ended grant of future authority to be deployed in unforeseen circumstances to address unanticipated problems. It is also appropriate for the Court to ask whether the agency is claiming delegated authority in an area within its expertise and the expertise it had at the time of the enactment.

Ambiguous language and the passage of time should not present an opportunity for agencies to "bootstrap" authority over previously unregulated concerns.[106] Merely because a given word (say, "system"), taken out of context, may seem to be a capacious vessel for a convenient power is no reason to green-light a newfound regulatory power. There is good reason for courts to be skeptical when agencies (or outside litigants) purport to identify previously undiscovered and unused authority to address emergent mischief. Agency departures from past practice or prior understandings of their own authority should be particularly suspect. Indeed, where an agency seeks to enter a new field or exercise long dormant powers, this should create a presumption against the existence of a delegation.

Both for deciding *West Virginia v. EPA* and for bequeathing a manageable doctrine to the lower courts, the Court would have done better to engage in a holistic statutory inquiry into the nature of the agency power asserted and the sufficiency of evidence to support the agency's claim of delegated power. Instead, it offered a one-off escape hatch dependent on a contested judgment about whether

---

[106] See Adams Fruit Co. v. Barrett, 494 U.S. 638, 650 (1990) ("It is fundamental 'that an agency may not bootstrap itself into an area in which it has no jurisdiction.'") (cleaned up).

a given action is sufficiently "major" or "extraordinary." The latter course invites unprincipled and politically contingent inquiries outside of judges' core competencies and invites the complaint that courts are making political judgments rather than legal ones.

Questions about EPA's Remaining Authority

West Virginia v. EPA bars the EPA from adopting expansive regulations under Section 7411 that would require existing power plants to engage in generation shifting. The decision does not bar the EPA from continuing to regulate GHGs, however. The Court took no steps toward overturning *Massachusetts v. EPA* and raised no questions about the legal viability of other GHG regulations on the books. *West Virginia v. EPA* does not even bar the regulation of GHGs under Section 7411. It simply bars the EPA from reinterpreting longstanding regulatory authority in new and expansive ways, particularly insofar as such reinterpretation is intended to adopt regulatory measures that the enacting Congress had not anticipated. In this sense, *West Virginia v. EPA* is a clear sequel to *UARG v. EPA*, which likewise reaffirmed the EPA's traditional regulatory authority while simultaneously invoking the major questions doctrine to reject the agency's effort to unilaterally update its authority to more effectively control GHGs.

While a Section 7411(d) rule requiring generation shifting is off the table, the EPA is likely to adopt a new set of rules governing GHG emissions from coal-fired power plants. In late June, the EPA indicated that it had already begun working on a new rule, with plans to release a proposed rule in March 2023 and a final rule in 2024.[107] These new rules will not replicate the CPP or anything like it, but the agency retains a range of options beyond a narrow focus on heat-rate improvements and other plant-specific efficiency improvements. Possibilities include basing BSER on co-firing, which would require power plants to incorporate greater use of natural gas or other lower-carbon fuels.[108] While the Trump administration rejected co-firing as an option in promulgating the ACE rule, co-firing is used at a

---

[107] Lisa Friedman, E.P.A. Describes How It Will Regulate Power Plants after Supreme Court Setback, N.Y. Times (July 7, 2022), https://nyti.ms/3SrYvdm.

[108] See Maya Domeshek & Dallas Burtraw, Reducing Coal Plant Emissions by Cofiring with Natural Gas, Resources for the Future (May 2021), https://bit.ly/3Q6qAVS.

substantial percentage of fossil-fuel-fired power plants.[109] Thus the EPA could argue that it has been adequately demonstrated as a system of emission reduction that can be adopted at individual stationary sources. Another possibility would be to identify carbon capture and sequestration as the BSER, though this might be challenged as either not adequately demonstrated or too costly.

While the EPA's options are much narrower than they would have been under the D.C. Circuit's interpretation of Section 7411, the agency retains some residual flexibility to draft a new Section 7411(d) rule governing GHG emissions from power plants. And nothing in *West Virginia v. EPA* precludes states from authorizing cap-and-trade or generation shifting as a means of complying with more traditional standards of performance. Indeed, the chief justice seemed to go out of his way to make clear that the Court was not embracing the rigid interpretation of Section 7411 the Trump administration had adopted, noting the Court had "no occasion to decide whether the statutory phrase 'system of emission reduction' refers exclusively to measures that improve the pollution performance of individual sources, such that all other actions are ineligible to qualify as the BSER."[110] The only question the Court decided was "whether the 'best system of emission reduction' identified by EPA in the Clean Power Plan was within the authority granted to the Agency in Section 7411(d) of the CAA."[111]

As noted, *West Virginia v. EPA* does nothing to curtail the EPA's use of other existing authorities to regulate GHG emissions directly, such as has been done with vehicular emissions in the wake of *Massachusetts v. EPA* and with major sources already subject to regulation under Section 165. *West Virginia v. EPA* may, however, make it more difficult for the EPA to deploy other CAA provisions against GHGs.

The CAA provisions establishing and enforcing National Ambient Air Quality Standards (NAAQS) for criteria air pollutants are the "heart" of the act.[112] Ever since *Massachusetts v. EPA*, environmentalist organizations have urged the EPA to utilize these provisions more

---

[109] *Id.* at 1.

[110] West Virginia, 142 S. Ct. at 2615–16.

[111] *Id.*

[112] See Union Elec. Co. v. EPA, 427 U.S. 246, 249 (1976) (characterizing NAAQS provisions as the "heart" of the CAA).

aggressively to mitigate climate change. Some have even proposed listing GHGs as criteria air pollutants for purposes of the NAAQS provisions.[113] Given that the NAAQS provisions were written and structured to ensure that each portion of the country achieves a set national standard for *ambient* air quality, and not to control emission levels generally or stabilize atmospheric concentrations of a globally dispersed pollutant, any such effort would be likely to fail in the wake of *West Virginia v. EPA*.

GHGs need not be listed as criteria air pollutants for the NAAQS provisions to be useful in reducing GHG emissions, however. Tightening the national ambient air quality standard for particulate matter, for example, would not only reduce soot and fine particles in the air. It would put the squeeze on many large sources of GHGs, coal-burning facilities in particular, reducing GHG emissions as well. This strategy would appear to be viable, so long as the EPA does not lead courts to believe that such regulatory measures are adopted for the purpose of GHG control.

West Virginia v. EPA and the covid cases highlight the Court's concern that the executive branch sometimes seeks to expand and repurpose existing statutory authority to address broader (and perhaps worthwhile) policy goals beyond those with which Congress was focused when the statute was enacted. There is no problem if an agency action that addresses A (particulates) necessarily addresses B (GHGs) at the same time. In such cases, B is an added benefit of addressing A. If, however, the agency decides to address A for the purpose of B—and Congress has not authorized B—this raises the prospect of what we might call "regulatory pretext."

Concern for pretext is common in administrative law, but the rule against it is rarely enforced with much vigor. Provided that an agency can offer a reasoned explanation of its actions and justify the choices it made in terms aligned with its statutory authority, that is usually good enough to survive judicial review. In the census case, however, Chief Justice Roberts suggested courts should look more

---

[113] See, e.g., Ctr. for Biological Diversity, Petition to Establish National Pollution Limits for Greenhouse Gases Pursuant to the Clean Air Act (Dec. 2, 2009). The EPA denied this petition in January 2021, but then subsequently withdrew and reversed the denial in March 2021 "as the agency did not fully and fairly assess the issues raised by the petition." See Letter from Acting Administrator Jane Nishida, Mar. 4, 2021, https://bit.ly/3Q9Vdti.

closely when there is reason to suspect an agency's explanation is "contrived."[114] What judicial review requires, Roberts explained, is that agencies provide "genuine justifications for important decisions," and not "distractions" or subterfuge.[115]

Whereas pretext analysis is often used to ferret out truly nefarious motives, such as racial or religious discrimination, the Roberts Court is suspicious of agency attempts to use regulatory authority delegated for one purpose to address another. For example, it appears the Court's majority in *NFIB* was concerned that the Biden administration was trying to use OSHA's authority to set workplace safety standards as a means of increasing vaccination more generally.[116] Lacking any clear statutory authority to impose a nationwide covid-19 vaccination requirement, the Biden administration sought to use the OSHA rule as part of (what the president described as) "a new plan to require more Americans to be vaccinated."[117] Likewise, in *West Virginia*, the Court's majority showed some concern that the Biden administration was seeking to use provisions authorizing the imposition of source-specific pollution control standards as a way to "drive a[n] . . . aggressive transformation in the domestic energy industry."[118] Thus, were the EPA to tighten the particulate NAAQS standards for the stated purpose of reducing coal consumption and thereby reducing GHG emissions, this might raise a red flag.

More broadly, *West Virginia v. EPA* suggests that efforts to encourage an "all-of-government" approach to climate change through executive order and presidential directive are likely to face stiff headwinds in court.[119] Congress retains the authority to direct any and all federal agencies to do more to mitigate the threat of climate change. But unless and until it does so, the authority of individual

---

[114] Dep't of Com. v. New York, 139 S. Ct. 2551, 2575–76 (2019).

[115] *Id.* at 2556.

[116] See Michael C. Dorf, Pretext Explains (But Does Not Justify) the SCOTUS Invalidation of the OSHA Vaccine Rule, Dorf on Law (Jan. 17, 2022), https://bit.ly/3Jq0knd.

[117] See NFIB, 142 S. Ct. at 663.

[118] West Virginia, 142 S. Ct. at 2604 (quoting White House Fact Sheet on Clean Power Plan).

[119] See White House Office of Domestic Climate Policy (Jan. 27, 2021), https://bit.ly/3ORhgnG (establishing the office which "implements the President's domestic climate agenda, coordinating the all-of-government approach to tackle the climate crisis, create good-paying, union jobs, and advance environmental justice").

administrative agencies to pursue climate goals is limited, particularly where it involves taking pre-existing authorities and redirecting them toward climate change.

One regulatory proposal sure to get additional scrutiny in the wake of *West Virginia v. EPA* is the Security and Exchange Commission's (SEC) proposal to "enhance and standardize climate-related disclosures for investors."[120] Insofar as such disclosure requirements represent an extension of SEC authority beyond its core mission of protecting investors and force it to address matters outside of its traditional areas of expertise, that would seem to implicate the major questions doctrine and be vulnerable to challenge under *West Virginia v. EPA*.[121] To defend its rule, the SEC will likely argue that climate disclosures merely represent an update of traditional disclosure requirements in light of recent developments. Efforts by other regulatory agencies, including the Federal Energy Regulatory Commission, to focus their pre-existing regulatory authority on climate change would seem potentially vulnerable to major questions as well.

The implications of *West Virginia v. EPA* extend beyond environmental policy, however. As the chief justice noted, such questions of extraordinary importance may arise from any corner of the administrative state, and the opinion makes clear that courts are to be suspicious when agencies engage in self-aggrandizing behavior or otherwise seek to pour new wine from old bottles. Wherever an agency opts to update, redirect, or repurpose its authority in light of technological or other changes, it risks implicating the major questions doctrine. Agencies such as the Federal Communications Commission and Federal Trade Commission are on notice too.

Conclusion

When the Supreme Court concludes that an agency action exceeds the scope of the agency's delegated authority, it invites Congress to consider whether the agency *should* have such authority. After the Court rejected the FCC's claimed authority to relieve long-distance

---

[120] See Enhancement and Standardization of Climate-Related Disclosures for Investors, 87 Fed. Reg. 21,334 (Apr. 11, 2022).

[121] See Paul Atkins & Paul Ray, The SEC's Climate Rule Won't Hold Up in Court, Wall. St. J. (July 12, 2022), https://on.wsj.com/3bpHUGk.

carriers of tariff filing obligations in *MCI v. AT&T*,[122] Congress enacted the 1996 reforms to the Communications Act, providing the FCC with the authority to relieve regulatory burdens so as to enhance competition in telecommunications services.[123] Similarly, after the Court rejected the Food and Drug Administration's claimed authority to regulate tobacco as a "drug" under the Food, Drug, and Cosmetic Act,[124] Congress soon enacted a new tobacco-control statute providing the agency with new authority to regulate tobacco products, tailored to the particulars of the tobacco industry.[125] In both cases, the new authorities delegated by Congress were different from the authority the agencies had sought to exercise.

The Supreme Court's decision in *West Virginia v. EPA* need not be the last word on whether generation shifting should play a role in mitigating the threat of climate change. There is broad consensus that more flexible, outcome-based strategies are more cost effective and efficient than facility-by-facility permitting. If legislative majorities support federal regulation of the power sector to reduce greenhouse gas emissions, Congress can still take that step. What Congress cannot do is sit back and hope that agencies discover how to unearth broad regulatory powers in the deepest regions of statutes it passed decades ago.

[122] 512 U.S. 218 (1994).

[123] Telecommunications Act of 1996, Pub. L. No. 104-104, 110 Stat. 56.

[124] FDA v. Brown & Williamson Tobacco Corp., 529 U.S. 120 (2000).

[125] Family Smoking Prevention & Tobacco Control Act, Pub. L. No. 111–31, 123 Stat. 1776 (2009).

A Major Question of Power: The Vaccine Mandate Cases and the Limits of Executive Authority

*Ilya Somin**

Introduction

In January 2022, the Supreme Court decided two major cases reviewing the legality of sweeping covid-19 vaccine mandates imposed by the Biden administration. In *National Federation of Independent Business (NFIB) v. Occupational Safety and Health Administration*,[1] a 6-3 ruling invalidated a regulation requiring employers with 100 or more workers to compel nearly all of them to get vaccinated against covid or wear masks on the job and take regular covid tests. In *Biden v. Missouri*, decided the same day, a 5-4 Court upheld a Centers for Medicare and Medicaid Services (CMS) policy requiring health care workers employed by institutions receiving federal Medicare and Medicaid funds to get vaccinated.[2]

Both cases addressed large-scale policies that were significant in their own right. The rule invalidated in *NFIB* would have affected some 84 million workers,[3] while the CMS health care worker mandate covered some 10 million employees of hospitals and other health care facilities around the country.[4] The two cases also have important implications for the scope of executive power to set regulations

*Professor of law, George Mason University. For helpful suggestions and comments, I would like to thank Jonathan Adler, Thomas Berry, Bernard Black, Trevor Burrus, Simon Lazarus, John Meurer, and David Thaw. I would like to thank Emily Brenn Bordelon and Tyler Lardieri for helpful research assistance. A few passages in this article are adapted from Ilya Somin, Supreme Court Blocks Vaccine Mandate for Businesses, Exposing Biden's Overreach, NBC (Jan. 13, 2022), https://nbcnews.to/3cZ2xcP.

[1] 142 S. Ct. 661 (2022).

[2] 142 S. Ct. 647 (2022).

[3] NFIB, 142 S. Ct. at 670.

[4] Biden v. Missouri, 142 S. Ct. at 656 (Thomas, J., dissenting).

(*NFIB*) and impose conditions on federal grants to state and local governments (*Biden v. Missouri*).

Reaction to the two decisions has been largely polarized along left-right ideological lines, with most on the left believing that the Court should have upheld both vaccination mandates, and most on the right believing both should have been struck down. I am, perhaps, one of the relatively few observers who believe the Court got both cases right. The majority was justified in striking down the Occupational Safety and Health Administration (OSHA) employer mandate because Congress had never clearly authorized it, and also justified in upholding the CMS mandate because it was backed by far more unequivocal statutory authorization.

NFIB v. OSHA reaffirmed important constraints on the executive's power to decide a "major question" of policy on its own, while also giving an indirect boost to constitutional nondelegation constraints on the transfer of legislative power to the White House and the administrative state. For its part, *Biden v. Missouri* makes clear that the executive can exercise reasonable discretion when Congress does clearly authorize it, particularly in the context of attaching conditions to federal grants to state and local governments.

At the same time, there are notable flaws and omissions in the majority's reasoning in both cases. In *NFIB*, especially, I believe the majority got the right result in part for the wrong reasons. These mistakes highlight some of the downsides of addressing important issues via the "shadow docket"—the Court's practice of hearing cases on an expedited basis that gives only very limited time to consider arguments and prepare opinions.[5]

Part I of this article provides a brief overview of the history of the two cases, the policies they address, and a summary of the Court's rulings. Of particular note is that both were sweeping emergency measures enacted in response to the covid pandemic, and both reached the Supreme Court on a heavily expedited basis.

Part II defends the outcome in *NFIB v. OSHA* but also criticizes key elements of the Court's reasoning. While the majority was right to invalidate the large-employer vaccination mandate on the basis of the "major questions doctrine," its interpretation of the OSHA Act of

---

[5] See, e.g., Stephen I. Vladeck, The Supreme Court Needs to Show Its Work, The Atlantic (Mar. 10, 2021), https://bit.ly/3PPHeJy (criticizing the shadow docket on such grounds).

1970 is strained, and it overlooked a stronger statutory rationale for its conclusion.

Part III assesses *Biden v. Missouri.* In this case, the Court's statutory reasoning is compelling. But the justices erred in failing to address some crucial issues related to Congress's Spending Clause authority to set conditions on federal grants to state and local governments. It also overlooked the plaintiffs' argument that the CMS mandate runs afoul of the statutory federalism "clear statement" rule.

Finally, part IV considers some broader implications of the two rulings. While *NFIB* is usually seen as a victory for the right, and *Biden v. Missouri* as one for the left, this need not be the long-term legacy of either case. Rather, Americans across the political spectrum have much to gain from judicial enforcement of limits on executive power. The kind of sweeping unilateral authority the Biden administration claimed in *NFIB* could easily have been misused by a future Republican administration. The Court's sensible statutory interpretation in *Biden v. Missouri* also bodes well for the future. At the same time, the significant missteps in the reasoning of both cases—especially *NFIB*—reinforce arguments for reform of the shadow docket, though there may not be any easy solution for that problem.

I. Overview of the Vaccine Mandate Cases

The vaccine mandate cases arose out of regulations enacted by the Biden administration in the fall of 2021 after the rise of the more contagious Delta variant led to an increase in covid cases, despite the growing availability of effective vaccines.[6] The spread of Delta, combined with lagging vaccination rates in many parts of the country, led the Biden administration to enact sweeping vaccine mandates in an attempt to curb the spread of the virus.

The most wide-ranging of these mandates was OSHA's use of its emergency temporary standard (ETS) authority under the 1970 OSHA Act to institute a policy requiring employers with 100 or more workers to compel nearly all of them to get vaccinated against covid or wear masks on the job and test on a regular basis.[7] Put in

[6] See, e.g., Zachary Wolf, Biden's Six-Step Covid Plan, Explained, CNN (Sept. 10, 2021), https://cnn.it/3zlI75C (summarizing the administration's plans and the rationales for them).

[7] See COVID–19 Vaccination and Testing; Emergency Temporary Standard, 86 Fed. Reg. 61402 (Nov. 5, 2021).

place on November 5, 2021, the regulation affected some 84 million workers.[8] Because OSHA used its emergency ETS authority, the regulation could be adopted without going through the normal notice-and-comment process required under the Administrative Procedure Act (APA).[9] While the mandate had a few narrow exceptions, such as those for workers who work exclusively outside or 100 percent remotely,[10] it nonetheless had an extraordinarily broad scope, as the exemptions applied to only a small fraction of otherwise covered employees.[11]

The large-employer mandate went far beyond any measures previously enacted under OSHA's ETS authority.[12] The ETS provision of the 1970 OSHA Act gives the Secretary of Labor—acting through the agency—the authority to impose,

> an emergency temporary standard to take immediate effect upon publication in the Federal Register if he determines (A) that employees are exposed to grave danger from exposure to substances or agents determined to be toxic or physically harmful or from new hazards, and (B) that such emergency standard is necessary to protect employees from such danger.[13]

The question of whether OSHA's large-employer mandate falls within the scope of this power was the central issue in the litigation that began soon after the agency issued the rule.

Predictably, the ETS rule was challenged by a range of employer groups and conservative Republican state governments. One of these suits led to a decision by a U.S. Court of Appeals for the Fifth Circuit panel staying implementation of the mandate on the grounds that OSHA's regulation exceeded both the agency's authority under the 1970 act and also the scope of Congress's enumerated powers under

---

[8] NFIB, 142 S. Ct. at 670.

[9] *Id.* at 663.

[10] COVID–19 Vaccination and Testing, 86 Fed. Reg. at 61460.

[11] NFIB, 142 S. Ct. at 663–64.

[12] For an overview of previous uses, see Scott D. Szymendera, Cong. Rsch. Serv., R46288, Occupational Safety and Health Administration (OSHA): COVID-19 Emergency Temporary Standards (ETS) on Health Care Employment and Vaccinations and Testing for Large Employers 18–19 (2022).

[13] 29 U.S.C. § 655(c)(1).

the Constitution.[14] I do not address these constitutional questions here because the Supreme Court did not end up considering them. The stay imposed by the Fifth Circuit was quickly lifted after a statutorily required lottery process consolidated all the cases challenging the mandate into a single case in the U.S. Court of Appeals for the Sixth Circuit.[15] The Sixth Circuit proceeded to lift the stay in a 2-1 ruling upholding the legality of the mandate, in a decision issued on December 17, 2021.[16] Earlier, the circuit rejected a petition for immediate *en banc* consideration of the case by the full Sixth Circuit, despite a forceful dissent by Chief Judge Jeffrey Sutton.[17]

The cases challenging the mandate were then swiftly taken up by the Supreme Court, which overruled the Sixth Circuit in an unsigned *per curiam* shadow docket decision providing expedited consideration. The 6-3 ruling split the Court along ideological lines, with all six conservative justices in the majority, and all three liberals— Stephen Breyer, Elena Kagan, and Sonia Sotomayor—jointly dissenting. The majority concluded that the ETS provision of the OSHA Act did not authorize the mandate because the statutory text gave the agency the power to address only *"workplace* safety standards, not broad public health measures,"[18] and because attempting to address the latter would run afoul of the major questions doctrine, which requires Congress to "'speak clearly when authorizing an agency to exercise powers of vast economic and political significance.'"[19]

The CMS mandate for health care workers in facilities receiving federal Medicare and Medicaid funds was issued at the same time as the OSHA rule. On November 5, 2021, the Department of Health and Human Services (HHS) announced that, "in order to receive Medicare and Medicaid funding, participating facilities must ensure that their staff—unless exempt for medical or religious reasons—are vaccinated against COVID–19."[20] The authorizing statutes for Medicare

---

[14] BST Holdings, LLC v. OSHA, 17 F.4th 604 (5th Cir. 2021).

[15] 28 U.S.C. § 2112(a)(3).

[16] Mass. Bldg. Trades Council v. U.S. Dep't of Labor (In re MCP No. 165), 21 F.4th 357 (6th Cir. 2021), rev'd, NFIB v. OSHA, 142 S. Ct. 661 (2022).

[17] In re MCP No. 165, 20 F.4th 264 (6th Cir. 2021).

[18] NFIB, 142 S. Ct. at 665 (emphasis in original).

[19] *Id.* (quoting Ala. Ass'n of Realtors v. HHS, 141 S. Ct. 2485, 2489 (2021)).

[20] Biden v. Missouri, 142 S. Ct. at 650.

and Medicaid grants to state and private health facilities give the HHS secretary the power to impose such "requirements as [he] finds necessary in the interest of the health and safety of individuals who are furnished services in the institution."[21] The Biden administration cited these provisions as authorization for the health care worker mandate.[22]

The CMS mandate was quickly challenged in two separate lawsuits filed by a total of 25 Republican-controlled state governments; in both cases, district courts issued preliminary injunctions blocking enforcement of the mandate as litigation proceeded.[23] The U.S. Court of Appeals for the Fifth Circuit refused to lift the injunctions as applied to the 14 state plaintiffs in one of the cases, but did lift them as applied to the rest of the country.[24]

Unlike in the OSHA mandate case, the Supreme Court did not divide along ideological lines in *Biden v. Missouri.* Instead, Chief Justice John Roberts and Justice Brett Kavanaugh joined the three liberal justices in upholding the CMS mandate.[25] The majority's unsigned *per curiam* opinion indicates that "[t]he rule . . . fits neatly within the language of the statute" giving CMS the authority to impose regulations "the Secretary [of HHS] finds necessary in the interest of the health and safety of individuals who are furnished services."[26]

Because *Biden v. Missouri* was litigated at the same time as the OSHA mandate case and both rulings were issued on the same date, January 13, 2022, reaction to *Biden v. Missouri* was relatively muted. Nonetheless, it is a highly significant decision—both because it upheld a mandate affecting some 10 million people[27] and because of its implications for future cases.[28]

---

[21] See 42 U.S.C. § 1395x(e)(9) (hospitals receiving Medicare funds); § 1395x(cc)(2)(J) (outpatient rehabilitation facilities receiving Medicare funds); §§ 1395i–3(d)(4)(B) (nursing facilities receiving Medicare funds); § 1395k(a)(2)(F)(i) (ambulatory surgical centers receiving Medicare funds). See also §§ 1396r(d)(4)(B), 1396d(l)(1), 1396d(o) (similar provisions in Medicaid act).

[22] COVID–19 Vaccination and Testing, 86 Fed. Reg. at 61555.

[23] Louisiana v. Becerra, 571 F. Supp. 3d 516 (W.D. La. 2021), rev'd, 142 S. Ct. 647 (2022); Missouri v. Biden, 571 F. Supp. 3d 1079 (E.D. Mo. 2021), rev'd, 142 S. Ct. 647 (2022).

[24] Louisiana v. Becerra, 20 F.4th 260 (5th Cir. 2021).

[25] Biden v. Missouri, 142 S. Ct. at 652–55.

[26] *Id.* at 652.

[27] *Id.* at 656 (Thomas, J., dissenting).

[28] See discussion *infra*, Parts III, IV.

II. The OSHA Large-Employer Mandate Case

The Supreme Court's conservative majority reached the right decision in *NFIB v. OSHA*, but in part for the wrong reasons. The Court adopted a strained reading of the ETS provision of the OSHA Act while overlooking a much stronger alternative rationale.

The ETS statute allows OSHA to impose rules bypassing normal notice-and-comment procedures (which give members of the public an opportunity to comment on proposed regulations) only in cases where "employees are exposed to grave danger from exposure to substances or agents determined to be toxic or physically harmful or from new hazards."[29] The Supreme Court majority contends that the covid vaccination mandate does not fall within this category because "[t]he [OSHA] Act empowers the Secretary to set *workplace* safety standards, not broad public health measures."[30] They emphasize that "[t]he text of the agency's Organic Act . . . repeatedly makes clear that OSHA is charged with regulating 'occupational' hazards and the safety and health of 'employees.'"[31]

This theory is subject to the dissenting justices' rejoinder that "nothing in the Act's text supports the majority's limitation on OSHA's regulatory authority."[32] As the dissenters point out, "[c]ontra the majority, [the text] is indifferent to whether a hazard in the workplace is also found elsewhere."[33] The ETS provision of the OSHA Act only requires that the risk in question pose a "grave danger" within the workplace.[34] It doesn't matter whether similar dangers exist elsewhere.

But there is an alternative justification for the majority's position that both they and the dissenting justices overlook. It is, in fact, doubtful that covid posed a grave danger to employees when the vast majority of them could have easily minimized the risk by getting vaccinated voluntarily, thereby largely eliminating the threat of serious illness and death.[35] By the time OSHA issued its large-employer

---

[29] 29 U.S.C. § 655(c)(1).

[30] NFIB, 142 S. Ct. at 665.

[31] *Id.* at 664 (quoting 29 U.S.C. §§ 652(8), 654(a)(2), 655(b)–(c)).

[32] *Id.* at 673 (joint dissent).

[33] *Id.*

[34] 29 U.S.C. § 655(c)(1).

[35] For a recent summary, see Julia Ries, Omicron BA.5: Experts See Increase in Mild Cases, Vaccines Continue to Be Effective, Healthline (July 7, 2022), https://bit.ly/3znhe0Y.

vaccination mandate, covid vaccines were readily available for free to adults throughout the United States.

During oral argument, Biden administration Solicitor General Elizabeth Prelogar conceded that OSHA's "grave danger finding is limited to unvaccinated workers."[36] OSHA itself had concluded that "most *unvaccinated* workers across the U.S. economy are facing a grave danger posed by the COVID-19 hazard."[37] By the time of the ruling, workers could easily avoid that danger by getting vaccinated—a simple procedure that usually takes only a short time. The dissenting justices argue that OSHA's rule is justified in part because "in [workplace] environments, more than any others, individuals have little control, and therefore little capacity to mitigate risk."[38] In fact, however, by OSHA's own admission, employees could very easily mitigate risk simply by getting vaccinated. Indeed, the regulation does not even make it significantly easier for them to do so.[39] It merely punishes employers if they retain workers who do not get vaccinated or, alternatively, wear masks and test regularly.

But if a "grave danger" that justifies the use of emergency authority exists even when workers could easily avoid it, OSHA would have near-boundless authority to use its emergency powers to control almost any workplace practice, or indeed almost anything that might affect workplace conditions in any significant way. Virtually any activity poses grave dangers to at least some people if none of them take even minimal precautions. For example, parking a car in the employee parking lot creates a grave danger for people who refuse to move out of the way when they see it coming. Even walking down a flight of stairs can be dangerous if people refuse to slow down or hold on to railings when necessary.

This authority might still be constrained by the ETS statute's limitation to grave dangers caused by "exposure to substances or agents determined to be toxic or physically harmful or from

---

[36] Tr. of Oral Arg. at 108, NFIB v. OSHA, 142 S. Ct. 661 (2022) (No. 21A244).

[37] COVID–19 Vaccination and Testing, 86 Fed. Reg. at 61433 (emphasis added).

[38] NFIB, 142 S. Ct. at 674 (joint dissent).

[39] The OSHA regulation did require employers to give workers "reasonable" time to get vaccinated and recover from side effects. COVID–19 Vaccination and Testing, 86 Fed. Reg. at 61479. But that accommodation has very limited value, given the agency's own conclusion that getting vaccinated requires a total of only about four hours for the complete two-dose regimen and that side effects are generally minimal. *Id.* at 61479–81.

new hazards."[40] But almost any "substance or agent" can potentially be "physically harmful" if people cannot be expected to use minimal precautions in handling it. Even water could potentially be spilled on the floor, thereby leading people to slip on it and suffer injuries. Food and beverages can cause serious harm if consumed in excessive quantities, and so on. And a very wide variety of changes in workplace conditions could potentially be considered "new hazards" if they can be interpreted as posing a "grave danger" even when the danger might be avoided through simple common-sense precautions.

Of course, covid-19 can pose risks even to the vaccinated, as they too can become infected. But the degree of risk is vastly smaller.[41] Even OSHA itself did not conclude that these risks were severe enough to qualify as a grave danger to the vaccinated. A statement supporting the OSHA mandate endorsed by the American Medical Association and numerous other health care organizations and experts also noted that the danger in question overwhelmingly affected the unvaccinated.[42] The statement emphasized that "[v]accines are effective in preventing COVID cases, hospitalizations and, most importantly, deaths," and that "[c]ompared to the vaccinated, the unvaccinated are 11 times more likely to die."[43]

The argument advanced here is similar to that made by Chief Judge Sutton of the Sixth Circuit in his opinion, urging his court to hear the case *en banc*:

> This emergency power extends only to "necessary" measures, namely measures indispensable or essential to address a "grave" danger in the workplace. But this set of preconditions does not apply (1) when the key population group at risk

---

[40] 29 U.S.C. § 655(c)(1).

[41] Early data indicate that vaccination reduces transmission of covid-19 even with the more contagious Delta and Omicron variants, though to a lesser degree than with earlier versions of the virus. See, e.g., Chris Stokel-Walker, What Do We Know about Covid Vaccines and Preventing Transmission?, BMJ, Feb. 4, 2022, https://bit.ly/3zthgVf; David Eyre, et al., Effect of Covid-19 Vaccination on Transmission of Alpha and Delta Variants, 386 New Eng. J. of Med. 744 (2022); Nick Andrews et al., Covid-19 Vaccine Effectiveness against the Omicron (B.1.1.529) Variant, 386 New Eng. J. of Med. 1532 (2022).

[42] See Press Release, Health Care Organizations, Leading Health Care Experts and Professional Organizations: Businesses Should Support OSHA's COVID Vaccination Mandate (Nov. 18, 2021), https://bit.ly/3vx688J.

[43] *Id.*

> from COVID-19—the elderly—in the main no longer works, (2) when members of the working-age population at risk—the unvaccinated—have chosen for themselves to accept the risk and any risk is not grave for most individuals in the group, and (3) when the remaining group—the vaccinated—does not face a grave risk by the Secretary's own admission, even if they work with unvaccinated individuals.[44]

While Chief Judge Sutton overstates the extent to which the elderly "no longer work,"[45] the rest of his points are well-taken. Among other things, he is right that the statute indicates that ETS measures must be "necessary" to mitigate the grave danger at issue, and such necessity is highly questionable at a time when vaccination is readily available even without the mandate.

The exceptional emergency nature of the ETS authority further undercuts claims that OSHA has sweeping authority to regulate a vast range of ordinary workplace conditions. Such an interpretation of the law would make emergency power the rule rather than the exception.

The argument that OSHA exceeded its authority is also reinforced by the fact that ETS power had never previously been used so sweepingly in the 50-year history of the OSHA Act. As the majority points out, the ETS power had been used "just nine times before (and never to issue a rule as broad as this one)."[46] Six of the nine previous uses of the ETS power were challenged in court, and five were invalidated, at least in part.[47] This history of aggressive, nondeferential judicial review suggests that the ETS power was generally understood as strictly limited—not as a wide-ranging power for the agency to counter almost any potential threats to worker safety.

In sum, it is more reasonable to interpret "grave danger" as limited to threats that cannot be easily mitigated by simple precautions.

---

[44] In re MCP No. 165, 20 F.4th at 268 (Sutton, C.J., dissenting from denial of initial hearing en banc).

[45] Some one-third of Americans between the ages of 65 and 74 are in the workforce. See Nat'l Inst. of Occupational Safety & Health, Productive Aging and Work, Ctrs. for Disease Control & Prevention (Sept. 11, 2015), https://bit.ly/3zPDdyV.

[46] NFIB, 142 S. Ct. at 663. See also BST Holdings, 17 F.4th at 609 (reviewing these uses); In re MCP No. 165, 20 F.4th at 276 (Sutton, C. J., dissenting from denial of initial hearing en banc).

[47] See BST Holdings, 17 F.4th at 609 n.1 (summarizing these cases); see also Szymendera, *supra* note 12.

The threat of covid to the unvaccinated does not qualify at a time when it can easily be addressed by getting vaccinated.

At the very least, there is ambiguity over whether such an easily mitigated risk qualifies as a "grave danger" under the ETS authority. Such ambiguity triggers the major questions doctrine, which requires Congress to "speak clearly if it wishes to assign to an agency decisions of vast 'economic and political significance.'"[48] The power to use ETS to address threats that are subject to simple mitigation surely qualifies as a delegation of "decisions of vast economic and political significance," as it would give OSHA the power to use its emergency powers to restrict almost any workplace condition, and do so in a way that bypasses normal administrative-law procedures.

The ETS provision of the OSHA Act does not make clear whether easily mitigated risks qualify as grave dangers. The Court was therefore justified in rejecting the large-employer mandate under the major questions doctrine. Its reliance on the distinction between workplace hazards and general threats to public health is less secure. Undoubtedly, giving the agency the power to use ETS to address easily mitigated risks would allow it to make "decisions of vast economic and political significance," as it would give the agency sweeping control over a vast range of workplace activities. Whether such risks really qualify as grave dangers is not clear.

The major questions doctrine is the subject of significant controversy, with some calling for it to be abolished or significantly scaled back,[49]

---

[48] Util. Air Reg. Group v. EPA, 573 U.S. 302, 324 (2014); see also FDA v. Brown & Williamson, 520 U.S. 120, 159–60 (2000) (Congress cannot be assumed to have implicitly delegated the power to regulate "a significant portion of the American economy" because "we are confident that Congress could not have intended to delegate a decision of such economic and political significance" without explicitly saying so.).

[49] See, e.g., Jonas Monast, Major Questions about the Major Questions Doctrine, 68 Admin. L. Rev. 445 (2019) (arguing for it to be scaled back); Natasha Brunstein & Richard Revesz, Mangling the Major Questions Doctrine, 74 Admin. L. Rev. 217 (2022) (arguing for its use only in "exceptional" cases); Marla Tortorice, Nondelegation and the Major Questions Doctrine: Displacing Interpretive Power, 67 Buffalo L. Rev. 1075 (2019). A standard criticism of the doctrine is that it is difficult to distinguish between major questions and less significant ones. See, e.g., Cass R. Sunstein, Chevron Step Zero, 92 Va. L. Rev. 187, 243 (2006) ("[T]he difference between interstitial and major questions is extremely difficult to administer.").

even as others defend it.[50] Here, I do not attempt to defend or criticize the doctrine, but merely limit myself to making the point that if courts should use it at all, the OSHA ETS mandate is a relatively easy case. The broad interpretation of ETS authority needed to sustain the mandate would undeniably give the agency control over major issues of economic and social policy, and that broad interpretation is—at the very least—far from clearly required by the text of the statute.

Over the last year, the Supreme Court has used the major questions doctrine to invalidate three major government policies: the OSHA mandate, the Centers for Disease Control nationwide eviction moratorium enacted by the Trump administration and later revived and extended by the Biden administration under the guise of combating the spread of covid-19,[51] and potentially sweeping Environmental Protection Agency regulations intended to combat global warming.[52] The ideological valence of these three decisions has led to concerns that the major questions doctrine is merely a cover for a right-wing political agenda. The most recent ruling, *West Virginia v. EPA*, has drawn especially negative commentary on this score.[53] But a strong major questions doctrine could well benefit liberal causes as well as conservative ones.[54]

---

[50] See, e.g., Clinton Summers, Nondelegation of Major Questions, 74 Ark. L. Rev. 83, 84 (2021) (arguing that "the 'major questions' test from the major questions doctrine should become the new basis for enforcing the nondelegation doctrine"); Andrew Howayeck, The Major Questions Doctrine: How the Supreme Court's Efforts to Rein in the Effects of Chevron Have Failed to Meet Expectations, 25 Roger Williams U. L. Rev. 173 (2020) (arguing for a more robust version of the doctrine).

[51] Ala. Ass'n of Realtors v. HHS, 141 S. Ct. 2485 (2021). For my assessment and defense of the Court's ruling in this case, see Ilya Somin, Nondelegation Limits on COVID Emergency Powers: Lessons from the Eviction Moratorium and Title 42 Cases, 15 NYU J.L. & Liberty 658 (2022) (symposium on "Responding to Emergency: A Blueprint for Liberty in a Time of Crisis").

[52] West Virginia v. EPA, 142 S. Ct. 2587 (2022).

[53] See, e.g., Blake Emerson, The Real Target of the Supreme Court's EPA Decision, Slate, (June 30, 2022), https://bit.ly/3zL7PRh; Durwood Zaelke, West Virginia vs. EPA: A Political Tragedy Disguised as a Legal Farce, The Hill (July 8, 2022), https://bit.ly/3zQsZhO; Adrian Vermeule, There Is No Conservative Legal Movement, Wash. Post (July 6, 2022), https://wapo.st/3PUhxaG. For more measured assessments, see, e.g., Jonathan H. Adler's article in this volume: Jonathan H. Adler, West Virginia v. EPA: Some Answers about Major Questions, 2021–2022 Cato Sup. Ct. Rev. 37 (2022); Kristin E. Hickman, Thoughts on West Virginia v. EPA, Yale J. on Reg. (July 5, 2022), https://bit.ly/3QhgxNM.

[54] See Somin, *supra* note 51, at 696–97 (making this case); see also *infra* discussion in Part IV.

The major questions doctrine is also often seen as a tool for enforcing the constitutional nondelegation doctrine: The idea that there are limits to the extent to which Congress can delegate power to the executive branch, even if it does speak clearly. Justice Neil Gorsuch—arguably the Court's leading advocate of robust nondelegation rules—has noted that "[a]lthough it is nominally a canon of statutory construction, we apply the major questions doctrine in service of the constitutional rule that Congress may not divest itself of its legislative power by transferring that power to an executive agency."[55] Gorsuch reiterates that position in a concurring opinion in *NFIB v. OSHA*, joined by Justices Clarence Thomas and Samuel Alito.[56] He emphasizes that "the major questions doctrine is closely related to what is sometimes called the nondelegation doctrine" because both seek to ensure that "the national government's power to make the laws that govern us remains where Article I of the Constitution says it belongs—with the people's elected representatives."[57]

Gorsuch contends that the sweeping nature of OSHA's assertion of authority in this case should lead to the invalidation of the ETS rule under either nondelegation or major questions, especially since both rules serve "a similar function."[58] There is, however, a crucial distinction between the two. A sufficiently clear delegation by Congress can satisfy the demands of the major questions doctrine. By contrast, even the clearest possible statutory text cannot save an otherwise unconstitutional delegation.

Even more than the major questions doctrine, the idea of judicially enforceable nondelegation rules is controversial. The Supreme Court has only recently started to give serious consideration to reviving such rules, and commentators are deeply divided over the question of whether doing so is desirable.[59] As in the case of major questions,

[55] Gundy v. United States, 139 S. Ct. 2116, 2142 (2019) (Gorsuch, J., dissenting).

[56] NFIB, 142 S. Ct. at 668–69 (2022) (Gorsuch, J., concurring).

[57] *Id.*

[58] *Id.*

[59] For critiques of nondelegation, see, e.g., Julian Davis Mortenson & Nicholas Bagley, Delegation at the Founding, 121 Colum. L. Rev. 277 (2021) (claiming there are no nondelegation limits that can be justified on originalist grounds); Nicholas A. Parillo, A Critical Assessment of the Originalist Case against Administrative Regulatory Power: New Evidence from the Federal Tax on Private Real Estate in the 1790s, 130 Yale L.J. 1288 (2021) (arguing that original meaning allows broad delegations). For defenses of nondelegation doctrine, see, e.g., Michael McConnell, The President Who Would Not

I do not attempt to resolve this broader debate here. I merely suggest that if nondelegation doctrine should be a meaningful constraint on congressional and executive power at all, it strengthens the case for invalidating the ETS employer vaccination mandate.

In his influential exposition of nondelegation doctrine, Justice Gorsuch argues that the original meaning of Article I of the Constitution requires that "Congress make[] the policy decisions when regulating private conduct," though "it may authorize another branch to 'fill up the details'" and to engage in fact-finding.[60] It seems obvious that the ETS mandate is a policy "regulating private conduct" and that the power to regulate anything that might be considered a "grave danger," even if easily mitigated, is more than a matter of "filling up details" and fact-finding.

It is important to understand that the Court's decision in *NFIB* does not categorically bar the use of ETS authority to mandate vaccination in all cases. To the contrary, the majority specifically notes that "[w]here the virus poses a special danger because of the particular features of an employee's job or workplace, targeted regulations are plainly permissible" and highlights the example of "risks associated with working in particularly crowded or cramped environments."[61] What is impermissible is the kind of wide-ranging, largely indiscriminate mandate adopted by the agency.[62] This weakens claims that the ruling drastically undermines OSHA's authority, or even that of the federal government more generally.[63]

Be King: Executive Power under the Constitution (2020); Ilan Wurman, Nondelegation at the Founding, 130 Yale L.J. 1490 (2021); Philip Hamburger, Nondelegation Blues, 91 Geo. Wash. L. Rev. (forthcoming 2023), https://bit.ly/3SzhTW2; Ann Woodhandler, Public Rights and Taxation: A Brief Response to Professor Parrillo, Virginia Public Law and Legal Theory Research Paper No. 2022-09 (2022), https://bit.ly/3zV9mp6; Jed Shugerman, Vesting, 74 Stan. L. Rev. (forthcoming 2022), https://bit.ly/3paDkiN.

[60] Gundy, 139 S. Ct. at 2136 (Gorsuch, J., dissenting).

[61] NFIB, 142 S. Ct. at 665–66.

[62] For a rare acknowledgement of this distinction by a critic of the Court's ruling, see Simon Lazarus, Biden Misread the Supreme Court's Ruling against the OSHA Vaccine Rule, New Republic (Jan. 19, 2022), https://bit.ly/3JwDJ8w.

[63] See, e.g., William Harrison, The Supreme Court's Vaccine Mandate Decision Is a Deadly Power Grab, Alliance for Justice (Feb. 2, 2022), https://bit.ly/3JqkNYL (claiming the decision will lead to a "dramatic shrinking" of government authority); Stephen I. Vladeck, The Supreme Court's Vaccine Mandate Ruling Shows It's Ready to Second-Guess Government Policy, Wash. Post (Jan. 19, 2022), https://wapo.st/3cOsCv9 (claiming that it heralds a return to the "Lochner era" of supposedly nondeferential judicial review).

Some targeted vaccination mandates might also be permissible under the approach outlined in this article. While I have argued that covid-19 does not generally pose a grave danger of the kind the ETS statute is intended to counter, such a danger could potentially exist in situations with substantial numbers of especially vulnerable employees, particularly if voluntary vaccination is, for some reason, inadequate to protect them against the spread of disease from others around them who remain unvaccinated.

Interestingly, at least as of this writing (summer 2022), the Biden administration has not so far taken up the Court's implicit invitation to draft a narrower workplace vaccine mandate rule. If such a rule were truly as desperately needed as defenders of the initial ETS rule believe, one would think the administration might make at least some effort to salvage as much of it as they can.

Despite my critique of the OSHA policy, I should emphasize that I am not categorically hostile to vaccination mandates. To the contrary, I believe they can sometimes be justified, even from the standpoint of a libertarian approach to public policy that embodies a strong presumption in favor of bodily autonomy.[64] My reservations about the OSHA mandate are mainly focused on the dangers of giving the executive vast discretionary control over workplace activities of the kind that it would have had if the Biden administration had prevailed in this case.

Concentrating such enormous power in one branch of government—ultimately under the control of a single man or woman in the White House—is a dangerous menace. Those who believe President Biden can be trusted with such vast authority should ask whether they will have similar confidence in the next Republican president, and vice versa. Constitutional limits on executive power are an important safeguard against such dangers. As Chief Judge Sutton warned in his opinion unsuccessfully urging the circuit to consider the OSHA case *en banc*, "[s]hortcuts in furthering preferred policies, even urgent policies, rarely end well, and they always undermine, sometimes permanently, American . . . separation of powers, the true mettle of the U.S. Constitution, the true long-term guardian of liberty."[65]

---

[64] See, e.g., Ilya Somin, A Broader Perspective on "My Body, My Choice," The Volokh Conspiracy (June 30, 2022), https://bit.ly/3oOyc3x; cf. Jason Brennan, A Libertarian Case for Mandatory Vaccination, 44 J. of Med. Ethics 37 (2018).

[65] In re MCP No. 165, 20 F.4th at 269.

III. The CMS Health Care Worker Vaccination Mandate

The Court's ruling on the CMS vaccination mandate for health care workers in *Biden v. Missouri* attracted much less attention than *NFIB v. OSHA* did. It is nonetheless a significant decision—and one the Court got right.

The most obvious difference between the two cases is that, in the CMS case, the statutory language supports the executive much more clearly. The relevant statutes authorizing federal Medicare and Medicaid grants to hospitals and other medical institutions give the Secretary of Health and Human Services the power to impose such "requirements as [he] finds necessary in the interest of the health and safety of individuals who are furnished services in the institution."[66] Unlike the ETS provision of the OSHA Act, this authorization is not a special emergency power, nor is it limited to countering grave dangers. It seems to cover any regulations that might counter threats to the "health and safety" of patients, even if those dangers are relatively modest in scope.

At the same time, in order to prevail, the government need not adopt an interpretation of its powers broad enough to trigger the major questions doctrine or raise nondelegation concerns. The power to set conditions is limited to institutions receiving Medicare and Medicaid grants and to regulations that protect the "health and safety" of patients within those institutions. It is far from being a general power to address health or safety issues throughout every workplace in the country and therefore does not qualify as a decision of "vast economic and political significance."[67]

Likewise, it is hard to deny that vaccinating medical personnel against a potentially deadly contagious disease can help protect the "health and safety" of vulnerable patients in the Medicare and Medicaid systems. In support of that proposition, HHS cited multiple studies from the United States and abroad indicating that vaccinated health care workers were far less likely to become infected with the

---

[66] See 42 U.S.C. § 1395x(e)(9) (hospitals receiving Medicare funds); § 1395x(cc)(2)(J) (outpatient rehabilitation facilities receiving Medicare funds); §§ 1395i–3(d)(4)(B) (nursing facilities receiving Medicare funds); § 1395k(a)(2)(F)(i) (ambulatory surgical centers receiving Medicare funds); see also §§ 1396r(d)(4)(B), 1396d(l)(1), 1396d(o) (similar provisions in Medicaid act).

[67] NFIB, 142 S. Ct. at 665 (quoting Ala. Ass'n of Realtors, 141 S. Ct. at 2489).

covid-19 virus to begin with and less likely to transmit it to others if they did.[68]

Notably, a hugely disproportional share of U.S. covid fatalities occurred among long-term care (LTC) and nursing home facility patients, who perished at 10 times the rate of the general population.[69] The situation was likely even worse for Medicare patients, who are, by definition, elderly. The elderly have much higher covid hospitalization and fatality rates than younger people, even if vaccinated.[70] In addition, patients in hospitals and LTC facilities are more likely to be immunocompromised than members of the general population, and such people, too, are at far more risk from covid.[71] Finally, it seems reasonable to assume that the incapacitation of unvaccinated health care workers by covid might further imperil patients as a result of understaffing. Vaccination reduces the risk that workers will contract covid and that they will suffer hospitalization or death if they do.[72]

Adding up all these factors, it seems obvious that the Supreme Court majority was right to conclude that a vaccination mandate for

---

[68] Medicare and Medicaid Programs; Omnibus COVID–19 Health Care Staff Vaccination, 86 Fed. Reg. 61555, 61557–58 (Nov. 05, 2021).

[69] See, e.g., Priya Chidambaram, Over 200,000 Residents and Staff in Long-Term Care Facilities Have Died from COVID-19, KFF (Feb. 3, 2022), https://bit.ly/3PVKqTW (noting that some 200,000 residents of nursing homes and LTC facilities have died of covid, forming 23 percent of all U.S. covid fatalities as of January 16, 2022). As of early 2022, there were some 8.3 million LTC residents in the U.S. Emma Rubin, Long-Term Care Statistics, Consumer Affairs (Jan. 27, 2022), https://bit.ly/3vDgd3N. That amounts to about 2.5 percent of the total U.S. population of 332 million. See Derick Moore, U.S. Population Estimated at 332,403,650 on Jan. 1, 2022, Census Bureau, (Dec. 30, 2021), https://bit.ly/3PTim3n. Thus, LTC residents have a fatality rate from covid some 10 times higher than the general population. CMS cited this disproportionate death toll in its justification for the rule. See Medicare and Medicaid Programs; Omnibus COVID–19, 86 Fed. Reg. at 61566.

[70] See, e.g., Risk for COVID-19 Infection, Hospitalization, and Death by Age Group, Ctrs. for Disease Control & Prevention (July 29, 2022), https://bit.ly/3zRfbDI (noting that people ages 65–74 are five times more likely to be hospitalized and 60 times more likely to die of covid than those ages 18–29; the ratios for people ages 75–84 and 85 and above are even higher). CMS's justification for the rule cites this factor, as well. Medicare and Medicaid Programs; Omnibus COVID-19, 86 Fed. Reg. at 61566.

[71] See, e.g., Ed Yong, The Millions of People Stuck in Pandemic Limbo, The Atlantic (Feb. 16, 2022), https://bit.ly/3JEHFUR.

[72] See *supra* discussion in Part II.

health care workers "fits neatly within the language of the statute."[73] Indeed, it is hard to think of many rules that more clearly serve the purpose of protecting the "health and safety" of patients.

In his dissenting opinion, joined by three other conservative justices, Justice Thomas describes the statutes giving CMS the power to impose "health and safety" rules as a mere "hodgepodge" of "ancillary" provisions in which Congress would not "hide 'fundamental details of a regulatory scheme.'"[74] To my mind, the rules protecting the health and safety of patients are far from merely "ancillary" provisions of a program intended to facilitate the provision of health care. If anything is "fundamental" to such a program, it is the protection of patient health and safety.

Thomas similarly argues that the "health and safety" requirements actually refer to merely "administrative" requirements similar to other regulations in the same sections, such as "provid[ing] 24-hour nursing service," "maintain[ing] clinical records on all patients," or having "bylaws in effect."[75] But 24-hour nursing services, maintenance of clinical records, and other similar provisions all ultimately serve the same purpose as the vaccination requirement: improving the quality of patient care and reducing health risks.

In a separate dissent, also joined by all those justices who joined Thomas's opinion, Justice Alito argues that CMS was not justified in foregoing the notice-and-comment process normally required by the APA.[76] I must leave the details of this question to analysts with greater relevant expertise on the APA. But it seems to me the majority effectively responds to this argument by pointing to the pressing need to deal with a winter surge of covid cases as sufficient grounds to invoke the "good cause" exception to this requirement.[77]

While the Court's statutory analysis is compelling, insofar as it goes, the majority neglected crucial issues raised by the lower court opinions and the plaintiffs in the case. Many of the latter were state governments suing because many of the facilities subject to the CMS

[73] Biden v. Missouri, 140 S. Ct. at 652.

[74] Id. at 656 (Thomas, J., dissenting) (quoting Whitman v. Am. Trucking Ass'ns, Inc., 531 U.S. 457, 468 (2001)).

[75] Id. at 657 (quoting 42 U.S.C. §§ 1395x(e)(2), (3), (5)).

[76] Id. at 659–60 (Alito, J., dissenting).

[77] Id. at 654.

mandate are controlled by states and localities. Federal grants to state and local governments are subject to constitutional restrictions on Congress's Spending Clause powers. Conditions attached to federal grants to subnational governments must be "unambiguously" spelled out by Congress,[78] "related" to the purposes of the grant,[79] and limited in their scope so as to avoid "coercion" of state and local governments.[80]

Federal courts take these requirements seriously. The Trump administration's repeated violation of them led to numerous defeats in court for its efforts to use grant conditions to pressure "sanctuary cities" that refused to cooperate with federal efforts to deport undocumented immigrants.[81] Spending Clause issues were raised in one of the two trial court decisions the Supreme Court overturned in *Biden v. Missouri*, which cited the clear statement and coercion issues,[82] and in the plaintiffs' brief before the Supreme Court.[83] Yet the Supreme Court majority ignored this important issue.

The same can be said for the plaintiffs' reliance on the longstanding federalism "clear statement" rule that Congress must use "exceedingly clear language if it wishes to significantly alter the balance between state and federal power."[84] The plaintiffs also emphasized this rule in their brief.[85] Justice Thomas cited it in his dissent as well.[86] A plausible argument can be made that the federalism canon is implicated in this case because vaccination and public health are traditionally functions of state government.[87]

[78] See, e.g., Pennhurst State Sch. & Hosp. v. Halderman, 451 U.S. 1, 17 (1981).

[79] South Dakota v. Dole, 483 U.S. 203, 207–08 (1987).

[80] *Id.* at 211; see also NFIB v. Sebelius, 567 U.S. 519, 580–83 (2012) (Roberts, C.J.).

[81] For an overview, see Ilya Somin, Making Federalism Great Again: How the Trump Administration's Attack on Sanctuary Cities Unintentionally Strengthened Judicial Protection for State Autonomy, 97 Tex. L. Rev. 1247 (2019).

[82] Louisiana, 571 F. Supp. 3d at 542.

[83] Plaintiffs' Response to Application for Stay at 23–24, Biden v. Missouri, 142 S. Ct. 647 (2022) (No. 21A240).

[84] Ala. Ass'n of Realtors, 141 S. Ct. at 2489; cf. Gregory v. Ashcroft, 501 U.S. 452, 458–62 (1991) (leading case emphasizing the importance of this rule).

[85] Plaintiffs' Response to Application for Stay, *supra* note 83, at 23–24.

[86] Biden v. Missouri, 142 S. Ct. at 658 (Thomas, J., dissenting).

[87] *Id.*

But the majority ignores the problem, just like it did with the Spending Clause issues.

In my view, both the Spending Clause requirement of an "unambiguous" statutory authorization and the federalism clear statement rule are satisfied by the very clear connection between vaccination of staff members against deadly contagious diseases and the statutorily authorized protection of the "health and safety" of patients. We can easily imagine borderline cases where the connection between a regulatory condition and health and safety is tenuous in nature and therefore difficult for grant recipients to foresee ahead of time. For example, imagine a rule requiring health care workers to jog five miles every day, on the theory that doing so would increase their health and stamina, which in turn would improve their job performance and benefit patients. In such situations, the Spending Clause clear statement rule and federalism canon might bar CMS from imposing the condition in question. But covid-19 vaccination is not such a borderline case.

The coercion issue is more complicated. The Supreme Court has never clearly explained what qualifies as unconstitutional "coercion" in the Spending Clause context. In the famous case of *NFIB v. Sebelius,* which partly invalidated Affordable Care Act conditions on Medicaid grants, Chief Justice Roberts's controlling opinion concluded that "coercion" is present in a situation where the amount of federal funding at issue is so large that the threat to remove it amounts to a "gun to the head" of the state.[88] No such gun to the head is present in this case, as failure to comply with the CMS mandate would only threaten funding given to the specific facilities in question, not all the Medicare and Medicaid funding given to the state government as a whole.[89]

The CMS rule probably meets the requirements of the Supreme Court's Spending Clause jurisprudence and federalism clear statement rule. But the Court would have done well to address these issues explicitly, rather than ignore them (with the exception of a brief mention in Justice Thomas's dissent).

[88] NFIB v. Sebelius, 567 U.S. at 581 (Roberts, C.J.).

[89] Medicare and Medicaid Programs; Omnibus COVID–19, 86 Fed. Reg. at 61612–14 (describing penalties for noncompliance).

Biden v. Missouri is an important case not only because it upheld a large-scale vaccination mandate affecting millions of health care workers, but because it is likely to set a precedent for future CMS staff vaccination mandates. At least in the case of deadly contagious diseases, such mandates are amply justified by the statutory text. But the Supreme Court should have also addressed the associated Spending Clause and federalism canon issues. Sweeping the latter under the rug, as the justices did, could well cause confusion in future cases.

IV. Broader Implications

NFIB v. OSHA and *Biden v. Missouri* have significant implications that go beyond the specific policies at issue in these cases, which are both important in and of themselves. Both the OSHA large-employer vaccination mandate struck down by the Court and the CMS health care worker mandate upheld by it affected millions of people. The Court's resolution of these cases therefore had a large-scale immediate effect. But it also set important precedents for the future.

The Court's ruling in *NFIB* ensures that future ETS measures will be limited to those that target workplace-specific risks rather than "public health more generally."[90] The extent to which this decision genuinely constrains OSHA's authority remains to be seen. It doesn't necessarily prevent the agency from using the ETS authority to impose either large-scale measures generally or vaccination mandates specifically. OSHA could still do so in situations where such measures target a situation where a virus or other health risk poses "a special danger because of the particular features of an employee's job or workplace."[91] In some cases, the "special danger" could affect large numbers of workers in a specific industry or sector of the economy.

The distinction between what qualifies as a "special danger" caused by "particular features of the workplace" and what counts as a general public-health risk is far from completely clear. Can the agency impose restrictions to counter a risk that is 10 percent greater in the workplace than outside it? What about five percent or two percent? This sort of question might well come up in future litigation, if OSHA again tries to use its ETS authority to regulate dangers that exist in both the workplace and outside it.

90 NFIB, 142 S. Ct. at 665; see also *supra* discussion in Part II.
91 NFIB, 142 S. Ct. at 665.

Despite this uncertainty, the Court has clearly signaled that the agency bears the burden of proving that there is a "special danger" in the workplace. That will make it more difficult for OSHA to use ETS to enact sweeping rules that affect a wide swathe of workers in different occupations. Proving that "special dangers" exist in the many industries covered by the regulation in question will often be difficult or impossible.

The Court's limitations on OSHA ETS authority also help to ensure that this power will remain a relatively rarely used emergency measure, as opposed to a commonplace end-run around normal notice-and-comment requirements. ETS cannot and should not be a blank check for OSHA or the White House to enact large-scale workplace regulations as it sees fit.

In my view, the Court's interpretation of the ETS power—based on the distinction between workplace risks and general public-health dangers—has significant flaws; it would have been preferable to instead focus on the requirement that ETS can only be used to counter a "grave danger." But the Court's approach does still have the virtue of placing meaningful constraints on what might otherwise have become near-boundless agency authority to regulate a vast range of workplace activities.

The Court's ruling in *Biden v. Missouri* also has important implications for future health care policy. By upholding the CMS vaccination mandate, the majority made clear that CMS's power to protect the "health and safety" of patients in institutions receiving federal Medicare and Medicaid funds includes the authority to require health care workers to be vaccinated against deadly contagious diseases. That power could well be used in the future, if new covid variants or the spread of other contagious diseases leads the agency to conclude that additional vaccinations are needed to protect patients.

As I write these words in the late summer of 2022, there is concern about the spread of monkeypox in the United States and elsewhere.[92] Unlike covid-19, monkeypox generally spreads only through prolonged close physical contact between individuals.[93] But such contact may be unavoidable between some types of health care providers and their patients. If so, CMS could potentially use the same power

---

[92] See, e.g., Jason Gale, Understanding Monkeypox and How Outbreaks Spread, Wash. Post (July 26, 2022), https://wapo.st/3bznznDS.

[93] *Id.*

at issue in *Biden v. Missouri* to justify requiring some health care workers to get vaccinated against the monkeypox virus as well.

In combination with other recent decisions, *NFIB* also signals that the Court is serious about enforcing the major questions doctrine as a constraint on delegation. This obviously will make it difficult for the executive to use vague statutes as justifications for sweeping assertions of authority.

NFIB also heralds a potential revival of the nondelegation doctrine as a serious constraint on Congress's authority to delegate power to the executive branch. Whether a majority favors such an approach is not clear, though it seems like at least four justices—Gorsuch, Thomas, Roberts, and Alito—have embraced the idea in recent years.[94] If the doctrine is revived, it could potentially constrain the executive more than the major questions doctrine alone would. Unlike the latter, nondelegation constraints could not be overcome merely by enacting a statute that delegates power more clearly.

Critics claim that major questions and nondelegation constraints could hobble executive power to address public-health emergencies and other societal problems. But, as I have argued in greater detail elsewhere, such limitations are actually valuable to avoiding abuses of executive power and protecting civil liberties in times of crisis.[95] The experience of the covid pandemic shows that presidents of both parties have strong incentives to exploit emergencies to adopt dubious policy measures that inflict significant harm while doing little to actually address the emergency in question. Examples include the eviction moratorium invalidated by the Supreme Court on major question grounds and the Trump administration's policy (later continued by Biden) of using Title 42 powers to expel hundreds of thousands of asylum seekers at the southern border.[96]

Strong enforcement of nondelegation and other limits on executive power would not completely obviate this danger. But pushing severely abusive policies through Congress is relatively more difficult than adopting them through White House or executive agency action.[97]

[94] Somin, *supra* note 51, at 681.
[95] *Id.* at 694–98.
[96] *Id.*
[97] *Id.* at 696–98.

Critics of the *NFIB* decision and other major question rulings argue that they provide insufficient deference to the expertise of specialized executive agencies. The joint dissent by the three liberal justices emphasizes that "[a]n agency with expertise in workplace health and safety" is in a better position to judge "how much protection, and of what kind, American workers need from COVID–19" than a "court, lacking any knowledge of how to safeguard workplaces, and insulated from responsibility for any damage it causes."[98] Similarly, legal scholar Steven Vladeck takes the Court to task for failing to "defer to the political branches" on a matter of "economic" policy on which the latter have superior expertise.[99]

But, as Vladeck himself pointed out in an earlier article (coauthored with Lindsay Wiley), nondeferential judicial review of the government's use of emergency powers during a crisis is a valuable tool for ensuring that the claims to "expertise" aren't merely a pretext for undermining civil liberties and constitutional constraints on government power.[100] A policy of judicial deference to supposed expertise will predictably lead to gross abuses.

In addition, claims of expertise often can be pretexts for other purposes, as likely occurred in the eviction moratorium and Title 42 cases. If the government's policy is truly justified by evidence derived from superior expertise, it should be able to prove it in court without any special deference. Indeed, a nondeferential approach by the judiciary can strengthen the government's incentives to do just that.[101]

Even the most expert of government agencies may lack expertise on all the issues raised by large-scale policy measures. The CDC may have scientific expertise on the spread of viruses, but it does not have expertise on economic and social policy sufficient to evaluate the full societal impact of policies such as a nationwide eviction moratorium or the expulsion of hundreds of thousands of migrants. Similarly, it is questionable whether OSHA really had relevant knowledge

[98] NFIB, 142 S. Ct. at 676 (joint dissent).

[99] Vladeck, *supra* note 63.

[100] Lindsay Wiley & Stephen I. Vladeck, Coronavirus, Civil Liberties, and the Courts: The Case against "Suspending" Judicial Review, 133 Harv. L. Rev. Forum 179, 183 (2020); cf. Somin, *supra* note 51 (making similar arguments); cf. Ilya Somin, The Case for "Regular" Judicial Review of Coronavirus Emergency Policies, Volokh Conspiracy (Apr. 15, 2020), https://perma.cc/4U9F-XF6Z.

[101] See Somin, *supra* note 100.

sufficient to assess the economic and social effects of imposing a vaccine mandate on tens of thousands of employers in widely varying circumstances, affecting over 80 million workers.

Sadly, the ideological valence of the most high-profile recent major question and nondelegation rulings by the Supreme Court have raised fears that these doctrines are merely tools of the political right to use against the left. But it is important to emphasize that strong enforcement of these doctrines can be used to constrain Republican abuses of power no less than Democratic ones. President Donald Trump used the covid pandemic as a pretext for adopting the most sweeping immigration restrictions in American history. Many of his policies were vulnerable to nondelegation challenges,[102] and a federal district court invalidated his sweeping suspension of work visas partly on that basis.[103] In an age where many on the left rightly worry that Trump (in the event that he returns to power) and other Republicans might use executive power for authoritarian purposes, the left has at least as much to gain from rigorous judicial enforcement of limitations on sweeping assertions of executive authority as the right.[104]

While progressives are understandably disappointed with *NFIB's* invalidation of the OSHA vaccination mandate, they have reason to support the separation-of-powers principles on which the ruling was based. The Supreme Court's strengthening of those principles could help constrain Republican power grabs no less than Democratic ones.

In addition to their implications for health care policy and separation-of-powers doctrine, the vaccine mandate rulings also highlight some weaknesses of the Supreme Court's growing use of the shadow docket. Scholars have criticized the practice of deciding important issues on an accelerated timetable with relatively limited

---

[102] For an overview, see Ilya Somin, The Dangers of America's Coronavirus Immigration Bans, The Atlantic (June 28, 2020), https://bit.ly/3zroRUi.

[103] See Nat'l Ass'n of Mfrs. v. DHS, 491 F. Supp. 3d 549, 563 (N.D. Cal. 2020), appeal dismissed, 2021 WL 1652546 (9th Cir. 2021).

[104] See Somin, *supra* note 51, at 695–98. For an argument that progressives should embrace nondelegation principles as a safeguard against Trump and others like him, see Carlos A. Ball, Principles Matter: The Constitution, Progressives, and the Trump Era 178–82 (2021).

briefing.[105] In a recent dissenting opinion in another shadow docket case, Justice Kagan took the majority to task for using the shadow docket as just "another place for merits determinations—except made without full briefing and argument."[106]

Both *NFIB* and *Biden v. Missouri* arguably exemplify some of the risks of using the shadow docket to resolve major substantive issues. The decisions in both cases were issued on January 13, 2022, just six days after oral argument, and only about two months after the OSHA and CMS rules were promulgated on November 5, 2021. That gave the Court little time to consider the arguments and issues at stake.

While I believe the Court nonetheless reached the right outcomes in both cases, the majority opinion in each one suffers from significant errors and omissions. In *NFIB*, the Court relied on a dubious distinction between workplace risks and general public-health dangers, while overlooking the much stronger rationale for its decision offered by focusing on the meaning of the requirement that ETS authority may only be used to counter a "grave danger." This despite the fact that the latter argument was highlighted by Chief Judge Sutton's lower-court opinion in the Sixth Circuit. And in *Biden v. Missouri*, the Court neglected important Spending Clause and federalism clear statement rule issues, even though these questions had been raised in the brief of the plaintiffs and in one of the lower court rulings the Court ended up overturning. Would the Court have avoided these errors if it had had more time for consideration? That question is hard to answer. But these mistakes do seem like the kind of slipshod errors that are more likely to occur when judges and their clerks work under extreme time pressure.

It doesn't necessarily follow that the Court should abolish or severely curtail its use of the shadow docket. The dangers of swift decisions made without time for careful consideration must be weighed against the costs of letting illegal policies remain in force, which can

---

[105] For criticisms of the shadow docket, see, e.g., Vladeck, *supra* note 5; The Supreme Court's Shadow Docket: Hearing before the Subcomm. on Cts., Intell. Prop., and the Internet of the H. Comm. on the Judiciary, 117th Cong. *3–4 (2021) (statement of Stephen I. Vladeck); Stephen I. Vladeck, The Solicitor General and the Shadow Docket, 133 Harv. L. Rev. 123 (2019). Professor Vladeck is the leading academic critic of the Court's use of the shadow docket.

[106] Louisiana v. Am. Rivers, 142 S. Ct. 1347, 1349 (2022) (Kagan, J., dissenting).

sometimes cause grave harm that is difficult or impossible to repair. There is also sometimes value in quickly and definitively resolving disputes in favor of the government, thereby allowing key policies to proceed without a cloud of legal uncertainty hanging over them. The Court's swift upholding of the CMS health care worker vaccination mandate may be an example of the latter. I do not attempt to resolve these difficult tradeoffs here. But I note that the use of the shadow docket may have significantly reduced the quality of the Court's work in these two important cases.

Conclusion

The Supreme Court's January 2022 vaccine mandate rulings correctly resolved legal disputes over two important policies adopted for the purpose of combatting the covid-19 pandemic. In the process, they also set valuable precedents for future cases and strengthened separation-of-powers constraints on executive power. There is much to applaud in both rulings.

At the same time, however, there are also significant limitations and omissions in both decisions. The Court's decisions reached the right results and were certainly "good enough for government work." But the justices should have done still better.

The *Becerra* Cases: How Not to Do *Chevron*
*by William Yeatman**

The title of this article is meant both figuratively and literally. In the literal sense, the title refers to how the Supreme Court ducked deference in two similar (and similarly named) controversies, *American Hospital Association v. Becerra*[1] (*"American Hospital Association"*) and *Becerra v. Empire Health Foundation*[2] (*"Empire Health Foundation"*)— even though both cases seemed to be well-suited for the famous *Chevron* "two step." Although the Court confusingly applied elements of the two-step framework, the opinions make no mention of *Chevron*, and thereby demonstrate "how not to do" the doctrine.

The title's figurative meaning is prescriptive. By eliding *Chevron* (again), the Court continues its ongoing failure to police the deference that has run amok in the lower courts. Indeed, the *Becerra* controversies demonstrate the costs of the Court's passivity. In each case, lower courts applied an expansive gloss to the standard *Chevron* framework, effectively turning the doctrine into super-deference. For as long as the Court fails to explicitly rein in the *Chevron* doctrine, lower courts will continue to tilt the scales of justice in favor of administrative authority even beyond the already generous terms provided by deference doctrines under black-letter administrative law. Making matters worse, in at least one of the *Becerra* cases, the Court muddled its silent *Chevron* analysis, which incurs undue regulatory uncertainty. The upshot is that, in addition to the urgent imperative for cleaning up *Chevron* in the lower courts, the Court needs to tighten up its own interpretative methodology. Thus, the *Becerra* decisions' *sub silentio* and garbled application of the doctrine demonstrates "how not to do" *Chevron*.

* Research fellow in the Cato Institute's Robert A. Levy Center for Constitutional Studies

[1] 142 S. Ct. 1896 (2022).
[2] 142 S. Ct. 2354 (2022).

I. *Chevron's* Vanishing Act

Chevron v. Natural Resources Defense Council is the most cited—and most controversial—decision in administrative law.[3] The *Chevron* doctrine establishes a two-step analysis for reviewing agency interpretations of laws they administer. *Chevron's* first step asks whether Congress "has directly spoken to the precise question at issue."[4] If so, then "that is the end of the matter" because courts "must give effect to the unambiguously expressed intent of Congress."[5] If, however, the statute is ambiguous, then the court proceeds to *Chevron* step two, which inquires whether the agency's interpretation is "based on a permissible construction of the statute."[6]

By all appearances, *American Hospital Association* and *Empire Health Foundation* were tailor-made for *Chevron* deference. Both controversies involved the Medicare Act, a "complex statutory and regulatory regime" for public health insurance.[7] In *American Hospital Association*, the controversy centered around the calculation of a reimbursement rate for outpatient drugs.[8] In *Empire Health Foundation*, the interpretive dispute pertained to a mathematical fraction that establishes enhanced reimbursement rates for hospitals that serve a higher-than-usual percentage of low-income patients.[9] These kinds of complicated statutory questions typically invite deference. After all, the sine qua non of the *Chevron* doctrine is that agencies are comparatively competent (relative to courts) when it comes to interpreting highly technical statutes.

In both cases, moreover, the Department of Health and Human Services (HHS) had undertaken a resource-intensive rulemaking process to reach its interpretations.[10] Jumping through these

---

[3] 467 U.S. 837 (1984); see also, Abbe R. Gluck, What 30 Years of Chevron Teach Us about the Rest of Statutory Interpretation, 83 Fordham L. Rev. 607, 612 (2014) ("It is the most cited administrative law case in history and has been referenced in more than 7000 cases and more than 5000 law review articles.").

[4] 467 U.S. at 842.

[5] *Id.*

[6] *Id.* at 843.

[7] Good Samaritan Hosp. v. Shalala, 113 S. Ct. 2151, 2154 (1993).

[8] 42 U.S.C. § 1395l(t)(14)(A).

[9] 42 U.S.C. § 1395ww(d)(5)(F)(vi)(I).

[10] See 82 Fed. Reg. 52,362, 52,490 (Nov. 13, 2017) (setting forth interpretation in American Hospital Association); 69 Fed. Reg. 48,916, 49,098–99, 49,246 (Aug. 11, 2004) (issuing interpretation in Empire Health).

procedural hoops is "significant . . . in pointing to *Chevron* author-ity," under long-established Supreme Court precedent.[11]

In both *Becerra* cases, lower courts had applied the *Chevron* frame-work. In *American Hospital Association,* the D.C. Circuit upheld HHS's interpretation at *Chevron* step two,[12] while in *Empire Health Founda-tion,* the Ninth Circuit ruled against HHS at step one.[13]

Before the Supreme Court, the questions presented were worded in the language of the *Chevron* doctrine. In *American Hospital Associa-tion,* this framing was explicit: the question was "whether *Chevron* deference permits" the agency's interpretation. In *Empire Health Foundation,* the government's petition for certiorari asked whether the agency "has permissibly" interpreted the statute, which closely tracks *Chevron's* command for courts to uphold an agency's interpre-tation if it is "based on a permissible construction of the statute."[14]

For all the above reasons, *Chevron* deference was a hot topic dur-ing oral arguments. In *American Hospital Association,* Justice Clarence Thomas started the day's questions by asking if the Court should "overrule *Chevron*,"[15] and the doctrine was invoked more than 50 times during the hearing. During arguments for *Empire Health Foundation,* Justices Samuel Alito, Stephen Breyer, Neil Gorsuch, and Sonia Sotomayor engaged in extensive exchanges over *Chevron* with the government's counsel.[16]

Against this backdrop, proponents of administrative power wor-ried that either of the *Becerra* cases might provide an ideal vehicle for the "conservative" Court to undermine the *Chevron* doctrine. *Politico* reported that "many expect" the Court "to announce the death of *Chevron* deference."[17] At SCOTUSblog, Professor Nicholas Bagley warned that "the right wing of the court could use [*American Hospital*

[11] See United States v. Mead Corp., 533 US 218, 230–31 (2001).

[12] Am. Hosp. Ass'n v. Azar, 967 F. 3d 818 (D.C. Cir. 2020); Empire Health Found. v. Azar, 958 F.3d 873 (9th Cir. 2020).

[13] *Id.* at 884–86.

[14] 467 U.S. at 843.

[15] Tr. of Oral Arg. at 5, Am. Hosp. Ass'n v. Becerra, 142 S. Ct. 1896 (2022) (No. 20-1114), https://bit.ly/3d6HmWA.

[16] Tr. of Oral Arg. at 14–15, 24, 29, 44–45, Becerra v. Empire Health Found., 142 S. Ct. 2354 (2022) (No. 20-1312), https://bit.ly/3PYNlv7.

[17] David Bernstein, The Supreme Court Could Foster a New Kind of Civil War, Politico (June 14, 2022), https://politi.co/3zsxSMF.

Association] to narrow or even overturn *Chevron*, with potentially dramatic implications for the scope of executive-branch power."[18]

Then, in mid-June, the opinions came down and . . . nothing. *Chevron* was nowhere to be found. In terms of outcomes, the government lost *American Hospital Association* and won *Empire Health Foundation*. But there was no mention of *Chevron* or any variation of "defer." That's not to say the famed doctrine went entirely missing. Rather, both decisions seemed to silently adopt diluted versions of the *Chevron* steps.

Writing for a unanimous Court in *American Hospital Association*, Justice Brett Kavanaugh appeared to employ a step-one inquiry into whether the legislative language unambiguously evinces congressional intent. In his introduction, for example, he writes that the case was "straightforward" under "the text and structure of the statute."[19] He then performs a detailed discussion of the statutory provision before the Court. At the end of the opinion, he directly invokes *Chevron's* doctrinal language, writing that HHS's interpretation failed scrutiny under "the traditional tools of statutory interpretation," which is the exact turn of phrase used in *Chevron* to describe a properly functioning first step of the doctrinal framework.[20] Still, the opinion omits any of the words and concepts that are the hallmark of a step-one inquiry, such as textual ambiguity, plain meaning, or statutory clarity. As a result, Kavanaugh's judicial methodology isn't entirely clear.

A similar methodological coyness pervades Justice Elena Kagan's majority decision in *Empire Health Foundation*. For the most part, her opinion reads like a *Chevron* step-two inquiry into the reasonableness of the agency's interpretation, albeit one with a strong textualist flavor. After performing a detailed analysis of the statutory language, she concludes that the "[t]ext, context, and structure all support" HHS's position, and this tone ("support") is indicative of a step-two analysis.[21] At other places, however, Kagan's opinion appears more like a *Chevron* step one. For example, she says the statute "disclose[s]

---

a surprisingly clear meaning—the one chosen by HHS."[22] Phrases like "clear meaning" are commonly associated with *Chevron's* first step. In a similar vein, she writes that "[t]he structure of the relevant statutory provisions reinforces our conclusion that [the disputed text] means [what HHS says it means], and nothing more."[23] Taken at face value, this statement ("and nothing more") suggests that the agency's reading is the only available interpretation of the statute, which is a conclusion available only under a *Chevron* step-one analysis. The Court again was sending confusing signals about its interpretive reasoning.

II. Interpreting the Void

After the two *Becerra* cases came down with nary a word on *Chevron,* many understood the Court's silence as speaking to ulterior motives.

In a prepared statement, Professor Cary Coglianese wondered aloud if the Court's unanimous opinion in *American Hospital Association* is "part of a deliberate strategy of allowing *Chevron* to wither on the jurisprudential vine and ultimately die from desuetude."[24] Dan Deacon, a lecturer at the University of Michigan Law School, tweeted that the decision, "taken at face value . . . impl[ies] no deference whatsoever to the agency's interpretation," and he reiterated this sentiment on social media about the decision in *Empire Health Foundation.*[25]

At the popular legal blog "The Volokh Conspiracy," Professor Jonathan Adler posted that *American Hospital Association* "reinforces a message that the Court has been giving for several years now: The first task of a reviewing Court is to focus on the statutory language and follow Congress's instructions."[26] The idea here is that by performing an apparent *Chevron* step one without naming the doctrine, Kavanaugh was admonishing lower courts to put greater effort into the textual investigation at step one before they rush on to the

---

[22] *Id.*

[23] *Id.* at 2366.

[24] Profs. Cary Coglianese and Allison Hoffman Share Their Insights on American Hospital Association v. Becerra, Penn Law (Nov. 23, 2022), https://bit.ly/3PTecZr.

[25] @danieltdeacon, Twitter (June 15, 2022, 10:24 AM), https://bit.ly/3oT63It.

[26] Jonathan H. Adler, Supreme Court Decides Major Chevron Case without Citing Chevron, Volokh Conspiracy (June 15, 2022), https://bit.ly/3vBaDyL.

(easier) task of deciding whether to defer to the agency at step two. Jack Fitzhenry seconded this theory at the Federalist Society blog, where he argued that the *Becerra* cases imply "that courts should tighten up the statutory inquiry."[27]

Practitioners echoed these scholarly inferences. Regarding *American Hospital Association*, Samuel Rasche and Michael Showalter of the law firm ArentFox Schiff wrote that "[t]he Court appears to have applied a higher bar" at *Chevron* step one, meaning the government must make a greater showing of ambiguity before the Court will accept the agency's interpretation.[28] Attorneys at the Miller Canfield firm concluded that the *Becerra* cases "show an increased skepticism by the Court of agency interpretations of statutes and signal that going forward, the federal courts will more closely scrutinize administrative agency decisions in general."[29]

In sum, conventional wisdom holds that the *Becerra* decisions carried an implied message. Generalizing somewhat, scholars and practitioners have coalesced around two takes: To progressives, the Court is trying to starve *Chevron* to death; to conservatives, the Court is instructing lower courts to pay closer attention to the text.

Perhaps this speculation is right. Maybe the Court was indeed sending hidden messages. For my part, I'm not sold. Rather than implied intent, I suspect the Court's doctrinal silence is the product of two prosaic inputs, which I discuss in turn below.

A. Government's Self-Effacing Chevron Claims

One likely explanation for the Court's failure to mention *Chevron* is that the government sandbagged its own arguments for deference.

For example, in *Empire Health Foundation*, the solicitor general seemed to go out of her way to deemphasize the doctrine. In its merits brief, the government argued that the Court should "uphold [HHS's] interpretation simply because it is the better one, without

[27] Jack Fitzhenry, Has Chevron Step One Stepped to Center Stage?, FedSoc Blog (June 28, 2022), https://bit.ly/3zXTCBA.

[28] Samuel Rashe & J. Michael Showalter, Court Side-Steps Overturning Chevron Deference in Recent Health-Care Related Decision, JD Supra (June 24, 2022), https://bit.ly/3d5UTOa.

[29] Andrew Blum, Matthew Greenberg & Larry Saylor, Supreme Court Signals Move Away from Judicial Deference to Administrative Agencies, JD Supra (July 21, 2022), https://bit.ly/3zX5OT9.

addressing the additional weight due under *Chevron*."[30] In support of this unusual request, the government cited a footnote in *Coventry Health Care of Missouri, Inc. v. Nevils*, where the Court stated that "we need not consider whether *Chevron* deference attaches to" the agency's interpretation "because the statute alone resolves this dispute."[31]

As it did in *Empire Health Foundation*, the government in *American Hospital Association* reluctantly raised *Chevron* in an ancillary argument. Again, the solicitor general's brief is given mostly to arguing that the agency "can prevail without any deference to its interpretation."[32] To be precise, the brief broaches the *Chevron* doctrine only in its final three pages, and most of this argument is given to assurances that "[t]his case ... does not present the potential concerns about *Chevron* deference" that have troubled many of the justices.[33] During the hearing, the solicitor general went so far as to say, "I do not think *Chevron* is necessary in this case."[34] In this fashion, the government treated *Chevron* almost like a liability, which is remarkable considering the D.C. Circuit had sided with HHS on the strength of deference alone.

To be sure, there have been other recent signs that the Supreme Court bar is wary of pressing *Chevron* claims. In 2020, for example, the Justice Department waived deference in *Guedes v. Bureau of Alcohol, Tobacco, Firearms and Explosives*.[35] A year earlier, in *BNSF Railway, Co. v. Loo*, Justice Gorsuch made light of the (private-sector) petitioner's reluctance to seek *Chevron* deference for a government interpretation that mirrored its own.[36] But the *Becerra* cases are the first examples that I've seen of the solicitor general arguing for *Chevron* in such a backhanded manner.

It's obvious what's going on here. The government's self-effacing *Chevron* claims are part of a risk-averse litigation strategy. These days, deference is a losing argument for (at least) a critical mass of justices,

[30] Br. for the Pet. at 26, Becerra v. Empire Health Found., 142 S. Ct. 2354 (2022) (No. 20-1312), https://bit.ly/3Jqugj3.

[31] 137 S. Ct. 1190, 1198 n.3 (2017).

[32] Br. for Respondents at 47, Am. Hosp. Ass'n v. Becerra, 142 S. Ct. 1896 (2022) (No. 20-1114), https://bit.ly/3d54kx2.

[33] *Id.* at 48.

[34] Tr. of Oral Arg., *supra* note 15, at 69.

[35] 140 S. Ct. 789 (2020) (statement of Gorsuch, J., respecting denial of certiorari).

[36] See 139 S. Ct. 893, 908–09 (2019).

as Chief Justice John Roberts, Thomas, Gorsuch, and Kavanaugh have all publicly stated a willingness to reform, diminish, or upend the *Chevron* doctrine. The solicitor general, who is no fool, litigates accordingly.

B. Getting to Yes

Likely, the most important reason the Court didn't mention *Chevron* is also the blandest explanation. The vote tally for both cases indicates that any engagement with *Chevron* was bargained away as winning coalitions were cobbled together during the behind-the-scenes horse-trading.

Looking at the Court's unanimous opinion in *American Hospital Association*, the justices reached broad agreement that the statute, whatever it means, doesn't mean what the agency says. Rather than press the *Chevron* issue, and use the case to launch broadsides against deference, I suspect that the Court's *Chevron*-skeptics were willing to take the doctrine off the table—by name, at least—to obtain a 9-0 ruling.

A similar dynamic likely played out in *Empire Health Foundation*. Kagan's majority opinion was supported by a peculiar alliance of justices, including Sotomayor, Breyer, Thomas, and Amy Coney Barrett. If we take a closer look at that lineup, *Chevron*'s vanishing act starts to make a lot more sense. During oral arguments, Justices Sotomayor and Breyer expressed reservations about whether HHS warranted deference due to deficiencies in the agency's notice-and-comment rulemaking.[37] And Justice Thomas, of course, has gone as far as any Article III judge in questioning the constitutional propriety of *Chevron* deference. Because there was no constituency for *Chevron* on the Court, Kagan's majority opinion does not mention doctrine.

III. Fallout from the Void

Scholarship suggests that *Chevron*'s disappearance in the *Becerra* cases is the norm, not the exception. In a seminal survey of deference doctrines at the Supreme Court, Professors William Eskridge and Lauren Baer found that the Court applies the *Chevron* framework

---

[37] See Tr. of Oral Arg., *supra* note 16, at 15, 60 (Breyer: "I have an awful qualm about using *Chevron* here"; Sotomayor: "I don't see how we give you *Chevron* deference under those circumstances").

only about a quarter of the time the doctrine could apply.[38] As explained above, I don't think the Court's evident reluctance to resort to *Chevron* is part of some grand design. Yet just because there's no lurking intent, that doesn't mean the Supreme Court's doctrinal circumspection is not fraught with meaning. To the contrary, the Court's haphazard approach incurs several negative consequences, as discussed below.

A. Letting Lower Courts Run Riot

Even if the Court meant to admonish lower courts *sub silentio*, this muted strategy is unlikely to succeed. That's because lower courts have every incentive to ignore the high court's silence on *Chevron*. As explained by Professor Richard Pierce, "[i]t is much easier for a judge to apply the relatively simple *Chevron* standard and to uphold an agency interpretation of a statute as reasonable than it is to write a lengthy opinion" that elucidates the law.[39] Given this incentive structure, the only way for the Court to reform the *Chevron* doctrine is to do so explicitly—and such a course correction is sorely needed. To understand why it's necessary to rein in *Chevron*, look no further than the *Becerra* cases.

Consider, for example, the district court's bizarre, beefed-up *Chevron* framework in *Empire Health Foundation*.[40] Describing step one, the district court said it would employ the "[t]raditional tools of judicial statutory construction," including "the plain meaning of the language in the statute, dictionary definitions, canons of construction, *legislative purpose*, and *legislative history*."[41] By resorting to nontextual tools like legislative purpose and history at *Chevron*'s first step, the district court introduces a purposive influence into what is supposed to be textual analysis. At *Chevron* step two, the district court further distorted the doctrine. Rather than asking whether the agency's interpretation is reasonable under the statute, which is how this second step is supposed to operate, the district court asked

[38] William N. Eskridge, Jr. & Lauren E. Baer, The Continuum of Deference: Supreme Court Treatment of Agency Statutory Interpretations from Chevron to Hamdan, 96 Geo. L.J. 1083, 1124–25 (2008).

[39] Richard J. Pierce Jr., Is Chevron Deference Still Alive?, Reg. Rev. (July 14, 2022), https://bit.ly/3QjtvdO.

[40] Empire Health Found. v. Price, 334 F. Supp. 3d 1134 (E.D. Wash. 2018).

[41] *Id.* at 1148 (emphasis added).

whether the statute "precludes" the agency's reading.[42] The result is to condone any interpretation that isn't expressly forbidden by the law, which is far more generous to the government than standard *Chevron* deference. Indeed, the district court deferred despite having conceded that the agency's interpretation "does not appear entirely reasonable."[43] Under a "normal" *Chevron* step two, HHS's unreasonable interpretation would have failed. Yet under the district court's souped-up version of the *Chevron* doctrine, the government prevailed. The district court's *Chevron* shenanigans went unadmonished by the Ninth Circuit.[44]

Turning to *American Hospital Association*, the D.C. Circuit seemed to skip *Chevron* step one in reviewing the agency's interpretation of the operative statutory question. This apparent doctrinal short cut prompted Justice Gorsuch, during oral arguments, to question whether the D.C. Circuit's decision reflects a "troubling trend" of lower courts jumping straight to deference without first exhausting the traditional tools of statutory construction at *Chevron* step one.[45] At step two, the D.C. Circuit transformed *Chevron* into superdeference, just like the district court did in *Empire Health Foundation*. According to the D.C. Circuit, "we would need to conclude that Congress unambiguously barred HHS" to side against the government.[46] And because "the statute does not clearly preclude" HHS's interpretation, the agency carried the day.[47] Again, this formulation lowers the bar from the standard *Chevron* framework, by putting the burden on Congress to specify all that HHS cannot do, when the burden should be on the agency to demonstrate that its interpretation is reasonable.

Alas, there is nothing anomalous about the lower courts' expansive gloss on the *Chevron* doctrine. As observed by Sixth Circuit Judge Raymond Kethledge, "the federal courts have become habituated to defer to the interpretive views of executive agencies, not as

---

[42] *Id.* at 1153.

[43] *Id.*

[44] The Ninth Circuit ruled on *Chevron* step-one grounds, by way of the *Brand X* doctrine, without commenting on the district court's *Chevron* methodology. Empire Health Found., 958 F.3d at 884–85.

[45] Tr. of Oral Arg., *supra* note 15, at 33.

[46] 967 F.3d at 831.

[47] *Id.* at 834.

a matter of last resort but first."[48] Justice Anthony Kennedy, in one of his final opinions, bemoaned "reflexive deference," by which he meant that "some Courts of Appeals engag[e] in cursory" textual analyses before deferring to the government.[49] Unless and until the Supreme Court takes on *Chevron*, reflexive deference will remain unchecked in the lower courts.

B. Is the Justice Department Rigging the Game?

In the *Becerra* cases, there is a stark difference in how the lower courts and the Supreme Court applied the *Chevron* doctrine. Whereas the lower courts viewed these controversies through an overly deferential lens, the Supreme Court ignored the doctrine altogether.

Scholarship suggests that this dichotomy holds true overall in Article III courts. As noted above, survey data indicate that the Supreme Court applies the *Chevron* two-step in only about 25 percent of the cases in which the doctrine could apply. Circuit courts apply *Chevron* much more frequently—about 77 percent of the time, according to research by professors Chris Walker and Kent Barnett.[50] Based on this discrepancy, the professors hypothesize that "there may be 'a *Chevron* Supreme' and 'a *Chevron* Regular,'" meaning that "*Chevron* deference may not have much of an effect on agency outcomes at the Supreme Court, but our findings suggest that it seems to matter quite a bit in the circuit courts."[51]

If the professors' supposition is correct, then it would make sense for the government to adopt a Janus-faced litigation strategy for *Chevron* deference. Under such a scenario, lawyers at the Justice Department would argue zealously for deference before the lower courts and then, in the off chance that certiorari is granted, the solicitor general's office would pull its punches on *Chevron* before the high court.

---

[48] Valent v. Comm'r of Soc. Sec., 918 F.3d 516, 525 (6th Cir. 2019) (Kethledge, J., dissenting); see also Arangure v. Whitaker, 911 F.3d 333, 336 (6th Cir. 2018) ("[A]ll too often, courts abdicate th[eir] duty [to say what the law is] by rushing to find statutes ambiguous, rather than performing a full interpretive analysis.").

[49] Pereira v. Sessions, 138 S. Ct. 2105, 2120 (2018) (Kennedy, J., concurring); see also Valent, 918 F.3d at 525 ("In too many cases, courts do so almost reflexively, as if doing so were somehow a virtue, or an act of judicial restraint—as if [courts'] duty were to facilitate violations of the separation of powers rather than prevent them.").

[50] Kent Barnett & Christopher J. Walker, Chevron in the Circuit Courts, 116 Mich. L. Rev. 1, 29 (2017).

[51] *Id.* at 72–73.

I suspect such a cynical strategy was afoot in at least one of the *Becerra* cases. Above, I discussed how the solicitor general effaced the government's own *Chevron* claims in *Empire Health Foundation*. Before the Ninth Circuit, however, government lawyers sang a different tune. There, the Justice Department led with *Chevron*—the doctrine is introduced in the first sentence of the government's merits brief argument.[52]

The inescapable problem, of course, is that the Supreme Court hears only a tiny fraction of administrative law cases that are before the federal judiciary. And lower courts have every incentive to continue to reflexively apply *Chevron* deference, as it's a lot easier to defer than it is to perform a rigorous textual analysis.

The Justice Department seems to be exploiting—and exacerbating— this unfortunate status quo. Before the lower courts, government lawyers may press for ever more permissive glosses on the standard *Chevron* framework, knowing that the odds are exceedingly slim that the controversy will ever get before the high court. If certiorari is granted, the government can then basically discard its *Chevron* claims and count on the Court to leave the doctrine unchecked in the lower courts.

C. Regulatory Uncertainty

It's not just the lower courts that need to tighten up their judicial methodology. The Supreme Court's equivocal application of the *Chevron* doctrine, whatever the cause, creates regulatory uncertainty and is, therefore, deficient as a matter of interpretative technique.

In both *Becerra* cases, the Court never definitively established whether the underlying statutory provision is ambiguous—that is, the Court failed to perform a *Chevron* step-one analysis. This won't do. A robust step one is crucial if courts are to meet their duty to say what the law is. Even if the Court overturned *Chevron v. NRDC*—and it should—a step-one analysis must remain the starting point for whatever replaces deference. In every instance of statutory interpretation, all courts should begin with the text and then exhaust the tools of statutory construction.

Professors Kenneth Bamberger and Peter Strauss have advanced a public policy reason why it's incumbent upon courts to always

---

[52] Cross-Appellee Response Br. at 14, Empire Health Found. v. Azar, 958 F.3d 873 (9th Cir. 2020) (No. 18-35845).

search for unambiguously expressed legislative intent.[53] In determining that a statute is ambiguous, the court establishes that the agency may change its interpretation in the future. Obviously, the reverse also holds true: When the court fixes a statutory meaning, it binds the agency to a particular interpretation. It follows that a proper step one analysis provides important regulatory clarity. And a deficient step-one analysis will bring about undue regulatory uncertainty for the agency and the regulated community.

An example from the *Becerra* cases will help to demonstrate how a sloppy *Chevron* analysis can cause undue confusion.[54] In *Empire Health Foundation*, the Supreme Court "approve[d]" HHS's interpretation without first investigating whether the statute has an unambiguous meaning. Kagan's opinion sometimes implies the statute is ambiguous and at other times she hints that the statute unambiguously means what the government says it means. It's impossible to say for sure, even though the difference is highly significant for the regulatory regime. If the statute is unambiguous, then HHS is locked into that policy course. If the statute is unclear, then the agency is free to experiment with new policies.

It's easy to imagine how the resultant regulatory uncertainty might lead to administrative inefficiencies. For example, HHS could waste its limited resources implementing a new policy in the mistaken belief that the statute is ambiguous. Alternatively, HHS might be deterred from seeking regulatory changes warranted by sound policy due to the misimpression that *Empire Health Foundation* had identified the unambiguously expressed legislative intent of Congress. This uncertainty, and any attendant administrative waste, never would have been a concern if the Court hadn't muddled its step-one analysis.[55]

---

[53] Kenneth A. Bamberger & Peter L. Strauss, Chevron's Two Steps, 95 Va. L. Rev. 611, 617–18 (2009).

[54] This public policy concern is less of an issue in a decision like *American Hospital Association*, where the Court unequivocally rejected HHS's interpretation and, therefore, took that policy off the agency's menu of future discretionary choices.

[55] Professors Bamberger and Strauss argue that a proper step one is not exhausted "once a court has found statutory ambiguity," but instead entails the court "ascertaining . . . the range of meaning available to the agency." See Bamberger & Strauss, *supra* note 53, at 613–14. I suspect that's asking too much of courts. They probably would be satisfied with what they call a "point solution," which is basically a yes/no determination that the statute is either ambiguous or unambiguous.

The Court must do better. In addition to cleaning up *Chevron* for the lower courts, the Court should clean up its own statutory interpretation by faithfully exhausting the tools of statutory construction to discern whether Congress's intent is clear.

IV. Conclusion

Regarding Antonin Scalia's profound influence on the law, Justice Kagan famously said, "we are all textualists now." Among her peers on the Supreme Court, at least, she's undoubtedly correct, as demonstrated by the conspicuous commitment to textual analysis in both *Becerra* decisions. Outside the Court's chambers, however, Kagan's declaration rings hollow. In the lower courts, interpreting regulatory statutes remains a purposive affair that is characterized first and foremost by deference doctrines, as demonstrated by the amped up versions of *Chevron* employed by lower courts in the *Becerra* controversies. For its part, the government seems content to play both sides.

Because lower courts still haven't gotten the memo on textualism, the Supreme Court does a disservice to the law when, as in the *Becerra* cases, the Court declines to check the gross distortions of the *Chevron* framework that are running rampant in the federal judiciary. Ideally, the Court would overturn *Chevron v. NRDC* and nix the concept of binding judicial deference to self-serving agency interpretations. Short of that, the Court could explicitly call for lower courts to resolve more cases on *Chevron* step-one grounds; to the extent the Court already is sending implicit signals about step one, they're falling on deaf ears. Even a simple holding that the lower courts shouldn't expand on the standard *Chevron* framework would go far toward reining in worst practices. These much-needed reforms are the opportunity costs of the Court's doctrinal circumspection.

At the very least, the Court must tighten up its own method of statutory interpretation. Notwithstanding the Court's embrace of textualism, its opinions sometimes send mixed messages about whether the statute is ambiguous, which is what happened in *Empire Health Foundation*. This interpretive equivocation threatens to bring about undue regulatory uncertainty and, therefore, should be avoided by the Court.

Egbert v. Boule: Federal Officer Suits by Common Law

Jennifer L. Mascott* & R. Trent McCotter**

Smugglers, informants, border crossings, and drugs. In one of the more factually colorful cases of this term, the U.S. Supreme Court all but nailed the door shut on one of the modern era's last remaining vehicles for monetary damages to heap accountability on bad-acting federal officials. In a 5-1-3 decision in *Egbert v. Boule* during the final weeks of the term, the Court reversed the Ninth Circuit's approval of *Bivens* monetary damages against an officer for assault and retaliation stemming from a border confrontation at the location known as Smuggler's Inn.

This may trouble individuals concerned with history. Founding-era evidence suggests that damages suits against federal officers provided an important complement to impeachment as an accountability mechanism outside the hierarchical structure of executive branch direction and command.[1]

But while this case may superficially present as a dispute over whether federal officers should face accountability, the Court instead wrestled with a more fundamental core constitutional and structural question. The Court assessed which governmental institution can authorize federal officer damages suits. It concluded that Congress and not the courts must authorize such actions in the federal system.[2]

---

* Assistant professor of law and co-executive director, C. Boyden Gray Center for the Study of the Administrative State, Antonin Scalia Law School, George Mason University.

** Director, Separation of Powers Clinic of the Gray Center, Antonin Scalia Law School, George Mason University and partner, Boyden Gray & Associates.

[1] See Jennifer L. Mascott, The Ratifiers' Theory of Officer Accountability (manuscript), https://bit.ly/3bFIwrs (reviewed by the Legal Theory Blog at https://bit.ly/3Q5qRsa).

[2] Egbert v. Boule, 142 S. Ct. 1793, 1800 (2022); Br. of Prof. Jennifer L. Mascott as Amicus Curiae in Support of Petitioner at 20–28, Egbert v. Boule, 142 S. Ct. 1793 (2022) (No. 21-147), https://tinyurl.com/2w5z3fn2 (hereinafter, "Mascott Brief"); Br. for the United States as Amicus Curiae Supporting Petitioner at 19–33, Egbert v. Boule, 142 S. Ct. 1793 (2022) (No. 21-147), https://tinyurl.com/2t29f39u (hereinafter, "DOJ Brief").

This holding, speaking to the role of Article III courts versus policy-makers within federal institutions, applies whether the Constitution requires liability for federal misdeeds and whether such liability remains available under state law.[3]

For many decades after the ratification of the U.S. Constitution, federal officers faced lawsuits for damages under state common law when they allegedly engaged in unlawful acts, as multiple scholars have explained.[4] A not-uncommon fact pattern included an individual suing a federal officer for trespass connected with a search, seizure, or arrest, to which the officer would plead the defense of lawful federal authority connected with a federally authorized act. Constitutional questions sometimes arose because the contours of the federal officer's defense were subject to the constraint that the federal officer carrying out a search could not do so unreasonably under the Constitution's Fourth Amendment.[5] These common-law suits existed long before Congress established statutory general federal-question jurisdiction for federal courts in 1875. Congress did not analogously authorize any specific cause of action for monetary damages for the commission of federal officer constitutional violations. And whereas Congress had authorized suits against those acting under color of state law under 42 U.S.C. § 1983, Congress had enacted no companion act for federal officers. Nonetheless, common-law suits remained available against federal officers.

The Court attempted to bring its pragmatic vision of equity to this state/federal asymmetry in 1971 when it held in *Bivens v. Six Unknown Named Agents of Federal Bureau of Narcotics* that the text of the Constitution itself contained an implicit right to monetary damages in the event of a federal violation of individual rights. The pressure on this form of relief intensified in 1988 when Congress enacted the Westfall Act, removing the availability of state common-law remedies

---

[3] See Egbert, 142 S. Ct. at 1804; Mascott Brief, *supra* note 2, at 28–29; DOJ Brief, *supra* note 2, at 26; Br. of Project for Privacy & Surveillance Accountability & Protect the First Foundation as Amici Curiae Supporting Respondent at 18–26, Egbert v. Boule, 142 S. Ct. 1793 (2022) (No. 21-147), https://tinyurl.com/ymny4t78; Stephen I. Vladeck, The Disingenuous Demise and Death of Bivens, 2019–2020 Cato Sup. Ct. Rev. 263, 283–84 (2020).

[4] See, e.g., Jerry Mashaw, Creating the Administrative Constitution 26–27 (2012); William Baude, Is Qualified Immunity Unlawful?, 106 Cal. L. Rev. 45, 51–52 (2018); Akhil Reed Amar, Of Sovereignty and Federalism, 96 Yale L.J. 1425, 1506 (1987).

[5] See Baude, *supra* note 4, at 51–60.

for actions by federal officials other than claims alleging constitutional violations.[6] But in the years following *Bivens*, the Court has repeatedly reconsidered its contours, granting *Bivens* relief on three occasions between 1971 and 1980 in the context of Fourth, Fifth, and Eighth Amendment violations, and then uniformly rejecting *Bivens* claims 12 times in the 42 years since.[7]

Therefore, after *Egbert*, policymakers and theorists who believe that there is either a constitutional or good-governance mandate to ensure that federal officers violating rights face individual monetary liability must turn to Congress (or the courts, perhaps less ideally) to revisit the severity of the Westfall Act and its comprehensive bar on such individualized suits, or they must look for other state-law or statutory-driven solutions. The Court did not remove *Bivens* from the realm of governing precedents in the U.S. Reports. Neither did it show any proclivity for permitting *Bivens* suits in any but the precise factual contexts of that case and the several that nearly immediately followed.

This article delves into the historical role of monetary suits against federal officers, explains how such suits differed structurally in a constitutionally meaningful way from the suits that *Bivens* authorized, and unpacks the separation-of-powers implications of the Supreme Court's subsequent rejection of federal judicial creation of damages relief. The Court's decision in *Egbert* stands as a retrenchment of 20th-century claims of judicial authority to apply the law as the Court sees fit. As such, the ruling in *Egbert* ties into the central theme of the 2021–2022 Supreme Court term: which actor has the power to decide?[8] The Supreme Court in *Egbert* reaffirmed the scope of congressional authority to decide the contours of federal liability and recovery in federal courts. *Egbert* thus puts squarely on Congress the future question of the extent to which monetary damages recovery must be available against individual federal officials for unconstitutional acts not directly governed by *Bivens* and its several follow-on cases.

---

[6] See 28 U.S.C. § 2679(b)(1)–(2).

[7] See Egbert, 142 S. Ct. at 1799.

[8] See, e.g., Nat'l Fed'n of Ind. Bus. (NFIB) v. Dep't of Labor, Occupational Safety & Health Admin., 142 S. Ct. 661, 666 (2022) ("It is not our role to weigh such tradeoffs. In our system of government, that is the responsibility of those chosen by the people through democratic processes.").

I. Officer Suits within the Constitutional Scheme

The Supreme Court's October 2021 term highlighted a critical and recurring theme—the question of who, or which governmental actor, has authority to exercise power on behalf of the American electorate when reaching significant decisions. Federal judge and former Justice Antonin Scalia clerk Jeffrey Sutton poignantly framed this inquiry as "Who Decides" in his 2021 volume exploring the relationship between power exercised by states and power exercised by the federal government.[9] The Court this term explored that question, both with respect to that vertical breakdown of power as well as in the context of the horizontal breakdown of power between the three distinct federal branches.

The Court repeatedly considered which federal branch had authority to resolve the question in the particular case at hand or whether decisions in the matter remained with private, nongovernmental actors. This question often was more pressing in the Court's resolution of a case than the substantive question of whether the challenged governmental action was right, wise, or just.

Perhaps most prominently in one of the Court's more atypical oral argument sessions, in an emergency-docket case, the Court evaluated which, if any, governmental actor had the power to decide whether every U.S. employer of a particular size must mandate covid-19 vaccination or testing for employees to return to in-person work. There, in *NFIB v. Department of Labor*, the Court concluded that Congress held the policymaking power within the federal government to decide whether to imbue any federal agency with that level of authority.[10] The Court found that Congress had not done so, and that the Occupational Safety and Health Administration's (OSHA) general emergency workplace safety jurisdiction did not extend to authorize individual worker (personal) vaccine requirements on a nationwide scale across all industries within businesses of a certain size. In contrast, that same day the Court reached the opposite pro-regulatory determination in *Biden v. Missouri*. There, it held that Congress had authorized the Centers for Medicare and Medicaid Services to impose a covid-19 vaccine mandate on staff members of

---

[9] See Jeffrey S. Sutton, Who Decides? (2021).
[10] NFIB, 142 S. Ct. at 665–66.

health care facilities participating in Medicare and Medicaid, including those owned and operated by the states.[11]

Similar evaluations of the degree to which Congress versus a federal agency must dominate a particular federal policymaking decision grounded numerous other key 2021–2022 decisions as well, including *West Virginia v. EPA* (carbon dioxide emissions and "major questions")[12] and *Alabama Association of Realtors v. Department of Health & Human Services* (federal eviction moratorium and federalism).[13] Perhaps most prominently, albeit in the distinct vertical context of federalism, the theme also provided the setting of the Court's monumental overruling of *Roe* and *Casey* in *Dobbs*, where the Court released its grasp of the power to define the contours of proper abortion regulations.[14]

Egbert continued the interbranch theme but with a different flavor, examining the axis of power between Congress and federal courts. On the surface, the specific question before the Court seemed to begin and end with analysis about the degree to which courts can, and should, hold executive branch actors accountable. But really the core structural constitutional principles underlying the case hinged on the proper allocation of decisional authority between the federal legislature and the courts under Articles I and III of the federal Constitution.

The question is complex and perhaps tricky because Founding-era evidence suggests that the understanding, and even the practice within the states, was that federal officers very much were to remain accountable through the potential for common-law liability if they exceeded the proper bounds of their lawful authority.[15] But over the years, with legislative developments like the Westfall Act, Congress has so severely limited liability for federal officers that they no longer face potential personal liability for actions taken outside their lawful authority in the manner that they did when the Constitution was ratified. The U.S. Supreme Court had jerry-rigged a process to attempt

---

[11] Biden v. Missouri, 142 S. Ct. 647, 652 (2022).

[12] West Virginia v. EPA, 142 S. Ct. 2587, 2609–10 (2022).

[13] Ala. Ass'n of Realtors v. Dep't of Health & Hum. Servs., 141 S. Ct. 2485, 2488–89 (2021).

[14] Dobbs v. Jackson Women's Health Org., 142 S. Ct. 2228, 2283–84 (2022).

[15] See, e.g., Mashaw, *supra* note 4, at 26–27; Mascott, *supra* note 1, at 28–30.

to replicate historic common-law liability for officer misdeeds by inferring a constitutional right to monetary recovery for federal officer violations of the Constitution. The doctrine was first created in a 1971 case called *Bivens* in support of a claim brought under the Fourth Amendment providing protection against "unreasonable" searches and seizures. But since the 1980s the Court has exhibited significant uneasiness with its judge-made solution and seems to be returning to the pre-*Bivens* judicial understanding that courts generally should not manufacture causes of action in the federal system.

II. Background: *Bivens* and *Egbert*

The Court in *Egbert* ultimately had to evaluate whether Congress or the judiciary holds responsibility for creating the contours of federal causes of action and accompanying relief within the federal constitutional system. In *Bivens*, 50 years earlier, the Court had concluded that circumstances called for judicial creation of monetary damages in constitutional cases, reversing the Second Circuit's determination to the contrary on the basis of longstanding history and earlier Supreme Court precedent. *Egbert* continued a 40-year trend of reversing what the Court now apparently considers to be the *Bivens* Court's mistake.

A. The History of Bivens, Early Progenitor of "Who Decides?"

In *Bivens*, the Court held 6-3 that it could create a Fourth Amendment cause of action in a case involving a federal agent who allegedly threatened an arrestee's family and bound him during a criminal arrest.[16] The claim included allegations that the agents lacked probable cause, improperly carried out a search and arrest without a warrant, and used unreasonable force.[17] Bivens claimed harm from humiliation and mental suffering and sued for $15,000 in damages from each individual agent.[18]

The federal district court had dismissed the complaint, filed pro se, for failure to state a legal cause of action.[19] It rejected out of hand Bivens's claim to relief under 42 U.S.C. § 1983, which establishes

[16] Bivens v. Six Unknown Named Agents of Fed. Bureau of Narcotics, 403 U.S. 388, 389 (1971).

[17] *Id.*

[18] *Id.* at 389–90.

[19] Bivens v. Six Unknown Named Agents of Fed. Bureau of Narcotics, 409 F.2d 718, 719 (2d Cir. 1969).

federal jurisdiction for suits based on alleged constitutional violations only under a state source of law or custom.[20] The district court
gave closer consideration to Bivens's alleged cause of action under
28 U.S.C. § 1331, the general federal-question jurisdiction statute, for
civil actions "aris[ing] under the Constitution, laws, or treaties of the
United States."[21] The district court relied on Second Circuit precedent
by Judge Learned Hand and others to reject the claim on the ground
that "the right to be free from unreasonable searches and seizures is
a common-law right." It concluded that the limited purpose of the
Bill of Rights was to secure such rights against "invasion by the Federal Government."[22] A cause of action was not inherent in the Fourth
Amendment text, so there was no federal recovery mechanism over
which section 1331 could establish jurisdiction.[23]

The Second Circuit affirmed, agreeing that "the Fourth Amendment does not provide a basis for a federal cause of action for damages arising out of an unreasonable search and seizure."[24] The court
traced the Fourth Amendment's prohibition of unreasonable searches
to English trespass actions for damages from the mid-18th century.[25]
Relying on an 1886 Supreme Court opinion, the Second Circuit observed that the common law underlying those British cases was well
known when the ratifiers adopted the Fourth Amendment.[26]

Although Bivens claimed the common law as support for his
counsel's argument that courts could grant monetary relief for unlawful searches and seizures, the Second Circuit found the common law distinct. Nothing about the private damages actions in
state court necessarily translated into an understanding that there
would be a "wholly new federal cause of action founded directly
on the Fourth Amendment."[27] More likely, in the Second Circuit's
estimation, the Fourth Amendment ratifiers envisioned that Fourth

[20] Bivens v. Six Unknown Named Agents of Fed. Bureau of Narcotics, 276 F. Supp. 12,
13–14 (E.D.N.Y. 1971) (discussing and quoting 42 U.S.C. § 1983).

[21] *Id.*; see also 28 U.S.C. § 1331(a) (1958) (providing general federal jurisdiction over
civil actions arising under federal law so long as the matter in controversy, at the time,
was more than $10,000).

[22] Bivens, 276 F. Supp. at 15 (internal quotation omitted).

[23] *Id.*

[24] Bivens, 409 F.2d at 718–19.

[25] *Id.* at 721.

[26] *Id.*

[27] *Id.*

Amendment limitations would be administered through the state courts via the common law, as trespass claims had been handled prior to the Constitution's ratification. The great development of the Fourth Amendment was to "increase the efficacy of the trespass remedy by preventing federal law enforcement officers from justifying a trespass" that was otherwise unreasonable as permissible just because the federal government had greenlighted it.[28] The liability work shouldered by the enforcement of the federal constitutional provision via state courts, under state law remedies, would not be at all unusual according to the Second Circuit, as longstanding constitutional doctrine held that state courts "'are the primary guarantor of constitutional rights, and in many cases they may be the ultimate ones.'"[29] Federal courts, after all, received jurisdiction over general cases arising under the Constitution only in 1875.[30]

And the Second Circuit cleanly concluded that the federal question statute alone did not implicitly contain a federal common-law remedy of monetary damages for violation of a federal right.[31] Such rights of action previously had been inferred from explicit statutory condemnation of particular conduct and a concomitant general statutory authority to enforce liabilities that the act had created where existing remedies were utterly ineffectual. Such a right to recovery could also be derived "from a condemnation in the Constitution itself,"[32] but it was only when the absence of the suggested implied remedy would leave a "clearly declared right" entirely "wanting of remedies" and not a substantive right at all.[33]

The Second Circuit concluded that federal rights did include "an implied injunctive remedy for threatened or continuing constitutional

---

[28] Id.

[29] Id. (quoting Hart & Wechsler, The Federal Courts and the Federal System 339 (1953)).

[30] Id. at 721–22.

[31] Cf. id. at 722 (discussing Clearfield Trust Co. v. United States, 318 U.S. 363 (1943); Pope & Talbot, Inc. v. Hawn, 346 U.S. 406 (1953); Fla. Lime & Avocado Growers, Inc. v. Paul, 373 U.S. 132 (1963); and Banco Nacional de Cuba v. Sabbatino, 376 U.S. 398 (1964), among others).

[32] Id.

[33] See id. at 722–23 (citing sources like Mapp v. Ohio, 367 U.S. 543 (1961), and Hart & Wechsler).

violations."[34] Therefore, courts could keep federal officers accountable by enjoining their unlawful or unconstitutional acts when a right was violated, even if no federal statute had explicitly authorized the granting of injunctive relief.[35] The additional step of permitting a monetary damages award, however, would be an entirely separate thing. It was not "essential to the effective vindication of the right to be free from unreasonable search and seizure" as it was not necessary to prevent continuing violations or government benefit derived from a constitutional violation.[36] Plus, Congress had addressed officer wrongdoing in plenty of other statutes and could have provided monetary damages for constitutional violations if it had thought such a remedy was warranted.[37]

The Supreme Court disagreed. In a majority opinion written by liberal lion Justice William Brennan, the majority concluded that violation of the Fourth Amendment protection from unreasonable searches and seizures "by a federal agent acting under color of his authority gives rise to a cause of action for damages consequent upon his unconstitutional conduct."[38]

The respondent officers had continued to contend that Bivens had only a state common-law right to recovery. They did not claim *no* right to recover, but rather that Bivens's asserted rights properly fell under state law rather than federal law.[39] Therefore, the proper way to acquire relief would be to seek redress through a state tort action against which federal agents could defend themselves by contending that they had lawfully acted within the proper scope of their federal authority.[40] The government respondents had also suggested that the equitable relief of an injunction might be implicit within the

---

[34] *Id.* at 723.

[35] See *id.* (citing Marbury v. Madison on judicial review and rights and remedies and opining that a federal system of "limited governmental power" could not imaginably have "the specter of its courts standing powerless to prevent a clear transgression by the government of a constitutional right of a person with standing to assert it").

[36] *Id.* at 724.

[37] See *id.* at 724–26.

[38] Bivens, 403 U.S. at 389.

[39] *Id.* at 390.

[40] Cf. H.L.A. Hart, The Relations between State and Federal Law, 54 Colum. L. Rev. 489, 523–24 (1954) (explaining that an official "could be enjoined from taking action which in the absence of official justification would amount to a trespass" and noting that as of the 1950s, the "normal remedy for abuse of state authority, as of federal, [was] the last-ditch remedy of defense").

Constitution if required to provide a remedy, but did not go so far as to provide for monetary remedies.[41] The government brief, signed by current D.C. Circuit Judge Ray Randolph (when he was an assistant to the solicitor general) and Solicitor General Erwin Griswold, among others, had attempted to lay out the history of the Fourth Amendment to make their point. They detailed that the Fourth Amendment had originated in the English common law of trespass against officers who had offered the defense of a general warrant. The Fourth Amendment's purpose was to make that general defense unavailable to American officers. In the view of the government lawyers, the absence of general federal-question jurisdiction at that time and in much of early practice confirmed that the Fourth Amendment impacted only defenses to state common-law suits; the amendment did not create a new federal tort action.[42] Had it done so, federal courts would have been given jurisdiction to hear those claims.

Justice Brennan countered these points, and others, with the *In re Neagle* principle from 1890 that state law cannot limit a federal officer's authority. The idea was that after *Neagle*, state common-law schemes could no longer provide a check on federal power.[43] But Justice Brennan did not fully explain why state common-law actions would have limited lawful federal authority, either before or after *Neagle*. Rather, the existence of lawful federal authority to conduct a search or seizure thwarted the establishment of the relevant state-law tort claim.[44]

Finally, Justice Brennan argued that the awarding of damages for Fourth Amendment injuries should hardly be "surprising" and suggested that because the remedial mechanism of monetary damages was "normally available in the federal courts" such relief surely must be available for Fourth Amendment violations.[45] This pragmatic

[41] See Br. for the Respondents at 4–5, Bivens v. Six Unknown Named Agents of Fed. Bureau of Narcotics, 403 U.S. 388 (1971) (No. 301), 1970 WL 122211.

[42] See *id.* at 4.

[43] Bivens, 403 U.S. at 395.

[44] See Hart, *supra* note 40, at 523–24; Wise v. Withers, 7 U.S. (3 Cranch) 331, 335, 337 (1806); Little v. Barreme, 6 U.S. (2 Cranch) 170, 179 (1804). See also Br. for Petitioner at 7–10, Bivens v. Six Unknown Named Agents of Fed. Bureau of Narcotics, 403 U.S. 388 (1971) (No. 301), 1970 WL 116899 (explaining this system of common-law damages relief although ultimately contending that it was inadequate).

[45] Bivens, 403 U.S. at 395, 397–98.

sense of the need for a certain type of relief coursed throughout the opinion.

Justice John Marshall Harlan II concurred in the *Bivens* judgment, writing separately to clarify his theory of the source of the damages relief. He thought that injunctive relief would be inadequate because the sovereign itself was immune from suit and that relief boiled down to "damages or nothing."[46] In this case of necessity, he agreed that the Court should discern monetary relief derived from the Constitution itself.[47]

Chief Justice Warren Burger, Justice Harry Blackmun, and Justice Hugo Black each dissented separately. The chief justice suggested the best course of action was that Congress provide a statutory remedy.[48] Thus the theme of the 2021–2022 Supreme Court term, of "who decides," was implicit in judicial consideration of core cases back in the 1970s as well.[49] In his decision, the chief justice tied together monetary relief with the exclusionary rule on suppression of evidence in certain cases involving constitutional violations.[50] In the end he did not think that the Court's awarding of damages would work well, and he suggested that perhaps Congress consider an administrative remedy for recovery for constitutional violations rather than a judicial remedy.[51]

Justice Black's dissent likewise framed the issue as one about allocation of power: "[T]he point of this case and the fatal weakness in the Court's judgment is that neither Congress nor the State of New York has enacted legislation creating such a right of action. For us to do so is, in my judgment, an exercise of power that the Constitution does not give us."[52] Justice Blackmun's dissent echoed this point: "I had thought that for the truly aggrieved person other quite adequate remedies have always been available. If not, it is the Congress and not this Court that should act."[53]

---

[46] *Id.* at 409–10 (Harlan, J., concurring).

[47] *Id.* at 399.

[48] *Id.* at 414 (Burger, C.J., dissenting).

[49] See also, e.g., Bush v. Lucas, 462 U.S. 367, 380 (1983).

[50] Bivens, 403 U.S. at 412–13 (Burger, C.J., dissenting).

[51] See *id.* at 422.

[52] *Id.* at 428 (Black, J., dissenting).

[53] *Id.* at 430 (Blackmun, J., dissenting).

In the nine years immediately following *Bivens*, the Court extended the *Bivens* cause of action to a claim of sex discrimination under the Fifth Amendment[54] and to an Eighth Amendment cause of action based on a prisoner's claim of cruel and unusual treatment for the receipt of inadequate care.[55] In the subsequent 42 years, however, the Court has consistently denied the application of the *Bivens* framework to create causes of action in new contexts.[56]

B. Egbert *Reconsiders*

Respondent Robert Boule lives right on the U.S.-Canada border. For years he has maintained his property as a bed-and-breakfast titled the "Smuggler's Inn."[57] U.S. border patrol agents have repeatedly observed individuals crossing the northern U.S. border and entering right through the back door of Boule's inn. Federal agents have seized illegal narcotics shipments from the inn. And Boule has alternated between serving as a paid government informant on illegal border crossers and offering unlawful U.S. entrants a drive from his inn into American cities.[58]

Boule filed claims against a border patrol agent for assaulting him. Specifically, Boule contended that Agent Erik Egbert entered Boule's property to check the immigration status of a guest. Egbert then declined to leave the property, throwing Boule against an SUV and then to the ground.[59] Boule lodged a grievance and then filed an administrative claim under the Federal Tort Claims Act (FTCA) for excessive force and injury. He contends that Egbert then retaliated by reporting Boule's vehicle—the license plate of which bears the moniker "SMUGGLER"—as being involved in criminal activity, thereby prompting the Internal Revenue Service to audit him.[60] Nothing came of Boule's grievance or administrative claim.

---

[54] Davis v. Passman, 442 U.S. 228 (1979).

[55] Carlson v. Green, 446 U.S. 14 (1980).

[56] Egbert, 142 S. Ct. at 1802.

[57] *Id.* at 1800–01.

[58] See *id.* at 1801.

[59] *Id.*

[60] *Id.* at 1801–02.

Boule then sued Egbert in federal court, raising a Fourth Amendment excessive force claim and a First Amendment unlawful retaliation claim.[61] Boule requested monetary damages for each violation under *Bivens*, but the district court declined to extend a *Bivens* remedy to those claims.[62] The U.S. Court of Appeals for the Ninth Circuit reversed, reasoning that the Fourth Amendment claim involved an extension of *Bivens* because a different law enforcement agency was involved, but there were no reasons counseling hesitation against extending *Bivens* to cover Boule's claim.[63] In particular, Boule was "a United States citizen . . . bringing a conventional Fourth Amendment excessive force claim arising out of actions by a rank-and-file border patrol agent on Boule's own property in the United States."[64] As for the First Amendment claim, the panel agreed that recognizing a damages action would extend *Bivens* but again found no factors counseling against extension, as the Ninth Circuit had previously recognized such a claim (albeit in 1986), and "retaliation is a well-established First Amendment claim."[65] The Ninth Circuit subsequently denied rehearing *en banc*, but with 12 judges in dissent.[66]

Egbert petitioned the Supreme Court for consideration of three questions. The first two asked for a simple reversal of the Ninth Circuit's decision and a reaffirmation of the Court's consistent determinations over the past four decades not to extend *Bivens* to new contexts. The third question asked the Court to overrule *Bivens* altogether. The Court denied consideration of that final question but granted the first two.

In June 2022, the Court in *Egbert* delivered a 5-1-3 decision with the majority opinion authored by Justice Clarence Thomas.[67] The split in the vote totals perhaps belied the fairly workaday nature of the decision. Justice Neil Gorsuch went further, choosing to concur only in the judgment and writing separately to contend that *Bivens* should be

---

[61] *Id.* at 1802.

[62] *Id.*

[63] Boule v. Egbert, 998 F.3d 370, 387 (9th Cir. 2021).

[64] *Id.*

[65] *Id.* at 391.

[66] *Id.* at 373 (Bumatay, J., dissenting); *id.* at 384 (Owens, J., dissenting); *id.* (Bress, J., dissenting).

[67] Egbert, 142 S. Ct. at 1799.

thrown over altogether.[68] A three-justice block consisting of Justices Stephen Breyer, Elena Kagan, and Sonia Sotomayor concurred in the judgment in part, agreeing to reverse the lower court's creation of a new First Amendment retaliation *Bivens* claim but dissenting from the Fourth Amendment judgment.

In prior cases over the past several years, the Court had repeatedly explained the separation-of-powers concerns held by a majority of justices that the structure of the federal constitutional scheme does not readily countenance judicial creation of new damages actions.[69] Therefore, the majority decision here in *Egbert* primarily reiterated, and then expanded upon, those same constitutional structural concerns, explaining why they continue to govern here as they have for the past several decades.

Justice Thomas began by noting that in the past 42 years, the Court had declined on 11 occasions to imply *Bivens* causes of actions in relevant cases brought before it.[70] Despite the clear trend from the Supreme Court, the Ninth Circuit had permitted two constitutional damages actions against a federal border patrol agent. The Supreme Court reversed the Ninth Circuit, noting that its cases had "made clear that, in all but the most unusual circumstances, prescribing a cause of action is a job for Congress, not the courts."[71] Judicial creation of a new cause of action arrogated legislative power to the court itself.[72]

The Court had set forth two steps that it would use to determine whether to grant a proposed *Bivens* claim: whether the case was meaningfully different from prior *Bivens* contexts and, if so, whether there were special factors suggesting that the Court would be less equipped than Congress in that case to evaluate the merits of permitting a damages action. In *Egbert*, the Court noted that these two inquiries "often resolve to a single question: whether there is any

---

[68] *Id.* at 1810 (Gorsuch, J., concurring in the judgment).

[69] See Hernandez v. Mesa, 140 S. Ct. 735 (2020); Ziglar v. Abbasi, 137 S. Ct. 1843 (2017).

[70] Egbert, 142 S. Ct. at 1799 (majority op.).

[71] *Id.* at 1800; see *id.* at 1803 (citing cases like Hernandez, 140 S. Ct. 735; Abbasi, 137 S. Ct. 1843); and Nestlé USA, Inc. v. Doe, 141 S. Ct. 1931 (2021) (arguing in a non-*Bivens* plurality decision that the existence of even one ground on which to defer to Congress is enough to counsel against judicial creation of a remedy).

[72] See Egbert, 142 S. Ct. at 1800.

reason to think that Congress might be better equipped to create a damages remedy."[73] One such context is where a new defendant category is relevant. In such a situation, it would be hard to predict the consequences of permitting a damages cause of action to move forward against those defendants, so the Court has found that it makes sense to stay its hand and that Congress is better situated to determine whether a cause of action is appropriate and permissible. The Court also will not weigh in, under its more modern approach post-*Bivens*, where there are other methods for addressing a wrong.

Egbert consequently makes clear that one threshold requirement for even a modest expansion of *Bivens* is the absence of any alternative recovery mechanism for that new claimed category of cases. Applying those standards, the Court concluded that Boule's two claims clearly should fail.[74] In particular, the Court noted that alternative remedies are available to provide relief to plaintiffs like Egbert.[75] And such remedies are adequate under Supreme Court precedent to preclude the creation of a new *Bivens* cause-of-action context even if those alternative remedial schemes "do not provide complete relief."[76] Remedies such as internal investigations of executive branch officials and administrative grievance processes can be adequate. No right to appeal or direct involvement by the complainant is necessarily required.[77] The question for the court simply is "whether it, rather than the political branches, is better equipped to decide whether existing remedies should be augmented by the creation of a new judicial remedy," and the existence of some form of statutory remedial scheme is sufficient to demonstrate that courts are not better equipped.[78]

In addition to its across-the-board determination not to create new causes of action under *Bivens* unless absolutely essential to provide a bare minimum of potential relief, the Court noted special national security considerations at play here.[79] Those considerations put an even greater thumb on the scale against the judiciary charging itself

[73] *Id.* at 1798.

[74] *Id.* at 1803–04.

[75] *Id.* at 1806–07.

[76] *Id.* at 1804 (quoting Bush, 462 U.S. at 388).

[77] *Id.* at 1806–07.

[78] *Id.* at 1804 (internal quotation omitted).

[79] *Id.* at 1804–06.

with the determination of whether to step in and provide monetary relief for lawsuits against government officials taking security-related action.[80] The national security considerations related to the border-control agent at work here, in the Court's view, were plainly adequate to keep the policymaking determination of what kind of federal cause of action to provide within the congressional domain. National security considerations will counsel against judicial creation of a new cause of action under *Bivens* even where the relevant agent was situated on the U.S. side of the border, the arrestee had most recently traveled from another port of entry within the U.S. instead of from outside of the country, and the relevant investigations had taken place on U.S. soil.[81]

Finally, the Court majority also noted the more practical separation-of-powers consequences of courts readily inferring damages causes of action—significant disruption to governmental functions.[82] Congress is best equipped, and properly equipped, as the federal rule-making body, to determine the proper contours of judicial causes of action to address such concerns. These concerns of harassment and disruption come into even clearer focus in the context of Boule's First Amendment claim. The Court noted that litigants have an incentive to turn any kind of adverse governmental action into a retaliation claim. Such claims would be hard to disprove and could cause significant, unwarranted disruption through discovery and fear of liability that would "unduly inhibit officials in the discharge of their duties."[83]

The Court closed by noting the many justices, both currently serving and in the past, who had criticized *Bivens* despite its place as precedent. They included Chief Justices Burger and William Rehnquist and Justices Black, Blackmun, Gorsuch, Scalia, and Thomas.[84] That disdain is perhaps reminiscent of the disdain that many jurists had held for the reasoning of *Roe*, even by those who had not been calling for the reversal of that decision, which the Court overruled this term in *Dobbs*.

Justice Gorsuch wrote separately and did not join the Court's reasoning, although he joined both aspects of its judgment. He praised the Court majority for recognizing that the two-step assessment of

[80] See *id.* at 1805.
[81] *Id.* at 1806.
[82] *Id.* at 1807–08.
[83] See *id.* at 1807 (internal quotation omitted).
[84] *Id.* at 1809.

which new contextual circumstances call for the extension of *Bivens* relief really boils down to a singular inquiry: whether courts are better equipped than Congress to evaluate the proper creation of a new damages cause of action in a particular case. In Justice Gorsuch's view, the answer to that question is none—to his mind, the power "to create a new cause of action is to assign new private rights and liabilities—a power that is in every meaningful sense an act of legislation."[85] Such an authority is not a proper function for federal tribunals within an electoral, representative democracy, under textually limited federal constitutional power, standing in contrast to English common-law courts. The end of his opinion suggests that he thinks the Court should make it clear that it will never authorize a new *Bivens* context.[86]

Concurring in part and dissenting in part, Justices Sotomayor, Kagan, and Breyer agreed that Boule's First Amendment claim should fail because the potential of "invit[ing] claims in every sphere of legitimate governmental action" gives serious "reason to pause."[87] But the dissenters argued that Boule's Fourth Amendment claim did not "arise in a new context" distinct from *Bivens* itself and, even if it had, there were no special factors counseling against extending *Bivens* because the allegations here involved a "run-of-the-mill" investigation that just happened to take place near a border.[88]

Egbert featured a wide array of amicus briefs on both sides. Notably, the Cato Institute joined a brief by the ACLU arguing that *Bivens* should not be overruled and that there were no special factors counseling against Boule's Fourth and First Amendment claims.[89] And the authors of this article submitted a brief on behalf of the Separation of Powers Clinic at the Antonin Scalia Law School, George Mason University, arguing that there was no widespread historic tradition of courts authorizing damages actions for alleged constitutional claims.[90] Six former U.S. attorneys general urged the Court to clarify in *Egbert* that under the constitutional separation-of-powers

---

[85] *Id.* at 1810 (Gorsuch, J., concurring in the judgment).

[86] See *id.* at 1809–10.

[87] *Id.* at 1817 (Sotomayor, J., concurring in the judgment in part and dissenting in part) (internal quotation omitted).

[88] *Id.* at 1814–17.

[89] See generally Br. for American Civil Liberties Union et al. as Amici Curiae Supporting Respondent, Egbert v. Boule, 142 S. Ct. 1793 (2022) (No. 21-147), https://tinyurl.com/mvks9fdr.

[90] See generally Mascott Brief, *supra* note 2.

framework, and the Court's prior precedent, further expansion of *Bivens* in any factual context would be inappropriate.[91]

Although the Court in *Egbert* ultimately denied the petitioner's request to consider overruling *Bivens* in full, the Court's decision clearly showed aversion to approving *Bivens* relief in any context other than that found squarely within the four corners of *Bivens* itself and the several follow-on cases over the subsequent several years. And even that restraint could have been due to the Court's tactical assessment that it did not want to reach out to overrule *Bivens* during a term where it was to consider overruling *Roe* and *Casey* and made clear for the first time that it believed itself to have already overturned the longstanding First Amendment Establishment Clause case *Lemon v. Kurtzman*.[92]

III. Officer Suits without *Bivens*[93]

Individuals concerned with history and tradition may worry about *Egbert* shutting the door on *Bivens* claims for money damages, given that Founding-era evidence suggests that damages suits against federal officers were expected to provide a meaningful mechanism for accountability. But there was no widespread tradition of such cases premised on judicially crafted federal causes of actions, and plaintiffs rarely (if ever) directly alleged constitutional violations as standalone claims. This comports with the discrete assignment of powers in the Constitution, under which the task of creating new federal causes of action would lie with Congress, not with federal courts of limited subject-matter jurisdiction.[94] Thus, when considering "who decides?" in this context, history and text demonstrate that the answer is, and has been, Congress.[95]

---

[91] See generally Br. of Amici Curiae Former U.S. Attorneys General John D. Ashcroft, William P. Barr, Alberto R. Gonzales, Edwin Meese III, Michael B. Mukasey, and Jefferson B. Sessions III in Support of Petitioner, Egbert v. Boule, 142 S. Ct. 1793 (2022) (No. 21-147), https://tinyurl.com/p9dw5t2x.

[92] See Kennedy v. Bremerton Sch. Dist., 142 S. Ct. 2407, 2427 (2022).

[93] This section draws substantially from the amicus brief written and submitted by the authors at the Supreme Court in *Egbert*. See generally Mascott Brief, *supra* note 2.

[94] See U.S. Const. art. I, § 8, cl. 9; *id.* art. III, § 1. Cf. Stephen E. Sachs, The Unlimited Jurisdiction of the Federal Courts, 106 Va. L. Rev. 1703, 1704 (2020) (describing a "federal court's *subject-matter* jurisdiction" as "affirmatively limited by the Constitution" while noting the role of Congress in using enumerated powers to define other aspects of federal jurisdiction).

[95] See *infra* Parts III.B–C.

To be clear, the tradition of accountability for federal officer actions outside the scope of lawful authority is an important one, and it was even discussed during the ratification debates.[96] But it does not translate to the federal judiciary's fashioning of new forms of relief within an Article III system that the Constitution assigned to Congress to constitute and regulate. Accordingly, post-*Egbert*, those who believe that there should be individual liability for federal officers who violate rights could consider revisiting the Westfall Act's preclusion of state common-law tort actions against such officers or pursue other statutory-based solutions.[97]

A. *Historically, Officer Damages Suits Pursued Common-Law Claims and Rarely Involved Constitutional Questions.*

The tradition in early America as well as 17th- and 18th-century England was for plaintiffs to assert common-law violations, not to allege the violation of federal constitutional rights.

Historically, in England, individuals could claim damages against officers of the Crown acting in their official capacity but assertedly beyond their lawful authority—typically trespass or false-imprisonment claims, for example, to challenge improper arrests or searches.[98] In defense, the law would recognize an officer's contention that his actions had indeed remained within his legal authority.

For example, Matthew Hale described a false-imprisonment claim met with the defense that the officer had acted pursuant to a lawfully

---

[96] See, e.g., Archibald Maclaine, Convention of North Carolina (July 24, 1788), reprinted in 4 The Debates in the Several State Conventions on the Adoption of the Federal Constitution 46, 47 (Jonathan Elliot ed., 1836); John Marshall, Virginia Ratifying Convention (June 20, 1788), reprinted in 10 The Documentary History of the Ratification of the Constitution 1430, 1432 (John P. Kaminski et al. eds., 1993) (asserting that an individual could apply for redress in a local tribunal were a federal officer to assault him or trespass on his property). See Mascott, *supra* note 1, at 28–30.

[97] See *infra* notes 146–47 and accompanying text.

[98] See James E. Pfander & David Baltmanis, Rethinking Bivens: Legitimacy and Constitutional Adjudication, 98 Geo. L.J. 117, 134 (2009); Louis L. Jaffe, Suits against Governments and Officers: Sovereign Immunity, 77 Harv. L. Rev. 1, 1–2, 12 (1963) ("From time immemorial many claims affecting the Crown could be pursued in the regular courts if they did not take the form of a suit against the Crown. . . . If the subject was the victim of illegal official action, in many cases he could sue the King's officers for damages. . . . This was the situation in England at the time the American Constitution was drafted.").

valid warrant, but when the court concluded the warrant was void, the defense failed and the officer was liable.[99] Similarly, in the 18th-century matter *Entick v. Carrington*, the plaintiff brought a trespass claim against the King's chief messenger and several others who had broken into Entick's home with "force and arms," ransacked the residence, and departed with hundreds of documents.[100] The officers had acted pursuant to a general warrant issued by Lord Halifax.[101] Because the warrant was deemed illegal, Entick prevailed and recovered substantial sums against Halifax and the officers who had conducted the search.[102]

These English precedents were not premised on a right to sue directly for violating prohibitions against invalid warrants. Rather, the cases brought common-law causes of action against government officials, who then raised the authorization of the warrant as a defense, which failed in cases where the warrant was deemed unlawful.[103]

From the very start of the new federal government in America, similar to those English practices, government officers were subject to generally applicable common-law damages actions just like private parties.[104] Such claims were brought in state and federal courts for many years,[105] and federal officials introduced questions about the legality of government actions as a defense.[106]

---

[99] See, e.g., II Matthew Hale, History of the Pleas of the Crown 112 (1736) (writing that where a "warrant to apprehend all persons suspected" of a robbery was later determined to be "a void warrant," the official could not raise it as a "sufficient justification" against a common-law claim for "false imprisonment").

[100] Entick v. Carrington, (1765) 95 Eng. Rep. 807 (K.B.) 807.

[101] *Id.* at 808.

[102] See Boyd v. United States, 116 U.S. 616, 626 (1886) (describing Entick).

[103] See Br. for the Respondents in Bivens, *supra* note 41, at 9–11 (outlining the English tradition).

[104] Mashaw, *supra* note 4, at 26–27 (describing the relatively routine nature of suits against federal officials with relevant statutory authority claimed in defense, such as in suits against customs collectors for improper seizures and the collection of excessive duties). See also Hernandez, 140 S. Ct. at 748.

[105] See, e.g., § 28, Judiciary Act of 1789, 1 Stat. 73, 87–88 (discussing remedies for "the defaults and misfeasances in office" committed by a marshal's deputy and the degree to which marshals are held answerable for fulfilling certain duties).

[106] Wheeldin v. Wheeler, 373 U.S. 647, 652 (1963) (observing that federal law "supplie[d] the defense, if the conduct complained of was done pursuant to a federally imposed duty"); see also, e.g., An Act to Regulate the Collection of Duties § 36, 1 Stat. 29, 48 (1789) (providing that reasonableness of a seizure of goods would provide the basis for a defense against "liab[ility] to action, judgment or suit, on account of such seizure").

The mechanism of common-law liability to ensure federal officer accountability in lawfully performing their duties arose during the public debates on ratification of the U.S. Constitution, showing that officer suits were understood as an available mechanism for government accountability that would remain available under the constitutional system. During the North Carolina ratification debates, for example, Joseph Taylor expressed concern that impeachment would be impracticable for rank-and-file executive officers dispersed throughout the country. Archibald Maclaine replied that citizens harmed by such officers' behavior "would have redress in the ordinary courts of common law."[107] Future Supreme Court justice James Iredell concurred that it was very clear that "an officer may be tried by a court of common law."[108] In addition, Richard Dobbs Spaight opined that "if any man was injured by an officer of the United States, he could get redress by a suit at law." Spaight expressed strong certainty about this legal observation during the debates.[109]

During the First Congress, it was also clear that members understood the new constitutional system would preserve the ability of litigants to bring common-law claims for asserted wrongdoing by federal officials in carrying out their official responsibilities. Congress enacted several statutory provisions built on the implicit assumption that various principal officials and their deputies would be subject to personal liability for alleged harm related to governmental acts. For example, Congress provided that if a customs collector became unable to perform his duties or died, then those duties would devolve on the collector's deputy "for whose conduct the estate of such disabled or deceased collector shall be liable."[110] Similarly, federal marshals "had to assume personal liability for the misdeeds of their deputies."[111] But these provisions were not interpreted to create newly expansive federal rights implicitly justifying a new federal cause of action for monetary damages. In distinction, they simply

---

[107] 4 The Debates in the Several State Conventions, on the Adoption of the Federal Constitution 45–47 (Jonathan Elliot ed., 2d ed. 1836).

[108] *Id.* at 36–37.

[109] *Id.*

[110] § 8, Ch. 35, Act of Aug. 4, 1790, 1 Stat. 145, 155.

[111] § 27, Judiciary Act of 1789, 1 Stat. at 87.

assumed the continued existence and availability of common-law causes of action.[112]

Bivens and follow-on scholarship contends that this early practice established precedent for judicial creation of federal damages claims based on rights derived from constitutional protections, and thus overruling or even cabining *Bivens* is inconsistent with history.[113] But only two of the cases that *Bivens* claimed for support involved federal claims.[114] And both of those were drawn from a federal *statute* that had required federal marshals to post a bond and authorized suits against that bond for breach of a marshal's duties.[115]

Additional early American cases identified by scholars as involving federal law that are claimed as support for deriving causes of action directly from the Constitution typically invoked common-law causes of action. In these cases, the existence of federal statutory authority to commit the act was raised as a *defense*.[116] Constitutional claims did not arise directly in these matters, and the elements of the plaintiff's claim often did not invoke federal law.[117]

One case often identified as historical precedent for *Bivens* is *Little v. Barreme*.[118] But the claim in *Little* raised common-law trespass, not a violation of federal law. Captain George Little had captured a Danish boat in response to President John Adams's order to seize boats from French ports. The ship's owner sued for trespass to challenge the

---

[112] Cf. Hernandez, 140 S. Ct. at 742 (distinguishing between inference of authorization for a damages suit from enactment of a statutory prohibition on certain conduct from the actions of "a common-law court, which exercises a degree of lawmaking authority, flesh[ing] out the remedies available for a common-law tort"). See also Jennifer L. Mascott, Who Are Officers of the United States?, 73 Stan. L. Rev. 443, 515–20 (2018) (discussing the statutory provisions).

[113] See Bivens, 403 U.S. at 395–96; e.g., Vladeck, *supra* note 3, at 270 (asserting a historical "pattern of judge-made tort remedies" including "cases in which the plaintiff's underlying claim was that the defendant had violated the Constitution").

[114] See 403 U.S. at 395–96.

[115] See Lammon v. Feusier, 111 U.S. 17, 17–18 (1884); West v. Cabell, 153 U.S. 78, 84–85 (1894).

[116] See, e.g., Vladeck, *supra* note 3, at 267–70.

[117] Cf. Sachs, *supra* note 94, at 1712 ("Jurisdictional questions at the Founding were fundamentally questions of powers, not rights, and nothing has happened since to change that.").

[118] 6 U.S. (2 Cranch) 170 (1804). See, e.g., Richard H. Fallon, Jr., Bidding Farewell to Constitutional Torts, 107 Cal. L. Rev. 933, 943 (2019).

capture and sought damages. Little ultimately was found liable for "plain trespass" on the ground that the seizure was not authorized by federal law. The Court interpreted the underlying federal statute to permit only the seizure of ships on their way *to* French ports.[119] In the absence of a lawful order to form the legal basis for the capture, the ship's seizure was unlawful and Little had committed trespass.[120]

Wise v. Withers[121] has analogously been cited as justification for *Bivens* relief.[122] But here again, this case was based on a common-law claim. The Court found that the plaintiff's trespass action prevailed against the federal officer defendants on the ground that the court-martial authorizing entry to the plaintiff's home to collect a fine was statutorily invalid.[123] Other early cases surveyed in *Bivens*-related scholarship fare no better, as they, too, typically involve common-law claims without the allegation of a constitutional violation. Other cited early cases are similar, as they likewise involved common-law claims with no cause of action alleging that a federal official violated the plaintiff's constitutional rights.[124]

This survey demonstrates a telling absence of historical cases squarely on point. The distinction between these common-law cases

---

[119] Little, 6 U.S. at 170, 177–78.

[120] *Id.* at 179.

[121] 7 U.S. (3 Cranch) 331 (1806).

[122] See, e.g., Pfander & Baltmanis, Rethinking Bivens, *supra* note 98, at 124 & n.28.

[123] Wise, 7 U.S. at 337.

[124] See Vladeck, *supra* note 3, at 267–70. See also, e.g., Slocum v. Mayberry, 15 U.S. (2 Wheat.) 1, 2 (1817) (action for "replevin . . . for the restoration of the [plaintiff's] property," and the defense turned on whether the seizure of cargo was proper under the Embargo Act of 1808); The Apollon, 22 U.S. (9 Wheat.) 362, 363–64 (1824) (libel for *in rem* seizure of ship, and the defense turned on whether the Collection Act of 1799 authorized the seizure); Elliott v. Swartwout, 35 U.S. (10 Pet.) 137, 138 (1836) ("action of assumpsit" for overpaid duties, and the defense turned on whether the goods qualified as wool shawls under the federal import statute); Mitchell v. Harmony, 54 U.S. (13 How.) 115, 137 (1852) ("action of trespass," and the defense turned on whether the defendant could seize property pursuant to a military commander's order during the war with Mexico); Buck v. Colbath, 70 U.S. (3 Wall.) 334, 334–37, 346–47 (1866) (an action for trespass, and the defense turned on whether the property had been properly seized pursuant to a writ of attachment); Bates v. Clark, 95 U.S. 204, 205 (1877) (an action for trespass, and the defense turned on whether "this whiskey was seized in Indian country, within the meaning of the act of 1834 and the amendment of 1864"); Belknap v. Schid, 161 U.S. 10, 18 (1896) (involving a federal suit for patent infringement).

and federal recognition of constitutional claims meriting relief through monetary damages is significant. If pre-*Bivens* challenges to federal officer action had been based on a belief that the Fourth Amendment "created a federal damage remedy," then litigants "would have had no trouble" stating so in their complaints and "would not have relied upon state law."[125] But historical research suggests that litigants at the time did not conceive of their claims as constitutionally derived. Scholars James Pfander and Jonathan Hunt compiled a study on judgments reviewing decades of congressional records where early federal officials had sought indemnification from Congress for liability imposed in their individual capacity stemming from official acts. Nearly all the records involved indemnification requests arising from cases alleging "liability in trespass" in some form.[126]

B. Common-Law Suits Do Not Justify the Bivens Regime.

Given these distinctions, it is challenging to contend that longstanding history justifies the judicial fashioning of remedies to address allegations of unconstitutional acts by federal officials. The elements of common-law claims differed substantially from the contours of 20th-century *Bivens* claims. The accountability interests underlying those distinct causes of action differ significantly as well. The early common-law claims were not vehicles for the assertion of constitutional rights. Rather, the plaintiffs in those common-law suits desired recovery for governmental actions taken without lawful authority and relied upon common-law tort theories for redress.

These suits were aimed at providing accountability for federal actors to perform their duties consistent with legal constraints.[127] But, more fundamentally, the suits were not built on assertions of new federal mechanisms for relief beyond federal remedies enacted by Congress acting within its limited, enumerated areas of authority. Rather, the suits were grounded in law that preexisted the Constitution's ratification.

---

[125] Br. for the Respondents in Bivens, *supra* note 41, at 19.

[126] James E. Pfander & Jonathan L. Hunt, Public Wrongs and Private Bills: Indemnification and Government Accountability in the Early Republic, 85 N.Y.U. L. Rev. 1862, 1904–05 (2010).

[127] See, e.g., Br. for the Respondents in Bivens, *supra* note 41, at 10–11 (reporting on the ratification debate discussion about the importance of common-law causes of action for providing government officer accountability).

Moreover, even the "early republic damages liability doctrines" were not themselves "'judge-made'" causes of action. They originated in "statutes, international treaties, and executive practice" that had been around for "centuries" and, thus, were already part of the preexisting legal landscape at the time of the 1788 ratification of the new federal Constitution.[128] Consequently, at the time of ratification, such claims were no longer ongoing federal judicial creations. And the federal Constitution's imposition of separation-of-powers structural constraints would have curbed the ongoing fashioning of expansive implied causes of action in any event. The Article III judiciary's discrete role to resolve cases and controversies is distinct from the preceding role of common-law courts.[129] The new constitutional system assigned to Congress the task of creating lower federal courts and defining the contours of federal jurisdiction.

C. Constitutional Separation of Powers Explains the Lack of Historical Support for Judicially Creating New Federal Damages Actions.

Most fundamentally, the historical practice of federal courts has traditionally avoided creation of new damages actions absent congressional authority due to the exclusive vesting of federal "legislative Powers" in Congress subject to strict, interbranch procedural constraints.[130] Those rigid parameters on legislative authority extend not just to the pronouncement of new substantive binding legal standards but also to the imposition and generation of the methods for enforcing that substantive law.[131] The Supreme Court has expressly relied on those limits when interpreting and applying statutory limits on causes of action. In particular, the Court has warned that

---

[128] Andrew Kent, Lessons for Bivens and Qualified Immunity Debates from Nineteenth-Century Damages Litigation Against Federal Officers, 96 Notre Dame L. Rev. 1755, 1777–78 (2021).

[129] Compare, e.g., U.S. Const. art. I, § 1 (vesting of the legislative power to create binding policies in the federal legislature); *id.* § 8, cl. 9 (power to create inferior tribunals); *id.* art. III, § 1, cl. 1 (reference to congressional creation of inferior tribunals); with *id.* art. III, § 1, cl. 2 (grant to the federal courts of the discrete judicial power to resolve cases and controversies). See also, e.g., Alexander v. Sandoval, 532 U.S. 275, 286–87 (2001) (addressing the distinct powers and functions of Article III courts versus common-law courts).

[130] See U.S. Const. art. I, § 1 (legislative vesting clause); *id.* art. I, § 7 (bicameralism and presentment requirements).

[131] Alexander, 532 U.S. at 286.

"[r]aising up causes of action where a statute has not created them may be a proper function for common-law courts, but not for federal tribunals."[132]

From its first session, Congress accordingly enacted provisions creating and delineating the authority of lower federal courts. The Judiciary Act of 1789 painstakingly specified and crafted the structure and organization of inferior federal tribunals, and it regulated the causes of action to be heard within those courts.[133] For example, Congress specified venues for the consideration of causes of action including "suits for penalties and forfeitures incurred[] under the laws of the United States," suits against ambassadors, removal jurisdiction from state courts, forfeitures of bonds, "suits at common law where the United States sue," "civil causes of admiralty and maritime jurisdiction," certain "alien su[its] for a tort," and appeals from state court cases that "draw[] in question the validity of a treaty or statute of, or an authority exercised under the United States."[134]

The first Congress also enacted statutory provisions expressly authorizing damages actions for underlying substantive rights granted in the text of the Constitution, suggesting that Congress believed such statutory authorization was necessary to generate monetary damages relief in connection with underlying substantive law. The Patent Act of 1790, for example, established a patent infringement action enabling patent holders to recover "such damages as shall be assessed by a jury." The act also specified the requisite elements and available defenses for infringement claims and addressed forfeiture.[135] These actions previewed the Supreme Court's acknowledgment centuries later that similar to "substantive federal law itself, private rights of action to enforce federal law must be created by Congress."[136] Courts may not create a

---

[132] *Id.* at 287; see Gamble v. United States, 139 S. Ct. 1960, 1981–82 (2019) (Thomas, J., concurring) (contrasting "a common-law legal system in which courts systematically developed the law through judicial decisions apart from written law" from "our federal system" in which "[t]he Constitution tasks the political branches—not the Judiciary—with systematically developing the laws that govern our society").

[133] See generally Judiciary Act of 1789, 1 Stat. 73.

[134] *Id.* §§ 9, 12, 13, 25, 26.

[135] §§ 4 & 6, ch. 7, Act of April 10, 1790, 1 Stat. 109.

[136] Alexander, 532 U.S. at 286–87.

cause of action no matter how desirable one might be on policy grounds.[137]

Creating a damages remedy thus would also violate a second core structural constitutional feature: the limitation of federal judicial authority to the resolution of discrete and concrete "cases" and "controversies."[138] Article III's limits ensure that "federal courts exercise 'their proper function in a limited and separated government.'"[139] Under Article III, federal courts do not have power to "exercise general legal oversight of the Legislative and Executive Branches, or of private entities"[140] but to "decide only matters 'of a Judiciary Nature.'"[141]

This structural reality, combined with the constitutionally ordained role of Congress in the establishment of lower federal tribunals, specification of causes of action, and imposition of jurisdictional requirements courts, suggests that the entire *Bivens* enterprise of squinting to discern a cause of action from bare constitutional text is not only ahistorical but also at odds with the Constitution's limited role for the judiciary.

The structural impropriety of the judiciary manufacturing of damages actions is compounded by the fact that damages relief also implicates core political interests like how best to protect the public fisc.[142] *Bivens* claims, aimed at individual federal actors, often have the capacity for burdening the federal government with "substantial costs, in the form of defense and indemnification."[143] Decisions related to the scope and contours of monetary damages claims for officer wrongdoing therefore are particularly well suited for congressional and presidential resolution through statutory enactments.

As the Court has previously observed, elected federal policymakers bear significant responsibility for assessing the extent to which individual federal officers and employees should be subject

---

[137] *Id.*

[138] U.S. Const. art. III, § 1.

[139] TransUnion LLC v. Ramirez, 141 S. Ct. 2190, 2203 (2021).

[140] *Id.*

[141] *Id.* (Madison, J.) (quoting 2 Records of the Federal Convention of 1787, at 430 (M. Farrand ed. 1966)).

[142] U.S. Const. art. I, § 7, cl. 1 ("No Money shall be drawn from the Treasury, but in Consequence of Appropriations made by Law.").

[143] Abbasi, 137 S. Ct. at 1856.

to potential monetary and other liabilities.[144] Through its representation spread among districts and states bearing distinct geographical, economic, and cultural interests, Congress has the greatest institutional capacity for acting responsively to the broadest array of varied electoral interests at a granular level.[145] Accordingly, Congress is best equipped, and was intentionally assigned by constitutional design, to resolve these sorts of complex value judgments.

Conclusion

Given *Egbert's* cabining of *Bivens* and the lack of historical support for judicial creation of federal damages actions in the first place, policymakers and theorists who believe there is either a constitutional or good-governance mandate to ensure the availability of monetary relief against federal officers must look elsewhere for such relief.[146]

Egbert's narrowing of *Bivens*, premised on separation-of-powers principles, is supported by the historical record. Furthermore, the question of "who decides?" seeks to identify which actor in our governmental system has been authorized to take certain action. The Constitution's limited federal system intentionally imposes hurdles for the creation of new policy and new federal rights because of the robust role that state governments and private actors are supposed to play within our constitutional system.[147] *Egbert* and the cases preceding it return the Supreme Court and Congress to their original balance, which primarily seeks to preserve electoral representation

---

[144] *Id.*

[145] See Jennifer Mascott, Early Customs Laws and Delegation, 87 Geo. Wash. L. Rev. 1388, 1394–96, 1398–99, 1434–43 (2019).

[146] See, e.g., Carlos Manuel Vázquez & Stephen I. Vladeck, State Law, the Westfall Act, and the Nature of the Bivens Question, 161 U. Pa. L. Rev. 509, 575–76 (2013) (due process justification); Ann Woolhandler, The Common Law Origins of Constitutionally Compelled Remedies, 107 Yale L.J. 77, 148–49 (1997) (suggesting the potential constitutional necessity of trespass remedies for unlawful state official actions); but cf. Sachs, *supra* note 94, at 1711–12 (distinguishing due process claims from claims asserting a lack of enumerated authority).

[147] See, e.g., U.S. Const. art. I, § 7 (bicameralism and presentment requirements); Bradford R. Clark, Separation of Powers as a Safeguard of Federalism, 79 Tex. L. Rev. 1321 (2001) (explaining the connection between tough statutory enactment procedures, the Supremacy Clause's applicability to only federal law, treaties, and the Constitution, and the safeguards of federalism).

and accountability by empowering appointed judges to resolve only concrete disputes rather than reorienting the substantive contours of the federal legal system.

To the extent that some scope of monetary damages claims against federal officials in their individual capacity are deemed constitutionally necessary, the solution is not for courts to create *Bivens*-like actions, which are in tension with core constitutional requirements. Instead, Congress or the courts could reconsider the constitutionally proper scope of the Westfall Act's limitations on relief and preemption of traditional common-law damages actions against federal officials.[148] Currently, the Westfall Act imposes a significant roadblock to obtaining damages because it is interpreted to generally preempt state common-law claims against federal officials in their individual capacity for their official actions.[149] Congress could address the broad scope of the Westfall Act by enacting a new law to authorize such suits or by concretely narrowing the scope of the present law. Or perhaps courts may conclude through litigation that enforcement of the Westfall Act to bar the availability of constitutionally necessary relief is unlawful and may decline to apply the Westfall Act's preemption provision in such a case.[150]

Regardless of any action (or not) by litigants and Congress to fundamentally reexamine individual officer immunity provisions, the Constitution includes very significant constraints on which actor

[148] Cf. Michael Ramsey, Don't Fear Bivens, The Originalism Blog (Nov. 12, 2019), https://bit.ly/3bLVynx (contending that "absent a *Bivens* remedy the Westfall Act would be unconstitutional, as applied to state law claims" in analysis contending for the constitutionality of *Bivens*).

[149] The Westfall Act includes a carve-out for "a civil action against an employee of the Government . . . which is brought for a violation of the Constitution of the United States," 28 U.S.C. § 2679(b)(2), although the Supreme Court has stated that this provision neither endorsed nor enshrined *Bivens* but rather "simply left *Bivens* where it found it," Hernandez, 140 S. Ct. at 748 n.9.

[150] Cf, e.g., United States v. Arthrex, Inc., 141 S. Ct. 1970, 1987 (2021) (concluding that it would be unconstitutional to enforce the Patent Trial and Appeals Board's exclusive statutory rehearing power only "to the extent that its requirements prevent the Director from reviewing final decisions rendered by [administrative patent judges]"); Seila Law LLC v. Consumer Fin. Prot. Bureau, 140 S. Ct. 2183, 2219–20, 2224 (2020) (Thomas, J., concurring) (concluding that the nonenforcement of a challenged government action is a more appropriate judicial remedy than severance of the constitutionally problematic statutory provision).

may fashion federal jurisdiction to provide judicial relief.[151] Within a federalist system of limited enumerated power, and congressional responsibility for the generation of federal jurisdiction, the federal judiciary generally is not the appropriate entity to fashion new forms of relief. The Court's decision in *Egbert*, and those before it that denied expansion of new *Bivens* actions, have not been rulings on whether accountability for officers is warranted. Rather, those decisions have laid down markers acknowledging the limits of the power of the federal judiciary.

---

[151] See, e.g., U.S. Const. art. I, § 8 (assigning to Congress the power "[t]o constitute Tribunals inferior to the supreme Court"); *id.* art. III, § 1 (acknowledging the discretion of Congress to determine whether inferior courts are established); *id.* art. III, § 2 (limiting possible federal subject matter jurisdiction to admiralty, maritime jurisdiction, "[c]ases affecting Ambassadors, other public Ministers and Consuls" and to cases that "aris[e] under" the Constitution, federal law, or treaties made under their authority); *id.* art. III, § 2 (authorizing Congress to make exceptions and regulations impacting the Supreme Court's appellate jurisdiction).

The Content-Discrimination Two-Step Post-*Reed* and *Austin*

*Enrique Armijo**

Introduction

Decided in its 2021–2022 term, the U.S. Supreme Court's decision in *Austin v. Reagan National Advertising* held an ordinance that defined whether a sign was on- or off-premises based on the sign's message was content neutral, and thus should not be subjected to strict scrutiny by a court reviewing the law under the First Amendment.[1] To some, including the dissenters in *Austin* itself, the decision repudiated the Court's prior sign ordinance case, the 2014–2015 term's *Reed v. Town of Gilbert*. That case held that, for First Amendment purposes, a court should deem a speech-restrictive law content based, and thus presumptively unconstitutional, if the law "on its face draws distinctions based on the message a speaker conveys." *Reed* then applied that rule to invalidate an ordinance that treated signs differently based on their content. Both *Reed* and *Austin* address the proper application of the Court's "content-discrimination" doctrine, which dictates that under the First Amendment—and with a few exceptions not relevant here—government may generally not regulate speech because of what it says.

Reed set off a firestorm of criticism, with those opposed to the decision believing it threatened a range of existing rules and doctrines more forgiving of government action that affected speech, from commercial speech to compelled disclosures. These critics

* Professor, Elon University School of Law; affiliated fellow, Yale Law School Information Society Project; faculty affiliate, UNC-Chapel Hill Center for Information, Technology, and Public Life. Thanks to Ash Bhagwat and Alan Chen for comments, to Kaylee Faw for research assistance, and to the *Cato Supreme Court Review* for inviting me to write this article.

[1] City of Austin v. Reagan Nat'l Advert. of Austin, LLC, 142 S. Ct. 1464 (2022).

believed *Reed* thus called into question areas of regulation that were long thought to be of no First Amendment concern.[2] Similarly, some commenters welcomed *Austin* as a necessary but incomplete, if slightly disjointed, corrective.[3] By its own terms, the rule announced in *Austin* gives governments greater leeway in using speech as a basis for regulation. But by diluting *Reed*'s primary contribution to content-discrimination doctrine, *Austin* has cracked open a door that *Reed* was right to shut.

In setting out a content-discrimination rule that operates independently of government purpose, *Reed* rejected prior, more contextual interpretations of the Court's First Amendment cases. These interpretations had held governments could make facial references to a particular type or category of content in their laws and still avoid strict scrutiny, so long as those laws were not referring to that content in order to express disagreement with or disapproval of it. Contrary to how most lower courts had understood and applied content-discrimination doctrine, *Reed* held laws that treat different kinds of speech differently deserve strict scrutiny regardless of any asserted government purpose to justify doing so. Post-*Reed*, it was thought that even a benign governmental purpose could not save a law referring to content from the most rigorous constitutional standard of review.

However, *Austin*, in which the Court found a content-neutral purpose could cause a law referencing content to avoid such scrutiny, has now brought that principle back into question. The result of *Austin*'s partial unwinding of *Reed*'s core First Amendment holding will inevitably be an unwelcome return to judicial considerations of government purpose and intent behind regulations that facially and intentionally distinguish among types of speech. By permitting legislatures to treat speech differently through the use of statutory

[2] See, e.g., Adam Liptak, Court's Free-Speech Expansion Has Far-Reaching Consequences, N.Y. Times (Aug. 17, 2015), https://nyti.ms/3yM2U1B.

[3] See, e.g., Amanda Karras, Big Win for Local Government in Supreme Court Sign Case, International Municipal Lawyers Association (Apr. 21, 2022), https://bit.ly/3uT8sGx; but see, e.g., Eugene Volokh, Supreme Court on What Counts as a Content-Based Speech Restriction, Volokh Conspiracy (Apr. 21, 2022), https://bit.ly/3IEqbHD (*Austin* makes content discrimination test "somewhat fuzzier"); Laurence Tribe (@tribelaw), Twitter (April 27, 2022 7:31AM), https://bit.ly/3z9JPYN (*Austin* "made a total mess of 1st Am law").

references to content, it will also give governments that seek to punish speech they do not like more opportunities to do so.

Part I of this article details the shifting and uncertain role government purpose has traditionally played in content-discrimination doctrine. It argues *Reed* was correct in cabining the consideration of purpose in First Amendment cases to only those instances in which content-neutral regulations of speech are being used to discriminate against particular speech and speakers. Part II discusses *Austin,* in particular how and why the Court avoided the obvious conclusion that the ordinance at issue was content based on its face—a conclusion compelled not just by *Reed* but by common sense. Part III argues that nearly all the consternation around *Reed's* formalistic rule stems from a failure to disentangle content discrimination from another regulatory area of less traditional First Amendment concern, namely compelled disclosures and related information-forcing by the government in the interest of public health, safety, and protection. Unraveling those two threads reveals that the *Reed* two-step is not the anti-regulatory bludgeon that its detractors fear.

I. *Reed* and the Evils of Government-Purpose Tests

Reed v. Town of Gilbert was born out of a decades-long confusion, starting at the Supreme Court but then manifesting itself in dozens of federal appellate First Amendment cases, over the role government purpose should play in setting a standard of review for legislative uses of content categories. Content discrimination began as a doctrine applied in facial First Amendment challenges rather than as-applied ones. But, prior to *Reed,* courts regularly applied the doctrine in a way that permitted governments to regulate speech using laws whose text referred to the content of that speech, so long as the reference was not made in order to express official disagreement or disapproval of the particular content being abridged.

As early as 1972 the Supreme Court stated that "above all else, the First Amendment means that government has no power to restrict expression because of its message, its ideas, its subject matter, or its content."[4] However, the Court's assessment of government purpose in content-discrimination doctrine finds its roots, like many of its

---

[4] Police Dep't of Chi. v. Mosley, 408 U.S. 92, 95 (1972).

doctrinal wrong turns, in cases involving sexually explicit speech.[5] In 1976's *Young v. American Mini Theaters*, the Court adopted a lenient standard of review in assessing a statute that clearly and obviously treated adult theaters differently from other theaters. Writing for four members of the Court, Justice John Paul Stevens wrote that the essence of content-discrimination doctrine was the requirement of "absolute neutrality by the government" with respect to content; the government's "regulation of communication may not be affected by sympathy or hostility for the point of view being expressed by the communicator."[6] Stevens's point then became the primary inquiry under the doctrine: if there was no evidence that the government's reference to content was based on "hostility for the point of view being expressed," then the neutrality requirement was met and the reference to content was not constitutionally suspect. This principle reached its peak in influence 13 years later in 1989's *Ward v. Rock Against Racism*, in which the Court, in assessing the constitutionality of a facially content-neutral regulation, stated that "[t]he principal inquiry in determining content neutrality, in speech cases generally and in time, place or manner cases in particular, is whether the government has adopted a regulation of speech because of disagreement with the message it conveys."[7] In other words, if a statute treated a speaker differently due to a statutory reference to the content of that person's speech, that abridgement could nevertheless avoid strict scrutiny if there was no evidence the government passed the content-classifying statute out of hostility to the content being classified.

Following *Ward*, the Court continued to prioritize purpose testing over facial review in First Amendment cases, such as its statement in *Bartnicki v. Vopper* that "in determining whether a regulation is

---

[5] *Young v. American Mini Theaters*, along with its successor cases *City of Renton v. Playtime Theatres* and *City of Los Angeles v. Alameda Books*, also adopted the much-maligned secondary effects doctrine, under which a reviewing court can find a facially content-based restriction content neutral if the restriction is aimed at the "secondary effects" of the content. In fact, the doctrine is so maligned that the Court has never applied it outside of First Amendment challenges to zoning restrictions by adult theaters. But see Mark Rienzi & Stuart Buck, Neutral No More: Secondary Effects Analysis and the Quiet Demise of the Content-Neutrality Test, 82 Fordham L. Rev. 1187, 1189–92 (2013) (arguing that even without formal extension, the secondary effects doctrine has had negative, speech-averse effects on other areas of First Amendment law).

[6] Young v. Am. Mini Theaters, 427 U.S. 50, 68 (1976).

[7] Ward v. Rock Against Racism, 491 U.S. 781, 791 (1989).

content based or content neutral, we look to the purpose behind the regulation."[8] Armed with such language, the lower courts crafted content-discrimination tests that put purpose, not text, as the driving inquiry in assessing First Amendment facial challenges. And because of "the general reluctance [of courts] to impute illicit purpose," the government purpose part of the inquiry consistently led to laws that referred expressly to content being subjected to only intermediate scrutiny.[9] For example, the Fourth Circuit characterized its content-discrimination test as one that followed a "pragmatic rather than formalistic approach to evaluating content neutrality," under which a speech regulation "is only content based if it distinguishes content with a censorial intent."[10] And in the lower court decision in *Reed* itself, the Ninth Circuit upheld the town of Gilbert's sign ordinance despite its use of content to distinguish among regulatory treatment of signs because the town "did not adopt its regulation of speech because it disagreed with the message" of the statutorily disfavored signs.[11] A search for evidence of censorial intent by the government, rather than a facial review of a statute's text, was the driving force in setting the standard of review.[12] Indeed, in looking for such intent, some courts even considered a government's purpose *before* looking at the text of the statute at issue.[13]

The reason so many applications of pre-*Reed* content-discrimination doctrine focused on government purpose was due to judicial unease with the premise underlying the doctrine itself: that government references to categories of speech in law are constitutionally

[8] 532 U.S. 514, 526 (2001). The majority opinion in *Bartnicki* was also written by Justice Stevens.

[9] Leslie Kendrick, Content Discrimination Revisited, 98 Va. L. Rev. 231, 292 (2012); see also *id.* at 296 ("Where both suspect and neutral justifications [for a content-based classification] are present, [the Court] tends to give the government the benefit of the doubt.").

[10] Clatterbuck v. City of Charlottesville, 708 F.3d 549, 556 (4th Cir. 2013), abrogated by Cent. Radio Co. v. City of Norfolk, 811 F.3d 625 (4th Cir. 2016).

[11] Reed v. Town of Gilbert, 707 F.3d 1057, 1071 (9th Cir. 2013), rev'd and remanded, 576 U.S. 155 (2015).

[12] The leading constitutional law treatise of the time agreed. See Laurence Tribe, American Constitutional Law 794 (2d ed. 1998) (a law is content based "if on its face a governmental action is targeted at ideas or information *that government seeks to suppress*") (emphasis added).

[13] See, e.g., Wag More Dogs, LLC v. Cozart, 680 F.3d 359, 366 (4th Cir. 2012).

suspect regardless of the nature of the category. In particular, the unease arises from a tension between that premise and a broader feeling, recognized in many First Amendment cases, that all speech is not equally valuable.[14] As Ashutosh Bhagwat writes, treating all government references to content as triggering strict scrutiny runs into "an unstated discomfort with the implications of [the doctrine's] all-speech-is-equal premise," which meant that "judges regularly look[ed] to avoid labeling the law [under review] as content based, even when it is clearly so."[15] In other words, if one believes that some speech is more valuable than other speech—and that belief is supported by, indeed embedded in, not just many First Amendment cases, but the self-governance rationale for the First Amendment[16]— then government references in law to that kind of "more valuable" speech are more pernicious than references to content that is not as valuable. And the converse is also true; when the government refers in its laws to speech that is less valuable, it often means no harm, to that speech or to the First Amendment more generally, and so judicial review should be less strict. If one needs proof-of-concept for this theory, the tension Bhagwat identifies also fully explains why content-discrimination doctrine went so wrong in cases involving sexually explicit films and books.[17]

Purpose-based content-discrimination analysis is one approach to First Amendment problems, but it certainly does not treat all government references to content alike. Nor does it seem consistent with the text of the amendment itself, which does not distinguish among types of government speech abridgements based on their underlying purpose or motivation. And as is usually the case, theoretical confusion led to confusion in application. As I mentioned above, different courts were giving different weight to government purpose

---

[14] See, e.g., Snyder v. Phelps, 562 U.S. 443, 452 (2011) ("Not all speech is of equal First Amendment importance.") (cleaned up and quoting several cases).

[15] Ashutosh Bhagwat, In Defense of Content Regulation, 102 Iowa L. Rev. 1427, 1428 (2017).

[16] Garrison v. Louisiana, 379 U.S. 64, 74–75 (1964) ("Speech concerning public affairs is more than self-expression; it is the essence of self-government.").

[17] See also Alan E. Brownstein, Illicit Legislative Motive in the Municipal Land Use Regulation Process, 57 U. Cin. L. Rev. 1, 95 (1988) ("Although the Court never explicitly affirms the view that sexually explicit expression is a generally less valuable form of speech [in the secondary effects cases], no other explanation of Renton is plausible.").

in their applications of content-discrimination doctrine, with some applying text-based tests and some analyzing motive.[18] The question before the Court in *Reed*, therefore, was whether, to quote the proposed question presented in Clyde Reed's successful petition for certiorari, the purpose-focused lower courts were correct that a "mere assertion of a lack of discriminatory motive" could "render [a] facially content-based sign code content neutral."[19]

Reed's primary doctrinal contribution in response to these developments was to cabin analysis of government purpose. According to *Reed*, when assessing whether a law was content based or content neutral, a reviewing court was to take a two-step approach: First, assess whether the law on its face referred to content. If the answer to that question was yes, then the court should apply strict scrutiny, and—to borrow a term from the well-known administrative law two step from *Chevron v. Natural Resources Defense Council*—then "that is the end of the matter" for content-discrimination doctrine. In other words, despite the purpose-focused language in *Young* and *Ward* and the applications of that language in content-discrimination cases in lower courts, when analyzing a law on its face, a court should not inquire as to whether the law regulates speech "because of disagreement with the message [the affected speech] conveys." By contrast, if the law under review makes no facial reference to speech, *then* the reviewing court asks whether that facially neutral law was adopted because of disagreement with the speech the law regulates—that is, the court asks whether the "purpose and justification for the [content-neutral] law are content based." Government purpose, in other words, cannot save content-based laws from strict scrutiny; it can only doom content-neutral laws that are content-discriminatory in their purpose or intent. The guiding inquiry is not a search for governmental motive that reveals or disproves a commitment to neutral treatment, rather, the test is textual. The larger question in *Reed*, as

[18] See Bethany J. Ring, Comment, Ripples in the Pond: United States Supreme Court Decision Impact Predictions v. Reality, 23 Chap. L. Rev. 205, 219–20 (2020) (Fourth, Sixth, and Ninth Circuit tests permitted a content-neutral motive for a facially content-based law to avoid strict scrutiny, while First, Second, Eighth, and Eleventh Circuits looked to law's text and Third Circuit applied a "context-sensitive balancing" content-discrimination test).

[19] Petition for Writ of Certiorari by Pastor Clyde Reed & Good News Cmty. Church at i, Reed v. Town of Gilbert, 576 U.S. 155 (2015) (No. 13-502).

well as in the commentary following it, is how formalistically content discrimination should be applied—that is, whether, like overbreadth, the other facial doctrine for First Amendment challenges, it should begin and end with a statute's text, or rather whether functionalist inquiries of statutory interpretation like purpose and intent can inform, and even override, answers supplied by textual analysis. *Reed* planted the flag firmly in the former camp.

Even though *Reed* was unanimous in the judgment, several concurring justices expressed concerns about the consequences of adopting a content-discrimination rule that could not use a speech-benign government purpose to save content-based laws from strict scrutiny. Justice Stephen Breyer argued that a formalistic approach to content neutrality would place most government regulation at risk.[20] Justice Elena Kagan warned that the *Reed* approach would threaten a host of noncensorial laws that referred to content for reasons unrelated to that content's viewpoint.[21] And Justice Samuel Alito concurred in the judgment by listing other hypothetical sign regulations that he argued would survive the *Reed* two-step, including, most helpfully for the city of Austin six years later, a sign law "distinguishing between on-premises and off-premises signs."[22]

Reed represented a victory for the argument that government purpose or intent should not save facially content-based laws from strict scrutiny. The victory recognizes that the government's intent in passing a statute that references content bears no relation to the subsequent application of that statute's content distinction against a particular speaker because of what they say. By definition, content-based laws lend themselves to censorious applications. If a category of content is capable of being proscribed based on the face of a statute, nothing holds the government back from doing so, even for viewpoint-discriminatory reasons, so long as its true motivation is kept hidden from view. Motivation or intent with respect to a statute's passage, in other words, does not bear on motivation or intent with respect to its application. *Reed* decided that the First Amendment solution to that problem was to invalidate the government's opportunity to act on its discriminatory intent in application, rather

---

[20] Reed, 576 U.S. at 175 (Breyer, J., concurring in the judgment).

[21] *Id.* at 179 (Kagan, J., concurring in the judgment).

[22] *Id.* at 174 (Alito, J., concurring).

than force the speaker to wait for an as-applied challenge post-enforcement and proffer evidence of such intent *ex post*.

Take for example the sign ordinance in *Austin* itself, which is discussed in more detail below. If the city of Austin is permitted to treat off-site signs differently than onsite signs, and signs are classified in those categories based on what they say, what prevents the city from using that distinction to discriminate against offsite signs that it disagrees with? The answer is nothing, because overinclusiveness with respect to content discrimination is not a deterrent for the government. Neither a Catholic church nor a mosque can erect an offsite sign advertising its services within Austin's city limits. But a government that does not like Islam and is indifferent to Catholicism simply pays the cost of discriminating against speech it does not care about in order to discriminate against speech that it dislikes. And if a speaker of the disfavored content is less likely to be able to erect an onsite sign because it does not have property on which to build one, all the better for the government. In this example and many others, the facial content distinction has content-differential effects in application, and those content-differential effects may even be motivated by animus, let alone a lack of neutrality, toward certain content. But as shown in part II below, after *Austin's* limits on the facial inquiry set out in *Reed*, that does not matter.

Nor should this concern be alleviated by the fact that as-applied challenges can smoke out censorious applications of laws referencing content that a court has deemed content neutral on purpose grounds. With some notable recent counterexamples by the legislatures of Florida and Texas notwithstanding,[23] governments generally do not willingly give up evidence of censorious intent with respect to a content-referencing law's passage.[24] Legislative history

---

[23] See, e.g., NetChoice, LLC v. Moody, 546 F. Supp. 3d 1082, 1093–94 (N.D. Fla. 2021) (signing statements and bill sponsor statements demonstrating a "viewpoint-based motivation" for legislation, "without more, subjects the legislation to strict scrutiny"), aff'd, 34 F.4th 1196, 1228 (11th Cir. 2022) (disagreeing that expressing a viewpoint-based motivation for a law alone is sufficient to trigger strict scrutiny, but noting that "there's no legitimate—let alone substantial—governmental interest in leveling the expressive playing field").

[24] For an argument that purpose and motivation tests are both (1) difficult to apply, because legislators have a "collection of different motivations," and (2) futile, because the government is always free to supply a less constitutionally suspect motivation to the same legislative classification after judicial review, see Palmer v. Thompson, 403 U.S. 217, 224–25 (1971).

or its equivalent concerning the government's adverse *application* of a given law to a particular speaker is even harder to find.[25] And differential effects, in the First Amendment and elsewhere in constitutional law, are almost never enough. As Geoffrey Stone points out, "[e]ven when the Court does take the presence of a content-differential impact into account in its content-neutral balancing, it does not shift automatically to full content-based standards of review."[26]

In the end, as *Reed* correctly recognized, government purpose analysis suffers from a fatal and irredeemable flaw: One legislature's benign content-neutral purposes in passing a facially content-based law does not limit a future executive officer from then using that content distinction to apply that law in a discriminatory way against speakers of that content that the government does not like. Justifications offered for the content-based legislative distinction in litigation do not bind a future enforcer in any way; the distinction, having survived a lesser level of scrutiny, lies in wait to be used against speakers whose speech falls into the disfavored content category. As Justice Clarence Thomas wrote for the *Reed* majority:

> Innocent motives do not eliminate the danger of censorship presented by a facially content-based statute, as future government officials may one day wield such statutes to suppress disfavored speech. That is why the First Amendment expressly targets the operation of the laws—*i.e.*, the "abridge[ement] of speech"—rather than merely the motives of those who enacted them.[27]

To assess *Austin*, one must ask the degree to which it reaffirmed this principle. As I discuss below, the majority in *Austin* avoided the obvious

---

[25] The Court has deemed a law's textual "target[ing of certain] speakers and their messages for disfavored treatment" as support for the conclusion that a law's motivation is content- and viewpoint-based. See Sorrell v. IMS Health, Inc., 564 U.S. 552, 565 (2011). But that is motive analysis based on the text of the statute itself, not on extrinsic evidence of purpose or motivation. In fact, the Court in *Sorrell* essentially discounted the content-neutral interests asserted in support of the law in light of its application to a limited set of speakers. In other words, motivation analysis based on statutory text trumped motivation analysis based on asserted interests.

[26] Geoffrey R. Stone, Restrictions of Speech Because of its Content: The Peculiar Case of Subject-Matter Restrictions, 46 U. Chi. L. Rev. 81, 103 n.110 (1978) (citing United States v. O'Brien, 391 U.S. 367 (1968)).

[27] Reed, 576 U.S. at 167.

result on the narrow content-based versus content-neutral question before it, but its avoidance will come at a broader doctrinal cost.

II. Sign, Sign, Everywhere a Sign, Blockin' out the Scenery, Breakin' my Mind[28]

After *Austin*, a regulation that requires reading a sign to determine whether a restriction applies to that sign does not necessarily result in differential treatment of speech that should be of first-order First Amendment concern. This is the Court's point in distinguishing between the sign categories in *Reed*—"ideological," "political," "temporary directional"—and the on- versus off-premises categories in *Austin*. Differential treatment based on references to particular kinds of subject matter or viewpoint are problematic, but references to content *per se* are not. But the *Austin* ordinance itself disproves this point.

Though there was no evidence yet in the record that the ordinance was intended to treat offsite signs worse than onsite ones because of the particular kinds of messages offsite signs tended to carry, the ordinance by definition creates a preference for on-premises signs by subjecting them to fewer restrictions. And dispositively for content-discrimination doctrine purposes, whether those restrictions apply depends not just on the location of a sign, but on the connection between a sign's location and its content. This is so even though the interests Austin asserted in support of the ordinance in the litigation—"to protect the aesthetic value of the city and to protect public safety"[29]—are not any more adversely affected by off-premises signs than they are by on-premises ones.[30]

To further prove the point, compare an imaginary (and much shorter) sign ordinance that subjects all signs, regardless of location, to the same restrictions. As a general matter under First Amendment doctrine, the absence of a categorical approach to regulating speech usually scrubs any content-discrimination-related problems, at least

[28] Five Man Electrical Band, Signs (May 1971).

[29] Amended Joint Stipulation of Fact and Evidence, Reagan Nat'l Adv. & Lamar Adv. Holding Co. v. City of Austin, W.D. Tx. 1:17-CV-673-RP (filed June. 5, 2018), ¶ 13, J.A.61a.

[30] Mosley, 408 U.S. at 100 (holding a ban on nonlabor residential picketing underinclusive, and thus in violation of the First Amendment, when labor picketing affected government interest in residential peace just as adversely).

facial ones.[31] But by contrast, by distinguishing based on location, the actual Austin ordinance chooses among types of signs that would be so restricted and those that would not, and the enforcement of the choice depends on the content of the sign.

The Austin ordinance arguably makes speaker-based distinctions as well. It could safely be presumed that on-premises signs are often owned by (or at a minimum more often owned by than off-premises signs), and always under the control of, the owner or occupier of the premises where the sign is located.[32] So, given a connection between the message on the sign and its location, those who put signs on their own property are subjected to many fewer restrictions in Austin than those who put them elsewhere. That creates a preference for, if not a category of speech, then a certain category of speaker, namely those who use their own property for speech rather than the property of another.

By making a premises-based distinction, the city of Austin relied on, and was respectful of, longstanding principles in both common law property and First Amendment doctrine—particularly the notion that using one's own property for speech is consistent with the doctrine of exclusive possession and the liberty to use one's property to express one's views free of government interference. The fact that the *Austin* Court was untroubled by the ordinance's favored treatment of on-premises signs might have been proof that the Court, at least implicitly, agreed. As the Court said in *City of Ladue v. Gilleo*,

> A special respect for individual liberty in the home has long been part of our culture and our law; that principle has special resonance when the government seeks to constrain a person's ability to speak there. . . . Most Americans would be understandably dismayed . . . to learn that it was illegal to display from their window an 8-by-11-inch sign expressing their political views.[33]

---

[31] See Heffron v. Int'l Soc. for Krishna Consciousness, 452 U.S. 640, 649 (1981) (anti-solicitation ordinance "applied evenhandedly to all who wished to solicit funds" and was thus content neutral) (edits omitted) (quoted in Austin, 142 S. Ct. at 1473).

[32] The Austin sign ordinance defined an "off-premise sign" as "a sign advertising a business, person, activity, goods, products, or services not located on the site where the sign is installed, or that directs persons to any location not on that site." Austin J.A. 65.

[33] City of Ladue v. Gilleo, 512 U.S. 43, 58 (1994); see also Maureen E. Brady, Property and Projection, 133 Harv. L. Rev. 1143, 1172–73 (2020) (noting that *City of Ladue* and other cases "emphasize[] the importance of the private citizen's right to communicate on or from his or her property.").

To be sure, *Austin's* solicitousness of this principle isn't complete—the ordinance cuts in favor of property owner speech in a relative sense but against it in an absolute sense, since even on-premises sign owners are limited to speaking about only topics that relate to what is happening on their property.[34] But there is no real question that, under the ordinance, off-premises speakers' speech is more restricted, if not what they can say then how they can say it, than on-premises speech. Favoring one category of signs necessarily disfavors the other category. Property owners can put a billboard on their property, or later digitize it, so long as it advertises something for offer on their property. A billboard owner that owns the billboard alone, like the respondent companies in the *Austin* case itself, cannot do the same, unless the message on the billboard advertises something taking place on the property where the billboard is located. This obviously limits the content of such a billboard owner's message. And if the non-premises owner did not already have a billboard at the time of the sign ordinance's passage, they cannot build a billboard at all.

The Court, then, cannot dispute that the city of Austin is treating signs differently based on what a sign says. What it concludes, however—indeed what it must conclude to avoid the application of strict scrutiny—is that Austin is not doing so for a First Amendment–averse *reason.* And that is so here, according to the Court, because "on premises" may be a legislative category of *signs,* but it is not a category of "substantive" *speech content,* like "ideological" or "political."[35] According to the *Austin* majority, the restrictions triggered by the sign's content are not based on the sign's "topic or subject matter." Rather, they are triggered by whether or not the sign is advertising or promoting something on the same property as the sign itself. This, claims the Court, sounds more like a content-neutral time, place, and manner restriction than a restriction of speech because of its content.[36] Austin is regulating the sign based on its location, not its message. And if the ordinance's enforcer must read the sign's message to determine which location-based regulation to apply, that

[34] *Id.* at 1175 ("While it is an obvious point, what appears on property communicates about and from its owner, rather than anyone else.").

[35] Austin, 142 S. Ct. at 1472.

[36] *Id.* at 1471 (Austin's "off-premises distinction requires an examination of speech only in service of drawing neutral, location-based lines" and "is agnostic as to content.").

alone does not make the regulation content based. This conclusion, according to the *Austin* majority, is also consistent with *Reed's* instruction that a law is content based when it "applies to particular speech because of the topic discussed or the idea or message expressed," because the content of a sign as it relates to whether the sign is on- or off-premises is not a "topic," "idea," or "message" for purpose of applying the First Amendment rule.[37] Requiring a peek at (or as some post-*Reed* lower courts have said, a "cursory examination" of) content in order to apply a content-neutral regulation does not trigger strict scrutiny.[38]

But the problem with the Court's reasoning is that, in this instance, a peek at content is necessarily also a peek at purpose. What *Austin* really says is that content-based categories do not trigger strict scrutiny when the uses to which those categories are put are content neutral. In other words, discriminating on the basis of content is not constitutionally suspect so long as the government has a content-neutral *motive or purpose* in doing so. Don't worry, says the *Austin* Court, the enforcer is only reading the sign to ask if it advertises activity on the sign's premises. This is different, the Court goes on, than the enforcer of the ordinance in *Reed*, who is deciding whether a sign's content is political or ideological before applying the law's various restrictions. Whether or why the *Reed* enforcer's motivation is content based, however, is left unclear, except to the extent that the use of subject-matter categories *itself* indicates a latent hostility, or at least a potentiality for same, towards some of those subjects. So if the law categorizes content for differential treatment based on its subject matter, purpose remains irrelevant; but if the law categorizes content based on a category that is capable of containing lots of different subjects, then purpose becomes relevant again, because a content-neutral purpose can save the law from strict scrutiny.

The Court distinguished the two ordinances in *Reed* and *Austin*: per *Reed*, any references to specific categories of speech are always content based regardless of purpose, but per *Austin*, references to broad categories of speech that are not limited to particular types

---

[37] *Id.* (citing Reed, 576 U.S. at 163).

[38] Act Now to Stop War & End Racism Coal. & Muslim Am. Soc'y Freedom Found. v. District of Columbia, 846 F.3d 391, 404 (D.C. Cir. 2017).

of subject matter can be justified by content-neutral purposes.[39] The speech-averse incentives such a rule creates for the government are obvious: regulate speech by avoiding the use of targeted substantive subject-matter categories of content. If restricting speech through the use of categories like "political" or "ideological" triggers strict scrutiny per *Reed*, a government could, under the *Austin* rule, more easily restrict symbolic (e.g., "no visual obstruction of a historic building"[40]) or pictorial (e.g., "no murals on private property"[41]) speech, or distinguish between online and off-line speech (e.g., "no posts on social media"[42]). Those are categories of speech that do not themselves contain substantive content or describe the content therein, and so they likely don't receive automatic strict scrutiny review under the rule in *Austin*. This is so even though in each of the examples the content of the speech must be examined by the enforcer to apply the prohibition, since "visual obstruction," "mural," and "social media"

---

[39] Austin, 142 S. Ct. at 1472 ("Unlike the sign code at issue in *Reed*, however, the City's provisions at issue here do not single out any topic or subject matter for differential treatment."); Tr. of Oral Arg. at 17–18, City of Austin v. Reagan Nat'l Advert. of Austin, LLC, 142 S. Ct. 1464 (2022) (No. 20-1029) (Austin arguing that laws using "broad categor[ies] of speech] that [are] not limited as to particular types of subject matter" are content neutral, but the use of more specific categories of speech as in *Reed* are content based); see also Austin, 142 S. Ct. at 1485 (Thomas, J., dissenting) ("[T]he majority contends that a law targeting directional messages concerning 'events generally, regardless of topic,' would not be content based, but one targeting 'directional messages concerning *specific* events' (*e.g.*, 'religious,' 'political' events) would be.").

[40] See, e.g., Mark Tushnet, Art and the First Amendment, in Free Speech Beyond Words 81–82 (2017) (permitting a historic preservation ordinance to prevent the work of artists Christo and Jeanne-Claude, who, with permission from the property owner, "wrap buildings in cloth for short periods," on the ground the ordinance is content neutral could have First Amendment–averse consequences).

[41] Cf. Neighborhood Enterprises, Inc. v. City of St. Louis, 644 F.3d 728, 736–37 (8th Cir. 2011) (finding a zoning ordinance's definition of "sign" that exempted from its definition flags, civic crests, and similar objects was content based because "to determine whether a particular object qualifies as a 'sign' and is therefore subject to the regulations, or is instead a 'non-sign' . . . one must look at the *content* of the object") (emphasis in original).

[42] Packingham v. North Carolina, 137 S. Ct. 1730 (2017) (assuming a statute barring sex offenders from using social media sites available to children is content neutral, but finding it was not narrowly tailored because of its reach). To be clear, under the Court's current application of content-discrimination doctrine, a ban on online speech could be deemed content neutral because it applies only to the medium in which the speech takes place. See, e.g., Leathers v. Medlock, 499 U.S. 439 (1991) (state sales tax that exempted newspapers but not broadcasters was content neutral). But a speech restriction based on the type of website or platform that hosts the speech could also be deemed content based because such a restriction is applied based on the type of content the website hosts.

all lend themselves to content-based legislative definitions. Like "on-premises," those categories "do not single out any topic or subject matter for differential treatment," and the sign's "substantive message itself is irrelevant to the application of the provisions."[43] They are also, like the Austin ordinance, "content-agnostic."[44] But by not using a subject-matter category, they restrict speech *across* categories—and restrict more speech in the process. Subjecting laws that restrict more speech to less scrutiny is an unfortunate byproduct of content-discrimination doctrine generally, so long as those laws manage to avoid being found substantially overbroad.[45] But the *Austin* rule compounds that unfortunate problem by making it easier for the government to avoid strict scrutiny by defining the type of content it regulates through the use of broader, more cross-cutting categories of speech. Under *Austin*, generality works in the government's First Amendment favor.

It is possible to distinguish between on- and off-premises signs in a content-neutral manner. As the Fifth Circuit noted, quoting the Sixth Circuit, "a regulation that defines an on-premises sign as any sign within 500 feet of a building is content neutral."[46] This is so because in that example, the basis for the differential treatment of the sign, whether with respect to digitization rights or its existence altogether, is based purely on the sign's location, not on what it says, or on a connection between what it says and where it is. Likewise, if digitized billboards present a particular safety hazard to drivers, as several amici in *Austin* told the Court, then billboards or the digitization rights of same can be defined based on their size or location instead of their content.[47]

---

[43] Austin, 142 S. Ct. at 1472.

[44] *Id.* at 1475.

[45] See, e.g., Barr v. Am. Ass'n of Pol. Consultants, 140 S. Ct. 2335, 2355 (2020) ("A generally applicable robocall restriction would be permissible under the First Amendment," but a statutory carve-out for government debt collection robocalls from that restriction is not because it is based on the carve-out's content); Alan K. Chen, Statutory Speech Bubbles, First Amendment Overbreadth, and Improper Legislative Purpose, 38 Harv. C.R.-C.L. L. Rev. 31, 65–66 (2003) ("More broadly drafted speech regulations tend to reduce the dissemination of greater amounts and types of speech than do viewpoint- and content-discriminatory laws.").

[46] Reagan Nat'l Adv. of Austin v. City of Austin, 972 F.3d 696, 704 (5th Cir. 2020), rev'd and remanded, 142 S. Ct. 1464, 1489 (2022) (quoting Thomas v. Bright, 937 F.3d 721, 732 (6th Cir. 2019)).

[47] See Austin, 142 S. Ct. at 1479 (Breyer, J., concurring) (summarizing amici safety-related arguments).

There are a range of true time, place, and manner-based options for municipalities that want to regulate signs and billboards, none of which require an enforcer to assess what a sign says in order to do so.

If one returns to the facts of *Reed*, the result of all this is particularly incoherent. As "Temporary Directional Signs Relating to a Qualifying Event," Pastor Clyde Reed's signs in the public rights-of-way advertising the location of his Good News Community Church services could stay up in Gilbert, Arizona, for 12 hours before and an hour after Sunday service. Other types of signs are not similarly restricted, and so this differential treatment, per the *Reed* Court, violates the First Amendment. However, if Pastor Reed's church was in Austin, Texas, because it had no building (which of course was the whole reason he needed his signs in the first place), his signs would be "off-premises" signs and they could never be put up at all. The *Austin* Court says this presents no First Amendment problem, due to Austin's content-neutral purpose for using a content-based statutory category of signs.

Accordingly, and after *Austin*, the *Reed* content discrimination two-step is now more like a tango-backward-*ocho*: (1) look to the face of the statute; (2) if the face of the statute refers to content, then ask whether the facial reference is to either (a), a substantive and particular category of content, which renders the law content based, or rather (b), a broad category of speech not limited as to subject matter; (3) if the answer to (2) is (b), ask whether the government's use of that type of category furthers a content-neutral purpose; and finally, (4) if the answer to (3) is yes, then conclude the law is content neutral. The *Austin* Court tried to preserve the *Reed* two-step, but by letting assessment of government purpose back into the content-based part of the test, it tripped over its feet in the process.

* * *

What caused the Court—or to be more precise, those members of the Court who were in the majority in both *Reed* and *Austin*, namely Chief Justice John Roberts and Justice Sonia Sotomayor[48]—to say

---

[48] Justices Antonin Scalia and Anthony Kennedy were also in the *Reed* majority; of their replacements, Justice Brett Kavanaugh was in the *Austin* majority and Justice Neil Gorsuch dissented. And Justice Alito's concurrence in the judgment and dissent agreed that Austin's definitions of on- and off-premises signs were content based, thus agreeing with the *Austin* dissenters that the majority misapplied *Reed*. Austin, 142 S. Ct. at 1479–81 (Opinion of Alito, J.).

essentially in *Austin*, "don't worry, we didn't really mean what we said in *Reed*"? The answer can be found in the opinion's very first line. The prospect of subjecting the sign regulations of "thousands of jurisdictions across the country" to strict scrutiny would call into question the fact that "American jurisdictions have regulated outdoor advertising for well over a century."[49] As the National League of Cities' amicus brief told the Court, "at least thirty states and thousands of municipal governments," following the federal Highway Beautification Act, distinguish between on- and off-premises signs as part of their regulation of billboards, and finding the Austin ordinance content based would throw all of those laws into question, causing those governments to "expend tremendous time, money, and resources to amend their sign codes."[50]

Given the possibility of casting tens of thousands of ordinances into constitutional doubt, and the hundreds if not thousands of lawyer billable hours it would presumably take to resolve those doubts, perhaps the Court was justified in proceeding cautiously. Of course, the fact that all of these statutes and ordinances exist does not necessarily mean they distinguish between those signs *on the basis of a sign's content*. As discussed above, a sign or billboard can be defined as "off-premises" without reference to the content of that sign. But concern around that perceived upheaval, combined with an unstated presumption that government action with a long history and tradition of presumed constitutionality should earn that action deference with respect to constitutional challenges, led the Court to avoid an obvious result.[51]

III. Building a Wall Between *Reed* and (Some) Compelled-Speech Doctrine

Though the *Austin* majority's fears were motivated by the possibility of throwing thousands of sign ordinances into doubt, also driving the move from *Reed* to *Austin* is a concern that *Reed* exposed

---

[49] Austin, 142 S. Ct. at 1469.

[50] Brief of the National League of Cities et al. in Support of Petitioner at 2, 8, City of Austin v. Reagan Nat'l Advert. of Austin, LLC, 142 S. Ct. 1464 (2022) (No. 20-1029).

[51] See, e.g., Am. Meat Inst. v. Dep't of Agric., 760 F.3d 18, 32 (D.C. Cir. 2014) (Kavanaugh, J., concurring in the judgment) ("in First Amendment free-speech law, history and tradition are reliable guides" when determining whether an infringement on a speaker's speech rights is justified) (citing several Supreme Court cases).

consumer protection laws, in particular compelled disclosures, to constitutional overruling. For example, under the rule announced in *Austin,* content-discrimination doctrine no longer presents a barrier to labeling requirements, because even though requiring a private party to put specific information on a food or drug label is clearly content based, the motivation behind the compulsion is content neutral.

But *Austin* is a solution in search of a problem. There was no real danger of applying strict scrutiny to compelled-disclosure requirements rooted in traditional exercises of police power under *Reed.* Even pre-*Austin,* the First Amendment analysis of a consumer protection-based compelled disclosure would never proceed under an "if you have to read the label or the securities disclosure to assess compliance with the government's disclosure requirement, then scrutiny of the requirement is strict"–type test. That is because the law of compelled disclosures is distinct from content-discrimination doctrine.

Justice Breyer's opinions in *Reed* and *Austin* are right about one thing: *every* compulsion of speech by the government is content based. New Hampshire told George Maynard what speech had to be on his license plate.[52] West Virginia told the Barnett children the content of the pledge they had to say at the beginning of every school day.[53] The Securities and Exchange Commission tells prospective sellers of securities the content of the disclosure those sellers are required to make before any sale.[54] A public-school teacher who tells her social studies students to write a report on a great historical figure is compelling speech in a content-based way (and when the teacher gives the student who writes about Hitler an F, she is engaging in viewpoint discrimination as well). Similarly, deciding whether a given restriction should be subjected to commercial speech-applicable intermediate scrutiny is literally a content-dependent analysis, because the first step in such an inquiry is to decide whether the speech at issue is commercial. Those facts, however, do not turn every compelled or commercial speech case into a content-discrimination case to which the *Reed* two-step would have applied, because both

[52] Wooley v. Maynard, 430 U.S. 705 (1977).

[53] W. Va. State Bd. of Educ. v. Barnette, 319 U.S. 624 (1943).

[54] Securities Act, 15 U.S.C. § 77e.

pre- and post-*Reed*, all speech compulsions are not treated the same under the First Amendment.

Austin itself affirmed that neither it nor *Reed* displaced traditional commercial speech intermediate scrutiny.[55] "Purely factual" government information-forcing "about the terms under which" a speaker's "services will be available" has never been thought to trigger the same set of concerns as those instances in which the government is coercing individuals "into betraying their convictions" by involuntarily affirming the government's position with respect to certain viewpoints.[56] And in its first case applying *Reed*, a First Amendment challenge to the federal robocall solicitation statute's government-debt-collection exception in *Barr v. American Association of Political Consultants*, the Court expressly distinguished those "impermissible speech restrictions" that content-discrimination doctrine is intended to snuff out from "traditional or ordinary economic regulation of commercial activity that imposes incidental burdens on speech."[57] And even absent the unnecessary cabining in *Austin*, lower courts were likewise distinguishing between those references to content to which the *Reed* two-step applied from laws and regulations that "safeguard the health and safety of citizens" but only incidentally burden speech.[58]

---

[55] Austin, 142 S. Ct. at 1480 (Alito, J., concurring in the judgment in part and dissenting in part) ("Many [and possibly the great majority] of the situations in which the relevant [Austin sign ordinance] provisions may apply involve commercial speech, and under our precedents, regulations of commercial speech are analyzed differently.").

[56] Zauderer v. Off. of Disciplinary Couns. of Sup. Ct. of Ohio, 471 U.S. 626, 651 (1985); Janus v. Am. Fed'n of State, Cnty., & Mun. Emps. Council 31, 138 S. Ct. 2448, 2464 (2018).

[57] Barr, 140 S. Ct. at 2347; see also *id.* ("Our decision is not intended to expand existing First Amendment doctrine or to otherwise affect traditional or ordinary economic regulation of commercial activity.").

[58] Greater Phila. Chamber of Com. v. City of Philadelphia, 949 F.3d 116, 138 (3d Cir. 2020) ("[T]he Supreme Court has consistently applied intermediate scrutiny to commercial speech restrictions, even those that were content- and speaker-based."); see, e.g., Recht v. Morrisey, 32 F.4th 398, 405 (4th Cir. 2022) (statute regulating legal solicitations of clients in cases involving medications or medical devices "lies right at the heart of West Virginia's police power," namely its "one premier duty . . . to safeguard the health and safety of its citizens," and so district court's application of *Reed* rather than *Central Hudson*–based intermediate scrutiny for commercial speech to the statute was improper); see also *id.* at 409 ("*Reed* simply concerned a totally different context; it cannot be distorted to so unsettle the *Central Hudson* regime.").

Finally, the *Austin* Court said the fact that the First Amendment permits regulation of solicitation demonstrates that a rule is too broad if it deems a law content based if its enforcer must "read or hear" speech to enforce it. But the First Amendment law of solicitation actually proves the wisdom and utility of *Reed.* Laws that distinguish among kinds of solicitation and even types of solicitors should have been deemed content based even prior to *Reed.*[59] To the extent *Reed* instructs courts to ignore evidence of government intent justifying those distinctions, that is certainly a First Amendment–affirming result. And despite *Austin's* affirmation of the Court's solicitation-based jurisprudence as proof of First Amendment lenience, lower courts have increasingly found that "laws targeting speech involving requests for money are content based,"[60] and that strict scrutiny applies, even when those laws distinguish between places where certain kinds of solicitation may occur.[61] In other words, strict scrutiny applies to solicitation statutes whose enforcement "distinguish[es] on the basis of location" and are thus as analogous to "ordinary time, place, and manner distinctions" as the ordinance at issue in *Austin.* So the Court in *Austin* was quite correct to say that "the First Amendment allows for regulations of solicitation," but that statement is only true insofar as those regulations are themselves content neutral—that is, if they treat solicitation no worse than other kinds of speech.[62] And *Austin's* gloss on *Reed* will permit jurisdictions to avoid strict scrutiny by asserting content-neutral justifications for their content-based panhandling and solicitation bans, the very result that *Reed* itself precluded.

---

[59] But see Doucette v. City of Santa Monica, 955 F. Supp. 1192, 1204–05 (C.D. Cal. 1997) (upholding panhandling ban because there was no evidence that city disagreed with panhandlers' message).

[60] See, e.g., Kissel v. Seagull, 552 F. Supp. 3d 277, 289–90 (D. Conn. 2021) (citing Second, Eighth, and Ninth Circuit Courts of Appeals, as well as the district courts of the Eastern District of Louisiana and District of Minnesota).

[61] See Messina v. City of Fort Lauderdale, Fla., 546 F. Supp. 3d 1227, 1244–48 (S.D. Fla. 2021) (ordinance that prohibits panhandling in certain locations throughout city is content based because it defines "panhandling" as "any request for an immediate donation of money or thing of value").

[62] Austin, 142 S. Ct. at 1473 (citing Cantwell v. Connecticut, 310 U.S. 296 (1940) and Heffron v. Int'l Society for Krishna Consciousness, Inc., 452 U.S. 640 (1981)).

Conclusion

I end on a terminological note. Careful readers of this article who also follow the First Amendment will have noticed that throughout I use the term "content discrimination" rather than the more common doctrinal nomenclature "content neutrality." Part I above shows why. Characterizing the government's obligation under the doctrine as one that requires it to be "neutral" toward content led directly to the original sin of searching for governmental purpose and intent as a way of saving facially content-based laws. When a reviewing court's motivating doctrinal concern is to confirm government neutrality toward content referred to in law, searches for extratextual commitments to such neutrality—or more particularly, searches for the *absence* of any evidence of *non*-neutral motives—make perfect sense.

But nothing in the First Amendment grants government this degree of solicitousness. All references to content that are used to treat content differently constitute discrimination. The role of reviewing courts, as in other areas of constitutional law, is not to discern whether that discrimination is motivated by a cleansing neutral purpose and therefore unproblematic. Instead, courts should force the government to justify the differential treatment of speech with both a compelling interest and as narrow a fit as possible between the means and those ends. The *Reed* rule properly recognized the inherent constitutional problems presented when the government engages in content-based classifications of speech. The Supreme Court would be wise to return to it—and to make clearer those circumstances to which its level of highest scrutiny applies.

Using My Religion: *Carson v. Makin* and the Status/Use (Non)Distinction

*Michael Bindas**

For a brief, five-year period in American free-exercise jurisprudence, a curious theory gained sway over courts and commentators alike. It went something like this: Government can't discriminate against you because you are religious, but it can discriminate against you because you do religious stuff. Within a half decade of its positing, however, this theory of a "stuff" exception to the First Amendment's bar against religious discrimination has been discredited and discarded. The Supreme Court did the job in *Carson v. Makin*.[1]

The "stuff" exception also went by another name: the "status/use distinction." Although the Free Exercise Clause prohibits government from denying an otherwise available public benefit because of the religious status, or identity, of the recipient, the theory suggested, it allows government to deny the benefit because of the religious use to which the recipient might put it, or the religious conduct in which the recipient might engage with it. The distinction was born of a plurality footnote in 2017's *Trinity Lutheran Church of Columbia, Inc. v. Comer*,[2] and immediately, opponents of educational-choice programs—that is, programs that provide aid to families to choose private alternatives to a public education[3]—began wielding it as a

---

* Michael Bindas is a senior attorney at the Institute for Justice and was counsel of record for the Carson and Nelson families at the U.S. Supreme Court in *Carson v. Makin*.

[1] 142 S. Ct. 1987 (2022).

[2] Trinity Lutheran Church of Columbia, Inc. v. Comer, 137 S. Ct. 2012 (2017).

[3] Educational choice programs come in several forms: (1) voucher programs, which provide publicly funded scholarships that students can use to attend the private school of their parents' choice; (2) tax-credit scholarship programs, which also provide scholarships but are funded by private donations, incentivized by a tax credit to nonprofit scholarship-granting organizations; (3) education savings account programs, which may be publicly funded or tax credit–incentivized, and which provide government-authorized savings accounts that parents can use on a wide array of educational

weapon to try to deprive families of religious options in such programs. It seemed the weapon might be removed from their arsenal in *Espinoza v. Montana Department of Revenue*, but the status/use distinction lived to see another day.[4] In *Carson*, it could cheat death no more.

This article examines the short life and happy death of the status/ use distinction. The article begins with the distinction's origin story in *Trinity Lutheran*, then recounts the distinction's dodge of a bullet in *Espinoza*. Next up is a discussion of *Carson*, the case that killed the status/use distinction. Finally, the article considers what *Carson* portends for the future of the educational-choice movement, exploring what the decision does—and does not—resolve in the seemingly unending legal war that public school teachers' unions and their allies have waged on educational choice.

I. *Trinity Lutheran*, Wherein the Status/Use Distinction Is Born

The status/use distinction (or at least the idea of such a distinction) was born at 10:09 a.m. on June 26, 2017.[5] At that time, on that day, the Supreme Court handed down its decision in *Trinity Lutheran Church of Columbia, Inc. v. Comer*, and tucked away inside was Footnote 3, the villain of our story.

Trinity Lutheran concerned the exclusion of a church-run preschool from a Missouri playground resurfacing program. The program provided direct, monetary grants, awarded on a competitive basis, to preschools and other nonprofits to purchase rubber paving materials made from scrap tires.[6] In 2012, Trinity Lutheran Church Child Learning Center—a preschool and daycare center that operated under the auspices and on the property of Trinity Lutheran Church—applied for one of these grants. Despite ranking fifth among the 44 applicants that year, Trinity Lutheran did not receive one of the 14 grants ultimately awarded, because the state maintained "a strict and express policy of denying grants to any applicant owned or

---

services for their children; and (4) personal tax credit or deduction programs, which provide a tax credit or deduction to parents for educational expenses incurred for their own children's education.

[4] 140 S. Ct. 2246 (2020).

[5] Amy Howe, Trinity Lutheran Church of Columbia Inc. v. Comer, SCOTUSblog (June 26, 2017), https://tinyurl.com/fyzhccay (birth announcement by Amy Howe: "We have *Trinity Lutheran*, which is by the Chief Justice (for the most part, although not footnote 3).").

[6] Trinity Lutheran, 137 S. Ct. at 2017.

controlled by a church, sect, or other religious entity."[7] According to the state, this policy was mandated by a provision of the Missouri Constitution, commonly known as a "Blaine Amendment,"[8] that provides, "no money shall ever be taken from the public treasury, directly or indirectly, in aid of any church, sect or denomination of religion."[9]

Trinity Lutheran challenged its exclusion, and its case reached the Supreme Court. In an opinion authored by Chief Justice John Roberts, the Court held that Missouri's exclusion violated the Free Exercise Clause of the First Amendment. The Court began its analysis by examining past precedent, which "repeatedly confirmed that denying a generally available benefit solely on account of religious identity imposes a penalty on the free exercise of religion."[10] Missouri's policy did just that, "put[ting] Trinity Lutheran to a choice": "participate in an otherwise available benefit program or remain a religious institution."[11]

The Court then rejected Missouri's reliance on *Locke v. Davey* to support its exclusion.[12] In *Locke*, the Court *upheld* Washington's exclusion of "devotional theology" majors—students pursuing a degree in "religious instruction that will prepare [them] for the ministry"—from a state scholarship program for college students.[13] As the Court explained in *Trinity Lutheran*, Washington had "merely chosen not to fund a distinct category of instruction."[14] The plaintiff in that case, the Court added, "was not denied a scholarship because of who he *was*; he was denied a scholarship because of what he proposed *to do*—use the funds to prepare for the ministry," which is "an 'essentially religious endeavor.'"[15] Trinity Lutheran, by contrast, "was denied a grant simply because of what it is—a church."[16]

---

[7] *Id.*

[8] As discussed *infra* notes 27–31 and accompanying text. Blaine Amendments have a sordid history rooted in 19th-century, anti-Catholic bigotry.

[9] Mo. Const. art. I, § 7.

[10] Trinity Lutheran, 137 S. Ct. at 2019.

[11] *Id.* at 2021–22.

[12] 540 U.S. 712 (2004).

[13] *Id.* at 715, 719.

[14] Trinity Lutheran, 137 S. Ct. at 2023 (quoting Locke, 540 U.S. at 721).

[15] *Id.* (quoting Locke, 540 U.S. at 721) (emphasis in original); see also *id.* at 2024 ("The only thing he could not do was use the scholarship to pursue a degree in [devotional theology].").

[16] *Id.*

The Court then proceeded to hold that compliance with Missouri's state constitutional proscription on aid to schools controlled by a "church, sect or denomination of religion" could not justify the playground grant program's religious exclusion.[17] But before doing so, the Court—four justices of the Court, actually—dropped a little footnote.

Now, Supreme Court footnotes rarely gain notoriety and even less frequently, infamy. Those that manage to achieve such status are typically known simply by their number. "Footnote 4" in *United States v. Carolene Products Co.* is an example.[18] "Footnote 3" in *Trinity Lutheran* also made the cut, and it did not take long for it to do so: it was anointed "infamous" a mere nine minutes after the opinion was handed down.[18]

So, why the infamy? Here's what Footnote 3 had to say:

> This case involves express discrimination based on religious identity with respect to playground resurfacing. We do not address religious uses of funding or other forms of discrimination.[19]

In those 27 words[20] was born the "status/use distinction": the idea that although government may not withhold a benefit based on the would-be beneficiary's religious status, or identity, it may withhold a benefit based on the religious use to which the would-be beneficiary might put it.[21]

As mentioned above, Footnote 3 was not part of the majority opinion in *Trinity Lutheran*. It was appended to what was, in all other respects, the majority opinion, but the footnote itself was joined only by four justices, depriving it of precedential value. And even those four justices did not actually *embrace* a status/use distinction—they

---

[17] *Id.* at 2024–25.

[18] Howe, *supra* note 5. Thankfully, as we shall soon see, Footnote 3 did not have quite the staying power of Footnote 4, which continues to haunt us.

[19] Trinity Lutheran, 137 S. Ct. at 2024 n.3 (plurality).

[20] Like other members of the 27 Club, Footnote 3 was not long for the world. See The 27 Club: A Brief History, Rolling Stone (Dec. 8, 2019), https://tinyurl.com/yjx2ubyz.

[21] Under this view of the law, for example, government could not withhold social security benefits from a retiree because she is religious, but it could prohibit her from tithing part of her social security income to her church.

merely left open the possibility of one.[22] Meanwhile, Justice Neil Gorsuch, who, along with Justice Clarence Thomas, did not join Footnote 3, took issue with even the suggestion that a useful distinction between religious status and use could be made. In an opinion concurring in part, he said he "harbor[ed] doubts about the stability of such a line," because "[o]ften enough the same facts can be described both ways."[23] "Neither do I see," he continued, "why the First Amendment's Free Exercise Clause should care. After all, that Clause guarantees the free *exercise* of religion, not just the right to inward belief (or status)."[24] For this reason, Justice Gorsuch concluded, "I don't see why it should matter whether we describe that benefit, say, as closed to Lutherans (status) or closed to people who do Lutheran things (use). It is free exercise either way."[25]

But Justice Gorsuch's view didn't carry the day—yet. And because it didn't, the idea of a constitutionally meaningful status/use distinction was born.

Nevertheless, *Trinity Lutheran* was a great victory for religious liberty, and, although not an educational-choice case, it was also widely viewed as a victory for educational choice. After all, opponents of choice had long argued that Blaine Amendments like the one Missouri relied on also prohibited educational-choice programs that included religious options. For decades, they had been weaponizing these provisions, challenging educational-choice programs in state courts under them, usually unsuccessfully.[26] *Trinity Lutheran* seemed to finally remove this weapon from their arsenal.

---

[22] See Trinity Lutheran, 137 S. Ct. at 2025 (Gorsuch, J., concurring in part) ("[T]he Court leaves open the possibility a useful distinction might be drawn between laws that discriminate on the basis of religious *status* and religious *use*.").

[23] *Id.* at 2025–26.

[24] *Id.* at 2026 (emphasis in original).

[25] *Id.*

[26] See, e.g., Schwartz v. Lopez, 382 P.3d 886, 899 (Nev. 2016) (rejecting Blaine Amendment challenge to publicly funded education savings account program); Magee v. Boyd, 175 So. 3d 79, 131–37 (Ala. 2015) (rejecting Blaine Amendment challenge to refundable personal tax-credit program and tax-credit scholarship program); Meredith v. Pence, 984 N.E.2d 1213, 1227–30 (Ind. 2013) (rejecting Blaine Amendment challenge to voucher program); Kotterman v. Killian, 972 P.2d 606, 617–25 (Ariz. 1999) (rejecting Blaine Amendment challenge to tax-credit scholarship program); Jackson v. Benson, 578 N.W.2d 602, 620–23 (Wis. 1998) (rejecting Blaine Amendment challenge to voucher program); Niehaus v. Huppenthal, 310 P.3d 983, 985–89 (Ariz. Ct. App. 2013) (rejecting

But then there was the matter of Footnote 3, and, here, educational-choice opponents found an opening. They began arguing that the status/use distinction floated in the footnote meant state constitutions *could* bar religious options in educational-choice programs. Why? Because religious schools engage in religious instruction; they *do* religious *stuff.* Opponents of choice insisted that even if *Trinity Lutheran* meant a state constitution could not bar a family's choice of school because it *is* religious, it could still bar a family from putting their educational-choice benefit to the *use* of procuring a religious education. Justice Gorsuch's warning—"Often enough the same facts can be described both ways"—had quickly come to fruition.

II. *Espinoza v. Montana Department of Revenue*, wherein the Status/Use Distinction Dodges a Bullet

Meanwhile, it wasn't just the usual suspects (read: public school teachers' unions) making this argument. Government bureaucrats hostile to educational choice joined the party. In Montana, after the state legislature enacted an educational-choice program that offered parents the choice of religious and nonreligious schools alike, the state's department of revenue—the agency charged with administering the program—promulgated a regulation barring religious options from it.[27] Why? Like Missouri in *Trinity Lutheran*, the department insisted the religious exclusion was necessary to comply with the state's Blaine Amendment, which provides, in part: "The legislature . . . shall not make any direct or indirect appropriation or payment from any public fund or monies . . . to aid any . . . school . . . controlled in whole or in part by any church, sect, or denomination."[28]

Blaine Amendment challenge to publicly funded education savings account program); Green v. Garriott, 212 P.3d 96, 105–06 (Ariz. Ct. App. 2009) (rejecting Blaine Amendment challenge to tax-credit scholarship program); Toney v. Bower, 744 N.E.2d 351, 357–63 (Ill. Ct. App. 2001) (rejecting Blaine Amendment challenge to tax-credit scholarship program); see also Simmons-Harris v. Goff, 711 N.E.2d 203, 211–12 (Ohio 1999) (rejecting compelled support clause challenge to voucher program). But see Cain v. Horne, 202 P.3d 1178, 1183–85 (Ariz. 2009) (invalidating voucher program under Blaine Amendment); Bush v. Holmes, 886 So. 2d 340, 347–61 (Fla. Dist. Ct. App. 2004) (invalidating voucher program under Blaine Amendment), aff'd on other grounds, 919 So. 2d 392 (Fla. 2006).

[27] Espinoza, 140 S. Ct. at 2252.

[28] Mont. Const. art. X, § 6(1).

A quick word regarding such state constitutional provisions is in order. Blaine Amendments are found in 37 state constitutions and have a sordid lineage steeped in 19th-century anti-Catholic bigotry.[29] At the time these provisions were originally adopted, public schools were overtly religious and nondenominationally Protestant. Bible reading, hymn singing, and prayer recitation were common in the public schools, and it was the King James Version of the Bible that was read and Protestant hymns and prayers that were sung and recited.[30] It was not uncommon, moreover, for Catholic students to be beaten or expelled from their public schools for refusing to engage in these Protestant exercises.[31]

Despite the fact that the public schools were thoroughly religious, they were not controlled or operated by a church, sect, or denomination and, thus, not subject to the proscriptions on public funding contained in the Blaine Amendments. By contrast, Catholic schools— which the Church had begun establishing to provide an acceptable alternative to Catholic children—were. Thus, the twin aims of the Blaine Amendments: preserve the religious nature of the public schools while denying aid to Catholic schools.

Understanding this history is important. When opponents of parental choice in education rely on Blaine Amendments to take that choice away, they are not relying on some high-minded, noble principle of church-state separation. They are relying on vestiges of 19th-century anti-Catholic bigotry.

And the Montana Department of Revenue was all too happy to invoke such a vestige to justify banning religious options from the state's educational-choice program. But three mothers of children

[29] See Richard D. Komer, School Choice and State Constitutions' Religion Clauses, 3 J. Sch. Choice 331, 337, 341 (2009). These provisions are named for Representative James G. Blaine, who attempted unsuccessfully to amend the U.S. Constitution to include a similar provision. *Id.* at 341. "Although their language varies, and some interpretation is involved in classifying a provision as a Blaine Amendment, [the author] considers any provision that specifically prohibits state legislatures (and often other governmental entities) from appropriating funds to religious sects or institutions, including religious schools, to be a Blaine Amendment." Answers to Frequently Asked Questions About Blaine Amendments, Institute for Justice, https://tinyurl.com/3h9vpzun.

[30] See, e.g., Lloyd P. Jorgenson, The State and the Non-Public School, 1825–1925, 90 (1987); see generally *id.* 69–110; Philip Hamburger, Separation of Church and State 219–29 (2002).

[31] See, e.g., Donahoe v. Richards, 38 Me. 376, 377–78 (1854); Jorgenson, *supra* note 30, at 90; Joan DelFattore, The Fourth R 49 (2004).

eligible for the program and wanting to use it to attend religious schools challenged the religious exclusion, alleging, like Trinity Lutheran had in challenging the religious exclusion from Missouri's scrap-tire program, that it violated their rights under the Free Exercise Clause of the U.S. Constitution. The case reached the U.S. Supreme Court two years after *Trinity Lutheran,* and it appeared the Court was poised to resolve the status/use question raised in that case.

Except it didn't. To be sure, the Montana Department of Revenue insisted that Montana's Blaine Amendment "has the goal or effect of ensuring that government aid does not end up being used for 'sectarian education' or 'religious education'"—that is, ensuring government aid is not put to a religious *use.*[32] And without the exclusion, it maintained, the aid provided by the educational-choice program "could be used for religious ends by some recipients, particularly schools that believe faith should '*permeate*[ ]' everything they do."[33] In the department's view, then, it was all about religious use: by barring religious options, it was simply engaging in the good kind of religious discrimination, not the bad kind the Court denounced in *Trinity Lutheran.*

But Chief Justice Roberts, writing for the Court, saw things as more statusy than usey. Montana's Blaine Amendment, he explained, "bars religious schools from public benefits solely because of the religious character of the schools" and "bars parents who wish to send their children to a religious school from those same benefits, again solely because of the religious character of the school."[34] The provision thus "discriminates based on religious status just like the Missouri policy in *Trinity Lutheran,* which excluded organizations 'owned or controlled by a church, sect, or other religious entity.'"[35] Thus, in Roberts's view, the case "turn[ed] expressly on religious status and not religious use."[36]

The good news in this was that Montana's bar to religious options in the state's educational-choice program met the same fate as

---

[32] Espinoza, 140 S. Ct. at 2256 (quoting Espinoza v. Mont. Dep't of Revenue, 435 P.3d 603, 609, 613–14 (Mont. 2018), rev'd and remanded, 140 S. Ct. 2246 (2020)).

[33] *Id.* (alteration and emphasis in original) (quoting Br. for Respondents at 39).

[34] *Id.* at 2255.

[35] *Id.* at 2256 (quoting Trinity Lutheran, 137 S. Ct. at 2017).

[36] *Id.*

the religious exclusion in Missouri's playground resurfacing program: the Court held it unconstitutional. The bad news was that the status/use distinction lived to see another day, and to continue being wielded as justification for denying parents religious options in educational choice programs.

Opponents of those programs, while obviously unhappy with the outcome, found comfort in the fact that the Court had shown mercy on the status/use distinction. For example, Ron Meyer, a lawyer who has represented the Florida Education Association in legal challenges to educational-choice programs in that state, breathed a huge sigh of relief that the Court had "simply" concluded that benefits were "being withheld solely because of the religious character of the school" and didn't "reach into whether those monies were used to inculcate students."[37] There was no doubt that Meyer and his colleagues in the anti-parental-choice camp saw *Espinoza* as a green light to continue—or at least not a red light to stop—attacking educational-choice programs because of the religious use to which they allow a parent to put their child's benefit.

But if *Espinoza* wasn't a red light to stop use-based discrimination against religious schools and the parents who choose them, it was at least a yellow one. For one thing, the Court suggested that religious status and religious use were not mutually exclusive. "Status-based discrimination remains status based even if one of its goals or effects is preventing religious organizations from putting aid to religious uses," Chief Justice Roberts wrote for the Court.[38] As one commentator[39] suggested at the time, this statement "could indicate sympathy for Justice Gorsuch's position that status and use ultimately collapse into each other—that they are two sides of the same coin."[40] Moreover, the chief stressed that nothing in the Court's opinion was "meant to suggest that we agree with the Department [of Revenue] that some lesser degree of scrutiny applies to discrimination against

[37] Mary Ellen Klas, Ruling on Religious Schools Could Steer More Public Money to Private Schools, Tampa Bay Times (July 1, 2020), https://tinyurl.com/3u6vns45.

[38] Espinoza, 140 S. Ct. at 2256.

[39] Your scribe.

[40] Michael Bindas, The Status of Use-Based Exclusions & Educational Choice after Espinoza, 21 Federalist Soc'y Rev. 204, 216 (2020).

religious uses of government aid."[41] Finally, citing Justice Gorsuch's concurring opinion in *Trinity Lutheran*, the chief expressly acknowledged that "[s]ome Members of the Court . . . have questioned whether there is a meaningful distinction between discrimination based on use or conduct and that based on status."[42] These statements provided hope to educational-choice supporters that when the Court finally *did* reach the viability of the status/use distinction, it would put it to rest.[43]

And speaking of Justice Gorsuch . . . he again issued a concurring opinion, echoing the one he had authored in *Trinity Lutheran*.[44] "Maybe it's possible to describe what happened here as status-based discrimination," he opined, "[b]ut it seems equally, and maybe more, natural to say that the State's discrimination focused on what religious parents and schools *do*—teach religion."[45] In the end, however, he insisted that "[c]alling it discrimination on the basis of religious status or religious activity makes no difference: It is unconstitutional all the same."[46]

Justice Gorsuch was prescient.

III. *Carson v. Makin*, wherein the Status/Use Distinction Dies (Mostly)

While the Supreme Court was resolving *Espinoza*, another educational-choice case involving a religious exclusion was making its way through the lower courts. That case—the hero of our article— was *Carson v. Makin*.

---

[41] Espinoza, 140 S. Ct. at 2257. In reviewing the status-based discrimination in *Trinity Lutheran* and *Espinoza*, the Court applied "strict scrutiny"—the most searching level of judicial scrutiny and the one least deferential toward the government. "[I]n upholding the religious use-based exclusion in *Locke v. Davey*," by contrast, "the Court applied what many lower courts and commentators considered a standard short of strict scrutiny." Bindas, *supra* note 40, at 216.

[42] *Id.* (citing Trinity Lutheran, 137 S. Ct. at 2026 (Gorsuch, J., concurring in part)).

[43] See Bindas, *supra* note 40, at 117–18.

[44] Justices Thomas and Alito also authored concurring opinions. Justice Alito's focused on the bigoted origins of the Blaine Amendments. See Espinoza, 140 S. Ct. at 2267 (Alito, J., concurring).

[45] Espinoza, 140 S. Ct. at 2275 (Gorsuch, J., concurring) (emphasis in original).

[46] *Id.*

A. *The Program and the Exclusion*

Carson concerned a tuition assistance program for high school students in Maine. The Pine Tree State has a lot of pine trees; it's pretty rural. Consequently, many towns do not operate a public high school. If a school district neither operates its own high school nor contracts with a particular private or public high school to educate the resident students of the district, the district must pay tuition, up to a statutory maximum, "at the public school or the approved private school of the parent's choice at which the student is accepted."[47]

Participating families may send their children to schools inside or outside the state—even outside the country—and school districts have paid for students to attend some of the most elite, blue-blood prep schools (think Avon Old Farms, the Taft School, and Miss Porter's).[48] But although students can—and have—attended school in Santa Barbara, California, under the program, they cannot (or, before *Carson*, could not) attend a Jewish day school in their Maine hometown, or an Islamic school, or the school in their local Catholic parish in Augusta. That is because Maine, beginning in 1980, forbade parents from choosing any school the state deemed "sectarian."

Before 1980, parents were free to choose such schools, and hundreds of students attended them annually under the program. But the state barred sectarian options after the Maine attorney general, in 1980, opined that including them as a choice in the program violated the federal Establishment Clause.[49] The legislature then codified this bar in a statute providing that a student's chosen school must be "nonsectarian."[50]

Now, it wasn't at all clear that the Establishment Clause prohibited the participation of religious schools in educational-choice programs back in 1980. But even giving the attorney general the benefit of the doubt, once the U.S. Supreme Court held, in 2002, that the Establishment Clause did *not* prohibit the participation of religious schools in educational-choice programs, it should have been pretty clear that

---

[47] Me. Stat. tit. 20-A, § 5204(4).

[48] *Id.* §§ 2951(3), 5808.

[49] Me. Op. Att'y Gen. No. 80-2 (1980).

[50] 1981 Me. Laws 2177 (codified at Me. Stat. tit. 20-A, § 2951(2)). Maine also has a tuition assistance program for elementary school students, Me. Stat. tit. 20-A, § 5203(4), and the now-invalidated sectarian exclusion in Section 2951(2) applied to it, as well.

the Establishment Clause did not prohibit the participation of religious schools in educational-choice programs.[51] Yet the state went right on excluding them.

Enter the Carsons and Nelsons. These Maine families lived in towns that neither operated a public high school nor contracted with a school to educate the resident children of the town, so they were entitled to the tuition assistance benefit. Both families thought a religious school was the best fit for their children, but that was not an option under the program. The Carsons were able to afford tuition on their own and therefore decided to forgo the benefit and send their daughter to a religious high school. The Nelsons, however, could not afford to go without the tuition assistance and so made the difficult choice to send their children to a nonreligious high school, even though they knew it was not the best school for them.

The circumstances of these two families demonstrate well the fundamental constitutional problem with Maine's religious exclusion: A family could either exercise their right to choose a religious school for their children, in which case they had to forgo their statutory right to the tuition assistance benefit, or they could exercise their statutory right to the tuition assistance benefit, in which case they had to forgo their constitutional right to send their children to a religious school. They could have one or the other, but they could not have both.

B. Litigation in the Lower Courts

In 2018—shortly after *Trinity Lutheran* had been decided but while *Espinoza* was still making its way through the lower courts—the families challenged Maine's "sectarian" exclusion in federal court, claiming it violated, among other things, their rights under the federal Free Exercise Clause. They were not the first plaintiffs to challenge the exclusion. Four other challenges, dating back to the 1990s, had been filed, and each one failed.[52] But something had happened since those earlier cases: *Trinity Lutheran*, in which the Court held that the Free Exercise Clause prohibits discrimination in public

---

[51] See Zelman v. Simmons-Harris, 536 U.S. 639 (2002).

[52] Strout v. Albanese, 178 F.3d 57 (1st Cir. 1999); Bagley v. Raymond Sch. Dep't, 728 A.2d 127 (Me. 1999); Eulitt ex rel. Eulitt v. Maine Dep't of Educ., 386 F.3d 344 (1st Cir. 2004); Anderson v. Town of Durham, 895 A.2d 944 (Me. 2006).

benefits based on religious status. Maine had long applied its sectarian exclusion based on the religious status of the excluded schools, so, in light of *Trinity Lutheran,* the exclusion seemed sure to fail.[53]

But Maine wised up. Whereas, before *Trinity Lutheran,* the state excluded schools based on religious status, the state shifted its focus to religious use in the wake of the decision. Now, as the state's commissioner of education explained during discovery in *Carson,* "affiliation or association with a church or religious institution" is "not dispositive." Rather, the Department of Education examines whether the school, "in addition to teaching academic subjects, promotes the faith or belief system with which it is associated and/or presents the material taught through the lens of this faith."[54] "The Department's focus," according to the commissioner, is "on what the school teaches through its curriculum and related activities, and how the material is presented."[55] It was clear that Maine was going to ride the status/use distinction as far as it could.

The district court ruled against the Carsons and Nelsons and upheld the religious exclusion. According to the court, the last decision of the U.S. Court of Appeals for the First Circuit upholding the sectarian exclusion[56] had not been "unmistakably cast . . . into disrepute" by *Trinity Lutheran.*[57] And why had it not, according to the district court? Because of Footnote 3.[58] "It is certainly open to the

[53] See Colo. Christian Univ. v. Weaver, 534 F.3d 1245, 1257 n.4 (10th Cir. 2008) (explaining that Maine "declined funding the entire program of education at the disfavored schools, based on their religious affiliation"); Strout, 178 F.3d at 66 (Campbell, J., concurring) ("The Maine tuition statute was narrowed in 1981 to exclude religiously-affiliated schools[.]"); Bagley, 728 A.2d at 147 (Clifford, J., dissenting) (noting the state "excludes sectarian schools from the choices available to the parents *solely* because of religious affiliation").

[54] Def. Robert G. Hasson, Jr.'s Resps. to Pls.' First Set of Interrogs. No. 7, Carson v. Makin, 142 S. Ct. 1987 (2022) (No. 20-1088).

[55] *Id.*

[56] Eulitt, 386 F.3d 344.

[57] Carson v. Makin, 401 F. Supp. 3d 207, 211 (D. Me. 2019), aff'd, 979 F.3d 21 (1st Cir. 2020), rev'd and remanded, 142 S. Ct. 1987 (2022).

[58] As the district court explained, the four justices who joined the footnote did "not address religious uses of funding," *id.* (emphasis omitted) (quoting Trinity Lutheran, 137 S. Ct. at 2024 n.3 (plurality)), and Justice Stephen Breyer, in an opinion concurring in the judgment, "le[ft] the application of the Free Exercise Clause to other kinds of public benefits for another day." *Id.* (quoting Trinity Lutheran, 137 S. Ct. at 2027 (Breyer, J., concurring in judgment)).

First Circuit" to revisit its earlier ruling, the court concluded, but "it is not my role to make that decision."[59]

The Carsons and Nelsons appealed to the First Circuit, which heard oral argument in the case on January 8, 2020, two weeks before the Supreme Court heard argument in *Espinoza*. The First Circuit, however, did not issue its opinion until four months after *Espinoza* was decided, presumably wanting to see how the Supreme Court would resolve the constitutionality of Montana's religious exclusion before ruling on the constitutionality of Maine's. The Supreme Court, of course, struck down Montana's exclusion, and the First Circuit, in turn, *upheld* Maine's.

So, what gives? Footnote 3, of course, plus a recharacterization of the tuition assistance program itself.

The First Circuit began by acknowledging that it had to consider the constitutionality of Maine's sectarian exclusion "afresh in the light of" *Espinoza*, as well as *Trinity Lutheran*.[60] But unlike the religious exclusions in those cases, the court determined, Maine's exclusion did not turn solely on religious "status"—that is, "the aid recipient's affiliation with or control by a religious institution."[61] Noting the exclusion's "'focus on what the school teaches through its curriculum and related activities, and how the material is presented,'" the court concluded that it turned on "the religious use that [the school] would make of [a student's aid] in instructing children."[62]

Having determined that the exclusion fell on the "use" side of the status/use distinction (a distinction that, again, the Supreme Court had not actually endorsed, but merely posited), the First Circuit then addressed the appropriate level of scrutiny to apply in reviewing its constitutionality. The court noted that although *Espinoza* and *Trinity Lutheran* had held that strict scrutiny—the most searching form of judicial scrutiny[63]—applies to religious status-based discrimination, those decisions "expressly left unaddressed the level of scrutiny applicable to a use-based restriction."[64] With no holding from the

---

[59] *Id.*

[60] Carson, 979 F.3d at 32, rev'd and remanded, 142 S. Ct. 1987.

[61] *Id.* at 37.

[62] *Id.* at 40 (quoting Def. Robert G. Hasson, Jr.'s Resps. to Pls.' First Set of Interrogs. No. 7).

[63] See *supra* note 42.

[64] Carson, 979 F.3d at 34.

Supreme Court on this score, the First Circuit subjected the exclusion to mere rational basis review, the least searching form of scrutiny (that is, the most deferential toward the government).[65] This, notwithstanding that the Supreme Court, in *Espinoza* itself, stated that nothing in its opinion was "meant to suggest that . . . some lesser degree of scrutiny applies to discrimination against religious uses of government aid."[66]

The First Circuit then concluded that the exclusion survived such review. In so doing, it recharacterized the benefit at issue, defining it not as the relevant statute defined it (tuition to use at a public or private school of the parent's choosing[67]), but rather as the "rough equivalent of [a Maine] public school education."[68] And because Maine can "permissibly require" a public school education "to be secular," the Court then reasoned, it can "impose[] a use-based 'non-sectarian' restriction on the public funds that it makes available for the purpose of providing a substitute for . . . public educational instruction."[69]

The First Circuit's conclusion in this regard was curious. For one thing, the schools to which the Carsons and Nelsons wanted to send their children satisfied the state's compulsory attendance laws and thus provided all the substitute for a public education the state requires. Moreover, the First Circuit's reasoning—a secular education is a nonsectarian education—was utterly tautological. In the end, the court simply redefined the benefit in a way aimed at justifying the very discrimination that Maine was engaged in—a point that, as we shall see, would not be lost on the Supreme Court.

C. SCOTUS Does the Deed

The Supreme Court granted certiorari to review the First Circuit's decision and, after five years of birthing (the idea of) a status/use distinction, put it in the ground.

The Court began by pronouncing that the case was resolved by "[t]he 'unremarkable' principles applied in *Trinity Lutheran*

---

65 *Id.* at 40 n.7.
66 Espinoza, 140 S. Ct. at 2257.
67 See Me. Stat. tit. 20-A, § 5204(4).
68 Carson, 979 F.3d at 44.
69 *Id.* at 43, 44.

and *Espinoza*."[70] Like the church-run preschool in *Trinity Lutheran* and the excluded schools in *Espinoza*, it noted, the schools to which the Carsons and Nelsons wished to send their children with the tuition benefit were "disqualified from [a] generally available benefit 'solely because of their religious *character*.'"[71]

In this light, the Court held that strict scrutiny applied to the religious exclusion and, as in *Trinity Lutheran* and *Espinoza*, had no problem concluding that the exclusion failed such review. The state's original justification for the exclusion—the attorney general's 1980 opinion that barring religious options was necessary to comply with the Establishment Clause—was no justification at all, the Court explained, because the Court had already held, in *Zelman v. Simmons-Harris*,[72] that "a neutral benefit program in which public funds flow to religious organizations through the independent choices of private benefit recipients does not offend the Establishment Clause."[73] "Maine's decision to continue excluding religious schools from its tuition assistance program after *Zelman*," the Court continued, sought to "promote[] stricter separation of church and state than the Federal Constitution requires."[74] But the Court noted that it had already held, "in both *Trinity Lutheran* and *Espinoza*, [that] such an interest in separating church and state more fiercely than the Federal Constitution . . . cannot qualify as compelling" so as to satisfy strict scrutiny.[75] The exclusion, in short, was unconstitutional.

When he got to this point in the opinion the day it came down, your scribe (also counsel for the Carsons and Nelsons) was at once relieved ("We won!") and dejected ("What about the status/use distinction?!?!"). The Court, it seemed, had once again dodged the question of whether there is a constitutionally meaningful distinction between the two forms of discrimination, and it seemed we would have to continue fighting attempts to bar religious options from educational-choice programs as opponents of those programs, like Maine had done with respect to *Espinoza*, invited lower courts

---

[70] Carson, 142 S. Ct. at 1997 (quoting Trinity Lutheran, 137 S. Ct. at 2021).

[71] *Id.* (quoting Trinity Lutheran, 137 S. Ct. at 2021) (emphasis added).

[72] See Zelman, 536 U.S. at 652–53.

[73] Carson, 142 S. Ct. at 1997.

[74] *Id.* at 1998.

[75] *Id.* (omission in original) (internal quotation marks omitted).

to simply ignore the Supreme Court's decision in *Carson*: "*That* case? No, no, no. That case was all about religious *status*. We're talking religious *use*. Totally different."

But your scribe kept reading, and suddenly the opinion—heretofore "unremarkable," in the chief justice's words—warranted remark. "The First Circuit attempted to distinguish our precedent," the Court observed, "by recharacterizing the nature of Maine's tuition assistance program in two ways, both of which Maine echoes before this Court":

> First, the panel defined the benefit at issue as the "rough equivalent of [a Maine] public school education," an education that cannot include sectarian instruction. Second, the panel defined the nature of the exclusion as one based not on a school's religious "status," as in *Trinity Lutheran* and *Espinoza*, but on religious "uses" of public funds. Neither of these formal distinctions suffices to distinguish this case from *Trinity Lutheran* or *Espinoza*, or to affect the application of the free exercise principles outlined above.[76]

Now we were getting somewhere.

Regarding the first point—the First Circuit's recharacterization of the tuition assistance program as providing the equivalent of a public education—the Supreme Court curtly noted that "the statute does not say anything like that."[77] According to the statute, the Court explained, "[t]he benefit is *tuition* at a public *or* private school, selected by the parent, with no suggestion that the 'private school' must somehow provide a 'public' education."[78]

But it wasn't just the text of the statute that belied the First Circuit's characterization, it was also the operation of the tuition assistance program. "The differences between private schools eligible to receive tuition assistance under Maine's program and a Maine public school are numerous and important," the Court observed.[79] It proceeded to list some of them. Unlike Maine public schools, participating private schools "do not have to accept all students," while "[p]ublic schools

---

[76] *Id.* (quoting *Carson*, 979 F.3d at 44) (citations omitted) (alteration in original).

[77] *Id.*

[78] *Id.* at 1998–99 (emphasis in original).

[79] *Id.* at 1999.

generally do."[80] Unlike a public education, moreover, the education provided at private schools participating in the tuition assistance program "is often *not* free"; some "charge several times the maximum benefit that Maine is willing to provide."[81] "[T]he curriculum taught at participating private schools," meanwhile, "need not even resemble that taught in the Maine public school"; in fact, schools accredited by the New England Association of Schools and Colleges (NEASC) are entirely exempt from the public schools' curricular requirements and may implement "their own chosen curriculum."[82] And unlike Maine public schools, "[p]articipating schools need not hire state-certified teachers," and they "can be single-sex."[83] "In short," the Court concluded, "it is simply not the case that these schools, to be eligible for state funds, must offer an education that is equivalent—roughly or otherwise—to that available in the Maine public schools."[84]

With the utter mismatch between the First Circuit's characterization of the program and the program's actual operation laid bare, it became clear that the First Circuit had simply allowed Maine to describe the benefit provided by the program in a way that would justify the state's discrimination. "'[T]he definition of a particular program can always be manipulated to subsume the challenged condition,'" the Court noted, "and to allow States to 'recast a condition on funding' in this manner would be to see 'the First Amendment . . . reduced to a simple semantic exercise.'"[85] As the Court pointedly observed, Montana could have characterized its program in *Espinoza* as providing a substitute for, or rough equivalent of, a public education and, under Maine and the First Circuit's logic, carried on with its discrimination.[86] The Court did not intend such a flimsy holding

---

[80] *Id.*

[81] *Id.* (emphasis in original).

[82] NEASC has no curricular requirements of its own; it applies certain "standards and indicators" to assesses how a school implements whatever curriculum it has chosen to implement. *Id.* (citing NEASC, Standards—20/20 Process (rev. Aug. 2021)), https://tinyurl.com/2s5uj3mv.

[83] *Id.*

[84] *Id.*

[85] *Id.* at 1999 (quoting Agency for Int'l Dev. v. All. for Open Soc'y Int'l, Inc., 570 U.S. 205, 215 (2013)).

[86] *Id.* at 2000.

with such an easy workaround: "[O]ur holding in *Espinoza* turned on the substance of free exercise protections, not on the presence or absence of magic words."[87]

With the attempted recharacterization of the benefit out of the way, the Court turned to the main[88] event: the status/use distinction. The Court began its consideration of that issue by recalling two statements it had made in *Espinoza*: (1) "that the strict scrutiny triggered by status-based discrimination could not be avoided by arguing that 'one of its goals or effects [was] preventing religious organizations from putting aid to religious *uses*'"; and (2) "that nothing in our analysis was 'meant to suggest that we agree[d] with [Montana] that some lesser degree of scrutiny applies to discrimination against religious uses of government aid.'"[89] *Espinoza* (and *Trinity Lutheran* before it), the Court explained, "never suggested that use-based discrimination is any less offensive to the Free Exercise Clause."[90]

The Court then explained why it had never suggested that there was a constitutionally meaningful distinction between religious status and use in those cases: teaching and passing on the faith are part and parcel of *being* a religious school. Quoting its decision in *Our Lady of Guadalupe School v. Morrissey-Berru*, the Court stressed that "[e]ducating young people in their faith, inculcating its teachings, and training them to live their faith are responsibilities that lie at the very core of the mission of a private religious school."[91] Moreover, attempting to give effect to a status/use distinction "by scrutinizing whether and how a religious school pursues its educational mission would . . . raise serious concerns about state entanglement with religion and denominational favoritism."[92]

Finally, there was the matter of *Locke v. Davey*, in which the Supreme Court itself had upheld a religious exclusion that it subsequently described as turning on the "use" to which Joshua Davey wished to put his scholarship: vocational instruction for the ministry.

---

[87] *Id.*

[88] Maine?

[89] Carson, 142 S. Ct. at 2001 (quoting Espinoza, 140 S. Ct. at 2257) (alterations in original).

[90] *Id.*

[91] *Id.* at 2001 (quoting Our Lady of Guadalupe School v. Morrissey-Berru, 140 S. Ct. 2049, 2064 (2020)) (emphasis in original).

[92] *Id.*

"*Locke*'s reasoning," the Court noted, "expressly turned on what it identified as the 'historic and substantial state interest' against using 'taxpayer funds to support church leaders.'"[93] After explaining that there was no comparable state interest against allowing state aid to flow to religious schools generally, the Court declared, "*Locke* cannot be read beyond its narrow focus on vocational religious degrees to generally authorize the State to exclude religious persons from the enjoyment of public benefits on the basis of their anticipated religious use of the benefits."[94]

And with that, the Court invalidated Maine's religious exclusion, holding that "[r]egardless of how the benefit and restriction are described"—as turning on religious status or religious use—"the program operates to identify and exclude otherwise eligible schools on the basis of their religious exercise."[95] And unlike in *Trinity Lutheran* and *Espinoza*, there were no concurring opinions this time around, no disagreement among the justices in the majority. Even Justice Gorsuch, who had tried unsuccessfully to strangle the status/use distinction in its crib, was now satisfied.

However, there were dissenting opinions—two of them. Justice Stephen Breyer, whom Justice Elena Kagan joined and Justice Sonia Sotomayor partly joined, stressed the importance of recognizing some "play in the joints" between the religion clauses of the First Amendment—the idea that there is space between what the Establishment Clause permits and what the Free Exercise Clause requires.[96] This "play," "constitutional leeway," or "wiggle room," as Justice Breyer alternatively called it, permits states to include religious options in an educational-choice program but does not *compel* them to do so.[97] "State funding of religious activity risks the very social conflict based upon religion that the Religion Clauses were designed to prevent," he opined, and maintaining some leeway between the religion clauses was necessary to "allow[] States to enact laws sensitive to local circumstances while also allowing this Court

---

[93] *Id.* at 2002 (quoting Locke, 540 U.S. at 722).

[94] *Id.*

[95] *Id.*

[96] Carson, 142 S. Ct. at 2009 (Breyer, J., dissenting).

[97] *Id.* at 2005, 2009.

to consider those circumstances in light of the basic values underlying the Religion Clauses."[98]

Justice Sotomayor authored her own dissenting opinion, and she took us back to her dissenting opinion in *Trinity Lutheran*. Whereas, in that case, Justice Gorsuch had sought to kill the status/use distinction because of its instability and the fact that "free exercise" encompasses both belief *and* action, Justice Sotomayor had sought to kill it for the opposite reason: because she viewed both status- and use-based exclusions as perfectly permissible. She reiterated that point in *Carson*, saying the "Court should not have started down this path five years ago."[99]

Justice Sotomayor also bemoaned the "practical" result of the Court's decision: it "directs the State of Maine (and, by extension, its taxpaying citizens) to subsidize institutions that undisputedly engage in religious instruction" and, "while purporting to protect against discrimination of one kind, . . . requires Maine to fund what many of its citizens believe to be discrimination of other kinds," such as discrimination based on sexual orientation or gender identity.[100] The majority directly responded to these charges, noting that the Court's decision (1) does not *require* states to subsidize private education, but simply requires religious neutrality if they decide to do so;[101] and (2) does not address whether a state may exclude schools based on their "particular policies and practices."[102]

IV. What *Carson* Means for the Educational-Choice Movement . . . and What It Doesn't Mean

Carson is hardly a simple application of "[t]he 'unremarkable' principles applied in *Trinity Lutheran* and *Espinoza*," as Chief Justice Roberts suggested.[103] It killed the status/use distinction, killed the Blaine Amendments, and effectively left *Locke v. Davey* for dead.

[98] *Id.* at 2005, 2007.

[99] Carson, 142 S. Ct. at 2012 (Sotomayor, J., dissenting).

[100] *Id.* at 2014.

[101] *Id.* at 2000 (majority op.) ("As we held in *Espinoza*, a 'State need not subsidize private education. But once a State decides to do so, it cannot disqualify some private schools solely because they are religious.'") (quoting Espinoza, 140 S. Ct. at 2261).

[102] *Id.* at 1998 n.*. As the Court noted, "the law rigidly excludes any and all sectarian schools regardless of particular characteristics." *Id.*

[103] *Id.* at 1997.

And by putting these things to rest, the Court removed the most significant legal cloud that remained over educational-choice programs: the constitutionality of state bars to religious options.

Opponents of educational choice, however, are a dogged bunch, and they will not simply pack up and go home in the wake of *Carson*. They did not do so after *Zelman*, they did not do so after *Espinoza*, and they will not do so now. There are still legal questions surrounding educational choice that *Carson* did not resolve, and opponents of choice will undoubtedly seize on those issues in their relentless campaign to remove the educational opportunity that choice programs provide.

A. Carson *Removes the Most Significant Legal Cloud Lingering Over Choice . . .*

The status/use distinction, state Blaine Amendments, and *Locke v. Davey* have been an unholy trinity for the educational-choice movement. Three entities in one anti-choice object, that trinity has been invoked in statehouses and courthouses by those seeking to prevent new choice programs from passing or to smite those that do pass. No more.

1. The Status/Use Distinction: Gone

Perhaps the most obvious consequence of the *Carson* decision is that opponents of educational choice can no longer argue that religious use-based exclusions in educational-choice programs are permissible. Use-based discrimination is no less offensive to the Free Exercise Clause than status-based discrimination is, the Court explained, in part because "[e]ducating young people in their faith . . . lie[s] at the very core of the mission of a private religious school."[104] In other words, the religious "use" that Maine found offensive flows *directly from* the religious status of the excluded schools. Discrimination against them because of their religious conduct is discrimination against the religious status that impels that conduct. Of course, the same is true of the parents who choose such schools, whose religious status impels them to seek a religious education for their child.

Carson, moreover, eliminates the status/use distinction in areas beyond educational choice. Although the case concerned an

---

[104] *Id.* at 2001 (quoting Our Lady of Guadalupe, 140 S. Ct. at 2064).

educational-choice program, in which aid is provided to *individuals* and flows to schools only by the intermediating choice of parents, the language of the opinion reaches institutional aid scenarios as well. The Court, after all, dismissed the status/use distinction as one of "form[]," rather than substance, and one that did not "suffice[] to distinguish this case from *Trinity Lutheran* or *Espinoza,* or to affect the application of the free exercise principles outlined" in those cases.[105] While *Espinoza,* like *Carson,* was an educational-choice (individual aid) case, *Trinity Lutheran* was not: it involved direct, monetary assistance to a religious institution. Yet *Carson* says the same free-exercise principles apply in both contexts. Moreover, the Court stressed that the difficulty Maine encountered in enforcing its use-based exclusion "suggests that *any* status-use distinction lacks a meaningful application not only in theory, but in practice as well."[106]

This last point was not lost on Justice Sotomayor in dissent, who regretted that her "fear has come to fruition: The Court now holds for the first time that 'any status-use distinction' is immaterial in both 'theory' and 'practice.'"[107] In her view, it seems, *Carson* is an "unequivocal rejection of the status/use distinction," one that not only prevents reliance on a status/use distinction to bar religious options from educational-choice programs, but also "ensures that states and lower courts can no longer rely on arguments about religious 'use' to deny religious organizations equal access to generally available government funding programs."[108]

2. Blaine Amendments: Gone

Carson also finished the job of killing off the Blaine Amendments as obstacles to educational choice.[109] *Espinoza,* of course, had already done much of that work. Montana had argued that compliance with

---

[105] *Id.* at 1998.

[106] *Id.* (emphasis added).

[107] *Id.* at 2013 (Sotomayor, J., dissenting).

[108] Nick Reaves, Religious Autonomy in Carson v. Makin, Harv. J.L. & Pub. Pol'y Per Curiam (Summer 2022 No. 18), https://tinyurl.com/5aykasmy.

[109] Although *Carson* removed conventional Blaine Amendments (those that bar aid to religious schools) as obstacles to choice, there are Blaine variants, sometimes referred to as "public/private" Blaine Amendments, which prohibit aid to *all* private schools, whether religious or not. As discussed *infra* Part IV.B.2. these provisions remain an obstacle to choice in a small handful of states.

its Blaine Amendment justified its exclusion of religious options from the state's educational-choice program. The Supreme Court rejected that argument, observing that the text of the state's Blaine Amendment "discriminates based on religious status" and "bars religious schools from public benefits solely because of the religious character of the schools."[110] Applying that status-based provision to bar religious options from an educational-choice program, the Court held, violated the Free Exercise Clause of the federal Constitution.

But Blaine Amendments can be couched in more "use"-based language, as well. In addition to barring public funding to schools or other institutions that *are* religious (in the words of Montana's Blaine Amendment, schools "controlled in whole or in part by any church, sect, or denomination"[111]), many Blaine Amendments target specific religious conduct. Those of Arizona, Utah, and Washington, for example, provide that "[n]o public money or property shall be appropriated for or applied to any religious worship, exercise, or instruction."[112] After *Espinoza* was decided, educational-choice opponents could argue that such use-based language was still enforceable, given that *Espinoza* turned solely on the status-based proscription in the text of Montana's Blaine Amendment.

That argument, thankfully, is now gone. Interestingly, it is gone because of a decision in a case arising out of Maine, which, although the home state of James G. Blaine, does not have a Blaine Amendment. Rather, Maine's sectarian exclusion was rooted in statute alone. Yet the Supreme Court's invalidation of the statute makes perfectly clear that, even if the statute had instead been a state constitutional provision, it would have been just as doomed under the Free Exercise Clause. The Court, after all, directly analogized Maine's statute to Montana's Blaine Amendment: "While the wording of the Montana and Maine provisions is different," the Court noted, "their effect is the same." Both, in other words, impermissibly target religious exercise. So, although "*Espinoza* held that a provision of the Montana Constitution barring government aid to any school 'controlled in whole or in part by any church, sect, or denomination' violated the Free Exercise Clause," a Blaine Amendment that employs more

---

[110] Espinoza, 140 S. Ct. at 2255, 2256.

[111] Mont. Const. art. X, § 6(1).

[112] Ariz. Const. art. II, § 12; Utah Const. art. I, § 4; Wash. Const. art. I, § 11.

"usey" language (e.g., "religious worship, exercise, or instruction") will unquestionably meet the same fate in the wake of *Carson*.

3. *Locke v. Davey*: (Mostly) Gone

And although we cannot quite bid *Locke v. Davey* good riddance, that opinion is unlikely to show its face around the educational-choice debate anymore. For nearly two decades, it was the favorite case of the National Education Association (NEA) and other opponents of educational choice, who would trot it out to legislators and judges and say, "Look, state law *can* bar educational-choice programs that include religious options." And those legislators and judges were often convinced. In fact, the *last* time it upheld Maine's sectarian exclusion, the First Circuit read *Locke* "broadly," well beyond its focus on vocational religious instruction.[113] The court refused to "restrict its teachings to the context of funding instruction for those training to enter religious ministries," or to limit it "to certain education funding decisions but not others."[114] In other words, the court read it as authorizing the wholesale exclusion of religious options in educational-choice programs.

In *Carson*, the Supreme Court flatly rejected such a reading of *Locke* and expressly cabined the decision to the vocational religious instruction at issue in the case: "*Locke* cannot be read beyond its narrow focus on vocational religious degrees to generally authorize the State to exclude religious persons from the enjoyment of public benefits on the basis of their anticipated religious use of the benefits."[115] Short of overruling it or limiting it to litigants named Gary Locke and Joshua Davey, the Court could have done nothing more to make clear there is no more mileage left in *Locke*.

B. . . . *but the Legal Battles Regarding Choice Are Not Over*

With so much resolved, there is lots to celebrate. But as discussed below, several federal constitutional questions concerning educational choice remain unanswered after *Carson*: for example, whether participation in educational-choice programs may be conditioned on a school's compliance with nondiscrimination requirements

---

[113] Eulitt, 386 F.3d at 355.

[114] *Id.*

[115] Carson, 142 S. Ct. at 2002.

concerning sexual orientation and gender identity; the federal constitutionality of applying "public/private" Blaine Amendments to bar educational-choice programs; and the constitutionality of religious charter schools.

There are, to be sure, other issues that will need to be resolved. Robert Chanin, former chief counsel for the NEA, once vowed that educational-choice opponents would attack choice programs under any "Mickey Mouse provisions" they could find in state constitutions.[116] After their loss in *Carson*, the NEA and its cronies will no doubt get mousier, but the battles they wage will increasingly turn on state, not federal, law. Only the remaining federal issues are discussed below.

1. Sexual Orientation and Gender Identity Conditions

No sooner had the Court's Public Information Office made the *Carson* opinion available than Maine Attorney General Aaron Frey fired off a press release continuing to defend the very religious discrimination the Court had just held unconstitutional.[117] Rather than undertaking a sober reflection of the opinion and what it required of the state, Attorney General Frey attacked the schools that the Carsons and Nelsons desired for their children, criticizing them for their religious beliefs and calling them "inimical" to and "fundamentally at odds with values we hold dear," such as "tolerance," "understanding," and "divers[ity]."[118] Then, apparently not having learned the lesson of *Masterpiece Cakeshop*[119]—and apparently forgetting that it was an erroneous opinion of the Maine attorney general that embroiled the state in *Carson* and four other lawsuits spanning three decades—Attorney General Frey announced his "inten[t] to

---

[116] Clint Bolick, David's Hammer: The Case for an Activist Judiciary 138 (2007).

[117] Office of the Maine Att'y Gen., Statement of the Maine Attorney General Aaron Frey on Supreme Court Decision in Carson v. Makin (June 21, 2002), https://tinyurl.com/4vt3wacu.

[118] *Id.*

[119] Masterpiece Cakeshop, Ltd. v. Colo. Civ. Rights Comm'n, 138 S. Ct. 1719, 1732 (2018) (invalidating, under the Free Exercise Clause, a remedial order of the Colorado Civil Rights Commission ordering the defendant to serve same-sex couples, in part because public comments of the commission members evinced hostility toward the defendant's religious views). Note to public officials: If you don't like someone's religious views, don't say so publicly.

explore with Governor Mills's administration and members of the Legislature statutory amendments to address the Court's decision and ensure that public money is not used to promote discrimination, intolerance, and bigotry."

Commentators cheered on Attorney General Frey, urging him to "outmaneuver" the United States Supreme Court and "avoid the consequences of [its] ruling."[120] How? By banning the Carsons' and Nelsons' chosen schools because of their views and policies on sexual orientation and gender identity.

Now, this article is not going to attempt to resolve—or even wade into—the debate over whether state anti-discrimination laws can be enforced to bar religious persons or organizations from otherwise available public benefit programs because of their policies on things such as same-sex marriage or the nature of sex/gender. The Supreme Court will presumably resolve those issues in time, and your scribe trusts that it will resolve them with respect and tolerance for the concerns of both advocates for LGBTQ rights and advocates for religious liberty.[121] Suffice it to say that *Carson* did not resolve them, because Maine barred *all* religious schools, regardless of their policies on such issues[122]—a fact the Kent School found out when it was barred under the religious exclusion even though it does "not tolerate discrimination against students or employees based on," among other grounds, "religious creed," "sex," "sexual orientation," and "gender identity."[123]

2. "Public/Private" Blaine Amendments

Nor does *Carson* resolve the federal constitutionality of applying so-called public/private Blaine Amendments to bar educational-choice programs entirely. Public/private Blaine Amendments prohibit aid

---

[120] Aaron Tang, There's a Way to Outmaneuver the Supreme Court, and Maine Has Found It, N.Y. Times (June 23, 2022), https://tinyurl.com/2p8muhd6. Note to everyone, including public officials: If your goal is to "outmaneuver" the Supreme Court to "avoid" its rulings, don't say so publicly.

[121] Similar issues are already being litigated in the lower courts. See Reaves, *supra* note 109, at 7 & nn.53–54.

[122] Carson, 142 S. Ct. at 1998 n.*. One commentator, however, has observed that in resolving *Carson*, the Court relied on the religious autonomy principles underlying cases such as *Our Lady of Guadalupe* and *Hosanna-Tabor Evangelical Lutheran Church & School v. EEOC*, and, in his view, "confirmed that religious organizations must have the freedom to operate in accordance with their beliefs." Reaves, *supra* note 109, at 1, 4–5, 7.

[123] Welcome from Old Main, Kent-School.edu, https://tinyurl.com/bdzh3v9a.

to *all* private schools, whether religious or nonreligious. Alaska's is representative: "No money shall be paid from public funds for the direct benefit of any religious or other private educational institution."[124]

While quite a few states have such provisions, most state courts have appropriately interpreted them as barring only aid to private *schools*—not aid to students who attend private schools. Thus, jurisprudence in most states with these provisions allows for private educational choice. But in a few states—for example, Alaska, Massachusetts, and Hawaii—courts have interpreted them to preclude even programs that aid students.[125]

Applying these provisions to bar educational-choice programs violates the federal Constitution, notwithstanding the fact that, unlike conventional Blaine Amendments, they are neutral with respect to religion, at least in their language.[126] For one thing, they condition availability of a public benefit on parents' surrender of their constitutional right, recognized in *Pierce v. Society of Sisters*,[127] to send their child to a private school, much the same way Montana and Maine conditioned the availability of an otherwise available public benefit on the surrender of parents' right to choose a specifically religious private school for their child.[128] Moreover, the Supreme Court has long held that "the First Amendment bars application of [even] a neutral, generally applicable law" if it burdens conduct involving certain "hybrid" rights, including, specifically, the free exercise of

---

[124] Alaska Const. art. VII, § 1.

[125] See, e.g., Opinion of Justices to Senate, 514 N.E.2d 353 (Mass. 1987); Sheldon Jackson Coll. v. State, 599 P.2d 127 (Alaska 1979); Bloom v. Sch. Comm. of Springfield, 379 N.E.2d 578 (Mass. 1978); Spears v. Honda, 449 P.2d 130 (Haw. 1969).

[126] While they are neutral in their language, such provisions have the same object as, and were motivated by the same animus underlying, conventional Blaine Amendments, which can give rise to free exercise problems. See Masterpiece Cakeshop, 138 S. Ct. 1719; Church of the Lukumi Babalu Aye, Inc. v. City of Hialeah, 508 U.S. 520, 531–46 (1993).

[127] 268 U.S. 510 (1925).

[128] See Espinoza, 140 S. Ct. at 2261 (recognizing that parents have "the right[] . . . to direct the religious upbringing of their children," that "[m]any parents exercise that right by sending their children to religious schools," and that Montana's Blaine Amendment "penalizes that decision by cutting families off from otherwise available benefits if they choose a religious private school rather than a secular one") (internal quotation marks and citations omitted).

religion combined with "the right of parents . . . to direct the education of their children."[129] And "public/private" Blaine Amendments create a structural barrier that, like the state constitutional amendment invalidated by the Supreme Court in *Romer v. Evans*,[130] makes it "more difficult for one group of citizens than for all others to seek aid from the government," which "is itself a denial of equal protection of the laws in the most literal sense."[131] *Carson* does not speak to these issues, but they will undoubtedly be litigated in future cases.

3. Religious Charter Schools

Finally, and despite an abundance of media commentary suggesting otherwise, *Carson* was never going to resolve the question of whether states with charter school laws may or must allow for religious charter schools. Charter schools "are privately operated but publicly funded," and "they are universally designated by law to be 'public schools.'"[132] Some within the educational-choice movement, however, argue that they are not state actors for federal constitutional purposes and, thus, are "essentially programs of private-school choice."[133] Others within the educational-choice movement, including the National Alliance for Public Charter Schools, disagree strongly.[134]

Carson does nothing to resolve that disagreement. It did not involve charter schools and does not bear on the question of whether they are state actors and, thus, subject to the restrictions of the

---

[129] Emp. Div. v. Smith, 494 U.S. 872, 881 (1990); see also Danville Christian Acad., Inc. v. Beshear, 141 S. Ct. 527, 529 (2020) (Gorsuch, J., dissenting from denial of application to vacate stay).

[130] 517 U.S. 620 (1996).

[131] *Id.* at 633.

[132] Nicole Garnett, Are Religious Charter Schools Coming Soon?, N.Y. Daily News (June 27, 2022), https://tinyurl.com/bdz8yrfr.

[133] *Id.*; see also Nicole Stelle Garnett, Religious Charter Schools: Legally Permissible? Constitutionally Required?, Manhattan Inst. (Dec. 1, 2020), https://tinyurl.com/2p8brta4.

[134] See, e.g., Lisa Scruggs, Separation of Church and School: Guidance for Public Charter Schools Using Religious Facilities, Nat'l All. for Public Sch. (2015), https://tinyurl.com/yj49kmd7 ("Public schools, whether traditional or charter, are generally considered government entities. Accordingly, like all government actors, they must comply with the Establishment Clause, which is part of the First Amendment to the U.S. Constitution.").

Establishment Clause. The question of religious charter schools, therefore, will have to await another day.

Conclusion

Carson will forever be associated with *Trinity Lutheran* and *Espinoza*, and rightly so. But it is also the bookend to another decision: *Zelman*. In *Zelman*, the Court held that the Establishment Clause permits religious options in educational-choice programs, and in *Carson*, it held that the Free Exercise Clause prohibits their exclusion, regardless of whether that exclusion is couched in terms of status or use. The two primary federal constitutional issues that have plagued the modern educational-choice movement have now been resolved, and they have been resolved resoundingly in favor of choice. The war will go on, because, again, the enemies of choice are a dogged bunch. But the two major battles have been won.

The State Secrets Sidestep: *Zubaydah* and *Fazaga* Offer Little Guidance on Core Questions of Accountability

By Elizabeth Goitein*

Introduction

Since the Supreme Court first recognized the state secrets evidentiary privilege in 1953, courts have struggled with basic questions about the privilege and its application. Does the privilege have roots in Article II of the Constitution, or is it solely a common-law doctrine? Can the privilege render an entire case nonjusticiable, and if so, under what circumstances? When is it appropriate to dismiss a case based on an assertion that specific items of evidence are privileged? Does a law addressing the use of sensitive national security information in certain proceedings preempt the procedures that would otherwise apply when the government asserts the privilege? How much deference do courts owe the executive branch's claims of national security harm?

When the Supreme Court granted certiorari in two cases involving assertions of the state secrets privilege—*United States v. Husayn, aka Zubaydah, et al.*[1] and *FBI v. Fazaga*[2]—observers speculated that the Court might finally provide clarity on these matters. The Court, however, took pains to avoid the primary questions that have occupied courts and commentators. Indeed, the Court in *Fazaga* went so far as to concoct a false resolution to the parties' dispute as a means of avoiding the constitutional and statutory interpretation questions the case presented.

That's not to say that the Court left matters as they were before its rulings. In *Zubaydah*, the Court created a dangerous new precedent by upholding an invocation of the privilege to shield information

---

* Senior director, Liberty and National Security Program, Brennan Center for Justice at NYU School of Law.

[1] 142 S. Ct. 959 (2022).

[2] 142 S. Ct. 1051 (2022).

that is a matter of public record. In doing so, the Court exhibited an unwarranted degree of deference to the government's national security claims. The Court, however, was not faced with the question of whether to review the privileged evidence *in camera*—the context in which the issue of deference typically arises. Moreover, the Court's decision to order dismissal of the lawsuit turned on the unique nature of the proceedings authorized by the statute at issue and should have little precedential value for cases arising under other laws.

As for the Court's decision in *Fazaga*, it did not simply fail to shed light on the issues raised by the case. It further muddied the waters with a ruling that generates more conceptual problems than it resolves. The case involved a provision of the Foreign Intelligence Surveillance Act (FISA) that requires courts to follow certain procedures in cases involving FISA surveillance when the executive branch claims that disclosure of evidence through litigation would harm national security. The question before the Court was whether these statutory procedures take precedence over conflicting common-law procedures that may be triggered by a claim of privilege. Rather than decide this question, the Court held that the two procedural schemes are not irreconcilable precisely because they are different. This incoherent conclusion leaves the district court—and future courts faced with similar dilemmas—with no workable guidance for handling the cases before them.

This article proceeds as follows. Part I describes the two versions of the state secrets privilege—one a nonjusticiability rule, the other an evidentiary doctrine—and the foundational cases that established them. Part II presents the thorny questions raised in recent decades by the application of the privilege. Parts III and IV discuss the Court's rulings in *Zubaydah* and *Fazaga*, showing how they fail both on their own terms and as answers to the questions outlined in part II. The conclusion briefly argues that Congress should step in to supply the clarity the Court failed to provide.

I. The Foundational Cases: *Totten* and *Reynolds*

There are two distinct version of the state secrets privilege. First, it can operate as a bar to justiciability in an extremely narrow category of cases that generally involve government contracts. Second, and far more commonly, it can operate as an evidentiary privilege, preventing the introduction of privileged evidence in civil lawsuits or criminal cases. *Zubaydah* and *Fazaga* involve the latter version, but it is important to understand both, as the executive branch has made a concerted effort, with some success, to conflate the two.

A Civil War-era case, *Totten v. United States*,[3] established the first version of the privilege. In *Totten*, the administrator of a Union spy's estate alleged that the United States had defaulted on an espionage contract signed by President Abraham Lincoln. The Court noted that "[t]he service stipulated by the contract was a secret service . . . the employment and the service were to be equally concealed."[4] Thus, "[b]oth employer and agent must have understood that the lips of the other were to be for ever sealed respecting the relation of either to the matter."[5] The Court concluded that "[t]he secrecy which such contracts impose precludes any action for their enforcement. The publicity produced by any such action would itself be a breach of contract of that kind, and thus defeat a recovery."[6] In what was arguably *dicta*, the Court went on to state: "It may be stated as a general principle, that public policy prohibits the maintenance of any suit in a court of justice, the trial of which would inevitably lead to the disclosure of matters which the law itself regards as confidential, and respecting which it will not allow the confidence to be violated."[7]

The Supreme Court has described *Totten* as articulating a rule "prohibiting suits against the Government based on covert espionage agreements."[8] Reflecting that understanding, courts generally have limited their application of *Totten* to cases involving secret contracts with the government, where the contracting party was on notice that the contract was unenforceable in court. The Supreme Court has invoked *Totten* in only one case that did not involve such a contract: *Weinberger v. Catholic Action of Hawaii/Peace Education Project*.[9] There, the goal of the suit was to compel the preparation and public disclosure of an environmental impact statement (EIS) for a Navy storage facility that the plaintiffs believed would house nuclear weapons. Such a statement would

---

[3] 92 U.S. 105 (1875).

[4] *Id.* at 106.

[5] *Id.*

[6] *Id.* at 107.

[7] *Id.*

[8] Tenet v. Doe, 544 U.S. 1, 3 (2005).

[9] 454 U.S. 139 (1981).

only be required, however, if the Navy in fact planned to store nuclear weapons at the facility—a fact the Navy could neither confirm nor deny without harming national security. The Court thus held that the question was not subject to judicial scrutiny under the logic of *Totten*.[10]

The second version of the privilege was established in 1953 in the case of *United States v. Reynolds*.[11] The lawsuit was brought by the widows of three civilian observers who were killed when a B-29 aircraft caught fire and crashed during a test flight. The widows sued the Air Force, alleging negligence, and sought to obtain the official accident report during discovery. The government invoked "the privilege against revealing military secrets,"[12] claiming that the aircraft was on a "confidential mission" and carried "confidential equipment on board."[13]

The Court noted that the asserted privilege "is well established in the law of evidence."[14] It observed that the privilege "is not to be lightly invoked," and that there must be a formal claim of privilege lodged by the head of the relevant agency after personal consideration of the matter.[15] At that point, "[t]he court itself must determine whether the circumstances are appropriate for the claim

---

[10] See *id.* at 146–47. It is difficult to reconcile this invocation of *Totten* with the Supreme Court's pronouncements in other cases, most recently *General Dynamics Corp. v. United States*, to the effect that *Totten* is limited to cases involving secret contracts. See Gen. Dynamics Corp. v. United States, 563 U.S. 478, 485 (2011). Indeed, the Court's description of the dilemma in *Weinberger* more closely tracks the application of *United States v. Reynolds* in situations where the privilege shields evidence that the plaintiffs would need to establish a prima facie case. United States v. Reynolds, 345 U.S. 1 (1953). Compare Weinberger, 454 U.S. at 146 (observing that "it has not been and cannot be established that the Navy has proposed the . . . action that would require the preparation of an EIS") with Mohamed v. Jeppesen Dataplan, 614 F.3d 1070, 1083 (9th Cir. 2010) (holding that a privilege claim under *Reynolds* may lead to dismissal of the case "if the plaintiff cannot prove the prima facie elements of her claim with nonprivileged evidence") (internal quotation marks and citation omitted). For this reason, scholars have suggested that the citation to *Totten* in *Weinberger* is best seen as an anomaly rather than a reframing of the rule. See, e.g., Matthew Plunkett, The Transformation of the State Secrets Doctrine through Conflation of Reynolds and Totten: The Problems with Jeppesen and El-Masri, 2 U.C. Irvine L. Rev. 809 (2012).

[11] 345 U.S. 1 (1953).

[12] *Id.* at 6.

[13] Herring v. United States, 424 F.3d 384, 392 (3d Cir. 2005) (quoting from the formal privilege claim entered in *Reynolds*).

[14] Reynolds, 345 U.S. at 6–7.

[15] *Id.* at 7.

of privilege."[16] In some cases, "it may be possible" for the court to rule on the claim without reviewing the evidence itself; in others, *in camera* review might be necessary.[17] The nongovernment party's need for the information in question "will determine how far the court should probe in satisfying itself that the occasion for invoking the privilege is appropriate."[18]

The Court upheld the government's privilege claim without reviewing the accident report. It found that "there was a reasonable danger that the accident investigation report would contain references to the secret electronic equipment which was the primary concern of the mission."[19] It further found that the plaintiffs had other means by which they could prove negligence and therefore had not made the showing of necessity that would have justified further probing by the Court. Notably, the Court did not order the case dismissed; it remanded the case to the district court for further proceedings, and the plaintiffs ultimately reached a settlement with the government.

As recently as 2011, the Supreme Court in *General Dynamics Corp. v. United States*[20] underscored that *Totten* and *Reynolds* are separate doctrines. *General Dynamics* presented a dispute over a government contract that involved classified matters. The government asserted the state secrets privilege and sought dismissal of the suit. Citing *dicta* in *Reynolds*, the parties argued over whether the government should have to forfeit the claim to which the privileged evidence pertained. A unanimous Court, however, noted that "*Reynolds* has less to do with these cases than parties believe."[21] In *Reynolds*, the Court had "decided a purely evidentiary dispute by applying evidentiary rules: The privileged information is excluded and the trial goes on without it."[22] In contrast, the Court observed, "[w]hat we are called upon to exercise is not our power to determine the procedural rules of evidence, but our common-law authority to fashion contractual remedies in Government-contracting disputes."[23] That authority was

---

[16] *Id.* at 8.
[17] *Id.* at 10.
[18] *Id.* at 11.
[19] *Id.* at 10.
[20] 563 U.S. 478 (2011).
[21] *Id.* at 485.
[22] *Id.*
[23] *Id.*

the subject of *Totten* and its progeny, which established the rule that "public policy forbids suits based on covert espionage agreements."[24]

II. Concerns Arising from Post-9/11 Uses

A. Dismissal on the Pleadings

During the 50 years that followed *Reynolds*, the privilege was invoked relatively sparingly and with little public controversy. In the wake of 9/11, however, there was a marked uptick in the number of state secrets privilege assertions by the executive branch.[25] At the same time, the George W. Bush administration began to explicitly conflate the *Reynolds* and *Totten* doctrines. It argued that lawsuits having nothing to do with contract disputes could not be litigated, and must be dismissed at the outset, because the "very subject matter" of the suit—language the *Reynolds* Court had used to describe the reasoning in *Totten*[26]—was a state secret.[27] The administration made this claim in lawsuits challenging a range of government abuses and constitutional violations that took place after 9/11, most notably "extraordinary rendition" (the practice of kidnapping individuals and sending them to other countries to be tortured)[28] and illegal surveillance.[29]

President Barack Obama criticized the Bush administration's frequent use of the privilege to get cases thrown out of court and

[24] *Id.* at 486 (internal quotation marks and citation omitted).

[25] See generally Daniel R. Cassman, Keep It Secret, Keep It Safe: An Empirical Analysis of the State Secrets Doctrine, 67 Stan. L. Rev. 1173 (2015).

[26] Reynolds, 345 U.S. at 11 n.26.

[27] See generally Amanda Frost, The State Secrets Privilege and the Separation of Powers, 75 Fordham L. Rev. 1931 (2007).

[28] See, e.g., Mem. of the United States In Sup. of Motion to Dismiss at 2, Mohamed v. Jeppesen Dataplan, Inc., 539 F. Supp. 2d 1128 (N.D. Cal. 2008) (No. C-07-02798-JW), ECF No. 43; Appellee's Br. at 13, El-Masri v. United States, 479 F.3d 296 (4th Cir. 2007) (No. 06-1667), ECF No. 80; Reply of the United States of America to Plaintiffs' Opp. to United States' Invocation of the State Secrets Privilege at 7, Arar v. Ashcroft, 414 F. Supp. 2d 250 (E.D.N.Y. 2006) (No. 1:04-cv-00249-DGT-SMG), ECF No. 72.

[29] See, e.g., In Sup. of the United States' Assertion of the Mil. and State Secrets Privilege at 7, Al-Haramain Islamic Foundation v. Bush, 451 F. Supp. 2d 1215 (D. Or. 2006) (No. 06-274-KI), ECF No. 59; Mem. of the United States In Sup. of the Mil. and State Secrets Privilege and Motion to Dismiss at 15, Hepting v. AT&T Corp., 439 F. Supp. 2d 974 (N.D. Cal. 2006) (No. 4:06-cv-00672-JSW), ECF No. 124; Mem. of Points and Authorities In Sup. of the United States' Assertion of the Mil. and State Secrets Privilege at 5, American Civil Liberties Union v. NSA, 438 F. Supp. 2d 754 (E.D. Mich. 2006) (No. 2:06-cv-10204-ADT-RSW), ECF No. 34.

promised to use the privilege more judiciously.[30] In September 2009, Attorney General Eric Holder issued a policy that purported to establish a higher standard for invoking the privilege and required privilege assertions to go through various layers of internal approval.[31] In practice, however, the policy changed nothing. Following a review of pending cases, the Department of Justice decided to continue pressing the Bush administration's arguments in all of them.[32] The department took a similar approach in subsequent lawsuits, urging courts to dismiss plaintiffs' claims on the pleadings before any discovery had taken place—that is, before the relevant evidence had been identified, let alone reviewed for privilege.

Some courts were receptive to the executive branch's attempts to erase the distinction between the *Reynolds* and *Totten* doctrines. They agreed that the subject of the lawsuit was a state secret, and they dismissed the case without ever reviewing or ruling on any specific items of evidence. Other courts insisted that they must rely on *Reynolds* alone and treat the state secrets doctrine as an evidentiary privilege, not a justiciability bar. Yet they, too, frequently dismissed cases or claims at the pleadings stage. Over time, three scenarios emerged[33] in which courts were willing to dismiss claims at the outset of litigation based on a purported application of the *Reynolds* privilege:

(1) Plaintiffs cannot make out a prima facie case without using privileged evidence.[34]

(2) Defendants cannot mount their defense without using privileged evidence.[35]

---

[30] See Andrew Malcolm, Obama White House Breaks Another Promise to Reject Bush Secrecy, L.A. Times (Jul. 22, 2009), https://lat.ms/3JsIKyW.

[31] See Dep't of Justice, Mem. from the Att'y Gen., Policies and Procedures Governing Invocation of the State Secrets Privilege (Sept. 13, 2009), https://bit.ly/3Q4DHGW.

[32] See Letter from Ronald Weich, Ass't Att'y Gen., to Patrick J. Leahy, Chairman, S. Comm. on the Judiciary (Apr. 29, 2011), https://bit.ly/3cU3i73.

[33] These three scenarios are succinctly summarized by the Ninth Circuit in Mohamed v. Jeppesen Dataplan, 614 F.3d 1070, 1083 (9th Cir. 2010).

[34] See, e.g., Halkin v. Helms, 690 F.2d 977 (D.C. Cir. 1982).

[35] See, e.g., Molerio v. FBI, 749 F.2d 815, 822 (D.C. Cir. 1984). Some courts have required that the defense be "meritorious," not merely "colorable," on the ground that "it would be manifestly unfair to a plaintiff to impose a presumption that the defendant has a valid defense that is obscured by the privilege." In Re Sealed Case, 494 F.3d 139, 149–50 (D.C. Cir. 2007).

(3) Privileged information is so central to the case that any attempt to disentangle it from nonprivileged information might fail, leading to inadvertent disclosures of privileged information.[36]

Of these three scenarios, only the first reflects the proper application of an evidentiary privilege, and even then only in part. When evidence is subject to a legal privilege—whether attorney-client, therapist-patient, marital confidence, or any other—the general rule is that the case simply proceeds without that evidence. In a situation where removal of the privileged material leaves plaintiffs with insufficient evidence to establish a prima facie case, they will be unable to overcome a motion for summary judgment, and the lawsuit will be dismissed.

Even in such cases, however, dismissal should not take place at the pleadings stage. Until the relevant evidence has been identified through discovery and the court has determined which evidence is privileged, the court cannot fairly conclude that plaintiffs lack sufficient nonprivileged evidence to continue. Without following this process, the court is simply making a prediction—or, more accurately, accepting the government's prediction—as to what the evidence in the case will be. Whatever one might think of this approach, it is not how evidentiary privileges ordinarily work. In no other context do courts dismiss cases based on parties' predictions of how the evidentiary disputes in the case will be resolved.

The second scenario is even less defensible. If courts were truly treating the state secrets doctrine as an evidentiary privilege, it would be irrelevant whether defendants needed privileged evidence to mount a valid defense. The evidence would simply drop out of the case, and the chips would fall where they may.[37] In some cases, the general rule that the lawsuit goes forward without the privileged evidence might result in grievous wrongs against plaintiffs going unrighted; in others, defendants might be held accountable

---

[36] See, e.g., Jeppesen, 614 F.3d at 1087–88; El-Masri v. United States, 479 F.3d 276, 308 (4th Cir. 2007).

[37] See Charles T. McCormick, McCormick's Handbook of the Law of Evidence 233 (E. Cleary ed., 1972) ("[T]he result" of a successful claim of privilege "is simply that the evidence is unavailable, as though a witness had died, and the case will proceed accordingly, with no consequences save those resulting from the loss of the evidence.").

for wrongs they did not commit. The courts' approach to the state secrets privilege, by contrast, imposes a "heads-we-win, tails-you-lose" rule, where the harms of withdrawing the evidence are always visited on the plaintiff, never the defendant. That approach is particularly unsound when the defendant is the party invoking the privilege and can accordingly choose whether asserting it is worth forfeiting a defense.

The third scenario is simply the subject-matter privilege by another name. Some courts have acknowledged this, while others have gamely attempted to distinguish this circumstance from *Totten*. In fact, there is no functional distinction between dismissing a case at the outset because the "very subject matter" of the case is a state secret, and dismissing a case at the outset because state secrets are so central to the case that they are bound to arise. And once again—as in the first and second scenarios—the court's assessment of the centrality of state secrets turns on a *prediction* about the evidence in the case, uninformed by the actual evidence itself. In short, nothing about this scenario resembles the manner in which courts apply any of the other evidentiary privileges that routinely come before them in civil or criminal cases.

B. Common Law or Constitution?

In addition to conflating *Reynolds* and *Totten*, the lawsuits challenging unlawful surveillance after 9/11 surfaced two foundational questions about the state secrets privilege that the Supreme Court has never answered: To what extent does the privilege have roots in the Constitution, as well as the common law, and how should that affect courts' analysis of legislation touching on the privilege?

In *Reynolds*, the Court asserted that the state secrets privilege is "well established in the law of evidence"; the Court did not find that the privilege also had origins in the Constitution. However, in another context—involving the president's authority to withhold security clearances from federal employees—the Court held that the president's "authority to classify and control access to information bearing on national security . . . flows primarily from [the Commander-in-Chief Clause's] constitutional investment of power in the President."[38] In addition, in a case involving the presidential communications privilege,

---

[38] Dep't of the Navy v. Egan, 484 U.S. 518, 527 (1988).

the Court noted in *dicta* that "military or diplomatic secrets" implicate "Art. II duties" and that "the courts have traditionally shown the utmost deference to [these] Presidential responsibilities."[39] Extrapolating from these statements, some lower courts have asserted that the state secrets privilege has "a constitutional dimension."[40]

Of course, even if the privilege were entirely constitutional in origin, that would not mean Congress could not regulate it. Under the famous three-part test Justice Robert Jackson set forth in his concurrence in *Youngstown Sheet & Tube Co. v. Sawyer*, Congress is barred from constraining a president's exercise of constitutional powers only where those powers are "conclusive and preclusive," and Congress itself is without any constitutional authority to act.[41] In the many areas in which the president and Congress share power, Congress may exercise its own constitutional authorities even if they tread on those of the president. Control of national security information falls into this shared-power category, as is evident from the many laws Congress has passed on this subject over the past century—including the National Security Act of 1947 (requiring protection of national-security information but also requiring disclosures to Congress), the Atomic Energy Act of 1954 (establishing a system for protecting information about nuclear weapons and capabilities), and the Freedom of Information Act (authorizing courts to review governmental withholding of classified information).

Nonetheless, in post-9/11 lawsuits involving foreign intelligence surveillance, the government has cited the privilege's (purported) constitutional roots in arguing for a cramped interpretation of 50 U.S.C. § 1806(f), a provision of FISA. As discussed in part IV.A, § 1806(f) establishes a procedure for courts to follow when the government asserts that disclosure of FISA surveillance materials in litigation would harm national security. Contrary to the plain text of the provision, the government interprets it to apply only when the government seeks to use evidence against the opposing party. It grounds this interpretation partly in the doctrine of "constitutional avoidance," arguing that a literal reading of the provision would interfere with the constitutional prerogatives protected by the state secrets privilege.

---

[39] United States v. Nixon, 418 U.S. 683, 710 (1974).

[40] El Masri, 479 F.3d at 303.

[41] Youngstown Sheet & Tube Co. v. Sawyer, 343 U.S. 579, 638 (1952) (Jackson, J., concurring).

C. Deference

A third concern about courts' implementation of the privilege since 9/11 is the level of deference courts have shown the executive branch. Courts usually begin their analyses by acknowledging that they have the final word on whether the privilege applies and underscoring the importance of their review. In one decision, for instance, the Ninth Circuit stated, "[w]e take very seriously our obligation to review the [claim] with a very careful, indeed a skeptical, eye, and not to accept at face value the government's claim or justification of privilege."[42] In that same decision, however, the court also stated: "[W]e acknowledge the need to defer to the Executive on matters of foreign policy and national security and surely cannot legitimately find ourselves second-guessing the Executive in this area."[43] Other Ninth Circuit decisions have gone even further, proclaiming that assertions of the state secrets privilege must be accorded "utmost deference."[44] Examining these statements, the three-judge panel of the Ninth Circuit in *Zubaydah* observed that "[o]ur guidance on evaluating the need for secrecy has been contradictory."[45] This tension is evident in almost every decision addressing the privilege—and is almost always resolved in favor of deference.

To date, the issue of deference has arisen largely in the context of courts' willingness to rely on executive officials' affidavits without reviewing the actual evidence. Indeed, in cases where the government seeks dismissal on the pleadings, there is generally no evidence for the court to review. Courts point to the Supreme Court's statement in *Reynolds* that when "the occasion for the privilege is appropriate," the court "should not jeopardize the security which the privilege is meant to protect by insisting upon an examination of the evidence, even by the judge alone, in chambers."[46] However, this statement followed an important caveat: Such restraint is in order only when the court is "satisf[ied] . . . from all the circumstances of the case, that there is a reasonable danger that compulsion of the evidence will expose military matters which, in the interest of national

---

[42] Jeppesen, 614 F.3d at 1082 (quotation marks and citation omitted).

[43] *Id.* at 1081–82 (quotation marks and citation omitted).

[44] Kasza, 133 F.3d at 1166.

[45] Husayn v. Mitchell, 938 F.3d 1123, 1131 (9th Cir. 2019).

[46] Reynolds, 345 U.S. at 10.

security, should not be divulged."[47] The Court stated only that *ex parte, in camera* review of the evidence should not be "automatic"[48]—not that it was never, or even rarely, appropriate.

Reynolds itself is an object lesson in the importance of reviewing the evidence. Nearly half a century after the Court's ruling, the accident report was declassified. The Supreme Court, without looking at the report, had concluded that there was "a reasonable danger that [it] would contain references to the secret electronic equipment which was the primary concern of the mission."[49] In fact, the report contained no such references—but it did support the plaintiffs' claims of negligence. Although the Third Circuit later speculated that some other facts contained in the report might legitimately have been deemed sensitive, the few facts the court identified (for example, the fact that the aircraft could fly at an altitude of more than 20,000 feet[50]) easily could have been redacted—as the *Reynolds* Court would have seen had it examined the document.

As *Reynolds* illustrates, federal agencies are not neutral actors in lawsuits that allege they have violated the law. They have a conflict of interest and a clear motive to stretch the permissible bounds of privilege claims. When courts insist on reviewing the evidence, they are not disputing the executive branch's judgments about what might cause harm to national security. They are acknowledging the fact that the executive branch sometimes uses claims of national security to withhold information for reasons *other than* national security.

This simple reality is evident in the phenomenon of overclassification. The standard for classifying information is roughly the same as the standard for invoking the state secrets privilege: Information may be classified if its disclosure could reasonably be expected to harm national security. Yet there is little dispute that much of the information classified by executive officials does not meet this standard. The current Director of National Intelligence has acknowledged that overclassification is a significant problem,[51] and former executive

---

[47] *Id.*

[48] *Id.*

[49] *Id.*

[50] Herring, 424 F.3d at 391 n.3.

[51] Dustin Volz, Vast Troves of Classified Info Undermine National Security, Spy Chief Says, Wall St. J. (Jan. 27, 2022), https://on.wsj.com/3OUKW3g.

branch officials have estimated that anywhere from 50–90 percent of classified information could safely be released.[52]

According to the Brennan Center's analysis, overclassification often occurs because busy officials classify documents by rote rather than engaging in an analysis of the national security implications.[53] But there are also multiple examples, going back many decades, of officials classifying documents to hide misconduct or avoid embarrassment. In 1947, the Atomic Emergency Commission classified information on nuclear radiation experiments it was conducting on human beings because disclosure "might have [an] adverse effect on public opinion or result in legal suits."[54] In the 1960s, the FBI classified information about its wiretapping of Dr. Martin Luther King, Jr.'s telephone as "top secret," even though the sole purpose of its activities was to gain information about King's personal life that could be used to "completely discredit [him] as a leader of the Negro people."[55] In 2019, White House officials placed the transcript of Donald Trump's call to Ukrainian President Volodymyr Zelenskyy in a system for top secret information, even though such readouts are routinely classified at a much lower level, to minimize the number of people who might learn that Trump had pressured Zelenskyy to investigate the son of his political rival, Joe Biden.[56]

Against this backdrop, courts are on solid ground when they insist on reviewing evidence that is subject to claims of privilege. As a general matter, courts may not have the expertise to assess whether disclosing facts X, Y, or Z will harm national security (although even then, there may be exceptions), but they surely can assess whether

[52] See Hearing on the Espionage Act and the Legal and Constitutional Implications of Wikileaks, H. Comm. on the Judiciary, 111th Cong., 2d sess. 8 (2010) (statement of Thomas Blanton, Dir., Nat'l Sec. Archive), https://bit.ly/3cUKapz.

[53] Elizabeth Goitein & David M. Shapiro, Reducing Overclassification through Accountability, Brennan Ctr., Oct. 5, 2011.

[54] Mem. from O.G. Haywood, Jr., Colonel, Corps of Engineers, to Dr. [Harold] Fidler, Atomic Energy Comm'n, Med. Experiments on Humans (Apr. 17, 1947), https://bit.ly/3PWnCU7.

[55] Senate Select Comm. to Study Gov't Operations, Final Report Intell. Activities and the Rights of Americans, Book III, S. Rep. No. 94-755, at 125 (1976).

[56] Julian E. Barnes, Michael Crowley, Matthew Rosenberg & Mark Mazzetti, White House Classified Computer System Is Used to Hold Transcripts of Sensitive Calls, N.Y. Times (Sept. 27, 2019), https://nyti.ms/2mnvo0K.

documents actually include facts X, Y, or Z, or whether facts X, Y, and Z can readily be redacted. Nonetheless, courts frequently forgo this review, deferring not only to the government's claims of national security harm but to its representations about the evidence in the case.

III. The *Zubaydah* Decision

Two of the questions discussed in part II were at issue in *Zubaydah*: how much deference to grant the executive branch's predictions of national security harm and when the invocation of the privilege may lead to dismissal of a lawsuit. On the first question, the Court established a disturbing new precedent. On the second, it made a wrong turn—but in a way that is unlikely to recur in future cases, given the unusual nature of the statute under which the litigation was brought.

A. Background and Lower Courts

After 9/11, Zayn al-Abidin Muhammad Husayn, otherwise known as Abu Zubaydah, was mistakenly believed to be a high-level al Qaeda operative. He was taken to several CIA black sites and subjected to torture, including 83 waterboarding sessions in the span of one month, hundreds of hours in a coffin-sized "confinement box," mock burials, sleep deprivation, and exposure to insects to trigger his "entomophobia." As a result of this treatment, Zubaydah sustained "permanent brain damage and physical impairments, including over 300 seizures in the span of three years and the loss of his left eye."[57]

The European Court of Human Rights found "beyond a reasonable doubt" that some of this torture took place at a CIA black site in Poland between December 2002 and September 2003—confirming allegations long made by the media, nongovernmental organizations, and even former Polish officials. This finding led Polish authorities to open a criminal investigation into various Polish actors who might have been complicit in the human rights violations. Polish prosecutors sought to depose James Mitchell and John Jessen, the American contractors who helped develop the CIA's torture program. They requested assistance from the United States under a Mutual Legal Assistance Treaty (MLAT), but the United States denied the request.

[57] Husayn, 938 F.3d at 1127.

To secure the contractors' deposition testimony, Zubaydah and his attorney filed suit under 28 U.S.C. § 1782, which allows U.S. courts to issue subpoenas requiring people to give testimony in foreign or international tribunals. The United States intervened and claimed the state secrets privilege, seeking to quash the subpoena. The district court held that some of the information the subpoena sought to elicit was privileged and some was not, but that the two categories could not be "disentangled"—the third scenario discussed in part II.A, above. Accordingly, it granted the government's motion to quash.

On appeal, the Ninth Circuit reversed. It held that the existence of a CIA black site in Poland and the treatment Abu Zubaydah suffered there were matters of public record and therefore could not qualify as "state secrets." The panel rejected the government's argument that Mitchell and Jessen's testimony would serve as "official confirmation" that the CIA had operated a black site in Poland, thus erasing any remaining doubt on that fact and betraying the trust of the Polish government. For one thing, the district court had found that Mitchell and Jessen were not agents of the government—a finding that the government did not contest—and so their testimony could not provide "official confirmation" of U.S. government activity. Furthermore, the former Polish president himself had acknowledged the existence of a CIA black site in Poland, and it was current Polish authorities who sought Mitchell and Jessen's testimony.

On the other hand, the Ninth Circuit held that the names of Polish officials involved in the torture, operational details about the facility, and other such matters remained nonpublic and sensitive, and that they were properly subject to the privilege. The privileged and non-privileged evidence could be disentangled, the panel reasoned, because such evidence *had* previously been disentangled: Mitchell and Jessen had given similar testimony in another lawsuit, *Salim v. Mitchell*.[58] As in that case, Mitchell and Jessen could answer deposition questions "us[ing] code names and pseudonyms, where appropriate."[59]

B. State Secrets and "Official Confirmation": A Dangerous New Precedent

In a splintered ruling with three concurring opinions and a strongly worded dissent, the Supreme Court reversed. Departing from both

[58] Salim v. Mitchell, 268 F. Supp. 3d 1132 (E.D. Wash. 2017).

[59] Husayn, 938 F.3d at 1137.

the district court and the Ninth Circuit, the Court upheld the government's assertion of the state secrets privilege over any testimony that would confirm the existence of a CIA black site in Poland. In doing so, it created a disturbing new precedent: The government may assert the state secrets privilege over matters that are well-known to the public based on the claim that "official confirmation" of established facts would itself harm national security.

The existence of a CIA black site in Poland is, in all relevant respects, a matter of public record. Initially, this fact was discovered and widely reported as a result of investigations performed by journalists and nongovernmental organizations. It has since been confirmed by more authoritative sources, including the European Court of Human Rights, which reviewed a wealth of evidence and issued a determination "beyond a reasonable doubt." Even former Polish officials have publicly acknowledged the existence of the black site.

The Court, however, ruled that "[s]ometimes information that has entered the public domain may nonetheless fall within the scope of the state secrets privilege."[60] This ruling represents an expanded conception of the doctrine. Previously, lower courts had assumed that public information was not subject to the privilege—in the Ninth Circuit's words, "In order to be a state secret, a fact must first be a secret."[61] Indeed, in another Ninth Circuit case, the government had conceded that the privilege "does not extend to public documents."[62] Nonetheless, the Court held that "official confirmation" of facts in the public domain—which, according to the Court, could encompass confirmation by government contractors such as Mitchell and Jessen—could cause sufficient harm to national security to justify invocation of the privilege.

The Court identified two reasons why "official confirmation" of the existence of a CIA black site in Poland could harm national security. First, it accepted the government's argument that the government's "refus[al] to confirm or deny . . . public speculation about its cooperation with Poland . . . leav[es] an important element of doubt about the veracity of that speculation."[63] This notion is specious. The finding of

---

[60] Zubaydah, 142 S. Ct. at 968.

[61] Husayn, 938 F.3d at 1133.

[62] Jeppesen, 614 F.3d at 1090.

[63] Zubaydah, 142 S. Ct. at 969 (internal quotation marks and citation omitted).

the European Court of Human Rights is not "speculation." Neither is the statement of the former president of Poland. In light of the sheer number of respected sources that have confirmed the black site's existence, including individuals with first-hand knowledge, there is simply no doubt remaining on this point. Contrary to the Court's implication, a statement by a United States government official is not the sole means—or even the primary means—by which a fact, even a fact about the U.S. government's activities, may be established.

Second, the Court agreed with the government that "the CIA's refusal to confirm or deny its cooperation with foreign intelligence services plays an important role in and of itself in maintaining the trust on which those relationships are based."[64] In other words, foreign intelligence services might be less willing to cooperate with the CIA in the future if they thought the CIA would betray its confidences. This argument fails for the same reason the first one does: There are, quite simply, no confidences left to betray. Whatever reputational harm Poland might suffer as a result of its cooperation with the CIA, and whatever adverse consequences might flow from the lifting of the veil, have happened already.

The sole exception might be the legal liability of Polish individuals who were complicit in Zubaydah's torture. By invoking the state secrets privilege, the U.S. government could impede or delay legal accountability for those acts. Here, though, it was incumbent on the Court to ask: Does it truly serve national security to honor a promise to conceal participation in war crimes? Would it not better serve national security, in the long run, to adopt a rule—analogous to the crime-fraud exception to the attorney-client privilege[65]—that the protection courts accord to secret U.S. agreements with foreign intelligence services does not extend to the commission of human rights violations? This is one area where courts, with their commitment to the rule of law and the vindication of legal rights, might indeed have a broader and more complete perspective on national security than the executive branch. At a minimum, the Court was well within its rights to question this assessment of national security harm—but failed to do so.

---

[64] *Id.*

[65] See United States v. Zolin, 491 U.S. 554, 562–63 (1989).

By accepting the government's "official confirmation" argument without probing its validity under the specific facts of this case, the Court exhibited undue deference to the government's claim of national security harm. It did so without shedding light on the more common question of whether courts should defer to claims of national security harm without reviewing the evidence in question.[66] Nonetheless, there are two silver linings to the decision when it comes to the question of deference.

First, seven justices rejected the efforts of Justices Clarence Thomas and Samuel Alito to further gut judicial inquiry into state secrets privilege assertions through a bizarre reading of *Reynolds*. Under this reading, the court would be required to accept the government's claim of privilege, no questions asked, unless the non-government party could show that the evidence was "immediately and essentially applicable" to its case.[67] If the nongovernment party made such a showing, the court could then ask whether "there is a reasonable danger that military secrets are at stake," affording "utmost deference" to the government's assessment.[68] Although they do not say so directly, Justices Alito and Thomas clearly believe that *in camera* review of the evidence is rarely, if ever, appropriate.

The Court had little difficulty disposing of this proposed approach. Parsing *Reynolds*, it observed that the proper steps for asserting and reviewing the privilege are as follows: (1) The government must formally invoke the privilege; (2) the court must determine whether the circumstances are appropriate for the claim of privilege; and (3) after determining that the government has offered a valid reason for invoking the privilege, the court should inquire into

---

[66] Justice Gorsuch did suggest that the Court should have remanded the case to the district court "for *in camera* review of any evidence the government might wish to present to substantiate its privilege claim." Zubaydah, 142 S. Ct. at 998 (Gorsuch, J., concurring). But the privileged evidence itself—at least, the evidence that formed the core of the Court's opinion—was evidence confirming that the CIA operated a black site in Poland. Once the Court determined that any answer to discovery questions posed in that investigation, regardless of whether the answer referenced a CIA black site in Poland, would necessarily confirm the black site's existence, the question of whether to conduct *in camera* review of the privileged evidence was effectively mooted.

[67] *Id.* at 975 (Thomas, J., concurring) (quoting United States v. Burr, 25 F. Cas. 30, 37 (No. 14,692d) (C.C. Va. 1807) (Marshall, C.J.)).

[68] *Id.*

the nongovernment party's need for the evidence, which will then inform whether the court should probe more deeply into the government's claim—for example, by conducting an *in camera* review of the evidence, if the court has not done so already.

The second silver lining is the dissent authored by Justice Neil Gorsuch and joined by Justice Sonia Sotomayor—two justices who do not often join forces. The dissent is a powerful rebuke of excessive deference to the executive branch in national security matters. It begins, "[t]here comes a point where we should not be ignorant as judges of what we know to be true as citizens."[69] It bluntly names the government's true motive for invoking the privilege: "[I]t seems that the government wants this suit dismissed because it hopes to impede the Polish criminal investigation and avoid (or delay) further embarrassment for past misdeeds."[70] And it ends with a powerful appeal to the role of the courts: "[E]mbarrassing as these facts [of Zubaydah's torture] may be, there is no state secret here. This Court's duty is to the rule of the law and the search for truth. We should not let shame obscure our vision."[71]

Beyond its compelling rhetoric, the dissent raises important objections to the majority's approach that few courts have identified. Perhaps most crucially, it cautions that the president's Article II interest in protecting information through the assertion of a state secrets privilege claim "must be carefully assessed against the competing powers Article I and Article III have vested in Congress and the Judiciary."[72] By shutting down litigation, the dissent explains, the privilege curtails Congress's Article I authority to authorize lawsuits (which Congress did here through 28 U.S.C. § 1782) and the judiciary's Article III responsibility to decide cases and controversies.

The dissent also foregrounds a reality that too few judges are willing to openly acknowledge: "[E]xecutive officials can sometimes be tempted to misuse claims of national security to shroud major abuses and even ordinary negligence from public view."[73] It lists examples of this phenomenon, both historical and more recent. And it highlights

---

[69] *Id.* at 985 (Gorsuch, J., dissenting) (internal quotation marks and citations omitted).

[70] *Id.* at 1001.

[71] *Id.*

[72] *Id.* at 991.

[73] *Id.* at 992.

the phenomenon of overclassification discussed above. Without suggesting nefarious motives on the part of executive branch officials, it concludes that judicial skepticism of national security claims is necessary to safeguard the constitutional separation of powers:

> It may be understandable that those most responsible for the Nation's security will press every tool available to them to maximum advantage. There has always been something of a hydraulic pressure inherent within each of the separate Branches to test the outer limits of its power. It may be nothing less than human nature. But when classification standards are so broadly drawn and loosely administered, temptation enough exists for executive officials to cover up their own mistakes and even their wrongdoing under the guise of protecting national security. This Court hardly needs to add fuel to the fire by abdicating any pretense of an independent judicial inquiry into the propriety of a claim of privilege and extending instead "utmost deference" to the Executive's mere assertion of one. Walking that path would only invite more claims of secrecy in more doubtful circumstances—and facilitate the loss of liberty and due process history shows very often follows.[74]

In its broad rejection of excessive deference to executive claims of national security, the dissent holds potential significance for future cases on a wide range of subjects.

C. The Dismissal Remedy: Wrong but Not Precedential

Having held that the existence of a CIA black site in Poland was a state secret, the Court remanded the case to the Ninth Circuit "with instructions to dismiss Zubaydah's current application for discovery under § 1782."[75] It concluded that there was no way to revise the discovery questions to avoid official confirmation of the black site. This was plainly wrong as a factual matter. However, given that conclusion, the decision to dismiss should be understood as a reflection of the unusual nature of § 1782 proceedings and not as a precedent for other types of lawsuits.

In dismissing the case, the Court observed that "any response Mitchell and Jessen gave to Zubaydah's subpoenas would tend to

---

[74] Id. at 993–94.
[75] Id. at 972.

confirm (or deny) the existence of a black site in Poland," given that "12 of Zubaydah's 13 document requests contain the word 'Poland' or 'Polish,'" and 10 of them specifically sought documents concerning the Polish detention site.[76] "If Mitchell and Jessen acknowledge the existence of documents responsive to these requests, they will effectively acknowledge the existence of the detention facilities referenced therein."[77] Merely answering the requests, in other words, would reveal state secrets.

The Court's logic may be sound with respect to the original discovery requests. However, Zubaydah offered to revise the requests to omit reference to the location of the detention site, focusing instead on conduct that took place within a certain time period (December 2002 to September 2003) and leaving it to other witnesses to establish where this conduct took place. Although there is ample information about Zubaydah's treatment in the public domain, very little of that information relates specifically to the time period in question. Bafflingly, the Court held that these revisions would be insufficient, suggesting that "the nature of this case (an exclusively discovery-related proceeding aimed at producing evidence for use by Polish criminal investigators)" would inevitably tie the discovery responses to Poland.[78]

As Justices Elena Kagan and Gorsuch noted, the Court's reasoning was flawed. True, prosecutors would not be asking Mitchell and Jessen what they did between 2002 and 2003 if they did not believe the conduct happened in Poland. But the belief of Polish authorities—presumably to be confirmed by witnesses other than Mitchell and Jessen—is not "official confirmation" by the United States, and therefore does not trigger any of the national security harms the government posited. Mitchell and Jessen's testimony, limited to what took place at an undisclosed location during a specific time period, would provide neither confirmation nor denial of the existence of a CIA black site in Poland.

The questions remain: Given the Court's conclusions that (1) the existence of a CIA black site in Poland was a state secret and (2) answering the document requests would necessarily have confirmed

[76] *Id.* at 968.
[77] *Id.*
[78] *Id.* at 972.

or denied that fact, was dismissal an appropriate remedy? And what does the Court's approach here signify for future cases?

On these questions, the key factor is the unusual nature of a proceeding under § 1782. The Ninth Circuit panel observed that, "[u]nlike our prior cases, this is a pure discovery matter where there are no claims to prove or defenses to assert."[79] The Supreme Court similarly described it as "an exclusively discovery-related proceeding aimed at producing evidence for use by Polish criminal investigators."[80] Once the Court determined (albeit wrongly) that the mere act of responding to the discovery requests would necessarily reveal state secrets, there was no reason to assess whether the plaintiff had sufficient nonprivileged evidence to make out a prima facie case. As the Court stated, "[this] is a purely evidentiary proceeding and thus unlike most litigation, which may, after a successful assertion of the state secrets privilege, continue without the government's privileged proof."[81]

Accordingly, had the Court been correct that responding to the discovery requests would necessarily have entailed revealing privileged information, the decision to order dismissal would have been sound. More important, it should not be seen as setting a precedent for other types of lawsuits. The Court was clear that the remedy it imposed turned on "the nature of this litigation," in which the discovery requests themselves were "the proceeding's sole object."[82] In lawsuits where that is not the case, the proper remedy—as the Court acknowledged—would be to "continue without the Government's privileged proof."[83] This acknowledgment, and not the dismissal of Zubaydah's case, should inform courts' analyses in future cases.

IV. The *Fazaga* Decision

Fazaga, on its face, raised the issue of whether a statutory provision of FISA displaces the procedures that would otherwise apply when the government claims the state secrets privilege—which in turn raised the question of whether the privilege is constitutional

---

[79] Husayn, 938 F.3d at 1135.

[80] Zubaydah, 142 S. Ct. at 972.

[81] *Id.* (internal quotation marks and citation omitted).

[82] *Id.*

[83] *Id.* (internal quotation marks omitted).

in nature. The Court, however, managed to avoid these questions entirely by wishing away the conflict between the FISA procedures and those that flow from state secrets privilege claims. Its ruling is likely to generate substantial confusion among lower courts.

A. Background and Lower Courts

At issue in *Fazaga* was a surveillance campaign the FBI conducted in 2005 and 2006 against Muslim American communities in southern California. The plaintiffs, three Muslim Americans who were caught up in this operation, alleged that the FBI's surveillance violated their constitutional rights under the First, Fourth, and Fifth Amendments, as well as FISA, which governs surveillance for foreign intelligence purposes that takes place on U.S. soil and/ or targets U.S. persons.

The FBI moved to dismiss the case on multiple grounds. With respect to the religious freedom claims, the FBI invoked the state secrets privilege. It was undisputed that the plaintiffs could make out a prima facie case using nonprivileged evidence. However, the attorney general, as the head of the agency in which the FBI is housed, submitted an affidavit asserting that defending against these claims would require the FBI to present sensitive evidence about its investigation, the disclosure of which would harm "national security interests."[84]

The plaintiffs argued that dismissal of the religious freedom claims based on the state secrets privilege was foreclosed by 50 U.S.C. § 1806(f), a provision of FISA that establishes special procedures for handling sensitive national security information in cases involving electronic surveillance. Those procedures may be triggered whenever (1) the government intends to "enter into evidence or otherwise use or disclose" any information obtained or derived from electronic surveillance;[85] (2) the target of electronic surveillance seeks to suppress evidence obtained or derived from such surveillance;[86] or (3) the target of surveillance makes a motion or request to "discover or obtain" materials relating to electronic surveillance or to "discover,

[84] Decl. of Eric H. Holder, Att'y Gen. of the U.S. at 1, Fazaga v. FBI, 885 F. Supp. 2d 978 (C.D. Cal. 2012) (No. 8:11-cv-00301-CJC-VBK), ECF No. 32-3.
[85] 50 U.S.C. §§ 1806(c), (d) (2018).
[86] *Id.* § 1806(e).

obtain, or suppress" information obtained or derived from electronic surveillance.[87]

In such cases, the attorney general may submit an affidavit attesting that disclosure or an adversary hearing would "harm the national security of the United States."[88] The court must then review, *in camera* and *ex parte*, "such . . . materials relating to the surveillance as may be necessary to determine whether the surveillance . . . was lawfully authorized and conducted."[89] The court may disclose some or all of the information to the nongovernment party "under appropriate security procedures and protective orders," but "only where such disclosure is necessary to make an accurate determination of the legality of the surveillance."[90] If the court determines that the surveillance was unlawful, it must suppress the unlawfully obtained evidence "or otherwise grant the motion" of the nongovernment party.[91]

At the time the case came before the Ninth Circuit, only two courts had previously considered whether these statutory procedures preempt contrary procedures under the state secrets privilege; both held that they do.[92] The FBI argued, however, that FISA's alternative procedures apply only when litigants challenge the admissibility of evidence that the government seeks to introduce—despite the law's broad language stating that the provision applies "whenever any motion or request is made by [the target of surveillance] pursuant to any . . . statute or rule of the United States or any State to . . . discover, obtain, or suppress evidence or information obtained or derived from electronic surveillance."[93] A literal reading of that language, the government claimed, would be inconsistent with the statute's overall structure, which suggests an intent to provide a suppression remedy rather than a mechanism to resolve the merits of claims in civil litigation.

[87] *Id.* § 1806(f).

[88] *Id.*

[89] *Id.*

[90] *Id.*

[91] *Id.* § 1806(g).

[92] See Jewel v. Nat'l Sec. Agency, 965 F. Supp. 2d 1090, 1105–06 (N.D. Cal. 2013); In re Nat'l Sec. Agency Telecomms. Records Litig., 564 F. Supp. 2d 1109, 1117–24 (N.D. Cal. 2008). Since then, the Fourth Circuit has held that § 1806(f) does not preempt the usual operation of the state secrets privilege. See Wikimedia Found. v. Nat'l Sec. Agency, 14 F.4th 276 (4th Cir. 2021).

[93] 50 U.S.C. § 1806(f) (2018).

In support of this interpretation, the FBI asserted that the state secrets privilege is rooted not only in the common law, but also in the president's authority under Article II of the Constitution to safeguard national security information. Absent a clear statement from Congress, the government argued, the court should not interpret § 1806(f) as "displacing" procedures or remedies available under the state secrets privilege, as such a reading would infringe on the president's exercise of Article II powers and therefore raise constitutional questions.

In reply, the plaintiffs pointed out that the FBI's reading ignored the plain text of the statute, which makes clear that § 1806(f) is triggered by *any* government use of sensitive information, or any request by the target of surveillance to discover or obtain such information, in *any* case. As for the structure and purpose of the law, the plaintiffs noted that FISA established a means to challenge unauthorized electronic surveillance through civil litigation, and that the FBI's reading of § 1806(f) would essentially prevent courts from adjudicating such cases. That, in turn, would subvert the purpose of FISA itself: reining in unilateral and unreviewable executive branch surveillance.[94]

On the constitutional question, the plaintiffs disputed the government's characterization of the privilege. They argued that the *Reynolds* version of the privilege is squarely rooted in the common law and not the Constitution. They also pointed out that the government could choose whether to present the privileged information in its defense, and because the government retained the option of nondisclosure, there could be no infringement on whatever constitutional authority the president might have.

---

[94] The Brennan Center for Justice, joined by several other organizations, submitted an amicus brief underscoring this conclusion. The brief demonstrated that the primary alternative means for challenging unlawful FISA surveillance—review by the Foreign Intelligence Surveillance Court (FISC) and challenges to the government's evidence in criminal proceedings—have proven ineffective. FISC oversight is fatally constrained by the absence of adversarial proceedings and what the FISC itself has called an "institutional lack of candor" on the government's part. In criminal cases, the government has frequently failed to comply with its statutory obligation to notify defendants when it relies on evidence "obtained or derived" from FISA surveillance; even when such notification occurs, defendants cannot meaningfully challenge the surveillance because they are not permitted to see the underlying materials. Accordingly, if civil litigation were effectively foreclosed through the government's reading of § 1806(f), there would be no meaningful avenues left for holding the government accountable. See Br. for Brennan Center for Justice et al. as Amici Curiae In Support of Respondents, FBI v. Fazaga, 142 S. Ct. 1051 (No. 20-828), https://bit.ly/3JmQgeF.

The district court essentially punted on the question, holding (erroneously) that § 1806(f) applies only to claims alleging violations of FISA, whereas the government had asserted the state secrets privilege only with respect to the plaintiffs' religious freedom claims.[95] It nonetheless dismissed *all* the plaintiffs' claims based on the state secrets privilege, even though the government had not sought this remedy.

On appeal, the Ninth Circuit clarified that § 1806(f) applies in any case involving a challenge to the lawfulness or use of electronic surveillance, "whether the challenge is under FISA itself, the Constitution, or any other law."[96] It went on to side with the plaintiffs/ appellants in their interpretation of the provision. Relying on the statute's text, structure, legislative history, and overall purpose, the panel ruled that § 1806(f) is not limited to instances in which the government seeks to introduce evidence and the nongovernment party seeks to suppress it. Moreover, it concluded that "Congress intended FISA to displace the state secrets privilege and its dismissal remedy with respect to electronic surveillance."[97] The panel acknowledged that the privilege "may have a constitutional core or constitutional overtones," but emphasized that, "at bottom, it is an evidentiary rule rooted in common law, *not* constitutional law."[98] To regulate a common-law privilege, Congress need only "speak[] directly to the question otherwise answered by federal common law,"[99] and Congress had done that through § 1806(f)—a provision that clearly establishes procedures for handling information that could harm national security if disclosed through litigation.

B. *The Supreme Court's Incoherent Resolution*

The Supreme Court granted certiorari "to decide whether § 1806(f) displaces the state secrets privilege."[100] The respondents, however, raised an additional issue. They argued that even if FISA's procedures did not control, the district court erred in holding that dismissal is

[95] Fazaga v. FBI, 884 F. Supp. 2d 1022, 1037–38 (C.D. Cal. 2012).
[96] Fazaga v. FBI, 965 F.3d 1015, 1052 (9th Cir. 2020).
[97] Id.
[98] Id. at 1045.
[99] Id. at 1044 (emphasis, internal quotation marks, and alterations omitted).
[100] 142 S. Ct. at 2720.

appropriate when the government requires privileged evidence to mount a defense. The respondents had not briefed this issue in the courts below—and those courts therefore had not addressed it—because it was foreclosed by Ninth Circuit precedent, but they offered it before the Supreme Court as an alternative ground for affirmance.

The Supreme Court thus appeared to have two options for resolving the case. First, it could rule on the correct interpretation of FISA—a decision that would determine whether civil lawsuits constitute a viable means of challenging unlawful foreign intelligence surveillance, or whether courts would effectively lose the ability to hold the government accountable for such violations. This approach might also require the Court to weigh in on whether the privilege has "constitutional overtones" and how that affects Congress's ability to regulate its exercise. Alternatively, the Court could hold that the state secrets privilege, outside the *Totten* contract context, should be treated like other evidentiary privileges, resulting only in the removal of the privileged evidence from the case. Such a ruling would return the privilege to its origins and help ensure that national security policies cannot categorically escape judicial review.

The Court did neither. Instead, it held that, "even as interpreted by respondents"—and the Court expressly declined to decide which party's interpretation was correct—FISA "does not displace the state secrets privilege."[101] It reached that conclusion because, in the Court's estimation, "nothing about the operation of that provision is at all incompatible with the state secrets privilege."[102] In other words, neither approach displaced the other; they could simply (the Court posited) coexist. Having thus disposed of the FISA question, the Court remanded the case for unspecified "further proceedings consistent with this opinion."[103]

The Court's conclusion that FISA and the state secrets privilege effectively operate on separate tracks was based on several observations. First, it asserted that "the state secrets privilege will not be invoked in the great majority of cases in which § 1806(f) is triggered," as that provision "is most likely to come into play when the Government seeks to use FISA evidence in a judicial or administrative proceeding, as

---

[101] Fazaga, 142 S. Ct. at 1060.

[102] *Id.* at 1061.

[103] *Id.* at 1063.

the Government will obviously not invoke the state secrets privilege to block disclosure of information that it wishes to use."[104]

This statement betrays the Court's lack of familiarity with how the government actually uses FISA surveillance in criminal cases. Although FISA requires the government to notify defendants when using evidence "obtained or derived from" FISA surveillance,[105] the government historically has managed to avoid that obligation through a creative interpretation of the words "derived from."[106] In particular, the government engages in a well-documented practice of "parallel construction," using less controversial authorities to recreate evidence obtained under FISA and thus avoiding notification.[107] In such cases, the government is simultaneously using FISA-derived evidence *and* attempting to shield any materials that would reveal the role played by FISA.

The Court's next set of reasons for concluding that "there is no clash between § 1806(f) and the state secrets privilege" was that "[t]he statute and the privilege (1) require courts to conduct different inquiries, (2) authorize courts to award different forms of relief, and (3) direct the parties and the courts to follow different procedures."[108] On the first point, the Court noted that § 1806(f) does not allow the court to assess the validity of the government's claim of national security harm; rather, the court must assume that the information is sensitive and determine whether it reveals unlawful surveillance. By contrast, the state secrets privilege requires courts to determine whether disclosure of the information would indeed harm national security; on the other hand, it does not authorize or require an assessment of whether the information indicates unlawful government conduct.

On the second point, the Court observed that the state secrets privilege, unlike § 1806(f), "sometimes authorizes district courts to dismiss claims on the pleadings."[109] The Court declined to address what circumstances, beyond those presented in *Totten*, would justify

---

[104] *Id.* at 1061.

[105] 50 U.S.C. § 1806(c) (2018).

[106] See Patrick C. Toomey, Why Aren't Criminal Defendants Getting Notice of Section 602 Surveillance—Again?, Just Security (Dec. 11, 2015), https://bit.ly/3d0uSQj.

[107] See Human Rights Watch, Dark Side: Secret Origins of Evidence in US Criminal Cases (Jan. 9, 2018), https://bit.ly/3SkllDJ.

[108] *Fazaga*, 142 S. Ct. at 1061.

[109] *Id.* at 1062.

dismissal, leaving the central controversy posed by the state secrets privilege unresolved.

On the third point, the Court highlighted certain differences between § 1806(f) proceedings and the proceedings that accompany assertions of the state secrets privilege. First, § 1806(f) is triggered by the attorney general, while the state secrets privilege is invoked by the head of the relevant agency. Second, under § 1806(f), the court must review, *in camera* and *ex parte*, such materials as are necessary to determine the lawfulness of the surveillance. By contrast, when the government invokes the state secrets privilege, a review of the information "even by the judge alone, in chambers" should not take place if the court is satisfied, "from all the circumstances of the case," that there is a "reasonable danger" that compulsion of the evidence would harm national security.[110]

The Court's conclusion that § 1806(f) and the state secrets privilege do not conflict because they operate differently borders on the nonsensical. The clash between § 1806(f) and the state secrets privilege exists precisely *because* they require the courts to do different things when faced with the same threshold circumstance—namely, information that could harm national security if disclosed through litigation. Critically, the Court identified no substantive difference between the type of information addressed by § 1806(f) and the state secrets privilege; both apply to information that allegedly requires protection in the interest of national security. What differs is how the court should respond to such a claim, both in terms of the procedures it applies and the relief it grants.

Those differences are what render § 1806(f) and state secrets fundamentally incompatible. A court cannot both rule on the validity of a claim of national security harm (state secrets) and not rule on it (§ 1806(f)). It cannot both assess whether sensitive information reveals unlawful surveillance (§ 1806(f)) and not make that assessment (state secrets). It cannot both review sensitive materials *in camera* and *ex parte* (§ 1806(f)) and refrain from such review (state secrets). It cannot both grant relief to the nongovernment party (§ 1806(f)) and dismiss that party's claims (state secrets).

In this regard, it might have been a poor choice for the respondents to frame § 1806(f) as "displacing" the state secrets privilege. That characterization obscures the fact that the information addressed in

---

[110] Reynolds, 345 U.S. at 10.

§ 1806(f) *is* information subject to the state secrets privilege—namely, information that would allegedly harm national security if disclosed through litigation. Section 1806(f) does not displace the privilege so much as it establishes procedures courts should follow when faced with claims of privilege in cases involving electronic surveillance. As the district court put it in *Jewel v. NSA,* one of the previous cases addressing this issue, § 1806(f) "is, in effect, a 'codification of the state secrets privilege for purposes of relevant cases under FISA, as modified to reflect Congress's precise directive to the federal courts for the handling of [electronic surveillance] materials and information with purported national security implications.'"[111] Viewed in such a manner, it becomes clear that the procedures set forth in § 1806(f) and the procedures established in the common law cannot coexist.

Going forward, any time information that may be subject to the state secrets privilege is at issue in electronic surveillance cases, the government will simply choose which set of procedures gives it the greater litigation advantage. If the government believes the information will help its case—for instance, if it seeks to introduce FISA-derived evidence against a criminal defendant (and has not obscured the evidence's origins through parallel construction)—it will file an affidavit signed by the attorney general and ask the court to proceed under § 1806(f). If, however, the information would give the nongovernment party an advantage—likely because it reveals unlawful surveillance—the government will instead file an affidavit signed by the head of the relevant agency asserting the state secrets privilege.

That outcome is bad enough. Among other things, it eviscerates the availability of civil litigation to challenge unlawful surveillance just as surely as would a ruling that adopted the government's cramped interpretation of § 1806(f). The shortcomings of the Court's opinion become even more clear, however, when one considers how district courts will apply the ruling in future cases involving challenges to unlawful surveillance by the Department of Justice or its components. The government will surely file an affidavit invoking the state secrets privilege and claiming that information about the surveillance cannot be disclosed without harm to national security. But because the head of the defendant agency happens to be the attorney general, that same affidavit should trigger the procedures set

---

[111] Jewel, 965 F. Supp. 2d at 1106 (quoting In re NSA, 564 F. Supp. 2d at 1119).

forth in § 1806(f). As the Supreme Court so clearly outlined, those are different procedures. Which will the court follow?[112]

Had the Court acknowledged that § 1806(f) and the common law provide different and often conflicting ways of handling sensitive national security information in litigation involving electronic surveillance, it would have had to decide which set of procedures must prevail. The answer would be clear: If Congress has directly weighed in on matters that would otherwise be governed by the common law, the common law must yield.[113] Moreover, even if the Court were to hold that the state secrets privilege is squarely rooted in Article II, that would not weigh against the application of § 1806(f). Congress may restrict the president's exercise of Article II authority unless that authority rests solely with the president. Even Justice Brett Kavanaugh, whose questions at oral argument made clear his belief that the state secrets privilege is rooted in Article II, expressed "real doubts" as to whether the president's authority in this area is "exclusive and preclusive."[114]

V. Conclusion: The Need for Congressional Action

As *Zubaydah* and *Fazaga* show, the Supreme Court is in no hurry to resolve the main questions triggered by lower courts' decisions over the past 20 years. We are no closer to knowing when the Court thinks dismissal is an appropriate remedy in a case involving a *Reynolds* claim, or the extent to which the Court views the privilege as rooted in the Constitution. Moreover, we are left with little clarity as to how courts should apply *Fazaga* in future cases involving electronic surveillance by the Department of Justice or its components.

The solution is for Congress to step in and resolve these issues. As noted above, even if the privilege has constitutional dimensions,

---

[112] Indeed, it is unclear how the district court in *Fazaga* itself should proceed. The district court had held that § 1806(f) does not apply to claims brought under laws other than FISA. The Ninth Circuit disagreed, holding that § 1806(f) applies to any case where FISA surveillance is at issue, regardless of the nature of the claims. The Supreme Court does not appear to have disturbed that aspect of the Ninth Circuit's decision. Accordingly, on remand, the district court presumably must decide which set of procedures to follow in response to the attorney general's affidavit.

[113] See, e.g., Pasquantino v. United States, 544 U.S. 349, 359 (2005).

[114] Tr. of Oral Arg. at 124, FBI v. Fazaga, 142 S. Ct. 1051 (2022) (No. 20-828).

Congress may regulate the privilege's exercise in light of Congress's own authority to act in the areas of national security and access to information by the courts and the public.[115] Congress's reforms should be centered around two principles: treating the state secrets doctrine as an evidentiary privilege and ensuring that judicial deference does not turn into judicial abdication. The following measures would put those principles into practice.

First, Congress should prohibit rulings that are based on *predictions* about what the evidence might be, rather than an assessment of the actual evidence. Accordingly, no case should be dismissed based on the privilege before the parties have had a chance to conduct discovery and identify the relevant evidence that will be used in the case. If responding to a discovery request would entail revealing information the government asserts is privileged, the court may rule on the privilege claim in that context.

Second, Congress should ensure that courts scrutinize claims of privilege more carefully than they have done to date—not for the purpose of questioning national security judgments, but for the purpose of assessing whether national security is in fact the basis for the claim. There should be two facets to this increased scrutiny:

- Congress should require courts to review the evidence itself, or a sample of the evidence if the total amount is too voluminous, in all cases. This contradicts the Supreme Court's guidance in *Reynolds*. Whether the privilege is viewed as a common-law privilege or a constitutional one, however, Congress is entitled to modify its implementation as long as it is acting within its own constitutional authorities. It need only be clear about its intent to do so.
- Congress should direct the courts to use the many tools at their disposal to make the process as adversarial as possible. Congress can look to the Classified Information Procedures Act[116] (CIPA) as a model: the law contemplates various ways of protecting classified information in an adversary setting. For instance, in cases where disclosure to the nongovernment

---

[115] See generally Vicki Divoll, The "Full Access Doctrine": Congress's Constitutional Entitlement to National Security Information from the Executive, 34 Harv. J.L. & Pub. Pol'y 493 (2011).

[116] Pub. L. No. 96-456 (1980) (codified as amended at 18 U.S.C. Appendix §§ 1–16).

party and/or that party's counsel would risk national security harm even with protective orders in place, courts may appoint cleared counsel to represent the nongovernment party in the proceedings.

Third, Congress should similarly take a page from CIPA in fashioning remedies when privileged information is vital to either party's case. Where possible, courts should order nonprivileged substitutes for the privileged evidence, such as redacted versions, summaries, or admissions of fact that steer clear of privileged information. Only if no adequate substitute is possible, and only if plaintiffs lack sufficient nonprivileged evidence to make out a prima facie case, should the court dismiss the lawsuit. In civil cases where the defendant is the government, the government's need for privileged evidence to mount a defense should not justify dismissal of the claim. Such an outcome is inconsistent with how evidentiary privileges are treated in other contexts, and it ignores the fact that the government can always choose which evidence to present in its defense.

Finally, Congress should amend § 1806(f) to incorporate by reference the more robust judicial review procedures described above, while stating clearly that in cases where the court finds that disclosure would harm national security, it must determine the lawfulness of the surveillance described in the privileged materials.

Many of these reforms are embodied in the State Secrets Protection Act, first introduced by Senator Ted Kennedy and Representative Jerrold Nadler in 2008.[117] Since that time, the courts have continued to struggle with the privilege. The Supreme Court finally has weighed in, with two decisions that raise more questions than they answer. There is no reason for Congress to wait any longer. Legislation is needed to prevent national security policies from entering an accountability-free zone in which judicial review is effectively unavailable, no matter how grievous or unconstitutional the wrongs inflicted.

---

[117] S. 2533, 110th Cong. (2008); H.R. 5607, 110th Cong. (2008).

Vindicating Cassandra: A Comment on *Dobbs v. Jackson Women's Health Organization*

*Evan D. Bernick**

Introduction

In *Dobbs v. Jackson Women's Health Organization*, the Supreme Court of the United States overruled *Roe v. Wade* and held that the U.S. Constitution does not guarantee the right to terminate a pregnancy.[1] The decision triggered abortion bans in 11 states.[2] Nine other states have pre-*Roe* abortion bans on the books, and it's unclear what will happen with them.[3] It is certain that no Supreme Court decision has so quickly resulted in the prohibition of so much private conduct that was once afforded the highest constitutional protection.

Dobbs is shocking—not just because of the circumstances in which a draft of Justice Samuel Alito's opinion for the Court was leaked to the public.[4] *Dobbs* will have an impact on the lives of millions; it will create new legal conflicts (which are already happening); and it creates uncertainty for other rights. The most alarmist predictions from reproductive-rights supporters proved accurate.[5] Like Cassandra,

---

* Assistant professor of law, Northern Illinois University College of Law.

[1] See 142 S. Ct. 2228 (2022).

[2] See Elizabeth Nash & Isabel Guarnieri, 13 States Have Abortion Trigger Bans— Here's What Happens When Roe Is Overturned, Guttmacher Inst. (June 6, 2022), https://tinyurl.com/529zdcj6.

[3] *Id.*

[4] About which this essay will not speculate.

[5] Compare Kathleen Parker, Calm Down. Roe v. Wade Isn't Going Anywhere, Wash. Post (June 3, 2018), https://tinyurl.com/e3ch9z73 with How Activists Can Prepare for a Post-Roe World, Reproaction (Sept. 21, 2018), https://tinyurl.com/2p8ts3jt.

who warned in vain of the impending fall of Troy, they have been vindicated by devastation.[6]

Of course, the fall of Troy ended the Trojan War. *Dobbs* is a victory for one side in an ongoing constitutional conflict. It strives to be more than that, but the moment slips without decisive resolution. This essay explains why and describes and criticizes *Dobbs*'s reasoning.

Part I summarizes the history of abortion in the United States. Part II describes and evaluates *Roe*'s reasoning; explains how *Roe* became a focal point of constitutional conflict; and maps the political and legal landscape prior to *Dobbs*. Part III summarizes the opinions in *Dobbs*. Part IV argues that Alito's opinion for the Court fails to achieve three of its major goals. The opinion lands some justified blows on *Roe* but falls well short of demonstrating that it was "egregiously wrong." Its own constitutional interpretation suffers from crippling flaws, with the result that it fails to show that the Constitution doesn't protect abortion rights. And it not only fails to extricate the federal judiciary from abortion-related conflict but also invites attacks on other rights, from contraception to sexual intimacy to marriage.

I. Abortion in America, From the Founding to *Roe*

A. Abortion at the Founding

No abortion statutes existed in the United States when the Constitution was ratified. State courts followed the common law, distinguishing between abortion before and after "quickening"—the perception of fetal movement, roughly 14–20 weeks after pregnancy. A fertilized egg couldn't be the victim of a homicide, but the common law did criminally punish the termination and expulsion of a "quick" fetus.[7]

Abortion was widely practiced but not publicized. Observers generally believed that abortion was chosen by (as one doctor put it) "unmarried females, who, through imprudence or misfortune, have become pregnant, to avoid disgrace which would attach to them from

---

[6] See Hyginus, Fabulae 93 ("Cassandra, daughter of the king and queen, in the temple of Apollo, exhausted from practising, is said to have fallen asleep; whom, when Apollo wished to embrace her, she did not afford the opportunity of her body. On account of which thing, when she prophesied true things, she was not believed.").

[7] See James C. Mohr, Abortion in America 3–4 (1978).

having a living child."[8] It wasn't understood as a means of family limitation, with one important exception: enslaved African women. Enslaved African women, through childbearing, fulfilled an economic function for enslavers, particularly after Congress banned the international slave trade in 1808.[9]

In opposition to their "function" as child bearers, enslaved women used abortion as a means of resistance.[10] Prominent southern medical journals published essays about "the unnatural tendency in the African female to destroy her offspring" and described numerous "domestic remedies" that could be used to terminate pregnancy.[11] But white, married women didn't abort—or so it was thought.

By the 1840s the social perception of abortion had transformed. Abortion-inducing drugs were advertised in the popular press.[12] Newspaper exposés revealed that abortion was a daily practice among the upper and middle class in northern cities.[13] Physicians across the country lamented that abortion involved not "the unfortunate only, who have been deceived and ensnared by the seducer" but also "the virtuous and intelligent wife and mother."[14] Sensationalized cases led to new restrictions, as some states challenged the quickening line.[15]

---

[8] John B. Beck, An Inaugural Dissertation on Infanticide 67 (1817).

[9] See Sara Clarke Kaplan, The Black Reproductive: Unfree Labor and Insurgent Motherhood 13 (2021) ("Following the legal end of its participation in the transatlantic slave trade, the United States became the only slaveholding society in the Americas to successfully rely on . . . the multigenerational growth of an enslaved labor force and expansion of a plantation economy solely through the procreation of existing captives."); Thomas Jefferson, "Extract from Letter to John Wayle Eppes" (June 30, 1820), https://tinyurl.com/887xhr2s ("I know no error more consuming to an estate than that of stocking farms with men almost exclusively. I consider a woman who brings a child every two years as more profitable than the best man of the farm. What she produces is an addition to the capital, while his labors disappear in mere consumption.").

[10] See Stephanie Camp, Closer to Freedom: Enslaved Women and Everyday Resistance in the Plantation South 63 (2005).

[11] E.M. Pendleton, On the Susceptibility of the Caucasian and African Races to the Different Classes of Diseases, S. Med. & Surgical J. 338 (1949).

[12] See Mohr, *supra* note 7, at 49.

[13] See *id.* at 125.

[14] Jesse Boring, Foeticide, 2 Atlanta Med. & Surgical J. 257–58 (1857).

[15] See Mohr, *supra* note 7, at 145.

B. The Physicians' Campaign

Beginning in the 1850s, "regular" physicians who were associated with the country's better medical schools and well-organized local medical societies pursued an anti-abortion campaign. The goal was "educating up" the public to abortion as an "evil" that would "undermine the very foundation of all domestic morals."[16]

Why? While many "regulars" had earnest objections to abortion, they also had an economic interest in stricter abortion restrictions: They faced competition for their services from midwives, herbal healers, and other "irregular" practitioners.[17] But there's no evidence of a grand scheme to dupe the public. Rather, the regulars appear to have sincerely affirmed the (today, scientifically uncontroversial) fact that quickening is an insubstantial stage of gestation.[18] They then sincerely drew the (then and now, fiercely controverted) conclusion that all abortion was morally unjustifiable.[19] Like many today who believe abortion is murder, they found it difficult, if not impossible, to find a sufficiently counterbalancing value to stopping perceived murder.

Sincerity notwithstanding, it's important to situate the regulars' campaign in social context when evaluating the legislation that they inspired. This context included hostility to immigrants, Catholics, and people of color, as well as support for traditional gender norms.[20] Leading physicians proclaimed that "[t]he true wife" did not *seek* "undue power in public life, . . . [u]ndue control in domestic affairs, . . . [or]

---

[16] *Id.* at 171.

[17] *Id.* at 30–39.

[18] *Id.* at 36. See also Justin Buckley Dyer, Slavery, Abortion, and the Politics of Constitutional Meaning 116 (2013) ("[B]y mid-century the quickening requirement was increasingly thought to be in tension with the best medical science and with the principles underlying the traditional common law categories.").

[19] *Id.*

[20] See Leslie J. Reagan, When Abortion Was a Crime: Women, Medicine, and Law in the United States, 1867–1973, 11 (1997); Melissa Murray, "Roe v. Wade," in Critical Race Judgments: Rewritten U.S. Court Opinions on Race and the Law 531 (Bennett Capers, Devon W. Carbado, R.A. Lenhardt, & Angela Onwuachi-Willig eds. 2022). See also Michelle Goodwin, Policing the Womb: Invisible Women and the Criminalization of Motherhood 4 (2020) ("In southern states many . . . midwives or women trained in pregnancy delivery and termination were African American. It is estimated that 50 percent of births in the United States were attended by Black midwives.").

privileges not her own[.]"[21] White women were vital because "upon their loins depends the future destiny of the nation," and the regulars lamented the loss of "national characteristics" as a result of declining "American" birth rates.[22] They also emphasized the (alleged) prevalence of abortion among Protestant women.[23]

As Reva Siegel has shown, regulars unfolded a political-economic vision that tracked the general view of a woman's role at the time.[24] Women were to perform the work of gestation and nurturance, and men—especially male physicians—supervised reproduction for the sake of national prosperity.[25] As campaign leader Horatio Storer put it, "medical men are the physical guardians of women and their offspring; from their position and peculiar knowledge necessitated in all obstetric matters to regulate public sentiment, and to govern tribunals of justice."[26] Between 1860 and 1880, at least 40 new anti-abortion statutes were enacted, with most states eliminating the quickening distinction.[27] Campaigners worked closely with legislators, petitioning for reform and familiarizing legislative committees with Storer's major publications during their deliberations.

C. The Rise of Reproductive Rights

The birth-control movement of the 1920s stemmed from early feminists' "voluntary motherhood" demand—a demand for more control

---

[21] Horatio Storer, Why Not? A Book for Every Woman (1868), reprinted as A Proper Bostonian on Sex and Birth Control 85, 184 (1974); James S. Whitmire, Criminal Abortion, Chi. Med. J. 385, 392 (1874).

[22] Whitmire, *supra* note 21, at 392.

[23] See Mohr, *supra* note 7, at 167.

[24] See also Silvia Federici, Caliban and the Witch: Women, the Body and Primitive Accumulation 74–75 (2004) (arguing that the transition from a subsistence to a capitalist economy saw the reproductive work of women "being mystified as a natural vocation and labeled 'women's labor'" and women "excluded from many waged occupations." The result was a "sexual division of labor that . . . not only fixed women to reproductive work but increased their dependence on men.").

[25] See Reva B. Siegel, Reasoning from the Body: A Historical Perspective on Abortion Regulation and Questions of Equal Protection, 44 Stan. L. Rev. 261, 318 (1992).

[26] Horatio R. Storer, On Criminal Abortion in America 56 (1860).

[27] Mohr, *supra* note 7, at 200. See also James S. Witherspoon, Reexamining Roe: Nineteenth-Century Abortion Statutes and the Fourteenth Amendment, 17 St. Mary's L.J. 29, 34 nn.18–19 (1985) (listing state statutes that increased punishments based on proof of quickening).

over when and how women became pregnant.[28] Birth-control advocates demanded access to resources by which reproductive control could be achieved. In 1921 Margaret Sanger founded what would become the Planned Parenthood Federation of America to provide contraception and information about contraception.[29] But as Melissa Murray notes, Sanger opposed abortion, believing it to be "unsafe and dangerous."[30]

If the birth-control movement descended from the voluntary-motherhood demand, it fell importantly short in ways that did enduring damage to the cause of reproductive freedom. Leading progressive birth control advocates believed in the science of eugenics and defended birth control as a means of population control.[31] Whatever the motivations, Dorothy Roberts has observed that "[b]irth control became a means of controlling a population rather than a means of increasing women's reproductive autonomy."[32] When the sterilization of Black, Puerto Rican, and Native women became official policy in subsequent decades, "family planning" became associated with racial genocide.[33]

Planned Parenthood's first national conference on abortion was held in 1955. It was attended by elite physicians and focused on enabling physicians to provide therapeutic abortions. The final joint conference statement calling for reform of criminal abortion laws didn't discuss women's rights.[34]

In 1959 the American Law Institute proposed a model abortion law that tracked the Planned Parenthood joint statement.[35] By 1970, 12 states had passed abortion-reform measures.[36] But transformative

---

[28] See Melissa Murray, Race-ing Roe: Reproductive Justice, Racial Justice, and the Battle for Roe v. Wade, 134 Harv. L. Rev. 2025, 2038 (2021).

[29] Id.

[30] Id.

[31] See id. at 2039 ("With eugenics as a frame, Sanger and the birth control movement could emphasize contraception not only as conducive to women's health and autonomy, but also as a means of promoting the national welfare.").

[32] Dorothy Roberts, Killing the Black Body 113 (1993).

[33] See id. at 142.

[34] See Reagan, supra note 20, at 220.

[35] See Herbert F. Goodrich & Paul Wolkin, The Story of the American Law Institute, 1923–1961, 5–7 (1961).

[36] Judith Hole & Ellen Levine, Rebirth of Feminism 284 (1971).

change remained elusive, leading nonprofessional women to pursue more radical options.[37] An example: the Chicago-based "Jane," which negotiated with illegal abortion providers to lower prices, created a "scholarship" fund to help low-income abortion-seekers and even provided abortions themselves within an environment that was designed for and to empower women.[38]

Simultaneously, "women's liberation" groups emerged from protest movements in which women were marginalized by fellow leftists.[39] A feminist consensus developed around the need for abortion access.[40] And feminists took their arguments public—to politicians, medical professionals, judges, and ordinary people, pushing for abortion access as necessary for all women, everywhere.

By the late 1960s, a majority of Americans believed that abortion shouldn't be a crime.[41] But decriminalization efforts stalled. Influential pro-lifers[42] elaborated constitutional arguments for prenatal rights.[43] Robert Byrn, a Fordham law professor, published in 1966 an article arguing that abortion violated the Fourteenth Amendment's Equal Protection Clause by denying unborn "person[s] . . . the equal protection of the laws."[44] In December 1971 a New York judge appointed Byrn as the official legal "guardian" of all fetuses between 4 and 24 weeks of development that were scheduled for abortions in New York City hospitals.[45] Along with some high-profile legislative defeats, constitutional arguments for prenatal

[37] See Reagan, *supra* note 20, at 222–45.

[38] See Jenny Brown, Without Apology: The Abortion Struggle Now, 132–39 (2019).

[39] See Reagan, *supra* note 20, at 228–30.

[40] See *id.* at 233.

[41] See Changing Morality: The Two Americas, A Time-Louis Harris Poll, Time (June 6, 1969), https://tinyurl.com/3vb9devb.

[42] At this juncture, predominantly Catholics who regularly participated in national, statewide, and local organizations See Jennifer L. Holland, Tiny You: A Western History of the Anti-Abortion Movement 28–31 (2020).

[43] See, e.g., David Louisell, The Practice of Medicine and the Due Process of Law, 16 UCLA L. Rev. 16 (1968); A. James Quinn & James A. Griffin, The Rights of the Unborn, 3 Jurist 578 (1971). See also Mary Ziegler, Abortion and the Law in America: Roe v. Wade to the Present 17 (2020) (discussing how "[p]ro-lifers looked to both [the Due Process Clause and the Equal Protection Clause] in advocating for fetal rights").

[44] See Robert Byrn, Abortion in Perspective, 5 Duquesne L. Rev. 125 (1966).

[45] See David G. Garrow, Liberty and Sexuality: The Right to Privacy and the Making of Roe v. Wade 522 (1994).

personhood encouraged proponents of abortion rights to develop constitutional arguments of their own and to shift to litigation as a movement strategy.[46]

II. The Law and Politics of *Roe*—and Anti-*Roe*

Roe didn't "start" a national conflict over abortion, but it was a significant battle in a longer war. This part discusses the *Roe* litigation; Justice Harry Blackmun's opinion for the Court; and *Roe*'s emergence as a focal point of constitutional conflict and an inspiration for litigation, legislation, and judicial selection efforts that eventually produced *Dobbs*.

A. The Road to Roe

On March 3, 1970, lawyers Sarah Weddington and Linda Coffee filed a constitutional challenge to an 1857 Texas law banning all abortions not necessary to save a pregnant woman's life. Weddington and Coffee represented three plaintiffs: Marsha and David King, who had medical reasons to avoid pregnancy, and Norma McCorvey, a 21-year-old high-school dropout and survivor of an abusive relationship who was in the midst of her third pregnancy.[47]

For Weddington in particular, abortion rights were at once personal, political, and constitutional. When Sarah became pregnant during her final year of law school, she and her husband, Ron, drove together across the U.S.-Mexico border to procure an abortion.[48] That experience made her responsive to inquiries by Judy Smith and Bea Vogel, two University of Texas-Austin students who were seeking to provide information about safe abortions in Mexico without facing criminal prosecution in Texas.[49] It was at the UT Law snack bar that Judy first suggested a constitutional challenge to Texas's anti-abortion statute.[50]

Meanwhile, lawyers at the ACLU of Georgia were litigating a constitutional challenge to Georgia's abortion restrictions on behalf of Sandra Bensing.[51] The 22-year-old "Mary Doe," like "Jane Roe," was a high-school dropout, was a survivor of abusive relationships, and

---

[46] See *id.* at 495.

[47] See *id.* at 405–06.

[48] See *id.* at 393–94.

[49] See *id.* at 394.

[50] *Id.* at 395.

[51] *Id.* at 428.

had given birth to multiple children before being denied an abortion.[52] The all-female team litigating *Doe v. Bolton* included Margie Hames, Tobi Schwartz, Elizabeth Rindskopf, and Ruste Kitfield.[53]

The principal briefs in *Roe* deploy constitutional reasoning that had long informed contestation over abortion inside and outside the courts. *Roe's* brief focused on whether the right to privacy that was held in *Griswold v. Connecticut*[54] and *Eisenstadt v. Baird*[55] to include contraception also included abortion.[56] Texas's brief articulates the then-dominant pro-life constitutional position that the "unborn child" has a constitutionally guaranteed "personal right . . . to life" protected by the Fourteenth Amendment's Due Process and Equal Protection Clauses, both of which guarantee rights to "life" and "protection" to "person[s]."[57] Both sides were asking the Court to resolve the conflict over abortion by declaring one political movement's position unconstitutional.

B. The Roe *Opinion*

Roe and *Doe* were 7-2 decisions, each authored by Nixon-appointed Justice Harry Blackmun and joined by three other Republican appointees. *Roe* begins with abortion history—like, a *lot* of abortion history, ranging back to the Persian Empire.[58] The gist of it: (1) Attitudes about abortion have changed over time; (2) the common law didn't prohibit pre-quickening abortion and may not have even prohibited post-quickening abortion; and (3) American law followed the common law regarding abortion until the late-19th century.

---

[52] See *id.* at 425–28.

[53] *Id.* at 425.

[54] 381 U.S. 479 (1965).

[55] 405 U.S. 438 (1972).

[56] See Br. for Jane Roe et al., in Linda Greenhouse & Reva B. Siegel, Before Roe v. Wade: Voices That Shaped the Abortion Debate before the Supreme Court's Ruling 233–34 (2012). Notably, the brief doesn't make equal protection arguments. This seems a glaring omission from today's vantage point, but arguments that abortion restrictions discriminated against poor people who were less able to obtain permission for therapeutic abortions had been rejected by a number of lower courts. See, e.g., United States v. Vuitch, 305 F. Supp. 1032, 1035 (D.D.C. 1969); Steinberg v. Brown, 321 F. Supp. 741, 748 (N.D. Ohio 1970); Doe v. Bolton, 319 F. Supp. 1048, 1056 (N.D. Ga. 1970). And the Court's sex-discrimination doctrine had only just begun to develop. See Reed v. Reed, 404 U.S. 71 (1971); Frontiero v. Richardson, 411 U.S. 677 (1974).

[57] See Br. for Appellee Henry Wade, in Greenhouse & Siegel, *supra* note 56, at 243–44.

[58] Roe v. Wade, 410 U.S. 113, 129–50 (1973).

Justice Blackmun identifies three possible justifications for abortion restrictions: (1) discouraging illicit sex; (2) maternal health and safety; (3) the protection of prenatal life. Justice Blackmun quickly dismisses (1) because Texas didn't advance it; says that (2) is relevant only late in pregnancy; and reserves further analysis of (3).[59]

Blackmun then considers whether there exists a constitutional right to terminate a pregnancy. He states that the answer turns on the right to privacy but doesn't identify that right's constitutional source. He cites First,[60] Fourth,[61] Fifth,[62] and Fourteenth Amendment cases,[63] as well as Justice Arthur Goldberg's concurrence in *Griswold*,[64] which relied on the Ninth Amendment's command that "[t]he enumeration in the Constitution, of certain rights, shall not be construed to deny or disparage others retained by the people."[65]

Then comes a momentous declaration: "This right of privacy . . . is broad enough to encompass a woman's decision whether or not to terminate her pregnancy."[66] Why? Blackmun discusses physical, psychological, financial, and social "detriment[s]" that the state "would impose upon the pregnant woman by denying this choice."[67] He quickly adds that (1) the choice will be made by the "the woman and her responsible physician . . . in consultation"; (2) "a State may properly assert important interests in safeguarding health, in maintaining medical standards, and in protecting potential life"; and (3) "at some point in pregnancy, these respective interests become . . . compelling."[68] And he states that during the early stages of a pregnancy, strict scrutiny of abortion restrictions—the highest level of

---

[59] See *id.* at 148–50.

[60] See Stanley v. Georgia, 394 U.S. 557, 564 (1969).

[61] See Terry v. Ohio, 392 U.S. 1, 8–9 (1968); Katz v. United States, 389 U.S. 347, 350 (1967); Boyd v. United States, 116 U.S. 616 (1886).

[62] See Olmstead v. United States, 277 U.S. 438, 478 (1928) (Brandeis, J., dissenting).

[63] See Meyer v. Nebraska, 262 U.S. 390, 399 (1923); Pierce v. Society of Sisters, 268 U.S. 510, 535 (1925); Skinner v. Oklahoma, 316 U.S. 535, 541–42 (1942); Loving v. Virginia, 388 U.S. 1, 12 (1967); Eisenstadt, 405 U.S. at 453–54.

[64] 381 U.S. 479, 486 (1965) (Goldberg, J., concurring).

[65] U.S. Const. amend. IX.

[66] Roe, 410 U.S. at 153.

[67] *Id.*

[68] See *id.* at 153–54.

judicial scrutiny, reserved only for a handful of constitutional rights (on which more below)—is constitutionally required.[69]

Blackmun then sketches a framework for balancing abortion rights against states' interests in maternal health and the existence of "potential life."[70] The most important stage is viability—the point at which "the fetus . . . has the capability of meaningful life outside the mother's womb."[71] After viability, states can ban abortion except "where it is necessary, in appropriate medical judgment, for the preservation of the life or health of the mother."[72]

We have no record of any criticism of *Roe* from prominent reproductive-rights supporters. Pro-life criticism, however, followed immediately. Maryland Rep. Lawrence Hogan and New York Sen. James Buckley called for a constitutional amendment declaring that Fourteenth Amendment personhood began at conception.[73] The National Conference of Catholic Bishops issued a statement sharply criticizing the Court for rejecting prenatal constitutional personhood.[74] Pro-life legal scholars reiterated constitutional arguments for prenatal constitutional personhood.[75] Professor Charles Rice made the first of many comparisons of *Roe* to *Dred Scott v. Sandford*,[76] in which the Court denied that Black people could ever be citizens of the United States.[77]

The most important critique of *Roe* outside of pro-life circles was Harvard Law Professor John Hart Ely's essay, "The Wages of Crying Wolf."[78] Ely emphasizes that the Court had since 1938 singled

---

[69] See *id.* at 155.

[70] *Id.* at 154.

[71] *Id.* at 163.

[72] *Id.*

[73] Garrow, *supra* note 45, at 606. See Roe, 410 U.S. at 157–58 (determining that "the word 'person,' as used in the Fourteenth Amendment, does not include the unborn").

[74] See Pastoral Message, Feb. 13, 1973, https://tinyurl.com/ycxxr3kk.

[75] See, e.g., Robert M. Byrn, An American Tragedy: The Supreme Court on Abortion, 41 Fordham L. Rev. 807 (1973); Joseph O'Meara, Abortion: The Court Decides a Non-Case, 1974 Sup. Ct. Rev. 337 (1974).

[76] 60 U.S. 493 (1857).

[77] See Charles E. Rice, The Dred Scott Case of the Twentieth Century, 10 Houston L. Rev. 1059 (1973). On the *Roe-Dred Scott* comparison and its use by conservatives, see Dyer, *supra* note 18, at 3–12.

[78] John Hart Ely, The Wages of Crying Wolf, 82 Yale L.J. 920 (1973).

out for heightened judicial review only legislation affecting rights enumerated in the first eight amendments (the "Bill of Rights") or affecting politically vulnerable ("discrete and insular") minorities.[79] All other legislation, however, was subject to a lower "tier" of scrutiny. *Roe* had seemingly departed from this framework, and the Court hadn't adequately explained why. Questions raised but left unanswered included:

(1) Why is viability the critical constitutional line? To say that "the fetus . . . has the capability of meaningful life outside the mother's womb" is just to describe what viability is; it doesn't justify it.[80]

(2) Why does it matter whether zygotes or fetuses are constitutional persons? Can't states prohibit people from killing dogs and other non-human animals?[81]

(3) What does any of this have to do with privacy? *Griswold* emphasized how enforcement of a ban on contraceptives would require police to invade marital bedrooms. Is there a similar concern here?[82]

(4) Are women discrete and insular minorities? If zygotes or fetuses aren't, why not?[83]

Roe's failure to answer such basic questions was the basis for Ely's memorable charge that "[*Roe*] is not constitutional law and gives almost no sense of an obligation to try to be."[84] Ely doesn't say that *Griswold* or any of the other personal-liberty precedents upon which *Roe* had relied were "not constitutional law," but his critique resembled conservative then-Yale Law professor Robert Bork's critiques of *Griswold* and, later, *Roe*.[85] Both regarded the use of the Due Process

---

[79] See United States v. Carolene Products, 304 U.S. 144, 152 n.4 (1938). The literature on "Footnote Four" is dense, but one can hardly improve upon Jack M. Balkin, The Footnote, 83 Nw. L. Rev. 275 (1989). It's literally a footnote.

[80] See Ely, *supra* note 78, at 924.

[81] *Id.* at 926.

[82] *Id.* at 928–30.

[83] *Id.* at 935.

[84] *Id.* at 947.

[85] See Robert H. Bork, Neutral Principles and Some First Amendment Problems, 47 Ind. L.J. 1, 8–12 (1971); Robert H. Bork, The Tempting of America: The Political Seduction of the Law 116 (1990).

Clause of the Fourteenth Amendment to protect fundamental rights with great skepticism;[86] Bork considered "substantive due process" illegitimate.[87]

If substantive due process sounds silly, that's because the phrase was popularized by critics of the doctrine. The doctrine holds that the Constitution's guarantees that no "person" shall be "deprived of life, liberty, or property without due process of law" don't just require access to certain procedures (like notice and an opportunity to be heard) prior to the deprivation. They prohibit the government from depriving people of certain fundamental "liberty" rights—some listed in the Bill of Rights, others unwritten—without a compelling reason. The critique of substantive due process was first advanced by progressives who opposed the Court's enforcement of the (unenumerated) liberty to contract during the early 20th century.[88] But conservative critics of *Griswold* and *Roe* like Bork and eventual Justice Antonin Scalia eagerly took it up.

Any opinion recognizing a constitutional right to abortion would have been fiercely criticized. Still, *Roe*'s evident flaws lent credibility to a case for undermining and ultimately overruling it.

C. The Pro-Life Movement and Lifetime Appointments

As the above history suggests, it didn't take *Roe* to organize national movements around abortion rights. Further, as Linda Greenhouse and Reva Siegel have shown, Republican strategists seeking to appeal to pro-life Catholics whom they thought they could dislodge from the Democratic Party successfully lobbied Richard Nixon to campaign against "abortion on demand" prior to the 1972 presidential election.[89] What began as a strategy for targeting Catholics was

---

[86] John Hart Ely, Democracy and Distrust: A Theory of Judicial Review 18 (1980) (characterizing it as a contradiction in terms akin to "green pastel redness").

[87] See Bork, Tempting, *supra* note 85, at 43 (arguing that "substantive due process, wherever it appears, is never more than a pretense that the judge's views are in the Constitution").

[88] See, e.g., Charles Warren, The New "Liberty" Under the Fourteenth Amendment, 39 Harv. L. Rev. 431 (1926). For a discussion of this critique and its adoption by conservatives, see David E. Bernstein, Rehabilitating Lochner: Defending Individual Rights against Progressive Reform 118 (2011).

[89] See Linda Greenhouse & Reva B. Siegel, Before (and after) Roe v. Wade: New Questions about Backlash, 120 Yale L.J. 2028, 2046–47 (2011).

expanded to garner the support of conservatives more generally.[90] Partisan "sorting" on abortion didn't require Justice Blackmun's assistance.

Still, Mary Ziegler has documented how "the anti-abortion movement helped to make the Supreme Court a central issue for rank-and-file Republican voters" and "inspired the Republican Party to change its approach to judicial nominations."[91] These pro-life efforts included fighting to undo campaign finance restrictions in order to make it easier to raise money for conservative candidates who supported the appointment of conservative judges.[92] It also involved pressure on Republican legislators and presidents to undermine abortion rights until a human life amendment could be passed by a Republican Congress or a conservative Supreme Court could overrule *Roe*.[93] It was President Ronald Reagan who first prioritized anti-*Roe* judicial selection.

In the late 1970s, the Court issued three decisions that encouraged pro-lifers and dispirited reproductive-rights supporters. *Planned Parenthood v. Danforth* upheld a requirement that a woman seeking an abortion during the first 12 weeks of pregnancy certify that "her consent is informed and freely given and is not the result of coercion."[94] *Maher v. Roe*,[95] *Beal v. Doe*,[96] and *Poelker v. Doe*[97] upheld laws prohibiting the use of Medicaid funds or public hospital services for abortion. Finally, in *Harris v. McRae*, the Court held as constitutional a federal ban—the Hyde Amendment—on Medicaid reimbursement.[98] Pro-lifers took these decisions as signals to invest in constitutional litigation.[99]

In *Akron v. Akron Center for Reproductive Health*, a 6-3 majority struck down core provisions of an ordinance requiring parental consent

---

[90] *Id.*

[91] Mary Ziegler, Dollars for Life: The Anti-Abortion Movement and the Fall of the Republican Establishment 279 (2022).

[92] See *id.* at 177–224.

[93] See *id.* at 10.

[94] Planned Parenthood v. Danforth, 428 U.S. 52, 65 (1976).

[95] 432 U.S. 464 (1977).

[96] 432 U.S. 438 (1977).

[97] 432 U.S. 519 (1977).

[98] 448 U.S. 297 (1980).

[99] Ziegler, *supra* note 91, at 68.

and notification for abortions performed on unmarried minors; mandating a 24-hour waiting period; "informing" patients that "the unborn child is a human life from the moment of conception" and describing physical and psychological complication from abortion; and providing for the disposal of fetal remains.[100] But Justice Sandra Day O'Connor's dissent delivered a pleasant political surprise to the Reagan White House.[101] In it, O'Connor suggests jettisoning *Roe's* framework of strict scrutiny for pre-viability abortion restrictions.[102] She argues that the only relevant constitutional question is whether the state has imposed "absolute obstacles or severe limitations on the abortion decision."[103]

The White House used O'Connor's dissent to pitch pro-lifers on Reagan's 1984 reelection.[104] Reagan's next two nominees—Antonin Scalia and Robert Bork—were put forward in part because it was believed that they would meet with pro-life approval. Bork was specifically identified as someone who wouldn't hesitate to overturn *Roe.*[105]

Scalia was easily confirmed. Recognizing that the loss of two more members of the *Roe* coalition left no stable majority in favor of the precedent, the National Abortion Rights Action League vowed to spend $1 million to defeat Bork's nomination.[106] Hundreds of left-leaning organizations formed the Block Bork Coalition to paint Bork as an ideological extremist.[107] It succeeded; Bork was rejected by the Senate. After Reagan's next choice, Douglas Ginsburg, fell through when Ginsburg admitted to marijuana use, Reagan settled on Anthony Kennedy—despite some concerns about privacy-friendly language in his opinions.[108] When Reagan's successor in office, George H. W. Bush, found himself in a position to replace abortion-rights stalwarts William Brennan and Thurgood Marshall (with

[100] 462 U.S. 416 (1983).

[101] It was a surprise because O'Connor's nomination provoked a great deal of opposition from pro-lifers, who blamed her for obstructing abortion restrictions as an Arizona legislator. See Ziegler, *supra* note 91, at 77–78.

[102] See Akron, 462 U.S. at 461–66 (O'Connor, J., dissenting).

[103] *Id.* at 464.

[104] Ziegler, *supra* note 91, at 84.

[105] *Id.* at 96.

[106] *Id.*

[107] *Id.*

[108] *Id.* at 98.

David Souter and Clarence Thomas, respectively), *Roe's* overruling seemed certain.

D. Undue Burdens, TRAPs, and Tradition

In 1992, in *Planned Parenthood v. Casey*, five Republican-appointed justices voted to preserve *Roe*, but a three-justice plurality significantly modified judicial review of abortion restrictions.[109] The case arose from challenges to Pennsylvania abortion restrictions that included a 24-hour waiting period; a requirement that the person seeking an abortion be informed of the nature of the procedure, the health risks of the abortion and of childbirth, and the "probable gestational age of the unborn child"; a requirement that a minor seeking an abortion have the consent of one parent or a court order; and a requirement that a married woman inform her husband about the abortion.[110] The Court upheld all but the last requirement.

The *Casey* plurality—Justices O'Connor, Kennedy, and Souter—replaced *Roe's* trimester framework with an undue-burden standard applicable throughout the pregnancy. The undue-burden standard sought to determine whether "a state regulation has the purpose or effect of placing a substantial obstacle in the path of a woman seeking an abortion."[111] Before viability, states could promote informed choice and protect maternal health and safety.[112] But they couldn't ban pre-viability abortions.[113]

After performing the ordinary work of a court deciding whether to overrule a precedent—considering the workability of the rule, reliance interests, other developments in the law, changed facts or social understandings of those facts—the plurality identifies *Roe* as an extraordinary precedent demanding extraordinary analysis.[114] It describes *Roe* as one of only three cases—the others being *West Coast Hotel v. Parrish*[115] (holding constitutional minimum wage laws) and *Brown v.*

---

[109] 505 U.S. 833 (1992).

[110] *Id.* at 844 (plurality).

[111] *Id.* at 877.

[112] *Id.* at 878.

[113] *Id.* at 879.

[114] *Id.* at 855, 861.

[115] 300 U.S. 379 (1937).

Board of Education[116] (holding unconstitutional segregation in public education)—in which the Court had "call[ed] the contending sides of a national controversy to end their national division by accepting a common mandate rooted in the Constitution."[117] It concludes that none of the considerations above supported overruling *Roe*.[118]

Casey produced several separate opinions, the most significant of which was Justice Scalia's stirring dissent. What the plurality describes as its exercise of "reasoned judgment" concerning the meaning of "liberty," Justice Scalia calls "a collection of adjectives that simply decorate a value judgment and conceal a political choice."[119] The plurality isn't seeking to discern the path of the law in good faith—it's "systematically eliminating checks upon its own power."[120] And it's not courageously defending the Constitution—it's displaying "czarist arrogance" by "stubbornly refus[ing] to abandon an erroneous opinion."[121]

The central constitutional premise of Scalia's dissent is majoritarian democracy. Because the Constitution's text doesn't speak to abortion, Scalia argues that such "value judgment[s]" are left to democratic majorities.[122] And the people, Scalia intones, "love democracy . . . and are not fools."[123] He charges that "*Roe*'s mandate for abortion on demand destroyed the compromises of the past, rendered compromise impossible for the future, and required the entire issue to be resolved uniformly, at the national level."[124] And his rhetoric expresses his sympathy for those who "protest our saying that the Constitution requires what our society has never thought the Constitution requires."[125]

Scalia also casts *Roe* as a particularly damaging variation on a broader theme. He accuses the Court of "ignor[ing] a long and clear

---

[116] 347 U.S. 483 (1954).
[117] *Casey*, 505 U.S. at 867.
[118] *Id.* at 869.
[119] *Id.* at 983 (Scalia, J., dissenting).
[120] *Id.* at 981.
[121] *Id.* at 999.
[122] *Id.* at 982.
[123] *Id.* at 1000.
[124] *Id.* at 995.
[125] *Id.* at 999.

tradition clarifying an ambiguous text, as we did, for example, five days ago in declaring unconstitutional invocations and benedictions at public high school graduation ceremonies."[126] In case after case, then, the justices were disregarding *tradition* in constitutional interpretation.

In *Washington v. Glucksberg*,[127] in 1997, Chief Justice William Rehnquist wrote for a majority that rejected a substantive due process right to assisted suicide and enshrined Scalia's preferred tradition-centered approach to identifying fundamental rights.[128] *Glucksberg* held that only rights "deeply rooted in this Nation's history and tradition" and "implicit in the concept of ordered liberty" would qualify as fundamental.[129] For the purposes of determining whether a claimed right was deeply rooted, a claimed right had to be given a "careful description."[130] Rehnquist justified this "two-step"[131] on the ground that it would prevent judges from "plac[ing] matter[s] outside the arena of public debate and legislative action."[132]

In application, "careful" meant "narrow." Thus, the challengers to Washington's criminal ban on assisted suicide weren't—according to the Court—claiming "the right to die" or the right to "control one's last days."[133] Rather, they were claiming "the right to commit suicide which itself includes a right to assistance in doing so."[134] The Court rejected this claim because "for over 700 years, the Anglo-American

---

[126] *Id.* at 1000. This is a reference to Lee v. Weisman, 505 U.S. 577 (1992).

[127] 520 U.S. 702 (1997).

[128] The approach closely resembles Scalia's plurality opinion in Michael H. v. Gerald D., 491 U.S. 110, 122 (1989) ("In an attempt to limit and guide interpretation of the [Due Process] Clause, we have insisted not merely that the interest denominated as a 'liberty' be 'fundamental' (a concept that, in isolation, is hard to objectify), but also that it be an interest traditionally protected by our society."). A footnote indicates that the tradition is to be defined at "the most specific level at which a relevant tradition protecting, or denying protection to, the asserted right can be identified." *Id.* at 127 n.6.

[129] Glucksberg, 520 U.S. at 720–21.

[130] *Id.* at 721.

[131] See Randy E. Barnett, Scrutiny Land, 106 Mich. L. Rev. 1479, 1488 (2008). Barnett traces the *Glucksberg* test back to *Bowers v. Hardwick*, in which the Court upheld a ban on sodomy. *Bowers* was later overruled by *Lawrence v. Texas*.

[132] Glucksberg, 520 U.S. at 720.

[133] *Id.* at 722.

[134] *Id.*

common-law tradition has punished or otherwise disapproved of both suicide and assisting suicide."[135]

The Court's commitment to *Glucksberg* proved unstable, thanks to Justice Kennedy. A swing vote on a Court roughly evenly divided along ideological lines, Kennedy authored two key substantive due process opinions. In *Lawrence v. Texas*, the Court held unconstitutional a Texas ban on same-sex sodomy.[136] In *Obergefell v. Hodges*, the Court held that the Fourteenth Amendment's Due Process and Equal Protection Clauses guaranteed to same-sex couples the right to marry.[137] *Lawrence* didn't mention *Glucksberg; Obergefell* discussed it only to reject it as "inconsistent with the approach this Court has used in discussing other fundamental rights, including marriage and intimacy."[138]

But *Glucksberg* didn't disappear. The Court applied *Glucksberg* in incorporating against the states, via the Due Process Clause, the rights to keep and bear arms[139] and to not to be subjected to excessive fines.[140] Meanwhile, the pro-life movement worked to take full advantage of *Casey's* more deferential undue-burden test.

Several states enacted "informed consent" laws requiring people seeking abortions to undergo ultrasounds.[141] States also passed "fetal pain" laws requiring a person seeking an abortion 22 weeks into the pregnancy to be told about the possibility of fetal pain—even though medical evidence suggests that fetal pain is unlikely to occur until the 29th week.[142] Finally, states imposed facially neutral facility, equipment, and staffing regulations on abortion providers, purportedly to protect health and safety.[143] Critics referred to them as Targeted

---

[135] *Id.* at 711.

[136] 539 U.S. 558 (2003).

[137] 576 U.S. 644 (2015).

[138] *Id.* at 671.

[139] McDonald v. Chicago, 561 U.S. 742, 764 (2010).

[140] Timbs v. Indiana, 139 S. Ct. 682, 690 (2019).

[141] See Mary Ziegler, Liberty and the Politics of Balance: The Undue-Burden Test after Casey/Hellerstedt, 52 Harv. C.R.-C.L. L. Rev. 422, 451 (2017).

[142] *Id.* at 466.

[143] *Id.* at 451.

Regulation of Abortion Providers, or "TRAPs," because of the costly financial and administrative burdens that they imposed.[144]

At the federal level, pro-lifers in 2003 secured the enactment of the Partial Birth Abortion Ban Act, prohibiting the most common form of second-trimester abortions—dilation and evacuation (D&E)—without any health exception. Writing for the Court in *Gonzales v. Carhart*,[145] Justice Kennedy read *Casey* narrowly and emphasized as "central to its conclusion" the premise that "the government has a legitimate and substantial interest in preserving and promoting fetal life."[146]

E. "Pro-Life Justices"

The Court's next major abortion case, *Whole Women's Health v. Hellerstedt*, was decided shortly after Justice Scalia's death in 2016.[147] Here, Justice Kennedy joined a 5-3 majority to hold unconstitutional a Texas law imposing surgical-center and admitting-privilege requirements. Writing for the Court, Justice Stephen Breyer determined that the law imposed an undue burden because it produced no health benefits to justify its costs.[148] Those costs included closing around half of Texas's clinics and increasing travel distances for thousands of women by hundreds of miles.[149]

If *Gonzales v. Carhart* weakened *Casey*, *Hellerstedt* strengthened it. But *Hellerstedt* was decided by an eight-justice Court, and a Republican-controlled Senate declined to hold hearings on Democratic President Barack Obama's nominee for Justice Scalia's seat, D.C. Circuit Judge Merrick Garland. On the 2016 campaign trail, Republican nominee Donald Trump promised that if elected he would appoint "pro-life justices."[150] He put forward a list compiled with the aid of Leonard Leo, the longtime vice president of the Federalist Society,

---

[144] See Targeted Regulation of Abortion Providers (TRAP) Laws, Guttmacher Inst. (Jan. 2020), https://tinyurl.com/bdhhpx5p.

[145] 127 S. Ct. 1610 (2007).

[146] *Id.* at 1633.

[147] 136 S. Ct. 2292 (2016).

[148] See *id.* at 2300.

[149] See *id.* at 2301–03.

[150] Laura Bassett, Donald Trump Promises to Appoint Anti-Abortion Justices to Supreme Court, The Huffington Post (May 11, 2016), https://tinyurl.com/ycy2aswd.

an influential conservative-libertarian legal organization,[151] as well as the co-chairman of its board of directors.[152] As former Scalia clerk and president of the conservative Ethics and Public Policy Center Ed Whelan described him, "[n]o one has been more dedicated to the enterprise of building a Supreme Court that will overturn *Roe v. Wade* than the Federalist Society's Leonard Leo."[153] Trump's appointment for Scalia's seat, Neil Gorsuch, was on Leo's list.[154]

When Justice Kennedy retired, Trump in 2018 appointed Brett Kavanaugh. Then–D.C.-Circuit judge Kavanaugh's position on abortion was suggested by his dissent from a decision holding that the government's refusal to release a pregnant minor from custody constituted an undue burden.[155] In that dissent, Kavanaugh used the phrase "abortion on demand" three times.[156] Following the death of Justice Ruth Bader Ginsburg—a vigorous defender of *Roe*'s holding, though not its reasoning[157]—Trump appointed Amy Coney Barrett, a former Scalia clerk and law professor at Notre Dame who was known to be pro-life.[158]

---

[151] On the Federalist Society, see Stephen Teles, The Rise of the Conservative Legal Movement: The Battle for Control of the Law (2008); Amanda-Hollis Brusky, Ideas with Consequences: The Federalist Society and the Conservative Counterrevolution (2015).

[152] Ziegler, *supra* note 105, at 181.

[153] See Ed Whelan, Mistaken Attack by Andy Schlafly on Leonard Leo, Nat'l Rev. Online (Dec. 9, 2016), https://tinyurl.com/bdekw48h.

[154] See Shane Goldmacher, Josh Gerstein, & Matthew Nussbaum, Trump Picks Gorsuch for Supreme Court, Politico (Jan. 31, 2017), https://tinyurl.com/2u7273kn.

[155] See Garza v. Hargan, 874 F.3d 735 (D.C. Cir. 2017).

[156] *Id.* at 752, 755–56 (Kavanaugh, J., dissenting).

[157] See Ruth Bader Ginsburg, Speaking in a Judicial Voice, 67 N.Y.U. L. Rev. 1185 (1992). Justice Alito's opinion for the Court in *Dobbs* notes her criticism of the reasoning without acknowledging the equal protection argument that she advanced in defense of the holding. Compare *id.* at 1200 (arguing that *Roe* should have "honed in more precisely on the women's equality dimension of the issue and, correspondingly, attempted nothing more bold at that time than the mode of decision-making the Court employed in the 1970s gender classification cases") with Dobbs, 142 S. Ct. at 2279 (citing Ginsburg for the proposition that "*Roe* may have 'halted a political process,' 'prolonged divisiveness,' and 'deferred stable settlement of the issue'). As we'll see, he goes on to give the equal protection argument only cursory treatment.

[158] See Ariana de Vogue & Austin Bundy, Barrett Signed a "Right to Life" Letter in Ad That Also Called to End Roe v. Wade, CNN (Oct. 1, 2020), https://tinyurl.com/2fmbmzvb.

When the Court took up Mississippi's ban on abortion after 15 weeks—well before viability—most expected the Court to uphold the law. This would necessarily undermine *Casey*. But when Mississippi initially petitioned for review in *Dobbs*, it expressly stated that "the questions presented in this petition do not require the Court to overturn *Roe* or *Casey*."[159] Only after the Court granted review did it argue for their overruling in its principal brief.[160] And at oral argument, Chief Justice John Roberts—a potential swing vote—suggested that the viability line was inessential to *Roe* and *Casey*.[161]

On May 3, 2022, *Politico* published a leaked draft opinion indicating that the Court was about to overrule *Roe*.[162]

III. Reading *Dobbs*

Justice Alito's opinion for the Court in *Dobbs* closely resembles Justice Scalia's *Casey* dissent in its strident tone and majoritarian, tradition-bound substance. It drew an unsparingly critical dissent and yielded three concurrences. This part summarizes the opinions.

A. The Opinion of the Court

Alito comes out swinging at *Roe*. Previewing the critique to come, he states that *Roe* "did not claim that American law or the common law had ever recognized" a right to terminate a pregnancy; that "its survey of history ranged from the constitutionally irrelevant . . . to the plainly incorrect"; its trimester framework resembled "a statute enacted by a legislature"; and its bad reasoning justified Ely's charge that it was "not constitutional law."[163]

Constitutional analysis begins with Alito's summary dismissal of an argument that abortion restrictions violate the Equal Protection Clause by discriminating on the basis of sex. Alito pronounces this

---

[159] Pet. for Cert. at 5, Dobbs v. Jackson Women's Health Org., 142 S. Ct. 2228 (2022) (No. 19-1392).

[160] See Br. for Petitioners at 12–13, Dobbs v. Jackson Women's Health Org., 142 S. Ct. 2228 (2022) (No. 19-1392).

[161] See Tr. of Oral Arg. at 17–18, 51, Dobbs v. Jackson Women's Health Org., 142 S. Ct. 2228 (2022) (No. 19-1392).

[162] Josh Gerstein & Alexander Ward, Supreme Court Has Voted to Overturn Abortion Rights, Draft Opinion Shows, Politico (May 3, 2022), https://tinyurl.com/ywperwx7.

[163] Dobbs, 142 S. Ct. at 2240–41.

argument "squarely foreclosed by our precedents."[164] He discusses *Geduldig v. Aiello*[165] and *Bray v. Alexandria Women's Health Clinic,*[166] which he reads to hold that pregnancy-based distinctions don't trigger heightened judicial scrutiny and abortion restrictions don't constitute "invidiously discriminatory animus" against women.[167]

Up next is the main event—the substantive due process argument that "liberty" includes abortion rights. All "liberty" rights, says Alito, must be deeply rooted and implicit in ordered liberty under *Glucksberg* to be considered fundamental and receive heightened protection.[168] Alito then dives into abortion history, sweeping through common-law authorities spanning hundreds of years.[169] All authorities indicate that the abortion of a quick child was a common-law crime; none indicate that abortion was ever "a legal right."[170] Alito's survey of the Founding era yields similar results.[171]

By the time that the Fourteenth Amendment was ratified in 1868, Alito finds that toleration of pre-quickening abortion had ceased.[172] Alito isn't interested in why this happened. He explains his lack of interest in his response to an amicus brief by the American Historical Association (AHA).[173] Alito avers that "[t]his Court has long disfavored arguments based on alleged legislative motives" because different legislators have different motives.[174] He notes that the evidence in the AHA brief consists only of statements from supporters of the law—not legislators.[175] Finally, he expresses a broader, political concern about questioning motives in the context of abortion.

---

[164] *Id.* at 2245.

[165] *Id.* at 2246.

[166] *Id.*

[167] *Id.*

[168] *Id.*

[169] See *id.* at 2249–51.

[170] See *id.* at 2250.

[171] See *id.* at 2255.

[172] See *id.* at 2254–55.

[173] See Br. for Am. Historical Ass'n et al. as Amici Curiae at 27–28, Dobbs v. Jackson Women's Health Org., 142 S. Ct. 2228 (2022) (No. 19-1392), https://tinyurl.com/ytb5h223.

[174] Dobbs, 142 S. Ct. at 2255.

[175] *Id.* at 2254–55.

"Even *Roe* and *Casey*," he stresses, "did not question the good faith of abortion opponents."[176]

Next, Alito considers whether abortion rights, though not deeply rooted in history, fall within some broader right that *is* deeply rooted in history. For instance, the right to play violent videogames wasn't deeply rooted in 1791, but the Court (with Justice Scalia writing) held that "the freedom of speech" includes it.[177] Alito criticizes *Casey's* formulation of a broader substantive due process right to "liberty" that would include abortion: "the right to define one's own concept of existence, of meaning, of the universe, and of the mystery of human life."[178] *That* "liberty" is too broad, says Alito, because it might include "illicit drug use, prostitution, and the like,"[179] and *those* rights have no "claim to being deeply rooted in history."[180]

Alito then distinguishes abortion from other substantive due process rights. He doesn't say that rights to marry a partner of the same sex, use contraceptives, or have sex are deeply rooted.[181] But he says that they don't "involve[e] the critical moral question posed by abortion" because they don't implicate "fetal life."[182]

The Court doesn't overrule cases just because they were wrongly decided. Alito identifies "five factors that weigh strongly in favor of overruling *Roe* and *Casey*: the nature of their error, the quality of their reasoning, the 'workability' of the rules they imposed on the country, their disruptive effect on other areas of the law, and the absence of concrete reliance."[183]

The first reason that *Dobbs* overrules *Roe* and *Casey* is that they were "egregiously wrong and deeply damaging."[184] Citing Scalia's *Casey* dissent, Alito contends that the Court "usurped the power to address a question of profound moral and social importance that the

---

[176] *Id.* at 2256.

[177] See Brown v. Entm't Merch. Ass'n, 64 U.S. 786 (2011).

[178] Casey, 505 U.S. at 851.

[179] Dobbs, 142 S. Ct. at 2258.

[180] *Id.*

[181] As a dissenter in *Obergefell*, he could hardly affirm the first of those rights on *Glucksberg* grounds.

[182] *Id.*

[183] *Id.* at 2264.

[184] *Id.* at 2265.

Constitution unequivocally leaves for the people."[185] To add insult to constitutional injury, *Roe* and *Casey* lacked grounding in "text, history, or precedent."[186]

Regarding workability, Alito argues that Scalia was right about the undue-burden test being "inherently standardless."[187] He describes the Court's own shifting undue-burden doctrine, as well as persistent splits between federal appellate courts over various abortion restrictions.[188] Alito moves briskly through the fourth factor, "effect on other areas of law," after summarizing complaints that various justices have leveled against abortion doctrine.[189] The fifth factor, reliance, gets more extensive treatment.

How much are people's expectations tied up in *Roe/Casey* continuing to be the law? The *Casey* plurality acknowledged that "[a]bortion is customarily chosen as an unplanned response to the consequence of unplanned activity or to the failure of conventional birth control" and that "reproductive planning could take virtually immediate account" of *Roe's* overruling.[190] But, it stated that "for two decades of economic and social developments, people have organized intimate relationships and made choices . . . in reliance on the availability of abortion."[191] Alito rejects *Casey's* high-generality reliance in favor of the very "precise" reliance interests that *Casey* conceded were absent.[192] He argues that high-generality reliance "finds little support in our cases" and that the Court is ill-equipped to evaluate "generalized assertions about the national psyche."[193]

Finally, Alito criticizes *Casey's* concern about seeming to have "surrender[ed] to political pressure" if the Court decided to overrule *Roe*, as well as *Casey's* aspiration to bring "contending sides of a national controversy to end their national division."[194] To be "affected

---

[185] *Id.*

[186] *Id.* at 2266.

[187] *Id.* at 2272.

[188] See *id.* at 2274–75.

[189] See *id.* at 2264–65.

[190] Casey, 505 U.S. at 856.

[191] *Id.*

[192] *Id.*

[193] Dobbs, 142 S. Ct. at 2276.

[194] *Id.* at 2278 (quoting Casey, 505 U.S. at 866–67).

by any extraneous influences such as concern about the public's re-action to our work," Alito writes, is to go "beyond this Court's role in our constitutional system."[195]

So, how are judges to review abortion laws going forward? Schol-ars have long observed that the Court's "default" rule of judicial scrutiny of government restrictions on non-fundamental liberty rights—rational-basis review—can take two forms.[196] One form—"rationality review"—is deferential but not toothless. The Court has held unconstitutional under rationality review a number of govern-ment actions upon demonstration that the government sought to achieve an improper goal.[197] The other—"conceivable basis review"—essentially dictates victory for the government. It tells judges not to consider what government actions are actually designed to achieve and doesn't require the government to support with evidence claims that a rights-restriction is justified.[198]

Dobbs applies conceivable-basis review: "A law regulating abortion . . . must be sustained if there is a rational basis on which the *legislature could have thought* that it would serve legitimate state interests."[199] So, abortion laws can be defended and upheld for rea-sons that never crossed anyone's mind when they were enacted. Alito then provides a list of reasons that might justify abortion restrictions: "[R]espect for and preservation of prenatal life at all stages of develop-ment; . . . the protection of maternal health and safety; the elimination of particularly gruesome or barbaric medical procedures; the preser-vation of the integrity of the medical profession; the mitigation of fetal pain; and the prevention of discrimination on the basis of race, sex, or disability."[200] The Court easily upholds Mississippi's 15-week ban.[201]

---

[195] *Id.*

[196] See Gayle Lynn Pettinga, Rational Basis with Bite: Intermediate Scrutiny by Any Other Name, 62 Ind. L.J. 779, 780 (1987); Raphael Holoszyc-Pimentel, Reconciling Ra-tional Basis Review: When Does Rational Basis Bite, 90 N.Y.U. L. Rev. 2070 (2015); Clark Neily, Litigation without Adjudication: Why the Modern Rational Basis Test Is Unconstitutional, 14 Geo. J.L. & Pub. Pol'y 537 (2016).

[197] See, e.g., Dep't of Agric. v. Moreno, 413 U.S. 528 (1973); Cleburne v. Cleburne Living Ctr., Inc., 473 U.S. 432 (1985); Romer v. Evans, 517 U.S. 620 (1996).

[198] See FCC v. Beach Commc'ns, Inc., 508 U.S. 307, 314–15 (1993).

[199] Dobbs, 142 S. Ct. at 2284 (emphasis added).

[200] *Id.*

[201] *Id.*

A word on what the Court *didn't* say. It *didn't* say that any consideration of the health or safety of pregnant people was constitutionally required. Their health and safety are offered only as reasons for abortion *restrictions*. The silence is striking, particularly given that Chief Justice Rehnquist, dissenting in *Roe*, made clear that he thought an exceptionless abortion ban wouldn't survive rational-basis review.[202]

B. Concurrences

Justice Thomas and Justice Kavanaugh joined Alito's opinion but wrote separately to make points of interest. A longtime critic of substantive due process,[203] Thomas would "reconsider all of this Court's substantive due process precedents, including *Griswold*, *Lawrence*, and *Obergefell*."[204] Given that Thomas dissented in *Lawrence* and *Obergefell*, his opinion is not surprising. He does allow that the Fourteenth Amendment's Privileges or Immunities Clause might justify those decisions.[205]

Kavanaugh emphasizes that the Constitution is neither pro-life nor pro-choice. He mentions amicus briefs that endorsed prenatal constitutional personhood, only to say that they are—like *Roe* itself—wrong.[206] And he also anticipates future constitutional conflicts on the horizon. He briefly addresses two questions: (1) whether a state can "bar a resident of that State from traveling to another State to obtain an abortion" and (2) whether a state can "retroactively impose liability or punishment for an abortion that occurred before today's decision takes effect[.]"[207] His answers to both are "no."

[202] Roe, 410 U.S. at 173 (Rehnquist, J., dissenting).

[203] See Evan D. Bernick, Substantive Due Process for Justice Thomas, 26 Geo. Mason L. Rev. 1087, 1099–1102 (2018) (summarizing Thomas's criticism, which rests on originalist grounds). Randy Barnett and I have defended on originalist grounds a form of substantive review of government actions that deprive people of life, liberty, or property. See Randy E. Barnett & Evan D. Bernick, No Arbitrary Power: An Originalist Theory of the Due Process of Law, 60 Wm. & Mary L. Rev. 1599 (2018). But we agree with Thomas that the identification and protection of fundamental rights of U.S. citizens ought to take place under the Privileges or Immunities Clause.

[204] Dobbs, 142 S. Ct. at 2301 (Thomas, J., concurring).

[205] Since he dissented in *Lawrence* and *Obergefell*, this possibility seems remote.

[206] Dobbs, 142 S. Ct. at 2309 (Kavanaugh, J., concurring).

[207] Id.

Chief Justice Roberts concurred only in the judgment; he'd have upheld the Mississippi law but wouldn't have overruled *Roe/Casey*. He begins by criticizing Mississippi for disclaiming any intention to seek *Roe/Casey*'s overruling when petitioning for review and then doing precisely that once its petition was granted.[208] Anticipating the response that the Court couldn't uphold Mississippi's pre-viability ban without overruling *Roe/Casey*, Roberts asserts that "there is nothing inherent in the right to choose that requires it to extend to viability or any other point, so long as a real choice is provided."[209]

C. The Dissent

In their joint dissent, Justices Breyer, Kagan, and Sonia Sotomayor reject the majority's approach to substantive due process. They argue that constitutional rights shouldn't be frozen in the amber of tradition and contend that the result of the Court's reasoning will be "the curtailment of women's rights and of their status as free and equal citizens."[210]

The majority describes the harms of *Roe/Casey* in abstract terms— they harmed democracy. The dissent describes the concrete harms to individuals of overruling them. States can "force [a woman] to bring a pregnancy to term, even at the steepest personal and familial costs."[211] A woman may be forced "to bear her rapist's child or a young girl her father's"; to "carry to term a fetus with severe physical anomalies . . . sure to die within a few years of birth"; or to endure the "risk of death or physical harm."[212] These burdens will fall hardest on "the poor woman who cannot get the money to fly to a distant State for a procedure."[213] And the Court doesn't expressly "stop[] the Federal government from prohibiting abortions nationwide."[214]

To hear the dissent tell it, the majority fundamentally misunderstands how to interpret the Constitution. It's not the case that "we in

[208] Dobbs, 142 S. Ct. at 2310 (Roberts, C.J., concurring).

[209] *Id.* at 2314.

[210] Dobbs, 142 S. Ct. at 2318 (Breyer, Sotomayor, and Kagan, JJ., dissenting).

[211] *Id.* at 2317.

[212] *Id.* at 2318.

[213] *Id.*

[214] *Id.*

the 21st century must read the Fourteenth Amendment just as its ratifiers did."[215] Because the ratifiers "did not understand women as full members of the community[,]" privileging their understanding will necessarily "consign[] women to second-class citizenship."[216] The Constitution was "written as it is" to delegate to future generations the application of principles like liberty and equality "to new societal understandings and conditions."[217] So *Obergefell* was right to reject *Glucksberg's* narrow, tradition-bound approach to liberty.[218]

The dissent excoriates the majority's efforts to distinguish abortion from other substantive due process rights. If fundamental rights need to have been widely embraced in 1868, the dissenters argue that interracial marriage, same-sex intimacy and marriage, and contraceptive use wouldn't qualify.[219] The dissenters pointedly cite Justice Scalia's insistence in his *Lawrence* dissent that readers "not believe" the majority's assurances that recognizing a right to same-sex intimacy did "not involve" same-sex marriage—thus anticipating *Obergefell*.[220]

Next, the dissent criticizes the majority's approach to precedent. The dissent contends that *Casey's* undue-burden test is no less workable than any number of standards that the Court applies when reviewing everything from election laws to cantaloupe-crating requirements to seatbelt regulations issued by administrative agencies—*all* of the latter of which are scrutinized to determine whether they are "arbitrary or capricious."[221] By contrast, the majority's conceivable-basis approach and its identification of the protection of prenatal life as a legitimate interest invite a host of questions. Is the Court endorsing exceptionless abortion bans? If so, what's the constitutional basis for privileging prenatal life over the life of pregnant people? If not, what exceptions are constitutionally required? What's the line between abortion and contraception?

---

[215] *Id.* at 2324.

[216] *Id.* at 2325.

[217] *Id.*

[218] See *id.* at 2326.

[219] See *id.*

[220] See Lawrence v. Texas, 539 U.S. 558, 604 (2003) (Scalia, J., dissenting).

[221] See Dobbs, 142 S. Ct. at 2335 (joint dissent).

Casey's reliance analysis, the dissent argues, was sound. It's the majority that has gotten lost in abstractions and made "generalized assertions" that are ungrounded in "the reality American women actually live."[222] Take the majority's assertion that "'reproductive planning could take virtually immediate account of any sudden restoration of state authority to ban abortions.'"[223] The dissent responds that 45 percent of pregnancies in the United States are unplanned; contraceptives fail, and the most reliable ones aren't universally accessible; and sexual activity can be coerced.[224] There's nothing abstract about forcing people to make "different decisions about careers, education, relationships, and whether to try to become pregnant than they would have when Roe served as a backstop."[225]

The dissent concludes by expressing sorrow and indignation. The Court has deprived millions of a right that is "embedded in our constitutional law"[226] and "embedded in the lives of women—shaping their expectations, influencing their choices about relationships and work, supporting (as all reproductive rights do) their social and economic equality."[227] It has overruled decisions in which the Court performed its proper role and thrown who-knows-how-many other rights into jeopardy. That is simultaneously outrageous—a "betray[al]" of the Court's "guiding principles"—and an occasion for "sorrow," "for this Court, but more, for . . . many millions of American women."[228]

IV. A Critique of Dobbs

Alito's opinion for the Court is ambitious, and it has a number of goals. I will focus on three. The first goal is to demonstrate that Roe and Casey were badly reasoned. The second is to show that the Fourteenth Amendment doesn't protect abortion rights. And the third is to withdraw the Court—and the federal judiciary—from

[222] Id. at 2344.
[223] Id.
[224] Id.
[225] Id. at 2346.
[226] Id. at 2348.
[227] Id. at 2349.
[228] Id. at 2350.

the constitutional adjudication of abortion rights. This section argues that *Dobbs* fails to achieve any of these goals.

A. *Alito v.* Roe

On Alito's account, *Roe* and *Casey* were badly reasoned because they neglected history, text, and precedent. *Roe* made mistakes on history, and Alito's historical critique of *Roe* is compelling; the other critiques are not.

Roe prioritized the availability of pre-quickening abortion "at common law, at the time of the adoption of our Constitution, and throughout the major portion of the 19th century."[229] It made important errors about the common law—for example, raising unwarranted doubts about whether *post*-quickening abortion was unlawful. (It was.)[230] And it underappreciated the significance of the fact that pre-quickening abortion was widely prohibited when the Fourteenth Amendment was ratified. These are important shortcomings, and Alito rightly points them out.

But it's downhill from there. Alito's textual critique focuses on *Roe*'s trimester framework and the viability line. Obviously, neither is specified in constitutional text, but this criticism proves too much. The Court's constitutional decisions in virtually every major area of constitutional law are governed by what Professor Richard Fallon has called "implementing doctrines" that don't appear in any text.[231] That includes the tiers of scrutiny upon which Alito relies in dividing fundamental from non-fundamental rights, as well as the conceivable-basis test he applies to abortion rights.

Still weaker is Alito's criticism of *Roe/Casey* for neglecting precedent. Alito criticizes them for neglecting a prenatal-life distinction between abortion and other fundamental rights. But *why* is that distinction so significant? No text or history is offered in support of it. The only cases Alito cites for this distinction are *Roe* and *Casey*! And those now-overruled cases quite obviously *do not* categorically distinguish abortion rights from rights to contraception, procreation, and marriage.

---

[229] Roe, 410 U.S. at 140.
[230] Dobbs, 142 S. Ct. at 2236.
[231] See Richard H. Fallon, Jr., Implementing the Constitution (2001).

Alito correctly indicts *Roe* for its historical errors. But his textual and precedential critiques fall short. That doesn't mean that the Constitution protects abortion rights. Alito's own constitutional analysis might demonstrate that it does not.

B. Dobbs *as Conservative Living Constitutionalism*

Like Alito's critique of *Roe*, his positive case against abortion rights has textual, historical, and doctrinal components. Because the first two are practically indistinguishable, I'll treat them together before taking on the third.

1. Text and History

Alito's interpretation of the Fourteenth Amendment begins with a declaration: "Constitutional analysis must begin with 'the language of the instrument.'"[232] This tells us less than it might seem. Consider the following things that Alito might mean by "the language of the instrument":

(1) The literal string of words that appears on the document under glass at the National Archives.

(2) What kinds of things the framers/ratifiers of a constitutional provision originally intended or understood those words to express ("Search" in the Fourth Amendment might express "to look over or through for the purpose of finding something."[233]).

(3) What particular things the framers/ratifiers originally understood to be of the relevant kind ("The freedom of speech" might be understood to include, among other things, "newspapers critical of government policy.").

(4) What kinds of things the general public today associates with those words, given the way in which the Supreme Court has interpreted them ("Assistance of counsel" in the Sixth Amendment might express "at government expense, if you can't afford to hire an attorney.").

The first option isn't plausible. Text without context is meaningless. Different words and phrases come to be used in different ways,

---

[232] *Dobbs*, 142 S. Ct. at 2244.

[233] See N. Webster, An American Dictionary of the English Language 66 (1828) (reprint 6th ed. 1989).

to express different things. For instance, "domestic violence" wasn't taken to mean "intimate partner abuse" when it was incorporated into Article IV.[234] But that's the kind of thing those words bring to mind today.

The second and third options are associated with originalism—long the dominant theory of constitutional interpretation within the conservative legal movement from which the majority emerged.[235] Contemporary originalists favor (2). They distinguish between original meaning—what kind of things words/phrases express—and original expected applications—whether a particular thing was thought to be of that kind.[236] That's how Justice Scalia could conclude that the Fourth Amendment's prohibition against "unreasonable searches" applied to law enforcement using thermal imaging to detect drug use inside a home, even though no one imagined such technology at the Founding.[237]

Alito never specifies what he means by "language of the instrument." But his interpretive method is dictated by precedent—he applies *Glucksberg* because that's how the Court has identified fundamental "liberty" rights. And because the Court has prioritized positive law—the laws "on the books" at a given time, here 1868—in determining whether a right satisfies *Glucksberg*, so does he.

Is this originalism? One might hope that it would be, given that Alito, Barrett, Gorsuch, and Thomas have all identified as originalists. It seems obvious that focusing on legal history would help us understand what a constitutional provision guaranteeing "liberty" originally meant to people present at ratification. But *Glucksberg* doesn't *just* require an inquiry into whether a right is deeply rooted. It requires that rights be defined narrowly, at a low level of generality. So, it's a "right to terminate a pregnancy," not a "right to bodily integrity." This requirement invites questions that no originalist justice has persuasively answered.

---

[234] See U.S. Const. art. IV, sec. 4 ("The United States shall guarantee to every state in this union a republican form of government, and shall protect each of them against invasion; and on application of the legislature, or of the executive (when the legislature cannot be convened) against domestic violence.").

[235] For a brisk history of originalism, see Randy E. Barnett & Evan D. Bernick, The Letter and the Spirit: A Unified Theory of Originalism, 107 Geo. L.J. 1, 7–14 (2018).

[236] See Lawrence B. Solum, Triangulating Public Meaning: Corpus Linguistics, Immersion, and the Constitutional Record, 2017 BYU L. Rev. 1621, 1663–67 (2018).

[237] See Kyllo v. United States, 533 U.S. 27 (2001).

Consider Angel Raich, who challenged the constitutionality of the Controlled Substances Act under the Fifth Amendment's Due Process Clause.[238] She argued that the act infringed her fundamental "liberty" right to preserve her own life.[239] She claimed that it did so by prohibiting her from using marijuana to ameliorate a life-threatening wasting syndrome.[240] The U.S. Court of Appeals for the Ninth Circuit, applying *Glucksberg*, didn't look to history and tradition for a right to preserve one's own life.[241] Rather, it looked for a right to preserve one's own life *by using medical marijuana*. Unsurprisingly, it concluded that no such fundamental right existed.[242]

Why is framing rights at a low level of generality more likely to capture the original meaning of "liberty"? Why think that either the framers or ratifiers, or an ordinary member of the public, would be more likely to read "liberty" to encompass narrow rights than broad rights? How could one defend what most originalists take to be the uncontroversial proposition that *Brown v. Board of Education* is correctly decided, if one looked to determine whether there existed a narrow right to attend nonsegregated schools in 1868—as opposed to a more general right of citizens to be free from racist exclusion from public institutions?

Joel Alicea calls *Dobbs* originalist on the ground that the Court prioritizes the same evidence that any originalist would.[243] It focuses on 1868, when the Fourteenth Amendment was ratified, and it finds that most states prohibited pre-viability abortion, suggesting that they saw no constitutional problem with doing so.[244]

Randy Barnett and I argue that the positive law of the states is indeed the right place to look to determine whether a right is protected by the Fourteenth Amendment.[245] Widespread prohibitions on abortion in the positive law of the states in 1868 is compelling evidence

---

[238] See Raich v. Gonzales, 500 F. 3d 850 (9th Cir. 2007).

[239] *Id.* at 864.

[240] *Id.*

[241] *Id.*

[242] See *id.* at 864–66.

[243] See J. Joel Alicea, An Originalist Victory, City Journal (June 24, 2022), https://tinyurl.com/mw5k9ejx.

[244] See *id.*

[245] See Evan D. Bernick & Randy E. Barnett, The Original Meaning of the Fourteenth Amendment: Its Letter and Spirit 236–50 (2021).

that abortion isn't a fundamental right. Still, a level-of-generality problem lingers.

Think again of *Brown*. Originalists generally agree that the Fourteenth Amendment imposes some kind of anti-discrimination requirement on the states.[246] They've drawn extensively upon abolitionist and Republican constitutional argumentation in the years leading up to and following the Civil War.[247] There is not a *word* in Justice Alito's opinion about what abolitionists, Republicans, or anyone else said about discrimination in connection with the Fourteenth Amendment.

Which brings us to the anti-discrimination argument against abortion restrictions. It is *the* best-known, most-elaborated argument that *Roe* was correctly decided, despite the oft-criticized weaknesses of Justice Blackmun's reasoning.[248] In one leading form, it holds that abortion restrictions discriminate on the basis of sex because they force some people and not others to perform a particular social role: motherhood. Abortion restrictions create inequality by preventing people who would otherwise choose *not* to perform reproductive labor from avoiding it after conception. They require people to endure pregnancy, birth, and lactation, with attendant physical and psychological burdens that range from the nausea-inducing to the extremely painful to the life-threatening.[249] And (so the argument goes) they do so because of stereotypes concerning the social roles that *women* ought to perform.[250]

[246] See, e.g., John Harrison, Reconstructing the Privileges or Immunities Clause, 101 Yale L.J. 1385 (1992); Michael W. McConnell, Originalism and the Desegregation Decisions, 81 Va. L. Rev. 947 (1995); Steven G. Calabresi & Julia T. Rickert, Originalism and Sex Discrimination, 90 Tex. L. Rev. 1 (2011); Christopher R. Green, Equal Citizenship, Civil Rights, and the Constitution: The Original Sense of the Privileges or Immunities Clause (2015); Kurt T. Lash, Enforcing the Rights of Due Process: The Original Relationship between the Fourteenth Amendment and the 1866 Civil Rights Act, 106 Geo. L.J. 1389 (2017); Ilan Wurman, The Second Founding: An Introduction to the Fourteenth Amendment (2020).

[247] See sources cited *id.*

[248] For further discussion of these arguments, see Neil S. Siegel & Reva B. Siegel, Equality Arguments for Abortion Rights, 60 UCLA L. Rev. Discourse 160 (2012).

[249] See Chavi Eve Karkowsky, What Alito Doesn't Understand about Pregnancy, The Atlantic (May 21, 2022), https://tinyurl.com/3cxdxcam.

[250] For an elaboration of this argument by amici in *Dobbs*, see Br. of Equal Protection Constitutional Law Scholars Serena Mayeri, Melissa Murray, & Reva Siegel as Amici Curiae in Support of Respondents at 7–16, Dobbs v. Jackson Women's Health Org., 142 S. Ct. 2228 (2022) (No. 19-1392), https://tinyurl.com/nhj3r85n.

In *one paragraph*, Justice Alito dismisses this argument as "foreclosed by our precedents."[251] He discusses two cases, *Geduldig* and *Bray*, reading them to hold that "laws regulating or prohibiting abortion are not subject to heightened scrutiny."[252]

This won't do. The reasoning of *Gelduldig* is so inconsistent with subsequent decisions that it's doubtful it forecloses anything at all. In *United States v. Virginia*, the Supreme Court held that physical differences between men and women could not justify classifications that "create or perpetuate the legal, social, and economic inferiority of women."[253] Then, in *Nevada Department of Human Resources v. Hibbs*, the Court upheld the Family and Medical Leave Act as a means of enforcing the Equal Protection Clause, reasoning that state leave policies targeted by the FMLA were based on "the pervasive sex-role stereotype that caring for family members is women's work."[254] Further, neither *Gelduldig* nor *Bray* holds that abortion restrictions *can't* constitute unconstitutional sex discrimination. At most, they say they're not *inherently* sex discriminatory.[255] Both leave room for proof that a particular restriction was animated by discriminatory intent.

Of course, Alito disregards evidence of discriminatory intent.[256] But he doesn't do so for reasons that have anything to do with original

---

[251] Dobbs, 142 S. Ct. at 2245.

[252] *Id.* at 2246.

[253] 518 U.S. 515, 524 (1996).

[254] 538 U.S. 721, 731 (2003).

[255] See Geduldig, 417 U.S. at 496 n.20 (stating that "[a]bsent a showing that distinctions involving pregnancy are mere pretexts designed to effect an invidious discrimination against the members of one sex or the other, lawmakers are constitutionally free to include or exclude pregnancy from the coverage of legislation"); Bray, 506 U.S. at 274 (stating that "the goal of preventing abortion . . . *in itself*' does not constitute "invidiously discriminatory animus") (emphasis added).

[256] Or at least claims to. There's an extraordinary footnote in which Alito highlights amicus briefs that cast aspersions on the motives of proponents of abortion legalization—only to say that *those* motives don't matter either. Dobbs, 142 S. Ct. at 2256 n.41. It's extraordinary because even after saying that motives don't matter, Alito states that "[a] highly disproportionate percentage of aborted fetuses are Black[,]" *Id.* I can think of no reason why the racial identity of fetuses would be worth emphasizing if motives *really* don't matter. Alito also cites a concurrence by Justice Thomas from a prior abortion case in which he argues that support of abortion is closely associated with eugenics, racism, and racial genocide. See Box v. Planned Parenthood of Ind. and Ky., Inc., 139 S. Ct. 1780, 1783–87 (2019) (Thomas, J., concurring). For critiques of Thomas's history, see generally Murray, *supra* note 28; Mary Ziegler, Bad Effects:

meaning, which may not even require discriminatory intent.[257] And even taken on its own terms, the distinction Alito draws between the intentions of supporters of legislation and those of legislators is dubious. We've seen that legislators worked together with leading supporters of the campaign. As Alito observed in a concurrence documenting the anti-Catholic roots of state prohibitions on public aid to "sectarian" schools, "the resulting wave of state laws . . . cannot be understood outside this context."[258] Alito didn't cite a single legislator responsible for the Montana state constitutional prohibition at issue, but he made a convincing case that the prohibition was the product of bigotry.

There's a near-universal originalist consensus that *Roe* can't be plausibly defended on the ground of original meaning.[259] But *Dobbs* isn't originalism and gives almost no sense of an obligation to try to be. It focuses its attention on the right time period, but its inquiry into that period is limited by nonoriginalist doctrine, and Alito limits it still further in ways that aren't defended on originalist grounds.[260]

2. Doctrinal Disarray

Dobbs's arguments from constitutional doctrine are its strongest. The Court makes a compelling case that the right to terminate a pregnancy doesn't satisfy *Glucksberg*. Even here, however, there are flaws.

The Misuses of History in Box v. Planned Parenthood, 105 Cornell L. Rev. Online 165 (2020), https://tinyurl.com/2ywbr98p.

[257] See. e.g., Melissa L. Saunders, Equal Protection, Class, Legislation, and Color-blindness, 96 Mich. L. Rev. 245 (1997); Evan D. Bernick, Antisubjugation and the Equal Protection of the Laws, 110 Geo. L.J. 1 (2021).

[258] See Espinoza v. Mont. Dep't of Revenue, 140 S. Ct. 2246, 2270 (2020) (Alito, J., concurring).

[259] Jack M. Balkin, Abortion and Original Meaning, 24 Const. Comment. 291 (2007) and David H. Gans, Reproductive Originalism: Why the Fourteenth Amendment's Original Meaning Protects the Right to Abortion, 75 SMU L. Rev. F. 191 (2022) are the only scholarly defenses of *Roe* by avowed originalists of which I'm aware.

[260] It might be objected that the protection of prenatal life is a strong enough interest to justify abortion restrictions under any level of scrutiny, regardless of whether such restrictions discriminate on the basis of sex. But that's not an objection that Alito is in a position to make. The protection of prenatal life is treated only as a *legitimate* interest—sufficient under rational-basis review, but not under heightened levels of scrutiny. Ironically, prenatal life is thus downgraded in constitutional importance by *Dobbs*; *Roe* treated it as a *compelling* interest in the late stages of pregnancy.

First, Alito never acknowledges the Court's refusal to apply *Glucksberg* in *Lawrence* and *Obergefell*. True, *McDonald v. City of Chicago*[261] and *Timbs v. Indiana*[262]—incorporating via the Due Process Clause the rights to keep and bear arms and not be subjected to excessive fines, respectively—didn't discuss *Lawrence* and *Obergefell*. But they also didn't claim that *Glucksberg* was the exclusive means of identifying substantive due process rights or overrule any decisions in reliance upon *Glucksberg*.

Second, Alito frames *Glucksberg*'s "implicit in the concept of ordered liberty" language as a second requirement that all fundamental rights must satisfy.[263] This is a reasonable reading of *Glucksberg*, but the Court hasn't consistently adopted it.

Compare *McDonald* and *Timbs*:

McDonald:

> [W]e must decide whether the right to keep and bear arms is fundamental to *our* scheme of ordered liberty . . . or as we have said in a related context, whether this right is "deeply rooted in this Nation's history and tradition."[264]

Timbs:

> A Bill of Rights protection is incorporated, we have explained, if it is "fundamental to our scheme of ordered liberty," or "deeply rooted in this Nation's history and tradition."[265]

McDonald suggests that a right is *necessarily* implicit in ordered liberty if it's deeply rooted. By contrast, *Timbs* suggests that a right can be elevated to "fundamental" by being (a) implicit in ordered liberty OR (b) deeply rooted in history and tradition. Neither suggests that a deeply rooted right might not be fundamental. *Dobbs* does, without explanation.

---

[261] 561 U.S. 742 (2010).

[262] 139 S. Ct. 682 (2019).

[263] Dobbs, 142 S. Ct. at 2246 ("In deciding whether a right falls into either of these categories, the Court has long asked whether the right is 'deeply rooted in [our] history and tradition' and whether it is essential to our Nation's 'scheme of ordered liberty.'").

[264] McDonald, 561 U.S. at 764, 767.

[265] Timbs, 139 S. Ct. at 687.

Most importantly, Alito's prenatal-life distinction between abortion and other substantive rights isn't adequately explained or convincingly defended. It comes from the very cases that the Court is overruling. It's deployed alongside *Glucksberg* without discussion of how the distinction and the framework relate to one another in constitutional theory; how the distinction is to be applied in practice; or how the distinction and framework are to interact in case of conflict. Some questions that arise: Why are rights that don't implicate prenatal life more likely to be deeply rooted and implicit in ordered liberty? Who decides whether a right implicates prenatal life, and how? If a claimed right—to same-sex intimacy, for instance—doesn't implicate prenatal life but also does not satisfy *Glucksberg*'s criteria, what happens? *Dobbs* merely describes the prenatal-life distinction without justifying it, recalling *Roe*'s description-without-justification of viability.

Ultimately, *Dobbs* fails both as a critique of *Roe* and as a freestanding analysis of whether the Constitution protects abortion rights. This bodes ill for the last of *Dobbs*'s major aspirations: the Court's withdrawal from the field of abortion-related constitutional conflict.

C. New Battlegrounds, Old Battles

Dobbs seeks to turn back the clock to before *Roe* took one side of an issue about which the Constitution is silent. That's not going to happen.

We've seen the initial constitutional position of pro-lifers was prenatal constitutional personhood. *Dobbs* doesn't embrace prenatal personhood. But only Justice Kavanaugh explicitly rejects it, and Alito's prenatal-life distinction invites pro-life arguments that the Constitution protects prenatal life.[266]

These arguments are advanced by people whom some justices are likely to take seriously. They've been put forward by John Finnis, a titan of natural-law jurisprudence and Justice Gorsuch's thesis adviser at Oxford;[267] Robert George, a highly respected political philos-

---

[266] See Michael S. Paulsen, Three Very Enthusiastic Cheers for the Dobbs Draft, Nat'l Rev. Online (May 6, 2022), https://tinyurl.com/2s44rh59 ("The opinion goes as far as necessary to decide the case and no further; it does not deny, but (quite the reverse) seems to affirm, the humanity of the living human embryo or fetus, in the course of its discussion of the precise legal issues it treats; it would provide an excellent grounding for the next stage of the debate, in legislatures and in courts.").

[267] See Br. for Scholars of Jurisprudence John M. Finnis & Robert P. George as Amici Curiae in Support of Petitioners, Dobbs v. Jackson Women's Health Org., 142 S. Ct. 2228 (2022) (No. 19-1392).

opher at Princeton;[268] and Michael Stokes Paulsen, law professor at the University of St. Thomas and among the country's best-regarded originalists, among others.[269] Pro-life legal scholars have published op-eds and essays arguing that the Equal Protection Clause requires states to prohibit abortion and have called for Congress to enact prohibitory legislation.[270] If Congress does, the Supreme Court will need to decide whether Section Five of the Fourteenth Amendment gives Congress such power.

Nor will reproductive-rights advocates cede constitutional ground anytime soon. The view is ascendant[271] on the left that the Supreme Court offers only what Gerald Rosenberg described as a "hollow hope" of transformative social change.[272] But the prescriptions that follow from this critique often involve congressional and executive action. And congressional and executive action will necessarily find its way before the Court. A partial list of constitutional issues that might arise:

- Is abortion economic activity that has a substantial effect on interstate commerce? If so, can Congress exercise its Commerce Clause powers to forbid certain kinds of state interference with it?[273]

---

[268] *Id.*

[269] See Michael S. Paulsen, The Plausibility of Personhood, 74 Ohio St. L.J. 14 (2012).

[270] See, e.g., John Finnis, Abortion Is Unconstitutional, First Things (Apr. 2021), https://tinyurl.com/sm6fdfjy; Ramesh Ponnuru, What if a Fetus Has Constitutional Rights?, Bloomberg (Mar. 31, 2021), https://tinyurl.com/ms5nr2e7; Robert P. George & Josh Craddock, Even if Roe Is Overturned, Congress Must Act to Protect the Unborn, Wash. Post (June 2, 2022), https://tinyurl.com/275hu43c. See also Caroline Kitchener, The Next Frontier of the Anti-abortion Movement: A Nationwide Abortion Ban, Wash. Post (May 20, 2022), https://tinyurl.com/37fa9n37.

[271] See, e.g., Joseph Fishkin & William E. Forbath, The Anti-Oligarchy Constitution: Reconstructing the Economic Foundations of American Democracy (2022); Ryan D. Doerfler & Samuel Moyn, Democratizing the Supreme Court, 109 Cal. L. Rev. 1703 (2021); Nikolas Bowie & Daphna Renan, The Supreme Court Is Not Supposed to Have This Much Power, The Atlantic (June 8, 2022), https://tinyurl.com/22kwkbd6; Keeanga-Yamahtta Taylor, The Case for Ending the Supreme Court as We Know It, The New Yorker (Sept. 25, 2020), https://tinyurl.com/2htt3pbj.

[272] Gerald N. Rosenberg, The Hollow Hope: Can Courts Bring about Social Change? (2008).

[273] See United States v. Lopez, 514 U.S. 549 (1995); Gonzales v. Raich, 545 U.S. 1 (2005).

- Could Congress use its Spending Clause powers to condition certain kinds of federal grants to states on the lightening of abortion restrictions? If so, what kind, and to what extent?[274]
- If the Court says that either abortion rights or fetal personhood are not protected by the Fourteenth Amendment, can Congress exercise its Section Five enforcement power to protect it anyway?[275]
- The Court has interpreted the Thirteenth Amendment, abolishing slavery, to reach the "badges and incidents" of slavery. It has recognized broad congressional power to define badges and incidents—including racial discrimination in real estate sales.[276] Could Congress define forced birth— among the evils of chattel slavery—as a badge or incident of slavery?[277]

Moral urgency breeds constitutional creativity, and few if any issues match abortion in moral urgency for those invested in the struggle on both sides. It's telling that both pro-lifers and reproductive-rights supporters claim the legacy of the abolitionists, struggling against the forces of slavery, a struggle that ultimately saw both sides claiming that the Constitution established a national floor of fundamental rights below which states could not fall.[278] Constitutional arguments that were "off the wall" when advanced by abolitionists animated the work of the Reconstruction Congress after the Civil War. We can expect some seemingly radical arguments to get "on the table" in the years to come.

[274] See South Dakota v. Dole, 483 U.S. 203 (1987); Nat'l Fed'n of Indep. Bus. v. Sebelius, 567 U.S. 519 (2012).

[275] See Lopez, 514 U.S. 549; Gonzales, 545 U.S. 1.

[276] See Jones v. Alfred H. Mayer Co., 392 U.S. 409 (1968).

[277] For a sampling of the literature on the reach of the Thirteenth Amendment, see James G. Pope, Section 1 of the Thirteenth Amendment and the Badges and Incidents of Slavery, 65 UCLA L. Rev. 426 (2018); Pamela Bridgewater, Breeding A Nation: Reproductive Slavery, the Thirteenth Amendment, and the Pursuit of Freedom (2014); Rebecca E. Zietlow, James Ashley's Thirteenth Amendment, 112 Colum. L. Rev. 1697 (2012); Jennifer Mason McAward, Defining the Badges and Incidents of Slavery, 14 U. Pa. J. Const. L. 561, 571 (2012); Andrew Koppelman, Originalism, Abortion, and the Thirteenth Amendment, 112 Colum. L. Rev. 1917 (2012).

[278] See Barnett & Bernick, *supra* note 245, at 77–88.

As David Cohen, Greer Donley, and Rachel Rebouché have detailed, conflict over abortion will generate a range of legal questions owing to post-*Roe* political and technological developments.[279] There already exist "abortion deserts" across swaths of the country that are dominated by Republicans.[280] *Dobbs* has triggered abortion bans set to go into effect after *Roe*'s overruling, revived pre-*Roe* bans, and guaranteed that others will be enacted in nearly half of the country.[281] Michele Goodwin has documented how state laws criminalize unintentional harm to prenatal life through "feticide laws, drug policies, statutes criminalizing maternal conduct, and statutes authorizing the confinement of pregnant women to protect the health of fetuses."[282] As Republican states have harshly restricted abortion rights, Democratic states have enacted laws to protect abortion providers and out-of-staters seeking abortion care.[283]

As for technology, medication abortion—a two-drug regimen that ends a pregnancy through 10 weeks—now accounts for more than half of all U.S. abortions. It enables pregnant people to terminate their pregnancies without visiting a clinic.[284] It has also led anti-abortion states to enact new laws prohibiting medication abortion via telehealth and selling pills through the mail, as well as to ban certain drugs entirely.[285] What if an abortion-restricting state seeks to punish a local newspaper for advertising abortion care that's available in an abortion-permitting state? The Court that decided *Roe* held this unconstitutional under the First Amendment, but will that precedent hold up after *Dobbs*?[286] Such questions will be litigated.

---

[279] David S. Cohen, Greer Donley & Rachel Rebouché, The New Abortion Battleground, 122 Colum. L. Rev. ___ (forthcoming 2022).

[280] See Alice F. Cartwright, Mihiri Karunaratne, Jill Barr-Walker, Nicole E. Johns, & Ushma D. Upadhyay, Identifying National Availability of Abortion Care and Distance from Major US Cities: Systematic Online Search, 20 J. Med. Internet Res. 1 (2018); Caitlin Myers et al., Predicted Changes in Abortion Access and Incidence in a Post-Roe World, 100 Contraception 367, 369 (2019).

[281] See Cohen, Donley, & Rebouché, *supra* note 279, at *6–7.

[282] Michele Goodwin, Fetal Protection Laws: Moral Panic and the New Constitutional Battlefront, 102 Calif. L. Rev. 781, 787 (2014).

[283] See Cohen, Donley, & Rebouché, *supra* note 279, at *31–37.

[284] Rachel K. Jones et al., Abortion Incidence and Service Availability in the United States, Guttmacher Inst. (Sept. 2019), https://bit.ly/2W0ACgi.

[285] See Pam Belluck, Abortion Pills Take the Spotlight as States Impose Abortion Bans, N.Y. Times (June 27, 2022), https://tinyurl.com/mpucjjs7.

[286] See Bigelow v. Virginia, 421 U.S. 809 (1975).

State-federal conflicts will also arise. Federal law trumps ("pre-empts") conflicting state law. The FDA regulates medication-abortion drugs, but are states permitted to regulate a drug *more* harshly than the FDA?[287] The generic manufacturer of mifepristone—part of the two-drug regimen—has filed a lawsuit in Mississippi, arguing that the FDA's more-permissive regulation of mifepristone preempts certain provisions of Mississippi's abortion laws.[288] The outcome may inspire future litigation.

Finally, there will be conflicts over other substantive due process rights. As became clear in *Burwell v. Hobby Lobby Stores, Inc.*, some pro-lifers consider contraceptives—like Plan B and IUDs—that result in the destruction of fertilized eggs to be abortifacients.[289] Is a state's sincere belief that a drug acts as an abortifacient enough to justify a prohibition, even if that belief runs against the current scientific consensus? It may be hard to imagine the Court overturning *Obergefell* and *Lawrence*, thereby allowing states to ban marriage between same-sex couples and prohibit same-sex sodomy. Same-sex marriage polls well.[290] Then again, so did *Roe*.[291] It's reasonable to fear constitutional retrenchment on politically salient rights about which critics of substantive due process have always been skeptical.[292] And it's difficult to imagine those rights surviving *Glucksberg*, as applied in *Dobbs*.

Conclusion

We end where we began, with constitutional conflict. *Roe* didn't start it, and *Dobbs* won't finish it. No one will be persuaded by any judicial opinion—much less *Dobbs*—to stop arguing about abortion. In a political culture where urgent moral questions inevitably become constitutional ones, that means more constitutional argumentation. There will be more battles, and they won't just take place in

---

[287] See Cohen, Donley, & Rebouché, *supra* note 279, at *38–55.

[288] See Brendon Pierson, Abortion Drug Maker Says Mississippi Can't Ban Pill Despite Supreme Court Ruling, Reuters (July 1, 2022), https://tinyurl.com/2s7brfwn.

[289] 134 S. Ct. 2751 (2014).

[290] See Justin McCarthy, Same-Sex Marriage Support Inches Up to New High of 71%, Gallup (June 1, 2022), https://tinyurl.com/25m6hr9z.

[291] See Domenico Montanaro, Poll: Two-thirds Say Don't Overturn Roe; the Court Leak Is Firing Up Democratic Voters, NPR (May 19, 2022), https://tinyurl.com/4339d9tk.

[292] See Zachary Jarrell, Overview of over 300 Anti-LGBTQ+ Bills in 2022, Wash. Blade (Apr. 22, 2022), https://tinyurl.com/2zhch5ec.

state legislatures or state courts. They'll take place in Congress and administrative agencies. They'll take place in front of clinics and on the streets. And yes, they'll take place before the Supreme Court, again and again. Both sides will lay claim to the Constitution, and the Court will take sides. Perhaps the Court is aware of and prepared for this. But after *Dobbs*, it would be unwise to bet against Cassandra.

Ruan v. United States: "Bad Doctors," Bad Law, and the Promise of Decriminalizing Medical Care

*Kelly K. Dineen Gillespie**

Introduction

The Supreme Court's decision in the consolidated cases of *Ruan v. United States* and *Khan v. United States*[1] is a narrow but important decision that both emphasizes the role of scienter in separating innocent from criminal conduct and constrains federal law enforcement's ability to invade medical care under the Controlled Substances Act (CSA).[2] Section 841(a)(1) of the CSA is the general drug distribution provision under which prescribing practitioners and lay people alike are prosecuted. That section makes it unlawful *"except as authorized . . . for any person [to] knowingly or intentionally . . . distribute . . . a controlled substance."*[3] The *Ruan* decision corrected years of conflicting and eroding standards for what the government must prove to secure a conviction in 841(a)(1) prosecutions against doctors or other

* Professor of law, professor of medical humanities, Creighton University. I would like to thank Professor Jennifer D. Oliva for her collaboration on two amici briefs in this case and her ongoing support and scholarship in this area.

[1] Ruan v. United States, 142 S. Ct. 2370 (2022) (vacating and remanding United States v. Khan, 989 F.3d 806 (10th Cir. 2021) and United States v. Ruan, 966 F.3d 1101 (11th Cir. 2020)).

[2] Comprehensive Drug Abuse & Prevention & Control Act, 21 U.S.C. § 801 et seq. (1970).

[3] 21 U.S.C. § 841(a)(1) (emphasis added). Section 841(a) also includes unlawful dispensing or manufacturing or possession with intent to manufacture, distribute, or dispense any controlled substance or counterfeit substance. Prescribers are charged with distribution or dispensation under 841(a)(1), and a circuit split remains even after *Ruan* on the issue of whether they should be charged with distribution or dispensation. I use the language of distribution for simplicity because both petitioners were charged with distribution, and it does not change any of my assertions in this essay.

prescribing practitioners.[4] By holding that the requisite mental state (the *mens rea*, guilty mind, or scienter requirement) of "knowingly or intentionally" in the statutory text also applies to the "except as authorized" clause, the Court held that the government must prove not only that doctors acted outside the limits of their federal authorization to prescribe controlled substances, but also that they did so knowingly or intentionally.[5] In other words, prescribers can no longer be convicted under Section 841 for innovative, mistaken, negligent, or less-than-careful prescribing.

Despite the legal importance of this case, it didn't garner a lot of attention early on, and, when it did, the serious legal and policy issues were overshadowed by "bad doctor" narratives. To be clear, my claim is not that Drs. Ruan and Khan aren't bad doctors—I don't know, and I am not weighing in on that issue. And, of course, prescribing practitioners are sometimes imperfect in ways that should not merit a felony conviction. For example, they can be careful and still be mistaken, careless, and even negligent or "bad" in the sense of lacking competence or being compromised by their own impairment.[6] There are ample legal and quasi-legal remedies to address each of these problems, in context. Criminalizing all of them, rather than just the truly corrupt prescribers, wasn't and isn't the answer.

To be fair, given their positions of power, doctors are among the least sympathetic of all the victims of the profound injustices of the

---

[4] The defendants in both *Ruan* and *Khan* were physicians, but I refer to prescribing practitioners as well. Lawyers too often don't understand that other professionals prescribe, including advanced practice registered nurses (APRN) and physician assistants, in accord with their certificates of authorization from the Drug Enforcement Agency. See, e.g., 21 C.F.R. § 1301; Phillip Zhang & Preeti Patel, Practitioners and Prescriptive Authority (2021), https://bit.ly/3A5qabV. Even counsel for the government seemed confused. During oral arguments, he stated that nurse practitioners, one type of APRN, aren't authorized, when in fact they enjoy the ability to prescribe at least some classes of controlled substances in every state. Tr. of Oral Arg. at 48, Ruan v. United States, 142 S. Ct. 2370 (2022) (Nos. 20-1410 & 21-5261), https://bit.ly/3dnBUhS (Mr. Feigin describing a hypothetical type of doctor who should be subject to section 841 as one who, among other things, "trusts nurse practitioners, who aren't DEA registrants, aren't allowed to do this, don't have medical licenses, to do most of the prescribing").

[5] Ruan, 142 S. Ct. at 2376.

[6] Kelly K. Dineen & James M. DuBois, Between a Rock and a Hard Place: Can Physicians Prescribe Opioids to Treat Pain Adequately While Avoiding Legal Sanction?, 42 Am. J.L. &. Med. 1 (2016) (reviewing existing literature and suggesting a framework for misprescribers as careless, corrupt, and compromised by impairment).

War on Drugs.[7] The discourse surrounding the drug overdose crises[8] didn't exactly recruit a long list of champions for doctors accused of abusing their power to distribute drugs. Commentators initially focused on the particular facts—as presented by the government and framed by the circuit court opinions—to dismiss the defendants as corrupt "pill pushers," deserving of the harshest penalties available. A lot of media outlets still call *Ruan* & *Khan* the "pill mill" cases.[9] Most major medical organizations chose not to write amicus briefs despite multiple requests—even though the issue has implications for virtually every physician—for reasons that I can only guess included the risk of being viewed as advocating for "bad doctors." In briefs and at oral arguments, the government relied heavily on arguments based in indignation.[10] Implicitly government's counsel advanced the idea that doctors who had the benefit of the public trust and enjoyed a position of power had betrayed the social contract and shouldn't have the benefit of the typical principles of criminal law.[11] He also essentially argued that no matter what the standards were, those cases aren't "close calls"—the government only brought cases

---

[7] See, e.g., Deborah Small, The War on Drugs Is a War on Racial Justice, Soc. Res. 896–903 (2001); Brian D. Earp et al., Racial Justice Requires Ending the War on Drugs, 21 Am. J. Bioethics 4, 4–19 (2021).

[8] I avoid the term "opioid crisis" because it's inaccurate and perpetuates the use of the opioid heuristic. The overdose crises are multilayered and worsened by prohibition. See Nabarum Dasgupta et al., Opioid Crisis: No Easy Fix to Its Social and Economic Determinants, 108 Am. J. Pub. Health 2 (2018); Leo Beletsky & Corey S. Davis, Today's Fentanyl Crisis: Prohibition's Iron Law, Revisited, 46 Int'l J. Drug Pol'y 156–59 (2017).

[9] For example, Bloomberg Law, SCOTUSBlog, the New York Times, and others all refer to the cases this way.

[10] Indignation is a visceral bias that can drive irrational decisionmaking, especially when combined with feelings of betrayal and when shared by groups. See, e.g., Kelly K. Dineen, Addressing Prescription Opioid Abuse Concerns in Context: Synchronizing Policy Solutions to Multiple Complex Public Health Problems, 40 L. & Psych Rev. 1, 44–45 (2016) (synthesizing work by Cass Sunstein and applying it to pain treatment).

[11] At oral arguments, government's counsel offered a list of examples that really described careless, mistaken, and negligent doctors—including "egotistical doctors" who think they are "doing right by" their patients and an "absentee doctor"—as the types of defendants that should be convicted. Tr. of Oral Arg., *supra* note 4, at 45–48. He also suggested this is a rare type of case where doctors should be criminally punished for carelessness. *Id.* at 59.

against the really "bad doctors" and so inconsistency across circuits was practically inconsequential.[12]

This argument wasn't terribly surprising. We have been conditioned over the last century and certainly over the past decade to blame doctors who prescribe controlled substances for a hefty share of drug-related social harms. Their part in prescription opioid-related harms is particularly salient, and over the last 15 years we have imbued opioids with their own almost magical power of destruction. We continue to throw around terms like "overprescribing" and "misprescribing" without definition and let them serve as a heuristic for a wide range of behaviors,[13] all in a contextual void.[14] Stories of doctors' prosecutions elicit more cheers than concerns—in part because we believe they are "bad doctors" and in part because they provide a (false) reassurance that something is being done about the "opioid crisis." But truth is stranger than fiction and usually more complex.

This essay is an attempt to disentangle some of that complexity and proceeds in four parts. First, I share a few of my nursing experiences working with patients who took prescribed opioids and try to shed some light on the complexity of their care. I also describe the difficulties that arise from criminalizing care. In part II, I provide an overview of the federal criminalization of controlled substances prescribing over the past century, including Section 841(a)(1) prosecutions. I then review the conflicts that led the Court to take up the *Ruan* case and review the opinion in more detail in part III. I conclude by describing the relevance of *Ruan* for patients in need of care and their providers and summarizing the importance of the *Ruan* holding.

---

[12] *Id.* at 69–70.

[13] In an era of vigorous legal action aimed at misprescribing, not one jurisdiction had bothered to define the prescribing problems they sought to remedy. To that end, I offered a taxonomy that could help policymakers better attend to context and create a kind of cognitive-forcing strategy for bias correction. The taxonomy included inadvertent overprescribing, qualitative overprescribing, quantitative overprescribing, multi-class misprescribing, corrupt prescribing, and underprescribing. Kelly K. Dineen, Definitions Matter: A Taxonomy of Inappropriate Prescribing to Shape Effective Opioid Policy and Reduce Patient Harm, 67 U. Kan. L. Rev. 101, 961–1011 (2019).

[14] A series of my past law review articles have addressed these issues in depth. See Dineen & DuBois, *supra* note 6; Dineen, Addressing Prescription Opioid Abuse Concerns in Context, *supra* note 10 (applying behavioral economics to opioid policy and prescribing decisions and introducing the opioid heuristic); Dineen, Definitions Matter, *supra* note 13.

I. The Complexity of the Clinical Picture and the Perils of Criminalizing Care

I have a window into the difficult tradeoffs involved in taking care of patients with chronic or persistent pain (CPP)—not just from reading studies from my comfortable perch in the ivory tower, but firsthand from working as nurse in the late 1990s and early 2000s. I worked primarily for a neurosurgeon with a subspecialty in caring for patients with CPP syndromes refractory to medical care (a fancy way of saying treatments from many other doctors hadn't helped). Dr. Jaimie Henderson was and is an excellent physician—conscientious and empathetic, board certified and fellowship trained, a prolific scholar and thought leader in functional neurosurgery.[15] I would trust him with my life, as many have and still do, to this day.

Our patients' histories were always lengthy, complex, and riddled with trauma (much of it inflicted by the very medical systems they turned to for help). They had learned the hard way that practitioners often viewed them with more suspicion and skepticism than trust,[16] a problem amplified because many of our patients were also poor and disenfranchised in other ways.[17] As desperate for relief as most of them were by the time we met them, almost all of them were more desperate to be taken seriously and to be told the truth about the limits of medicine.[18]

I was their primary point of contact and a sort of medical gatekeeper.[19] I triaged their questions and concerns, programmed their medical devices, helped coordinate the timing and any changes

---

[15] Dr. Henderson is now at Stanford University, https://stanford.io/3JIInjA. I shared this essay with him and received his permission to publish it via email, which is on file with the author.

[16] See generally Megan Crowley-Matoka & Gala True, No One Wants to Be the Candy Man, 27 Cultural Anthropology 4 689–712, 701 (2012) ("[C]linicians offer[ed] up expressions of frustration, anger, and even disgust in vivid terms: 'Ugh, pain patients—I hate those back pain guys. I just want to turn and run when I see one coming.' And 'What a waste, the kind of energy they spend trying to get their meds—makes me sick.'").

[17] See, e.g., Liesa De Ruddere & Kenneth D. Craig, Understanding Stigma and Chronic Pain: A-State-of-the-Art Review, 157 Pain 8, 1607–10 (2016).

[18] See, e.g., Kelly K. Dineen, Moral Disengagement of Medical Providers: Another Clue to the Continued Neglect of Treatable Pain?, 13 Houston J. Health L. & Pol'y 2 (2013).

[19] See generally Elizabeth Chiarello, Medical versus Fiscal Gatekeeping: Navigating Professional Contingencies at the Pharmacy Counter, 42 J.L. Med. & Ethics 4, 518–34 (2014).

to their prescriptions—including long-term opioid therapy—and reviewed opioid treatment agreements with them.[20] It was the decade of pain and the era of Oxycontin, and some patients were on doses that are mostly unheard of today, but it was absolutely the standard of care for some people with CPP at the time.[21] For many of them, that medication was what allowed them to return to the activities of their daily lives. For a handful, access to those medications was problematic, and in hindsight the way we dealt with those issues was far from ideal.

I'd say we both had a lot of concern for these patients and were unusually comfortable with the complexity and uncertainty involved in taking care of patients with CPP. Our colleagues, like many providers,[22] often didn't understand how "we could stand taking care of these patients" and viewed us as outliers, a kind of association stigma. This paled in comparison to the way the patients themselves were and are still treated, too frequently dismissed as hysterical, difficult, noncompliant, or as "druggies."[23] I still regard patients with CPP as among the most marginalized and mistreated groups of patients in health care.

Only later did it dawn on me that there was another highly stigmatized group I had not regarded at all—those who use drugs or have substance use disorder (SUD). They were so marginalized that we simply didn't see them as our problem, except insofar as it concerned making sure they didn't "take advantage" of us again.[24] Contrary to common presumptions, most people with CPP do not have SUD, but

---

[20] These agreements spell out the terms under which the prescriber agrees to treat them. These exist to protect the provider from legal scrutiny, but evidence to support their use as a clinical tool is weak at best. See, e.g., Tuesday M. McAuliffe Staehler & Laura C. Palombi, Beneficial Opioid Management Strategies: A Review of the Evidence for the Use of Opioid Treatment Agreements, 41 Substance Abuse 2, 208–15 (2020).

[21] See, e.g., G.M. Aronoff, Opioids in Chronic Pain Management: Is There a Significant Risk of Addiction?, 4 Current Rev. Pain 112–21 (2000); M. Glajchen, Chronic Pain: Treatment Barriers and Strategies for Clinical Practice, 14 J. Am. Bd. Family Practice 3 (2001).

[22] See Dineen, Moral Disengagement, *supra* note 18.

[23] *Id.* The very use of terms (for someone who uses drugs or has a SUD) as a terrible insult illustrates the pervasive stigma that still exists. For a collection of first-person narratives from people with CPP and SUD, see Kelly K. Dineen & Daniel Goldberg (Symposium Editors), Living in Pain in the Midst of the Opioid Crisis, 8 Narrative Inquiry in Bioethics 3 (Winter 2018).

[24] Here again, indignation is a powerful driver of our decisions.

certainly some do.[25] And a subset of this group is those with opioid use disorder (OUD).[26] People with either or both conditions are deserving of appropriate, individualized, and compassionate health care, which may include prescribed controlled substances.[27]

I'm not proud of how I treated people who I discovered were using drugs other than as prescribed. When concerns were brought to our attention, our response was typical of how many providers respond even today, such as telling them they need to find a new doctor and dismissing them from the practice.[28] I personally don't recall having serious conversations about whether they may have had a SUD. I am reluctant to admit that the most effort I put into helping someone who had misused prescriptions was looking up drug treatment centers in the phone book for them. This is especially heartbreaking because, even at that time, there existed broadly effective treatments for OUD, although I can't say I was aware of them. Today, treatment with medication for OUD (MOUD) is lifesaving and more effective than those available for most other serious medical conditions.[29] Yet fewer than half of the people who would benefit from MOUD succeed in accessing it,[30] in part because

---

[25] In 2020, 14.5 percent of the population had a past-year SUD, with alcohol use disorder accounting for the largest share. SAMHSA, Key Substance Use and Mental Health Indicators in the United States: Results from the 2020 National Survey on Drug Use and Health (2021), https://bit.ly/3QdkAuB.

[26] The incidence of opioid addiction among those with SUD has been estimated at about 3.5 percent, with a greater percentage having mild or moderate OUD. See Joseph A. Boscarino et al., Opioid-Use Disorder among Patients on Long-Term Opioid Therapy: Impact of Final DSM-5 Diagnostic Criteria on Prevalence and Correlates, 6 Substance Abuse & Rehabilitation 83 (2015); see also Nora D. Volkow et al., Prevention and Treatment of Opioid Misuse and Addiction: A Review, 76 JAMA Psychiatry 2, 208–16 (2019).

[27] See, e.g., Micheal E. Schatman et al., No Zero Sum in Opioids for Chronic Pain: Neurostimulation and the Goal of Opioid Sparing, Not Opioid Eradication, 14 J. Pain Res. 1809–12 (2021). The gold standard of care for OUD is prescribed opioid medications. See, e.g., Nat'l Acad. of Sci., Eng'g, & Med., Medications for Opioid Use Disorder Save Lives (2019).

[28] See, e.g., Daniel G. Tobin et al., Responding to Unsafe Opioid Use: Abandon the Drug, Not the Patient, 36 J. Gen. Internal Med. 790–91 (2021) (describing a study in which 78 percent of primary care doctors had dismissed a patient for violating a controlled substances treatment agreement).

[29] See, e.g., Nat'l Acad., *supra* note 27.

[30] *Id.*

some health care providers still do not regard these patients as their responsibility.[31]

We could and should have done better by these patients, not just individually but as institutions and communities. I am also disappointed in the systems and structures that failed to educate us about addiction and model appropriate care and treatment. We simply didn't see addiction as within our scope or within the realm of health care as conventionally understood. I now know that laws related to controlled substances prescriptions and addiction treatment, especially criminal laws, are foundational to mutually reinforcing structural, institutional, and individual discrimination against people who use or are perceived as using drugs—including people with CPP and SUD.

A. Prescribing Decisions Are Fraught with Peril

Deciding what, when, how much, and to whom to prescribe controlled substances is one of the most fraught decisions practitioners make in the regular practice of medicine. All medicines carry both promise and peril for the patients to whom they are prescribed. Making the best judgments about when that balance tips in favor of issuing the prescription is rarely completely straightforward. When it comes to controlled substances, that calculation is especially knotty. It's the only area of medicine that borders criminal law so acutely and with so much variability about what separates lawful provider conduct from unlawful, criminal conduct. Prescribing controlled substances is uniquely personally risky to practitioners in a way that all other medical decisionmaking is not. And viewed in hindsight, imperfect but well-meaning decisions can be easily framed as malicious and criminal by law enforcement and other Monday-morning quarterbacks.[32]

When there isn't a bright line between lawful and unlawful conduct, claims ring hollow that only really "bad doctors" are at risk of criminal prosecution.

---

[31] See, e.g., Alexander C. Tsai et al., Stigma as a Fundamental Hindrance to the United States Opioid Overdose Crisis Response, PLoS Med 16(11): e1002969 (2019); Kelly K. Dineen & Elizabeth Pendo, Substance Use Disorder Discrimination and the CARES Act: Using Disability Law to Guide Part 2 Rulemaking, 52 Ariz. St. L.J. 1143–65 (Winter 2020).

[32] See generally Dineen & DuBois, *supra* note 6.

I offer just one example here of a patient, "Jane," that I think is illustrative. Jane had CPP, with a long history of back injuries and surgeries prior to coming into our care. About a year into the relationship, Dr. Henderson surgically placed a totally implanted, programmable and refillable pump that delivered highly concentrated opioid medication in small volumes into the cerebral spinal fluid space near her spine. Part of my job was refilling and programming those pumps in clinic. This required a small procedure in which I used a sterile, specially designed needle to access a port under the skin and empty any remaining volume of medicine. I then refilled the pump with 20ccs (4 teaspoons) of new medication and reprogrammed the pump to allow it to calculate how long that new volume would last given the concentration and dose. Jane's visits were uneventful for some time, and it seemed like the pump was really helping her pain.

Sometime over the next year, things changed. Over the course of three or four refills, I noted greater and greater discrepancies between the left-over amount I expected and what was actually remaining in the pump (that is, each time there was more liquid medication missing by a factor of a few more ccs). Dr. Henderson and I discussed the issue multiple times, and we also reached out to the device manufacturer, who had no other reports of similar irregularities although minor discrepancies were commonplace. A drug screen was not useful in this case because the pump was still delivering opioids. It wasn't impossible that the steadily increasing discrepancies were a chance pattern of normal variability. We also spent a lot of time talking to the patient about it. At the time, nothing else was amiss. She had been a model patient for years. I was more suspicious than Dr. Henderson, but I also knew it would require some medical skill and access to long needles to somehow access the medication. I was also less compassionate and more indignant, a product of the moralistic and punitive culture that criminalizes people who use drugs.

Weighing the options, I agreed with Dr. Henderson that in the absence of proof, we should trust the patient and continue her care. Dr. Henderson even replaced the pump in hopes that would solve the problem. When I saw the patient post-op, her wound had not fully healed, which was unusual, and the discrepancy was worse rather than better. But we went ahead and refilled and programmed the pump and talked to her again, openly sharing our concerns about diversion and giving her the opportunity to "confess"—as if she were a suspect and not a patient who may have developed a SUD. She denied any issues and despite our growing concerns, we erred on the side of trusting the patient.

Shortly thereafter, she returned with a seriously infected wound over the pump, leaving me with little doubt that she was accessing the pump and Dr. Henderson with little choice but removal after a course of antibiotics. The device company's analysis of that pump confirmed my suspicions. It found multiple breaches in the core of the access port caused by garden-variety hypodermic needles. The patient eventually admitted that a nurse relative had been extracting tiny amounts of the highly concentrated opioid medication for diversion. I don't know if I ever knew any additional details. I am not sure I cared. My reaction was indignant, smug satisfaction at having been correct rather than concerned for my patient's well-being. After a post-operative follow up, she was discharged from our care. I honestly don't recall if any referrals were made. I viewed Jane as detracting from the "good" patients with CPP, and I bought right into the misguided narratives and false binaries that distinguished patients with CPP as more deserving than people with SUD.

These kinds of absolutes and false binaries are part of what drive some in law enforcement to unfairly scrutinize prescribers. But false binaries, by definition, lack nuance and context. I can now imagine a description of Jane's case in the hands of law enforcement with the benefit of hindsight. It would probably focus on how we refilled that pump for months on end despite repeated "warning signs." We, especially Dr. Henderson, would certainly be accused of missing warning signs, maybe even of being what the government called the "egotistical doctor" who blindly believes he is just doing right by his patient—too caring for our own good.[33] They would have a field day with the pump replacement and certainly find some doctor—under the nonrigorous standards for expert testimony in these cases—to say that he had departed from the usual course of professional practice. They could make a convincing case, especially to the uninitiated (such as a jury), and if this happened a few years later, as the country fell under the moral panic of the overdose crisis, it could have been a travesty for everyone involved.

---

[33] See Tr. of Oral Arg., *supra* note 4.

At worst, we may have been a little slow to push the issue and a little naïve. Everything that transpired with Jane was in an honest, careful effort to treat her with respect and dignity and maintain a plan of care that helped her function. That she lied to us is not unexpected—she knew diversion is criminal behavior and viewed as deeply shameful to boot. She also knew she would lose her doctor because we, like most practices that treated people with CPP, didn't treat SUD. If the tables were turned, I would have lied to my providers too. That we were fooled, that we erred on the side of trusting a long-term patient, should not be criminal either. And even if we had made actual errors that had harmed her, those should be handled by the myriad state-based regimes better designed to address patterns of less-than-careful medical decisions.[34] Perhaps equally unjust is that there would be no legal scrutiny if we had been a substantial factor in harms from withdrawal or self-harm if we had discharged her after our first suspicions. Doctors are almost never held accountable for withholding care when it comes to opioids.[35] Jane's story is an example of what might be construed as nonnegligent (she arguably suffered no harm *caused* by the prescribing) but potentially criminal prescribing, at least under the standards in some circuits immediately before *Ruan*.

B. Criminalizing Care Causes Harm

Criminalizing medical care and the patients that need that care is state-sanctioned stigma. It can force doctors to choose between their patients' well-being and their own most basic freedoms. The power of legal entanglement or the threat thereof—especially within the criminal legal system—to push practitioners away from providing medically indicated but personally risky care has been particularly

[34] Although it is outside the scope of this essay and the *Ruan* decision did not address it, there are well written and compelling federalism arguments to exclude federal law enforcement from medical care. See, e.g., Br. of Cato Institute as Amicus Curiae Supporting Petitioner, Ruan v. United States, 142 S. Ct. 2370 (2022) (Nos. 20-1410 & 21-5261) (citing to other authorities); Br. of Professors of Health Law & Policy as Amici Curiae Supporting Petitioner at Sec. III, Ruan v. United States, 142 S. Ct. 2370 (2022) (Nos. 20-1410 & 21-5261) (Dec. 23, 2021); Br. of Professors of Health Law & Policy as Amici Curiae Supporting Pet. for Writ of Cert. at Sec. IV, Ruan v. United States, 142 S. Ct. 2370 (2022) (Nos. 20-1410) (May 7, 2021).

[35] See, e.g., Lynn Webster, Pain and Suicide: The Other Side of the Opioid Story, 15 Pain Med. 345 (2014).

salient in the immediate aftermath of *Dobbs v. Jackson Women's Health*,[36] with scores of reported delays and patient abandonments, even in emergencies, as practitioners and institutions struggle to understand the line between lawful or personally safe and unlawful or risky conduct.[37] Even mistaken beliefs about what the law sanctions can create powerful behavioral incentives for practitioners.[38] In the context of abortion, in some states practitioners have few assurances they won't face legal entanglement for appropriate care.[39] Practitioners who chose to keep treating patients associated with opioids and other controlled substances—such as people with CPP, SUD, or both—also operate in murky territory where good and ethical medical decisions may be at odds with legal risks to the provider.[40] They also do so in an environment of promised or actualized enhanced surveillance, including from prescription drug monitoring

---

[36] Dobbs v. Jackson Women's Health Org., 142 S. Ct. 2228 (2022) (overturning Roe v. Wade).

[37] See, e.g., Carrie Feibel, Because of Texas Abortion Law, Her Wanted Pregnancy Became a Medical Nightmare, NPR (July 26, 2022), https://n.pr/3JIKq7g (detailing the delays in performing an abortion for a woman who was 18 weeks pregnant whose water had broken and infection was progressing with a nonviable pregnancy); Caroline Kitchner, The Texas Abortion Ban Has a Medical Exception. But Some Doctors Worry It's Too Narrow to Use, The Lily (Oct. 21, 2021), https://bit.ly/3dmZLP2 (discussing the availability of surgical care for ectopic pregnancies under the abortion ban in Texas (SB 8) and the fears of legal scrutiny under that law among practitioners).

[38] This is certainly true in some of the reporting about delays in providing emergency surgical treatment for ectopic pregnancies, which probably aren't prohibited under even the strictest state law. For an excellent discussion of the way doctors behave in response to even inaccurate claims about the law, see Sandra H. Johnson, Regulating Physician Behavior: Taking Doctors' "Bad Law" Claims Seriously, 53 St. Louis U. L.J. 973 (2009).

[39] There may be some cold comfort of a narrow federal protection for medically indicated stabilizing emergency treatment under The Emergency Medical Treatment and Active Labor Act (EMTALA). See, e.g., U.S. Dep't of Justice, News: Justice Department Sues Idaho to Protect Reproductive Rights, August 2, 2022, https://bit.ly/3bLWo3E (describing a request for declaratory judgment against Idaho under EMTALA); Greer Donley & Kimberly Chernoby, How to Save Women's Lives after Roe, The Atlantic (June 13, 2022), https://bit.ly/3BWJU3Q (explaining how EMTALA could be used to prevent states from criminalizing emergency reproductive health care).

[40] Kate M. Nicholson & Deborah Hellman, Opioid Prescribing and the Ethical Duty to Do No Harm, Am. J.L. & Med. 297 (2020).

programs (PDMPs), of both their professional actions and their patients' confidential care.[41]

It is ultimately practitioners and patients who are casualties of laws and policies carved out of deeply entrenched moral, political, social, and religious ideologies. Law is simply too blunt an instrument to adequately manage the nuanced and constantly evolving nature of medicine. And when it tries to target broader social disputes at the bedside by invading the doctor-patient relationship, the law almost always ends up inducing substantial harms. These are often billed as "unintended consequences."[42] But the harms of overregulation and legal overdeterrence—whether (1) pregnant people with ectopic pregnancies are forced to wait until they are near death from a ruptured fallopian tube, or (2) the legal separation of addiction treatment from all the rest of medicine renders people with SUD invisible to doctors and untreated, or (3) the individuals with CPP who functioned well for years on long-term opioid therapy turn to riskier illicit drugs or become suicidal when doctors abruptly stop prescribing opioids in reaction to poorly conceived opioid policies—are almost always foreseeable, foreseen, and represent, at a minimum, an implicit choice about who and what matters more to society.

II. The History of Federal Controlled Substances Laws that Criminalize Prescribing

In an environment of overregulation, fears of criminal prosecution drive doctors away from patients, leading to more suffering and death among those most in need of medical care. This effect has been openly acknowledged for at least a century in the context of controlled substances prescribing, and yet policymakers continue to enact and enforce laws that induce harm.[43]

---

[41] For a chilling account of the combined reach, inaccuracy, and discriminatory nature of prescription drug monitoring programs, see Jennifer D. Oliva, Dosing Discrimination: Regulating PDMP Risk Scores, 110 Calif. L. Rev. 47–115 (2022).

[42] Alex Broom et al., The Administration of Harm: From Unintended Consequences to Harm by Design, Crit. Soc. Pol'y (Apr. 7, 2022), https://bit.ly/3p69pIi.

[43] The scope of this essay only allows me to include some of those federal criminal laws that directly bear on prescribing conduct.

A. The Harrison Narcotic Tax Act

The federal government began inserting itself into the doctor-patient relationship after the enactment of the Harrison Narcotic Tax Act in 1914.[44] The law created tracking, registration, recordkeeping, and taxing requirements for individuals and entities involved in the narcotics supply chain, with an exception for patients who possessed drugs prescribed to them "in *good faith* by a physician . . . registered under this Act."[45] The act also expressly allowed doctors to dispense or distribute narcotics to patients "*in the course of his professional practice only.*"[46] It was a general intent statute with a maximum fine of $2,000 and not more than five years in prison.[47] The act was aimed at the narcotics supply chain, not patients, who at the time of its enactment were viewed as

> "sufferers" or "patients" . . . [who] could and did get relief from any reputable medical practitioner, and there is not the slightest suggestion that Congress intended to change this beyond cutting off the disreputable "pushers" who were thriving outside the medical profession and along its peripheries.[48]

However, the law enforcement agency—here, the Treasury Department who would also soon be charged with enforcing the prohibition of alcohol—had other plans. Treasury officials quickly tried to play doctor and set clinical parameters on the meaning of "the course of professional practice" and "good faith" in the law, despite their utter incompetence to do so.[49] For example, they declared in 1915 guidance that when treating anyone with SUD, doctors' "prescriptions should show the good faith of the physician in the legitimate practice of his profession *by a decreasing dosage or reduction of the quantity* prescribed from time to time."[50] They also began sending in undercover agents and others to pretend to be a patient in serious pain or with addiction

---

[44] Harrison Narcotic Tax Act, Pub. L. 223, Stat. 785 (1914) (later codified at 26 U.S.C. § 4701 et seq.).

[45] *Id.* at § 8 (emphasis added).

[46] *Id.* at § 2(a) (emphasis added).

[47] *Id.* at § 9.

[48] Rufus G. King, The Narcotics Bureau and the Harrison Act: Jailing the Healers and the Sick, 62 Yale L.J. 5, 736–49, 737 (1953), https://bit.ly/3bGycjh.

[49] *Id.*

[50] Br. of Cato Institute, *supra* note 34 (citing to other authorities).

in an effort to "fool" the doctor into prescribing—later using the fact that the "patient" wasn't really suffering as proof that prescribing wasn't in good faith.[51] This practice remains pervasive today and the undercover patients appear with well-developed and documented medical histories consistent with CPP and SUD. This strategy is often effective in securing a conviction. I have written elsewhere how unjust this practice is because prescribers, as mere humans, aren't lie detectors.[52] Moreover, the practice undermines the orientation of mutual, relational trust so foundational to provider-patient relationships.[53]

In short order, federal courts across the country also got involved in the practice of medicine. In a series of cases the courts declared that prescribing opioids to people with SUD was not the "legitimate practice of medicine,"[54] for example, the Supreme Court's decision in *Webb v. United States* in 1919.[55] In the era of prohibition and punitive treatment, other powerful forces hopped on the bandwagon. The American Medical Association eventually issued a resolution in 1920 against the medical treatment of addiction with regular doses of opioids.[56] And in 1919, the Court reversed a lower court's dismissal of a prescribing case, describing the doctor as prescribing to a known "dope fiend" and "not for the treatment of any disease."[57] Emboldened by their judicial victories and prohibitionist orientations, and in concert with the moral panic over the "dope menace" across the country,[58] law enforcement began interpreting the act to prohibit doctors altogether from prescribing regular doses of opioids as a treatment for addiction, regardless of

[51] See, e.g., King, *supra* note 48, at 735–36 (describing the indictment of Dr. Linder based on prescribing a small dose of morphine to an "addict-stool pigeon who was working for the agents").

[52] It also may work only one way. Dr. Ruan refused to prescribe to people who turned out to be undercover agents multiple times, but the district court excluded that evidence on the grounds it wasn't relevant. Petition for Certiorari at n.3, Ruan v. United States, 142 S. Ct. 2370 (2022) (No. 20-1410).

[53] See Dineen & DuBois, *supra* note 6.

[54] *Id.* See also King, *supra* note 48, at 737–39 (describing the Treasury Department's actions and court decisions in Harrison Act cases against doctors, including Supreme Court opinions from 1919 to 1925).

[55] 249 U.S. 96 (1919).

[56] Institute of Medicine, Federal Regulation of Methadone Treatment, Nat'l Acad. Press (1995).

[57] United States v. Doremus, 249 U.S. 86, 90 (1919).

[58] King, *supra* note 48, at 737–38.

the circumstances or evidence of effectiveness. By 1925, it was widely known that doctors were abandoning patients out of reasonable fears of prosecution, and, in *Linder v. United States*, the Supreme Court tried to walk back its previous sweeping statements in Harrison Act cases.[59] The Court urged that its language about prescribing should be understood as applying only to cases with facts indicating the prescriber did not act in good faith in the usual course of professional practice (i.e., as applying only to "bad doctors"). In somewhat of an acknowledgment of the harms of driving doctors out of the business of caring for people with SUD, and perhaps the dawning knowledge that the law had in many ways created the illicit drug market,[60] the Court wrote:

> [The act] says nothing of "addicts" and *does not undertake to prescribe methods for their medical treatment.* They are diseased and proper subjects for such treatment, and we cannot possibly conclude that a physician acted improperly or unwisely or for other than medical purpose solely because he has dispensed to one of them, in the ordinary course and in good faith . . . for relief of conditions incident to addiction.[61]

But it was too late.[62] Prosecutions continued, and prescribers were left to choose between facing criminal prosecution for helping people with SUD and CPP or remaining safely avoidant. Medicine in the main decided that these patients simply weren't worth the risk. This attitude lingered for decades, and it's still pervasive. In the 1950s, the American Bar Association and the American Medical Association Joint Committee on Narcotic Drugs noted that

> the physician has no way of knowing before he attempts to treat, and/or prescribe drugs to an addict, whether his activities will be condemned or condoned. He does not have any criteria or standards to guide him in dealing with drug addicts, since what constitutes *bona fide* medical practice and good faith depends upon the facts and circumstances of each case.[63]

[59] 268 U.S. 5 (1925).

[60] Thomas M. Quinn & Gerald T. McLaughlin, The Evolution of Federal Drug Control Legislation, 22 Cath. U. L. Rev. 586 (1972).

[61] Linder, 268 U.S. at 18 (emphasis added).

[62] King, *supra* note 48, at 747–48.

[63] Morris Ploscowe, Interim and Final Reports of the Joint Committee of the American Bar Association and the American Medical Association on Narcotic Drugs, Appendix A (1950).

Through the 1960s, federal law enforcement continued to advise prescribers based on the language of *Webb* rather than *Linder*.[64] As enforced, the law solidified the ideas that doctors are criminally blameworthy for addiction and thus risk their very liberty in prescribing opioids to anyone, especially those with SUD. People who use drugs became almost the sole province of law enforcement as well as the poster children for anti-immigration and white-supremacist goals dressed up as drug policy.[65] Criminalization of the people who use drugs—which is highly racialized[66] and includes people who have CPP and SUD—made clarion that they are different, deviant, and defective, unworthy of compassion and appropriate medical care.

B. The Controlled Substances Act

The Harrison Act was widely viewed as "an unenlightened approach to a social problem."[67] The CSA of 1970 repealed the Harrison Act and a multitude of dispersed drug control laws and replaced them with a centralized statute enforced by the Department of Justice governing all narcotic and "dangerous drugs."[68] Leading up to its passage, concerns remained about the Harrison Act's overdeterrence of prescribing and its role in ending the medical treatment of SUD. The House hearings transcript includes the statement that "out of fear of prosecution many physicians refuse to use narcotics in the treatment of [people with SUD]. . . . In most instances they shun addicts as patients."[69] The legislative history does not otherwise provide

[64] Quinn & McLaughlin, *supra* note 60.

[65] See, e.g., andre douglas pond cummings & Steven A. Ramirez, Roadmap for Anti-Racism: First Unwind the War on Drugs Now, 96 Tulane L. Rev. 3 (2022); Doris M. Provine, Race and Inequality in the War on Drugs, 7 Ann. Rev. L. Soc. Sci. 1, 41–60 (2011).

[66] See, e.g., Br. of the Cato Institute and the ACLU of Pa. as Amici Curiae in Support of Appellees, United States v. Safehouse, 985 F.3d 225 (3d. Cir. 2021) (No. 20-1422) (July 6, 2020), https://bit.ly/3vTMrIg.

[67] Quinn & McLaughlin, *supra* note 60, at 597.

[68] The CSA places each controlled substance into one of five schedules based on currently accepted medical use and potential for abuse. Schedule I drugs have no currently accepted medical purpose and a high potential for abuse. Schedules II through V drugs all have a currently accepted medical use with varying potential for abuse, ranging from Schedule II (highest abuse potential) to Schedule V (lowest). 21 C.F.R. § 1308. See, e.g., Dineen & DuBois, *supra* note 6. There are serious questions about the utility and accuracy of this classification system.

[69] House Rep. No. 91-1444, 1970 U.S.C.C.A.N. 4580-4581 (1970).

a lot of background on the issue of prescribing. While the 1970 version of the CSA reflected an awareness of the need for rehabilitation rather than only repression and retribution in drug policy,[70] there remained a strong push for prohibitionist, supply-sided restrictions in much of the law and especially among law enforcement.

A few years later, Congress would eventually create extensive regulatory regimes for the treatment of OUDs with MOUDs—first for methadone administration,[71] and later for buprenorphine prescribing,[72] both of which have been regularly updated. The law also vested Health and Human Services, rather than a law enforcement agency, with the power to set the standards. This is the only instance in which Congress has placed in the hands of a federal agency the responsibility for setting standards for nuanced clinical care, which is contrary to important principles of federalism that properly place the regulation of medical practice solidly within the police powers of the states.[73] It also represents one of many examples of drug exceptionalism and addiction exceptionalism in the law. These regimes are burdensome, segregate care, involve excessive surveillance of providers and patients, continue to impede innovation and appropriate care of people with SUD, and further deter providers from assuming the risks.[74] Those prescribers who submit themselves to these enhanced OUD treatment regimens to provide appropriate, life-saving care to people with OUD also bear the risk of prosecution under Section 841(a)(1).[75]

---

[70] See Quinn & McLaughlin, *supra* note 60.

[71] Narcotic Addict Treatment Act of 1974, Pub. L. No. 93-281 (May 14, 1974).

[72] Drug Addiction Treatment Act of 2000, https://bit.ly/3QuI4ew.

[73] For an excellent explanation of the federalism concerns, see Br. of Professors of Health Law & Policy and Br. of Cato Institute, *supra* note 34.

[74] A comprehensive review of the regulation of opioid treatment programs and other medications for addiction is outside the scope of this essay. See, e.g., Ellen Weber, Failure of Physicians to Prescribe Pharmacotherapies for Addiction: Regulatory Restrictions and Physician Resistance, 13 J. Health Care L. & Pol'y 1, 49–76 (2010).

[75] See, e.g., United States v. Naum, 832 Fed. App'x 137 (4th Cir. 2020) (unpublished). Naum's petition for cert was granted and the case remanded for further consideration after the *Ruan* decision. Dr. Naum may have acted carelessly and out of compliance with the detailed regulatory requirements for buprenorphine prescribing, for which there are good administrative remedies. Yet he hardly met the standard of a corrupt prescriber—among other things, he enjoyed no real financial gain and his patients were actually helped rather than harmed.

Over the years, the CSA has been amended repeatedly, and, until very recently, generally in furtherance of punitive and retributionist rather than rehabilitative goals. The *Ruan* case focused specifically on one provision of the CSA: the felony drug distribution provision in Section 841(a)(1) under which prescribers are often prosecuted, which carries significantly stiffer penalties than the Harrison Act. The text of Section 841(a)(1) remains unchanged from 1970 as does the primary regulation that governs "effective prescribing." However, the standards for convicting prescribers thereunder have morphed over time in circular and conflicting ways that sometimes borrow from the ghosts of the Harrison Act more than the text of the CSA. This has complicated rather than clarified the standards for conviction.

C. Section 841(a)(1) and Pre-Ruan Supreme Court Opinions

Section 841(a)(1) makes it unlawful *"except as authorized . . .* for any person [to] *knowingly or intentionally . . .* distribute [] or dispense . . . a controlled substance."[76] For layperson prosecutions, the language is relatively straightforward—prosecutors must prove the defendant (1) knowingly or intentionally (2) distributed (3) a controlled substance. For a range of people to whom the "except as authorized" clause applies—including manufacturers, pharmacies, pharmacists, veterinarians, researchers, and others,[77] it is more complicated, especially because Congress did not provide much guidance. This essay and the *Ruan* case focus on what the government must prove to convict a prescriber under 841(a)(1). That depends, in large part, on what "as authorized" means. If practitioners act safely within the boundaries of "authorization," their conduct is lawful. The harder question to answer is where the boundary sits between less-than-careful prescribing or noncompliance with the CSA's technical requirements and unlawful felonious behavior punishable under 841(a)(1). The petitioners argued, as did most of the amici, that the line is set by the scienter of knowledge or intent explicit in the statutory text.

---

[76] 21 U.S.C. § 841(a)(1) (emphasis added).

[77] Entities such as manufacturers, pharmacies, and professionals such as pharmacists, researchers, veterinarians, etc. all have specific registration, recordkeeping, and reporting requirements and also fall under the "except as authorized" clause of 841(a)(1), but they are outside the scope of this essay. See 21 C.F.R. §§ 1300–1321.

1. When Is a Prescriber Authorized?

Acting "as authorized" requires compliance with registration mandates,[78] controlled substance prescription content and rules based on the drug's scheduling (technical requirements),[79] and the regulatory requirement of an "effective prescription."[80] Once a practitioner is licensed by the state to practice medicine (or another profession with prescriptive authority under state law),[81] she must apply for a certificate of registration (COR) from the Drug Enforcement Administration (DEA).[82] Practitioners with a COR possess a DEA number and are among those "authorized by this chapter" to dispense a "controlled substance *in the course of professional practice*"[83] and in "conformity with the other provisions of this title."[84] Those provisions include the central regulation defining an "effective" prescription,[85] which the attorney general promulgated without comment from practitioners in 1971.[86] An effective prescription is one "issued for a *legitimate medical purpose* by an individual practitioner acting in the *usual course of his professional practice*."[87] Practitioners do not violate Section 841(a)(1) if they are otherwise authorized and issue prescriptions for a legitimate medical purpose in the usual course of professional practice.

Discerning the limits and consequences for noncompliance has proved more elusive. In part, this is because there are a range of less-than-ideal prescribing behaviors for which prescribers should not be criminally culpable. It's quite easy to violate the technical requirements for prescriptions.[88] This could be something as simple as

---

[78] 21 C.F.R. § 1301.

[79] 21 C.F.R. § 1306. Violations of technical requirements, such as lax records or missing dates, are usually spotlighted in these cases as well.

[80] 21 C.F.R. § 1306.04.

[81] 21 C.F.R. § 1306.03.

[82] 21 U.S.C. §§ 822(a) & 823(f); 21 C.F.R. § 1301.

[83] 21 U.S.C. § 802(21) (emphasis added).

[84] 21 U.S.C. § 822(b).

[85] 21 C.F.R. § 1306.04.

[86] 36 Fed. Reg. 7776 (1971).

[87] 21 C.F.R. § 1306.04(a) (emphasis added).

[88] Once when Dr. Henderson was leaving the country for 10 days, I asked him to "pre-sign" a few prescriptions in case I failed to account for the regular timeline of opioid prescription renewals for one or more of our established patients. He did so

omitting some information or forgetting to sign a prescription. In the administrative realm, those who depart from the federal authorization (including the technical requirements) may face administrative sanctions, up to and including the denial, suspension, or revocation of the COR. [89] There are also myriad state civil, administrative, and lesser criminal remedies for inappropriate prescribing.[90] Section 841(a)(1) should be reserved for the most egregious behavior, especially considering the severity of the penalties. However, the federal courts have struggled in the 50 years since the CSA's enactment to elucidate clearly and consistently exactly what the government must prove to secure a conviction against a prescriber under Section 841(a)(1).

2. The Standards before the Overdose Crises

Prior to *Ruan*, only once had the Court addressed prescriber prosecutions under Section 841(a)(1)—in a 1975 case, *United States v. Moore*.[91] The question was whether a prescriber could *ever* be subject to 841(a)(1) because Dr. Moore had already admitted that he did not act for legitimate medical purposes.[92] The Court concluded that where a prescriber was acting "outside the bounds of professional practice" and prescribing not "for legitimate purposes, but primarily for the profits to be derived therefrom," he may be prosecuted under Section 841.[93] The Court did not reach the standards for judging whether and when a prescriber's conduct had shifted from legitimate to "illegitimate channels" but did note that the CSA fails to "unambiguously spell out" such standards.[94] In 2006, in *Gonzales v. Oregon*, the Court noted

---

with strict parameters that I would email him the details first and not deliver them to patients without his approval, which I did. We found out soon after that this was a violation of the CSA and didn't repeat it. But this kind of action has been used as a basis for felony conviction and a good example of why scienter is so important. See, e.g., United States v. Joseph, 709 F.3d 1082 (11th Cir. 2013).

[89] This wasn't added until 1984. 21 U.S.C. § 823(f)(1); 21 C.F.R. §§ 1301.35–1301.37.

[90] See, e.g., Dineen & Dubois, *supra* note 6.

[91] 423 U.S. 122 (1975).

[92] At the time of *Moore*, the DEA did not have authority to revoke or suspend a practitioner's COR. That was added in 1984. Absent the reach of 841(a)(1), the only remedies for misprescribing were found in state law. The DEA had no way to stop a practitioner from prescribing unless the state medical board acted first. See Gonzales v. Oregon, 546 U.S. 243, 261–62 (2006) (explaining the addition of the 1984 amendments).

[93] 423 U.S. at 135.

[94] *Id.* at 140.

that it had never considered "the extent to which the CSA regulates medical practice beyond prohibiting a doctor from acting as a drug pusher instead of a physician."[95]

The jury instructions from *Moore*, which the Supreme Court did not disturb, echoed the Harrison Act and became a model for future prescriber prosecutions. There, the jury was instructed

> that it had to find beyond a reasonable doubt that a physician, who *knowingly or intentionally*, did dispense or distribute [a controlled substance] by prescription, did so *other than in good faith* . . . in the *usual course of a professional practice and in accordance with a standard of medical practice generally recognized and accepted in the United States.*[96]

In the three decades following *Moore*, prescriber prosecutions proceeded across the country, and although there was variation in several of the standards, there was a sort of shaky consensus.[97] In general, and in line with the language of *Moore*, the government had to prove that the prescriber (1) acted outside their authorization, judged by a departure from prescribing for a legitimate medical purpose in the usual course of professional practice, and (2) did so knowingly or intentionally.[98] Initially, courts read this in the conjunctive—requiring *both* a departure from the usual course and no legitimate medical purpose.[99] Expert testimony is almost always used to establish the contours of the "usual course of professional practice." The usual course is judged by something of a watered down, national standard of care—prosecutors can show a departure from the usual course of professional practice far more easily

---

[95] Gonzales, 546 U.S. at 269 (internal quotations omitted).

[96] Moore, 423 U.S. at 149 (emphasis added).

[97] This is the term we used in our amici brief on the petition. See Br. of Profs. of Health Law & Policy Supporting Cert, *supra* note 34.

[98] Dineen & DuBois, *supra* note 6. See also Ronald W. Chapman II, Defending Hippocrates: Representing Physicians in the Wake of the Opioid Epidemic, 43 Champion 40 (2019).

[99] See, e.g., United States v. Varma, 691 F.2d 460, 462 (10th Cir. 1982) (the prosecution must show defendant "acted intentionally or knowingly and . . . prescribed the drug without a legitimate medical purpose *and* outside the usual course of professional practice") (emphasis added).

than establishing the actual standard of care in a malpractice case.[100] Therefore, also requiring the prosecutor to prove that there was no legitimate medical purpose (or that the defendant acted outside the "bounds of medical practice")[101] was necessary to save from criminal liability a well-meaning provider who had been careless with a prescription (putting them outside the usual course) but had issued it for her patient's legitimate medical needs.[102]

Second, courts allowed some type of good-faith defense for prescribers. Those were eventually described as falling into one of two camps. Some circuits, including the First, Seventh, and Ninth, adopted a subjective good-faith defense standard.[103] The subjective good-faith defense negated the *mens rea* showing of knowledge or intent by allowing the defendant to assert she intended to and honestly believed she was prescribing in the usual course of professional practice. Other circuits, including the Second, Fourth, and Sixth,[104] adopted an objective good-faith defense, which allowed a defendant to assert she honestly believed she had prescribed in the usual course of professional practice, but *only* if the belief was objectively reasonable. This reasonable belief standard rightly drew concern as a dressed-up negligence test that effectively criminalized standard-of-care departures.[105] Inserting the objectively reasonable standard into the good-faith defense circumvented, in some ways, what the jury already was charged with—judging the credibility of the evidence.

---

[100] For a direct comparison of those differences in Alabama, See Br. of Profs. of Health Law & Policy Supporting Petitioners at Sec. IV, *supra* note 34. See also Br. of Profs. of Health Law & Policy Supporting Cert at n.3, *supra* note 34.

[101] Some courts used this phrase instead of legitimate medical purpose. See, e.g., United States v. Schneider, 704 F.3d 1287, 1295–96 (10th Cir. 2013).

[102] See Petition for Certiorari, Naum v. United States, 832 Fed. App'x 137 (4th Cir. 2020), cert granted and remanded, 2022 U.S. LEXIS 3230 (U.S. June 30, 2022) (No. 20-1480); Chapman, *supra* note 98; John J. Mulrooney II & Katherine E. Legel, Current Navigation Points in Drug Diversion Law: Hidden Rocks in Shallow, Murky, Drug-Infested Waters, 101 Marq. L. Rev. 333, 425–26 (2017).

[103] United States v. Sabean, 885 F.3d 27 (1st Cir. 2018); United States v. Rosenberg, 585 F.3d 355, 357 (7th Cir. 2009); United States v. Feingold, 454 F.3d 1001 (9th Cir. 2006).

[104] United States v. Volkman, 797 F.3d 377, 387 (6th Cir. 2015); United States v. Hurwitz, 459 F.3d 463, 479 (4th Cir. 2006); United States v. Vamos, 797 F.2d 1146 (2d Cir. 1986).

[105] Deborah Hellman, Prosecuting Doctors for Trusting Patients, 16 Geo. Mason L. Rev. 3 (2009); Diane E. Hoffmann, Treating Pain v. Reducing Drug Diversion and Abuse: Recalibrating the Balance in Our Drug Control Laws and Policies, 1 St. Louis U. J. Health L. & Pol'y 231(2008).

It removed from their purview the ability to acquit a defendant they judged as credible but whose honest intention and belief that they had prescribed in the usual course was misguided or silly.

Overall, courts generally also expressed concern about maintaining a boundary between criminal and other prescribing conduct, such as negligent or mistaken prescribing, which they expressed in various ways.[106] But these standards began to erode after the early 2000s with a sharp uptick in the last several years, corresponding suspiciously with the growing awareness of the overdose crises.

III. The Conflicting Standards during the Overdose Crises and the *Ruan* Case

Section 841(a)(1)(a) prosecutions were long riddled with uncertainty as applied to people otherwise authorized to prescribe, dispense, distribute, and administer controlled substances. Shifting tides and enhanced concerns about prescribers' role in increased drug-related morbidity and mortality also induced legal actors to create and amend many prescription controlled substances laws. Law enforcement also used the tools at their disposal,[107] including the CSA, especially as Congress appropriated more resources to scrutinize prescribers.[108] In tandem, the standards in some circuits slowly shifted to the point that deviation from behavior akin to standard of care was sufficient for conviction, without regard to the prescriber's mental state. This was achieved by eliminating the legitimate medical purpose element, hollowing out the good-faith defense, and applying the *mens rea* requirement to the simple act of issuing a prescription—all of which is innocent conduct that is part of the everyday practice of medicine. Those courts had transformed a serious federal felony, with the potential for life in prison and fines up to a million dollars, into a strict liability offense—effectively

---

[106] Br. of Profs. of Health Law & Policy Supporting Cert at Sec. I.C., *supra* note 34.

[107] Michael C. Barnes, Taylor J. Kelly & Christopher M. Piemonte, Demanding Better: A Case for Increased Funding and Involvement of State Medical Boards in Response to America's Drug Abuse Crisis, 106 J. Med. Reg. 3 (2020) ("[I]nvestigating and prosecuting prescribers . . . has compromised access to treatment for individuals with legitimate medical needs. Enforcement efforts have created a chilling effect on prescribers, . . . who are decreasing and altogether ceasing their prescribing out of fear of investigation and prosecution.").

[108] See, e.g., Dineen, Definitions Matter, *supra* note 13.

criminalizing careless, mistaken, or even careful but innovative prescribing.

At the same time, patients associated with opioids, including people with CPP and OUD, were suffering. The supply-side-only, misaligned legal "solutions" that focused almost exclusively on prescription opioids alone had left people desperately in need of care, mistreated, undertreated, and abandoned.[109] Practitioners were not only concerned about the risks of prescription opioids for their patients; they were also worried about being blamed, about their prescription patterns standing out, and about institutional and legal scrutiny of their practices.[110] Patients who had done well on long-term opioid therapy found themselves involuntarily tapered, cut off altogether,[111] further stigmatized,[112] or without a doctor willing to care for them. Too many of these patients died by suicide or after overdosing on illicit opioids,[113] eventually leading the Food and Drug Administration and the Centers for Disease Control and Prevention to issue warnings.[114] Many people with OUD could not access care, in part because practitioners weren't willing to incur the heightened scrutiny or navigate the regulatory complexities involved in prescribing medications for OUD.[115] Past was prologue and, like the

---

[109] *Id.*

[110] See, e.g., Cara L. Sedney et al., "The DEA Would Come in and Destroy You": A Qualitative Study of Fear and Unintended Consequences Emerging from Restrictive Opioid Prescribing Policies in West Virginia, 17 Substance Abuse Treatment, Prevention, & Pol'y 1 (2022) (conducting qualitative interviews with prescribers who repeatedly identified the fear of the DEA as motivating patient avoidance).

[111] See, e.g., Jackie Yenerall & Melinda B. Buntin, Prescriber Responses to a Pain Clinic Law: Cease or Modify?, 206 Drug & Alcohol Dep. 107591 (2020) (after state law changes, 24 percent of prescribers stopped prescribing altogether, without regard for patient needs); Amelia L. Persico et al., Opioid Taper Practices Among Clinicians, 14 J. Pain Res. 3353, 3357 (2021) (describing the CDC guidelines as prompting tapering).

[112] See, e.g., Allyn Benintendi et al., "I Felt Like I Had a Scarlet Letter": Recurring Experiences of Structural Stigma Surrounding Opioid Tapers among Patients with Chronic, Non-Cancer Pain, 222 Drug & Alcohol Dependence (2021).

[113] Beth D. Darnall et al., International Stakeholder Community of Pain Experts and Leaders Call for an Urgent Action on Forced Opioid Tapering, 20 Pain Med. 429 (2019).

[114] See, e.g., Christine Vestal, Rapid Opioid Cutoff Is Risky Too, Feds Warn, PEW (May 21, 2019), https://bit.ly/3dmK6zh.

[115] Nat'l Acad., *supra* note 27.

Harrison Act in the 1920s, the law had succeeded in driving patients out of the medical system and into harm's way.

In tandem, it became far easier to convict a prescriber under Section 841(a)(1) even though the statute hadn't changed. By 2021, there was a long list of circuit splits such that *where* a prescriber-defendant was tried, rather than the prescribing conduct, determined whether she would be convicted or acquitted. In the amicus brief we filed in an effort to persuade the Court to hear *Ruan*, we detailed a non-exhaustive list of existing circuit splits in Section 841(a)(1) prescriber prosecutions. These included (1) whether the government must prove a practitioner departed from a legitimate medical purpose;[116] (2) whether the lack of a legitimate medical purpose is an element that must be included in the indictment;[117] (3) the availability and form of the good-faith defense;[118] (4) the relationship between good faith and *mens rea*;[119] (5) whether the jury must actually be instructed on the *mens rea*;[120] and (6) whether a prescriber may be convicted of dispensing, distributing, or both.[121] By the time the Court granted certiorari in *Ruan*, several circuits had successfully converted the drug distribution felony into a strict liability offense, but *only* when the defendant was a prescriber. The circuit courts did this in surprisingly confusing, conflicting, and overlapping ways that are hard to sort out—in part because of courts' reliance on good faith from the Harrison Act and in part because of the complexities of defining acting "as authorized." What the changes have in common, and what the *Ruan* decision corrects, is that most of the circuits

---

[116] Petition for Certiorari, Naum v. United States, *supra* note 102; Petition for Certiorari, Henson v. United States, 9 F.4th 1258 (10th Cir. 2021), cert granted and remanded (U.S. June 30, 2022) (No.19-3062) (also including a question of whether a willful blindness instruction was harmless error).

[117] Julia MacDonald, "Do No Harm or Injustice to Them": Indicting and Convicting Physicians for Controlled Substance Distribution in the Age of the Opioid Crisis, 72 Me. L. Rev. 197, 213–16 (2020).

[118] Petition for Certiorari, Ruan v. United States, 142 S. Ct. 2370 (2022) (No. 20-1410).

[119] United States v. Khan, 989 F.3d 806 (10th Cir. 2021) (concluding that objective good faith does not negate *mens rea* but simply explains the course of professional practice); but see, e.g., United States. v. Godofsky, 943 F.3d 1011, 1021 (6th Cir. 2019) ("Reasonable [good faith] conduct or beliefs, if proven, would necessarily prevent the jury from finding that he had a knowing or intentional *mens rea*.").

[120] Petition for Certiorari, Dixon v. United States, 141 S. Ct. 137 (2020) (No. 19-1313).

[121] Petition for Certiorari, Faithful v. United States, 141 S. Ct. 1742 (2021) (No. 20-7204).

had either (1) eliminated *any* scienter requirement or (2) lessened the scienter requirement to one of something akin to recklessness or negligence.[122] They did this in multiple ways.

A. Reading the Effective Prescribing Regulation as Disjunctive

Most circuits had switched to reading the effective prescription regulation in the disjunctive—meaning the government was required to prove that the defendant had *either* (1) departed from the "usual course of professional practice" *or* (2) not prescribed "for a legitimate medical purpose."[123] This was problematic in several ways. First, a departure from the usual course is very easy to prove;[124] moreover, some circuits required only proof of unreasonableness in usual-course departures leading prosecutors to favor that option over legitimate medical purpose departures, which required subjective knowledge.[125] Second, the "usual course" is a moving target. Although courts refer to this as an "objective standard" because it is based on expert testimony about "reasonable" prescriber practices, the acceptable standards of care are made up of a range of options from the almost out-of-date to the innovative.[126] These differences are tolerable in the civil context because of the rigorous expert testimony standards and because it is just one of several elements required for liability to attach, including for patient harm caused by acting outside the standard of care. Even then, the standards for treating people with conditions like CPP are especially complicated. They are subject to wildly divergent views, conflicting evidence of effectiveness, and policies and laws that encourage "reasonable" doctors to adopt practices that aren't in patients' best interests. And they are open to interpretations that are far from objective— a dangerous benchmark for criminal liability.

[122] See, e.g., Model Penal Code, § 2.02.

[123] Only the Ninth Circuit, in *United States v. Feingold,* has affirmatively stated that both showings are required. 454 F.3d 1001 (9th Cir. 2006). See also Naum, 832 Fed. App'x 137; Henson, 9 F.4th 1258. For an example of the reasoning for a disjunctive reading, see United States v. Nelson, 383 F.3d 1227, 1232 (10th Cir. 2004) (overruling precedent and concluding that neither *Moore* nor the effective prescription regulation required a showing of both).

[124] See briefs cited, *supra* note 34.

[125] See, e.g., Khan, 989 F.3d 806.

[126] See, e.g., Sandra H. Johnson, Customary Standards of Care, 43 Hastings Ctr. Rep. 6, 9–10 (2013).

Third, while "legitimate medical purpose" is a regulatory rather than statutory term, it has been understood by both Congress[127] and the Court as an essential component of effective prescribing.[128] The disjunctive reading is also a classic example of the professional arrogance that can infect some lawyers (here some prosecutors and judges) when it comes to the nuances of medicine. In this context, except for the Ninth Circuit, there has been widespread endorsement that the usual course of professional practice and a legitimate medical purpose are simply two ways of saying the same thing.[129] Practitioners do not see it the same way.[130] Imagine a doctor who is overworked and even careless; as a result she accidently provides a new prescription at 20 days rather than 30 days a few times and neglects to make detailed notes in the patients' records. Her patients truly benefit from the prescriptions, which they take as prescribed. In this instance, a provider would have a legitimate medical purpose but would not have acted in the usual course of professional practice—behavior that is better remedied outside the criminal system. Now, if the scienter requirement of knowledge or intent is preserved, either as an element or with a subjective good-faith defense, the defendant here would probably not be convicted.

When paired with a weak objective good-faith defense, the disjunctive reading is more troublesome. In those situations, the defendant could argue she intended and believed she was practicing in

[127] When Congress amended the CSA to account for both mail order and internet prescribing in recent decades, it included new statutory provisions that include "legitimate medical purpose" in the definition of a valid prescription. For mail order prescriptions, a valid prescription is "issued for a legitimate medical purpose by an individual practitioner licensed by law to administer and prescribe the drugs concerned and acting in the usual course of the practitioner's professional practice." 21 U.S.C. § 830(b)(3)(A)(ii) (2000). For internet prescriptions, among other things, a valid prescription is one "issued for a legitimate medical purpose in the usual course of professional practice." 21 U.S.C. § 829(e)(2)(A) (2008).

[128] Gonzales, 546 U.S. at 257 (describing C.F.R. § 1306.04 as a parroting regulation). Justice Antonin Scalia explained in his dissent that Section 1306.04 "gives added content to the text of the statute [§ 829]," such that a legitimate medical purpose is implicit in the requirements for an effective prescription. Id. at 279 (Scalia, J., dissenting) (citing Moore, 423 U.S. at 137 n.13 (1975)).

[129] That perception was aided greatly with active conflation by the DEA in guidance and policy. See Chapman, supra note 98.

[130] See, e.g., Mulrooney & Legel, supra note 102.

the usual course of professional practice. However, her belief would have to be reasonable, as judged again against the weak quasi-standard-of-care testimony allowed in these prosecutions. This is the very definition of circular reasoning: creating a situation in which the defendant can only be saved by convincing a jury it was reasonable to think she was behaving in ways the experts have already said are not reasonable.

Preserving or restoring a conjunctive reading is a work-around for the ways in which the objective good-faith defense weakens scienter. In the example above, the doctor's legitimate medical purpose could save her from the consequences of criminalized carelessness. This was the focus of the petition for cert in *Naum*, in which the doctor had taken on the treatment of people with OUD, including buprenorphine prescribing in hard hit and underserved West Virginia. He earned very little money and overstretched himself in the process. His patients benefited from the treatment—in fact, it's likely his prescriptions saved multiple lives. Nonetheless, it was true that he didn't act in the usual course of professional practice—he was careless in not adhering to the many regulatory requirements for OUD treatment and over-relied on a nurse. The Fourth Circuit allowed Naum an objective good-faith defense, but the jury didn't see his proffered belief as reasonable, and he was convicted. A conjunctive reading could have saved him, as he certainly had a legitimate medical purpose. While the *Ruan* Court did not weigh in on the specific conjunctive/disjunctive question, it was a question presented in the *Khan* petition as well. The Court's ultimate clarification of both scienter and to what elements it applies should provide reassurance.

B. Hollowing Out the Objective Good-Faith Defense

The issues that ultimately caught the Court's attention were the treatment by the Tenth and Eleventh Circuits, in *Khan* and *Ruan* respectively, concerning the objective good-faith defense (which was particularly dangerous because it was coupled with a disjunctive reading of the effective prescription regulation).[131] In both cases, the circuits had arrived at the conclusion that the objective good-faith defense was only available to defendants who already practiced within the usual course of practice. Intent didn't matter.

131 Khan, 989 F.3d at 825–26.

The Eleventh Circuit in *Ruan* upheld the district court's jury instructions that collapsed good faith into standard of care, saying:

> A controlled substance is prescribed by a physician in the usual course of a professional practice and, therefore, lawfully *if the substance is prescribed by him in good faith as part of his medical treatment of a patient in accordance with the standard of medical practice* generally recognized and accepted in the United States. The defendants in this case maintain at all times they acted in good faith and in accordance with [the] standard of medical practice generally recognized and accepted in the United States in treating patients. . . . Thus *a medical doctor has violated Section 841 when the government has proved beyond a reasonable doubt that the doctor's actions were either not for a legitimate medical purpose or were outside the usual course of professional medical practice.*[132]

The district court, in issuing those instructions, had rejected the defendant's proposed instructions as too subjective. Those said:

> Good faith in this context means good intentions and the honest exercise of professional judgment as to the patient's needs. It means that the Defendant acted in accordance *with what he reasonably believed to be proper medical practice.*[133]

The Eleventh Circuit agreed with the district court that those instructions were simply "too subjective." They endorsed the standard that would rest conviction on a simple showing that the prescriber's actions were not in the usual course of professional practice. The panel asserted that a good-faith defense was only available to defendants when their "conduct *also was in accordance with the standards of medical practice* recognized in the United States."[134] They had transformed Section 841(a)(1) into a strict liability offense such that even a mistake in prescribing was felonious.

The Tenth Circuit also created a strict liability offense for usual course departures in 2021, in *United States v. Khan,* by reconstructing the mechanism of the good-faith defense as having nothing to do with the culpable mental states. The court expressly stated,

---

[132] Petition for Certiorari, *supra* note 52, at 12 (emphasis added).

[133] *Id.* at 11 (emphasis added).

[134] *Id.* at 14 (emphasis added).

"[u]nlike other criminal offenses, good faith does not go to mens rea for § 841 offenses involving practitioners" and "the only relevant inquiry . . . is whether a defendant-practitioner objectively acted within [quasi-standard of care], regardless of whether he believed he was doing so."[135] In their estimation, knowledge only went *to the act* of writing a prescription—a standard met unless the prescriber did so in their sleep. Together, the Fourth, Tenth, and Eleventh Circuits had rewritten the CSA as applied to practitioners, grounding criminal liability in a mere departure from accepted medical practice.

C. It's the Scienter

Each of these issues was essentially about scienter in prescribing cases—both what it was and to what elements it applied. This was the focus of most of the briefs after the Court granted certiorari as well as of the Court's opinion. Viewed in that light and with the freedom to ask the Court for major clarifications, it seemed appropriate to explain that the circuits had managed to take a relatively straightforward statute and complicate it beyond recognition such that the elements of the crime for prescribers were no longer obvious. The boundary between innocent and unlawful conduct was clear as mud. In short, before *Ruan*, the defendants could not have knowledge of "all of the facts that make [their] conduct illegal."[136]

A culpable mental state requirement for criminal offenses is the default in the U.S. criminal legal system, and its existence grows in importance with the severity of the punishment.[137] The Court will also read in a *mens rea* requirement in a statutory void.[138] But there is no void here—knowledge or intent appear in the statute and interpreting the statute consistent with ordinary English usage means that the scienter requirement is one of knowledge or intent, just as it is for laypersons. The government, appealing to the "bad doctors" narrative again, asked the Court to ignore those words (but only when prescribers were defendants) in favor of a quasi-scienter which they struggled to articulate at oral argument. This left the justices

135 Khan, 989 F.3d at 825–26.

136 McFadden v. United States, 576 U.S. 186, 194–95 (2015).

137 Dennis v. United States, 341 U.S. 494 (1951).

138 Staples v. United States, 511 U.S. 600 (1994).

puzzled by the "no objectively honest effort" *mens rea* offered, which isn't a traditional mental state, and also because inserting reasonableness leads one back to a strict liability offense.[139]

In our amicus brief we argued that the government must prove beyond a reasonable doubt three material elements under Section 841(a)(1), whether prosecuting a layperson or a prescriber: that the defendant (1) knowingly (2) distributed (3) a controlled substance. Of course, prescribing controlled substances is part of everyday practice. Every time a doctor wrote a controlled substance prescription, she would be committing a crime if prescribing alone were enough for distribution. Proving a knowing departure from the authorization is what transforms conduct from innocent (regular prescribing) to unlawful (distribution).[140] Treating this as an element of the offense, rather than an affirmative defense, is the most straightforward reading of the statute. Holding that the *mens rea* applies to departures from authorization also is in line with several of the Court's previous cases that emphasize the role of scienter in separating innocent from criminal conduct.[141] The Court agreed, framing the question before them as "the state of mind that the government must prove to convict these doctors of violating the statute."[142]

---

[139] For example, at oral arguments, Justice Neil Gorsuch pushed the government's counsel on the implications of eliminating a *mens rea* for prescribers in the following exchange: "Justice Gorsuch: Just assume hypothetically [that the government brings a case against a doctor where their behavior is a close call] and that the jury believes that it's not legitimate medical purpose under your regulations. Even though it's an extremely close case, that individual stands, under the government's view, unable to shield himself behind any *mens rea* requirement and is subject to essentially a regulatory crime encompassing 20 years to maybe life in prison. Mr. Feigin: Well, Your Honor, I think— I think it's – Justice Gorsuch: I think the answer has to be yes, isn't it? Mr. Feigin: Your Honor, I think the answer is going to be yes." Tr. of Oral Arg., *supra* note 4, at 71–72.

[140] United States v. X-Citement Video, Inc., 513 U.S. 64, 79 (1994) ("[C]ourts ordinarily read a phrase in a criminal statute that introduces the elements of a crime with the word 'knowingly' as applied to each element.").

[141] See, e.g., Rehaif v. United States, 139 S. Ct. 2191, 2196 (2019) ("The cases in which we have emphasized scienter's importance in separating wrongful from innocent acts are legion."); Liparota v. United States, 471 U.S. 419, 426 (1985) (requiring knowledge that the possession of food stamps was unauthorized).

[142] Ruan, 142 S. Ct. at 2375.

IV. The *Ruan* Decision and Conclusion

In an opinion written by Justice Stephen Breyer, the Court held that the statute's knowingly or intentionally *mens rea* applies to the "except as authorized" clause, such that the government must prove that a doctor or practitioner defendant *knowingly* acted outside the limits of their federal authorization to prescribe controlled substances or *intended* to do so.[143] The Court treats the knowing departure from authorization as an element of the offense, based on the importance of the vicious will in criminal offenses, the long-standing presumption of scienter, and the importance of setting a clear boundary between innocent and criminal conduct.

Procedurally, however, the Court did not treat a knowing departure as an element that must be pled in the indictment because of Section 855 of the CSA, which states that the government does not need to:

> "negative"—i.e., refute—"any exemption or exception . . . in any complaint, information, indictment, or other pleading." This means that, in a prosecution under the Controlled Substances Act, the Government need not refer to a lack of authorization (or any other exemption or exception) in the criminal indictment . . . and that "the burden of going forward with the evidence with respect to any such exemption or exception shall be upon the person claiming its benefit," not upon the prosecution.[144]

The Court interpreted Section 885 to hold that the defendant retains the burden of production in raising the issue of authorization to prescribe controlled substances. Once raised, the government must prove beyond a reasonable doubt that the prescriber (subjectively) knew or intended to act outside her authorization (retaining the burden of persuasion).

In a concurring opinion by Justice Samuel Alito, joined in full by Justice Clarence Thomas and in part by Justice Amy Coney Barrett, the justices read Section 885 to preclude treating a departure from authorization as an element. They would treat it, instead, as an exception that would form the basis of an affirmative defense for which the defense would retain the burden of proving. The concurring

[143] *Id.* at 2375–76.
[144] *Id.* at 2379.

justices also argued that an authorization departure could not be an element because "except as authorized" preceded the words "knowingly or intentionally" in the statute, and basic grammar prohibits the adverbs of knowingly and intentionally from modifying the preceding clause.[145] This would make it far easier to convict a prescriber than a layperson and impose a different scienter requirement.

After *Ruan*, the government must prove not only that the prescriber did not act as authorized, but that she did so knowingly or intentionally. The decision should go a long way toward confining Section 841(a)(1) prosecutions to the corrupt among the "bad doctors" who knowingly used their authorization as a subterfuge for drug dealing as conventionally understood, a position that accords with the Court's previous treatment in *Moore*. It represents a victory for prescribing practitioners, who faced the threat of criminal investigation and prosecution for almost any prescribing behavior, including mistaken or careless controlled substances prescribing, whether their patients suffered any harm at all. While there is much work remaining to rationalize controlled substances prescribing law and policy, I hope *Ruan* will allow practitioners to fear criminal scrutiny a bit less and be slightly more willing to provide care that they believe is in their patient's interest such that patients with CPP, SUD, or both reap some benefit.

---

[145] This was the subject of some humorous back and forth between Justices Alito and Breyer about their grammar teachers in oral arguments. Tr. of Oral Arg., *supra* note 4, at 24.

Restoring the Right to Bear Arms: *New York State Rifle & Pistol Association v. Bruen*

David B. Kopel*

Justice Clarence Thomas's opinion for a 6-3 Supreme Court majority in *New York State Rifle & Pistol Association v. Bruen* vindicates the right of law-abiding Americans to carry handguns for lawful protection. That decision will directly affect three states where the right was entirely denied: New Jersey, Maryland, and Hawaii. It will also affect three other states where the right to bear arms was already respected by some local jurisdictions but denied by others: Massachusetts, New York, and California.

Perhaps even more important, *Bruen* announces a judicial standard of review that applies to all gun control laws throughout the United States. Gun control laws that are consistent with the history and tradition of the American right to keep and bear arms are constitutional. Gun control laws that are inconsistent with history and tradition are not.

One week after the *Bruen* opinion was released, the Court vacated decisions from federal courts of appeals that had upheld bans on common rifles or magazines in Maryland, California, and New Jersey. The Court remanded the cases to the lower courts and told the courts to reconsider their decisions in light of *Bruen*.[1]

---

* Adjunct scholar, Cato Institute; research director, Independence Institute; adjunct professor of constitutional law, University of Denver, Sturm College of Law. Coauthor of Professors of Second Amendment Law et al. amicus brief in *Bruen*; and of The "Sensitive Places" Doctrine: Locational Limits on the Right to Bear Arms, 13 Charleston L. Rev. 205 (2018), cited in *Bruen*.

[1] U.S. Supreme Court, Order List, June 30, 2022, https://bit.ly/3OBdFd7. The cases were: Bianchi v. Frosh, 858 Fed. Appx. 645 (4th Cir. 2021), vacated by 142 S. Ct. 2898 (2022) (Mem.) (Maryland ban on common semiautomatic rifles); Ass'n of N.J. Rifle & Pistol Clubs Inc. v. Att'y Gen. N.J., 974 F.3d 237 (3d Cir. 2020) (upholding confiscation of magazines over 10 rounds), vacated by 142 S. Ct. 2894 (2022) (No. 20-1507);

I. From *Miller* to *Heller* and *McDonald*

The Second Amendment has suffered from periods of judicial neglect: one was from 1940–2007, and another from 2011–2021. The first period began after the Court's 1939 decision in *United States v. Miller* upholding a federal tax and registration system for sawed-off shotguns.[2] For decades thereafter, the right to keep and bear arms appeared only in occasional cameo roles, such as in the second Justice John Marshall Harlan's famous explication of Fourteenth Amendment "liberty":

> This "liberty" is not a series of isolated points pricked out in terms of the taking of property; the freedom of speech, press, and religion; the right to keep and bear arms; the freedom from unreasonable searches and seizures; and so on. It is a rational continuum which, broadly speaking, includes a freedom from all substantial arbitrary impositions and purposeless restraints[.][3]

Starting in 1989, the Court began occasionally to take cases that vindicated the rights of gun owners—but always on grounds other than the Second Amendment.[4] One such case was 1997's *Printz v.*

Duncan v. Bonta, 19 F.4th 1087 (9th Cir. 2021) (also upholding magazine confiscation), vacated by 142 S. Ct. 2895 (2022).

Also granted, vacated, and remanded was Young v. State of Hawaii, 992 F.3d 765 (9th Cir. 2021) (en banc), which had held that Hawaii's ban on open carry was constitutional because there is no right to bear arms outside one's property. Presuming that Hawaii's local law enforcement officials comply with the state attorney general's advice to start issuing concealed carry permits, and given *Bruen*'s rule that states can decide whether carrying should be concealed or open, it is not clear what remains to be done with *Young* on remand. Presumably the plaintiff will be issued a concealed carry permit by his county of residence, Hawaii County (the Big Island).

[2] United States v. Miller, 307 U.S. 174 (1939).

[3] Poe v. Ullman, 367 U.S. 497, 543 (1961) (Harlan, J., dissenting). *Poe* was a predecessor to *Griswold v. Connecticut*. Unlike the majority in *Poe*, Justice Harlan believed the plaintiffs had standing, and he would have ruled in favor of the liberty rights of married couples to use birth control. Justice Harlan's words were quoted by Roe v. Wade, 410 U.S. 113, 167 (1973) (Stewart, J., concurring); Moore v. East Cleveland, 431 U.S. 494, 502, 542 (1976) (plurality op.) (White, J., dissenting); Planned Parenthood v. Casey, 505 U.S. 833, 848–49 (1992) (plurality op.); Albright v. Oliver, 510 U.S. 266, 306–08 (1994) (Stevens, J., dissenting).

[4] Michael P. O'Shea, The Right to Defensive Arms after District of Columbia v. Heller, 111 W. Va. L. Rev. 349, 390–91 (2009) (discussing United States v. Thompson/Ctr. Arms Co., 504 U.S. 505 (1992)); Florida v. J.L., 529 U.S. 266 (2000); Staples v. United States, 511 U.S. 600 (1994) (the "long tradition of widespread lawful gun ownership" includes firearms like the semiautomatic AR-15).

United States.[5] Back in 1993, Congress enacted a statute ordering local law enforcement officials to carry out background checks on handgun buyers. Sheriffs around the nation sued, arguing that Congress had no power to dragoon local officials into enforcing congressional statutes. If Congress wanted background checks, it could hire federal employees to conduct the checks.

By 5-4, the Supreme Court agreed, with Justice Thomas joining Justice Antonin Scalia's majority opinion. While *Printz* was about federalism, not the Second Amendment, Justice Thomas wrote a brief concurring opinion to point out the Second Amendment issue. He was dubious that the 1993 statute was compliant with the Second Amendment.

Justice Thomas hoped that the Court would again address the Second Amendment. Quoting one of the greatest justices of the 19th century, he wrote: "Perhaps, at some future date, this Court will have the opportunity to determine whether Justice Story was correct when he wrote that the right to bear arms 'has justly been considered, as the palladium of the liberties of a republic.'"[6]

Eleven years later, the Court did so in Justice Scalia's 5-4 opinion in *District of Columbia v. Heller*.[7] Then in 2010, the Court ruled in *McDonald v. City of Chicago* that the Fourteenth Amendment makes the Second Amendment enforceable against state and local governments, just as are most other provisions of the Bill of Rights.[8] Here, Justice Samuel Alito's plurality opinion for the Court relied on precedents from the 1890s onward that "incorporate" items in the Bill of Rights into the Fourteenth Amendment via the clause "nor shall any state deprive any person of life, liberty, or property, without due process of law." Ever the originalist, Justice Thomas agreed with the result, but concurred to explain that the Fourteenth Amendment clause that did the work was "No state shall make or enforce any law which shall abridge the privileges or immunities of citizens of the United States."[9]

---

[5] Printz v. United States, 521 U.S. 898 (1997).

[6] *Id.* at 939 (Thomas, J., concurring).

[7] District of Columbia v. Heller, 554 U.S. 570 (2008); Clark Neily, District of Columbia v. Heller: The Second Amendment Is Back, Baby, 2007–2008 Cato Sup. Ct. Rev. 127 (2008).

[8] McDonald v. City of Chicago, 561 U.S. 742 (2010).

[9] *Id.* at 805 (Thomas, J., concurring in part).

Almost immediately after *McDonald* was announced, the Court granted, vacated, and remanded a Second Circuit case that had upheld a ban on nunchaku (martial arts sticks connected by a chain).[10] After that, the Court entered another period of Second Amendment torpor.

II. "Justice Breyer's Triumph in the Third Battle over the Second Amendment"

Post-*Heller* some lower-court judges, including then-Judge Brett Kavanaugh of the D.C. Circuit, observed that the *Heller* decision had been based on text, history, and tradition. He argued that lower courts should follow the same methodology.[11]

But he was in the minority. Most of the lower federal courts adopted the test that Justice Stephen Breyer had proposed in his dissent in *Heller*, and which had specifically been repudiated by the *Heller* majority. Under this approach, judges engage in interest balancing; they decide for themselves if an infringement on traditional Second Amendment rights is acceptable.

Although the term "Breyer test" would have been accurate, the lower courts instead called it the "two-part test" or "two-step test."

While some lower courts applied the test conscientiously, many others set things up so the government would always win. In some courts, all the government needed to do was introduce some evidence in favor of a gun control law. The fact that the government's evidence was refuted by evidence from the other side was irrelevant. The Second, Fourth, and Ninth Circuits were particularly egregious.[12]

---

[10] Maloney v. Cuomo, 554 F.3d 56 (2d Cir. 2009) (per curiam), vacated and remanded by 561 U.S. 1040 (2010). On remand, the district court held that nunchaku were in common use by law-abiding persons; being considerably less dangerous than handguns, they could not be prohibited. Maloney v. Singas, 351 F. Supp. 3d 222 (E.D.N.Y. 2018). New York State did not appeal.

Then-Judge Sonia Sotomayor had been part of the *Maloney* Second Circuit panel. During her confirmation hearings, Sens. Orrin Hatch (R-UT), Russ Feingold (D-WI), and Jon Kyl (R-AZ) asked her about the *Maloney* case. She responded that the prohibition was legitimate because nunchaku could injure or kill someone. Tr. of the Sotomayor Confirmation Hearings, 37–38, 66, 248 (July 14, 2009), https://bit.ly/3PYc9Tp.

[11] Heller v. District of Columbia, 670 F.3d 1244 (D.C. Cir. 2011).

[12] David B. Kopel, Data Indicate Second Amendment Underenforcement, 68 Duke L.J. Online 79 (2018).

In the Ninth Circuit, civil rights advocates did sometimes win cases before three-judge panels. But the full circuit would then always order an *en banc* rehearing, even if none of the parties had requested it. *En banc*, the government would always win.[13] Of the 50 post-*Heller* Second Amendment cases decided by the Ninth Circuit, the government won all 50.[14]

In January 2022, a Ninth Circuit panel ruled in *McDougall v. County of Ventura* that Ventura County's pandemic lockdowns of gun stores and shooting ranges had violated the Second Amendment since the county had allowed other businesses with comparable (small) risks to stay open.[15] The three-judge panel had rigorously applied the Ninth Circuit's particular rules for the two-step test.

Judge Lawrence VanDyke, author of the *McDougall* panel opinion, knew it wouldn't last, so he also wrote a "concurring opinion" in which he predicted that *McDougall* would be reheard. Judge VanDyke's concurrence was a "draft" opinion for the future *en banc*, upholding the Ventura lockdown. As he explained, "Since our court's Second Amendment intermediate scrutiny standard can reach any result one desires, I figure there is no reason why I shouldn't write an alternative draft opinion that will apply our test in a way more to the liking of the majority of our court. That way I can demonstrate just how easy it is to reach any desired conclusion under our current framework, and the majority of our court can get a jump-start[.]"[16] The footnotes of the "concurring" opinion explained Judge VanDyke's disagreements with the sloppy and biased reasoning in the circuit's *en banc* gun cases.

As predicted, the *McDougall* decision was *en banc*ed a few weeks later, despite neither party having asked for *en banc* review.[17]

---

[13] Duncan v. Becerra, 970 F.3d 1133, 1138 (9th Cir. 2020), rev'd en banc sub nom. Duncan v. Bonta, 19 F.4th 1087 (9th Cir. 2021); Young v. Hawaii, 896 F.3d 1044, 1048 (9th Cir. 2018), rev'd en banc, 992 F.3d 765 (9th Cir. 2021); Teixeira v. Cnty. of Alameda, 822 F.3d 1047 (9th Cir. 2016), rev'd en banc, 873 F.3d 670 (9th Cir. 2017); Peruta v. Cnty. of San Diego, 742 F.3d 1144 (9th Cir. 2014), rev'd en banc, 824 F.3d 919 (9th Cir. 2016); Richards v. Prieto, 560 Fed. Appx. 681 (9th Cir. 2014), rev'd en banc sub nom. Peruta v. Cnty. of San Diego, 824 F.3d 919 (9th Cir. 2016).

[14] Duncan v. Bonta, 19 F.4th at 1165–66 (VanDyke, J., dissenting).

[15] McDougall v. County of Ventura, 23 F.4th 1095 (9th Cir. 2022).

[16] *Id.* at 1119–20.

[17] 26 F.4th 1016 (9th Cir. Mar. 8, 2022) (en banc). After the *Bruen* decision, the Ninth Circuit sent *McDougall* back to the district court, for reconsideration in light of *Bruen*. 38 F.4th 1162 (Mem.) (9th Cir. June 29, 2022).

Dissenting in *Heller* and *McDonald*, Justice Breyer had argued that Second Amendment cases should be decided on what he called "interest balancing."[18] Breyer interest balancing is similar to intermediate scrutiny, but without intermediate scrutiny's subrules. Law professor Allan Rostron accurately called the lower courts' behavior, "Justice Breyer's Triumph in the Third Battle over the Second Amendment."[19]

Meanwhile, the Supreme Court stood idle. Every year petitions for certiorari were filed, pointing out how the lower courts were violating *Heller* and *McDonald*. But the petitions were not granted, and the lower courts took the cert denials as a signal to become ever more aggressive in ruling against the Second Amendment. Justice Thomas, sometimes joined by Justices Alito, Neil Gorsuch, or Kavanaugh, dissented five times from the cert denials. Gorsuch and Kavanaugh had joined dissentals on the right to bear arms.[20]

But the majority of the Supreme Court acted in only one case after *McDonald*. In 2016 the Court vacated a Massachusetts case upholding a ban on electric stun guns, pointing out that the Massachusetts court's rationales—that stun guns did not exist in 1791 and are not militia arms—flagrantly contradicted *Heller*.[21]

---

[18] Heller, 554 U.S. at 689–90 (Breyer, J., dissenting).

[19] Allen Rostron, Justice Breyer's Triumph in the Third Battle over the Second Amendment, 80 Geo. Wash. L. Rev. 703 (2012). Professor Rostron was formerly an attorney for Handgun Control, Inc., so he was not complaining.

[20] Jackson v. City & Cnty. of San Francisco, 576 U.S. 1013, 1013 (2015) (Thomas, J., joined by Scalia, J., dissenting from denial of certiorari) ("Despite the clarity with which we described the Second Amendment's core protection for the right of self-defense, lower courts, including the ones here, have failed to protect it."); Silvester v. Becerra, 138 S. Ct. 945, 950 (2018) (Thomas, J., dissenting from denial of certiorari) ("[T]he lower courts are resisting this Court's decisions in *Heller* and *McDonald* and are failing to protect the Second Amendment[.]"); Friedman v. City of Highland Park, 577 U.S. 1039 (2015) (Thomas, J., joined by Scalia, J., dissenting from denial of certiorari) (discussed *infra*, Part IV.B); Peruta v. California, 137 S. Ct. 1995 (2017) (Thomas, J., joined by Gorsuch J., dissenting from denial of certiorari) ("The Court has not heard argument in a Second Amendment case in over seven years. . . . Since that time, we have heard argument in, for example, roughly 35 cases where the question presented turned on the meaning of the First Amendment and 25 cases that turned on the meaning of the Fourth Amendment. This discrepancy is inexcusable, especially given how much less developed our jurisprudence is with respect to the Second Amendment as compared to the First and Fourth Amendments."); Rogers v. Grewal, 140 S. Ct. 1865 (2020) (Thomas, J., partially joined by Kavanaugh, J., dissenting from denial of certiorari).

[21] Caetano v. Massachusetts, 577 U.S. 411 (2016) (per curiam). Concurring, Justices Alito and Thomas would have over-ruled the Massachusetts Supreme Judicial Court, rather than vacating and remanding. *Id.* at 412.

By 2020, the situation appeared bleak. That year, the Court had granted certiorari in a case challenging a New York City rule that licensed handgun owners in the city could not take their handguns out of the city—not to a nearby range in New Jersey, nor even to a second home in New York State.[22] The Second Circuit upheld the ban and claimed that it did not involve a Second Amendment issue, or even if the Second Amendment were implicated, the infringement was trivial. The Second Circuit said that the police department's worries about "road rage" were sufficient to uphold the law, even though the department could not point to a single instance of misconduct by a New York City licensee transporting a handgun.[23]

When the Supreme Court granted certiorari, the New York City and state governments partially relegalized transport outside the city, giving the plaintiffs some but not all of the relief they had sought. Five Democratic U.S. senators—Sheldon Whitehouse (RI), Mazie Hirono (HI), Richard Blumenthal (CT), Richard Durbin (IL), and Kirsten Gillibrand (NY)—sent the Court a threat letter in the form of an amicus brief. They warned that unless the Supreme Court dismissed the case as moot, they would "restructure" the Court.[24]

For whatever reason, six justices complied, while Justices Alito, Gorsuch, and Thomas dissented. A month later, the Supreme Court also dismissed all 10 pending Second Amendment cert petitions. According to CNN, Chief Justice John Roberts had warned his pro-civil rights colleagues that if they took up any gun case, he would vote to upheld the restriction.[25]

The replacement of Justice Ruth Bader Ginsburg with Justice Amy Coney Barrett changed everything. On the Seventh Circuit, Judge Barrett had written a 37-page dissent in *Kanter v. Barr*, in which the other two judges had upheld a lifetime gun ban for a man who had been convicted of mail fraud for selling shoe pad inserts that were

---

[22] N.Y. State Rifle & Pistol Ass'n v. City of New York, 140 S. Ct. 1525 (2020).

[23] 883 F.3d 45 (2d Cir. 2018).

[24] Br. of Sens. Sheldon Whitehouse et al. as Amici Curiae Supporting Respondents, N.Y. State Rifle & Pistol Ass'n v. City of New York, 140 S. Ct. 1525 (2020) (No. 18-280).

[25] Joan Biskupic, Behind Closed Doors during One of John Roberts' Most Surprising Years on the Supreme Court, CNN (July 27, 2020), https://cnn.it/3BuONku ("Roberts also sent enough signals during internal deliberations on firearms restrictions, sources said, to convince fellow conservatives he would not provide a critical fifth vote anytime soon to overturn gun control regulations. As a result, the justices in June denied several petitions regarding Second Amendment rights.").

too thin. In Judge Barrett's view, the history and tradition of the Second Amendment did not allow a lifetime ban for conviction of a nonviolent felony.[26]

III. The *Bruen* Decision

Soon after, the Court granted certiorari in *New York State Rifle & Pistol Association v. Bruen*.[27] Under New York law, an applicant for a carry permit needed to have "a proper cause."[28] In some counties, permits were issued reasonably, with lawful self-defense being considered a proper cause. But in others, such as Rensselaer County, applicants had to prove "a special need for self-protection distinguishable from that of the general community."[29]

In an opinion for six justices, including Chief Justice Roberts, Justice Thomas explained, "The constitutional right to bear arms in public for self-defense is not 'a second-class right, subject to an entirely different body of rules than the other Bill of Rights guarantees.' We know of no other constitutional right that an individual may exercise only after demonstrating to government officers some special need."[30] Hence, New York may not prevent "law-abiding citizens with ordinary self-defense needs from exercising their right to keep and bear arms."[31]

A. Bruen *Adopts Text, History, and Tradition*

Bruen affirmed that using text, history, and tradition as the basis for a decision is the correct methodology in Second Amendment cases, not interest balancing:

> [T]he Courts of Appeals have coalesced around a "two-step" framework for analyzing Second Amendment challenges that combines history with means-end scrutiny. . . .

---

[26] 919 F.3d 437 (7th Cir. 2019).

[27] N.Y. State Rifle & Pistol Ass'n v. Bruen, 142 S. Ct. 2111 (2022).

[28] N.Y. Penal Law § 400.00(2).

[29] Bruen, 142 S. Ct. at 2123.

[30] *Id.* at 2156 (quoting McDonald, 561 U.S. at 780).

Paul Clement and Erin Murphy were the winning lawyers in *Bruen*. Hours after the opinion was announced, their firm, Kirkland & Ellis, ordered them to cease representation of all Second Amendment clients. Rather than desert clients in ongoing cases, they formed the new D.C. firm of Clement & Murphy.

[31] *Id.* at 2150.

> Despite the popularity of this two-step approach, it is one step too many. Step one of the predominant framework is broadly consistent with *Heller*, which demands a test rooted in the Second Amendment's text, as informed by history. But *Heller* and *McDonald* do not support applying means-end scrutiny in the Second Amendment context. Instead, the government must affirmatively prove that its firearms regulation is part of the historical tradition that delimits the outer bounds of the right to keep and bear arms.[32]

The (Breyerish) two-step test failed because it put judges in the role of policymakers, as if their policy assessments could override the policy choice made by adoption of the Second Amendment:

> If the last decade of Second Amendment litigation has taught this Court anything, it is that federal courts tasked with making such difficult empirical judgments regarding firearm regulations under the banner of "intermediate scrutiny" often defer to the determinations of legislatures. But while that judicial deference to legislative interest balancing is understandable—and, elsewhere, appropriate—it is not deference that the Constitution demands here. The Second Amendment "is the very *product* of an interest balancing by the people" and it "surely elevates above all other interests the right of law-abiding, responsible citizens to use arms" for self-defense. It is this balance—struck by the traditions of the American people—that demands our unqualified deference.[33]

Thus, "[w]hen the Second Amendment's plain text covers an individual's conduct, the Constitution presumptively protects that conduct. The government must then justify its regulation by demonstrating that it is consistent with the Nation's historical tradition of firearm regulation."[34]

B. *Bruen's Rules for Analyzing Text, History, and Tradition*

1. How the Government Can Meet its Burden of Proof

The burden of proof is thus on the government, which "must affirmatively prove that its firearms regulation is part of the

[32] *Id.* at 2126–27.

[33] *Id.* at 2131 (quoting Heller, 554 U.S. at 635) (emphasis in original).

[34] *Id.* at 2129–30.

historical tradition that delimits the outer bounds of the right to keep and bear arms."[35] This does not mean that judges bear the burden of becoming legal history researchers. As with anything else that the government must prove, the government must present persuasive legal history to the court. "Courts are thus entitled to decide a case based on the historical record compiled by the parties."[36]

In practice, government production of historic evidence in support of gun control laws has long been outsourced to professional gun control organizations, such as Michael Bloomberg's "Everytown" or the Giffords Law Center. The groups often provide pro bono assistance to governments defending gun control laws, without formally displacing the government's own attorneys.

Sometimes, the government and its allies will win because there are many original-era laws that are twins of modern ones—for example prohibiting reckless discharge of a firearm in populated areas. Additionally, the government can prove its case by "analogical reasoning." This means "a well-established and representative historical *analogue*, not a historical *twin*. So even if a modern-day regulation is not a dead ringer for historical precursors, it still may be analogous enough to pass constitutional muster."[37]

2. The "How" and the "Why" of Burdens on Self-Defense

As the *Bruen* opinion states, "analogical reasoning under the Second Amendment is neither a regulatory straightjacket nor a regulatory blank check."[38] "[C]ourts should not 'uphold every modern law that remotely resembles a historical analogue,' because doing so 'risk[s] endorsing outliers that our ancestors would never have accepted.'"[39]

The first question is whether modern gun control and the alleged historical analogue are "relevantly similar." *Bruen* does not purport to "exhaustively" define how judges may consider similarity.

---

[35] *Id.* at 2127.

[36] *Id.* at 2130 n.5. "Of course, we are not obliged to sift the historical materials for evidence to sustain New York's statute. That is respondents' burden." *Id.* at 2150.

[37] *Id.* at 2133 (emphasis in original).

[38] *Id.*

[39] *Id.* (quoting Drummond v. Robinson, 9 F.4th 217, 226 (3d Cir. 2021)).

Instead, *Bruen* states that *Heller* and *McDonald* point to "at least two metrics: how and why the regulations burden a law-abiding citizen's right to armed self-defense."[40]

"How" means: "whether modern and historical regulations impose a comparable burden on the right of armed self-defense."[41]

"Why" means: "whether that burden is comparably justified."[42]

The second metric, the "why," is immensely important. It prevents historical, burdensome laws that were enacted for one purpose from being used as a pretext to impose burdens for other purposes. As Mark Frassetto, an attorney for Everytown for Gun Safety, writes, "[m]ilitia and fire prevention laws imposed substantial burdens on founding era gun owners." In his view, courts should uphold laws that impose equally substantial burdens "regardless of the underlying motivation for regulation."[43] *Bruen* expressly forbids this methodology.

Besides the two most central self-defense metrics from *Heller* and *McDonald*, there are certainly more. As both cases state, the right to arms is for all "lawful purposes."[44] For example, recreational arms activities, such as hunting or target shooting, are in themselves part of the right. Additionally, they build skills for defense of self and others.

3. Why originalism allows analogies

Why not limit modern gun control to only the twins of laws that existed in 1791, when the Second Amendment was ratified, or in 1868 when the Fourteenth Amendment made the Second Amendment enforceable against the states?

Justice Thomas answers: Although a constitutional provision's "meaning is fixed according to the understandings of those who

---

[40] *Id.* at 2132–33. *Heller* and *McDonald* declared that "whether modern and historical regulations impose a comparable burden on the right of armed self-defense and whether that burden is comparably justified are '*central*' considerations when engaging in an analogical inquiry." *Id.* at 2133 (citing McDonald, 561 U.S. 767).

[41] *Id.*

[42] *Id.*

[43] Mark Frassetto, The Duty to Bear Arms: Historical Militia Law, Fire Prevention Law, and the Modern Second Amendment, in New Histories of Gun Rights and Regulation: Essays on the Place of Guns in American Law and Society (Jacob Charles, Joseph Blocher & Darrell Miller eds., forthcoming).

[44] Heller, 554 U.S. at 625; McDonald, 561 U.S. at 78.

ratified it, the Constitution can, and must, apply to circumstances beyond those the Founders specifically anticipated."[45]

Does analogical analysis of self-defense burdens and gun control rationales just amount to interest balancing with new language? Justice Thomas says not:

> This does not mean that courts may engage in independent means-end scrutiny under the guise of an analogical inquiry. Again, the Second Amendment is the "product of an interest balancing by the people," not the evolving product of federal judges. Analogical reasoning requires judges to apply faithfully the balance struck by the founding generation to modern circumstances. . . . It is not an invitation to revise that balance through means-end scrutiny.[46]

"[N]ot all history is created equal."[47] Most important is the Founding era.[48] For the Fourteenth Amendment, this means Reconstruction.[49] Old English practices that ended long before American independence are of little relevance.[50] Postratification history is "secondary"; it can confirm or illuminate but not contradict or override the original public understanding.[51] The same is true for mid to late 19th century.[52]

C. The Nuances of Analogy

How to deal with technological or societal changes? Per Justice Thomas:

> While the historical analogies here and in *Heller* are relatively simple to draw, other cases implicating unprecedented societal concerns or dramatic technological changes may require a more nuanced approach. The regulatory challenges

---

[45] Bruen, 142 S. Ct. at 2132.

[46] *Id.* at 2133 n.7.

[47] *Id.* at 2136.

[48] *Id.*

[49] *Id.*

[50] *Id.*

[51] *Id.*

[52] *Id.*

posed by firearms today are not always the same as those that preoccupied the Founders in 1791 or the Reconstruction generation in 1868. Fortunately, the Founders created a Constitution—and a Second Amendment—"intended to endure for ages to come, and consequently, to be adapted to the various crises of human affairs." Although its meaning is fixed according to the understandings of those who ratified it, the Constitution can, and must, apply to circumstances beyond those the Founders specifically anticipated.[53]

It may be argued that mass murders are "unprecedented societal concerns." Actually, massacres of American settlers by Native Americans were unfortunately common for three centuries, as were massacres of Natives by Americans. As of 1791, it was well known that governments were more likely to massacre victims who had first been disarmed. In the 20th century, over 200 million disarmed victims (not soldiers killed in battle) were murdered by governments. Mass killing is a very serious problem, but it is definitely not unprecedented.

As for "dramatic technological changes," the 19th century saw a cascade. The century began with muzzle-loading single-shot flintlocks and concluded with semiautomatic rifles and handguns. The 1804 Lewis and Clark expedition carried the Girandoni rifle, which could shoot 22 rounds in 30 seconds. One round could penetrate an inch of wood, or take an elk.[54]

D. What Are Permissible Controls on Bearing Arms?

As of 1791, carrying a firearm openly was lawful in every state, and so was carrying a concealed firearm. The first state law against concealed carry was enacted by Kentucky in 1813 and was held to violate Kentucky's constitutional right to arms.[55] However, other states

---

[53] *Id.* at 2132 (citing McCulloch v. Maryland, 17 U.S. 316, 415 (1819)).

[54] Frederick J. Chiaventone, "The Girandoni Air Rifle: The Lewis and Clark Expedition's Secret Weapon," Warfare History Network, https://bit.ly/3S5s3NE; Nicholas J. Johnson, David B. Kopel, et al., The Evolution of Firearms Technology from the Sixteenth Century to the Twenty-first Century, chapter 23 in Firearms Law and the Second Amendment: Regulation, Rights and Policy (3d ed. 2022), https://bit.ly/3Q19tV6.

[55] Bliss v. Commonwealth, 12 Ky. 90 (1822).

passed similar laws, and these were held not to violate the right to bear arms, since open carry was still lawful.[56]

Based on the case law, *Heller* had implied that concealed carry might be outside the protection of the Second Amendment.[57] This was wrong for two reasons. First, the concealed carry cases cited by *Heller* had generally not gone so far; rather, they had simply affirmed legislative discretion to regulate the mode.[58] Second, a holding that open carry is a constitutional right while concealed carry has nothing to do with the Second Amendment would force states that want to (or must) comply with the Second Amendment to authorize open carry only. That would be perfectly fine for social norms in 1870, when some people considered concealed carry to be sneaky and not "manly." But in the 21st century, social norms are different. If you go to a crowded shopping mall in any of the 44 states that were already respecting the right to arms before *Bruen*, it is likely that at least several people will be carrying handguns, and all those handguns will be concealed. That is how many people like things these days. Peaceable lawful carry is now most socially harmonious when it is concealed carry.[59]

Wisely, *Bruen* accurately characterizes the 19th century concealed carry cases as recognizing legislative discretion on the mode of carry rather than requiring one particular mode.[60] So, for example, Florida since 1987 has issued concealed carry permits fairly, yet bans open carry.[61]

Another important limitation on the right to bear arms is that firearms may be forbidden in certain "sensitive places":

> Consider, for example, *Heller*'s discussion of "longstanding" "laws forbidding the carrying of firearms in sensitive places such as schools and government buildings." Although the

[56] Bruen, 142 S. Ct. at 2146–48.

[57] Heller, 554 U.S. at 626.

[58] Joseph G.S. Greenlee, Concealed Carry and the Right to Bear Arms, 20 Federalist Soc'y Rev. 32 (2019).

[59] James Bishop, Hidden or On the Hip: The Right(s) to Carry after Heller, 97 Cornell L. Rev. 907, 908, 926 (2012).

[60] "The historical evidence from antebellum America does demonstrate that *the manner* of public carry was subject to reasonable regulation. . . . States could lawfully eliminate one kind of public carry—concealed carry—so long as they left open the option to carry openly." Bruen, 142 S. Ct. at 2150.

[61] Norman v. State, 215 So.3d 18 (Fla. 2017) (upholding statute).

historical record yields relatively few 18th- and 19th-century "sensitive places" where weapons were altogether prohibited—*e.g.*, legislative assemblies, polling places, and courthouses—we are also aware of no disputes regarding the lawfulness of such prohibitions. . . . We therefore can assume it settled that these locations were "sensitive places" where arms carrying could be prohibited consistent with the Second Amendment. And courts can use analogies to those historical regulations of "sensitive places" to determine that modern regulations prohibiting the carry of firearms in new and analogous sensitive places are constitutionally permissible.[62]

However, analogies to "sensitive places" cannot be expanded wildly to, say, ban carrying in cities. As Justice Thomas wrote, "expanding the category of 'sensitive places' simply to all places of public congregation that are not isolated from law enforcement defines the category of 'sensitive places' far too broadly" and would "eviscerate the general right to publicly carry arms for self-defense."[63]

The sensitive places issue had taken a lot of time at oral argument. For modern analogies, the *Heller* and *Bruen* combined list is schools, government buildings, legislative assemblies, courthouses, and polling places. The *Bruen* text, if read strictly, would seem to limit additions to the list to "new" types of sensitive places. This would rule out carry bans in types of places that were well known in the 18th or 19th centuries, such as municipal parks. At present, there is much variance in state law on sensitive places, even in states that have generally respected the right to bear arms.

E. Fair Permitting Systems Are Constitutional

When the *Bruen* decision was issued, the right to bear arms was respected in 44 states. One of them, Vermont, has never required a permit for either concealed or open carry and does not issue permits.[64] In most states, open carry without a permit was lawful and had long

---

[62] Bruen, 142 S. Ct. at 2133 (citing David B. Kopel & Joseph G.S. Greenlee, The "Sensitive Places" Doctrine: Locational Limits on the Right to Bear Arms, 13 Charleston L. Rev. 205, 229–36 (2018), and Br. for Independent Institute as Amicus Curiae Supporting Petitioners, N.Y. State Rifle & Pistol Ass'n v. Bruen, 142 S. Ct. 2111 (2022) (No. 20-843)).

[63] Bruen, 142 S. Ct. at 2134.

[64] State v. Rosenthal, 75 Vt. 293 (1903).

been so.[65] *Bruen*, however, focused on concealed carry, for which laws are typically more restrictive. According to *Bruen*, 43 states had a "shall-issue" system for licensed concealed carry, mandating that the licensing authority shall issue a concealed carry permit to applicants who meet certain specific standards.[66] As previously noted, concealed carry permits are not necessary in 25 of the 44, as those states allow permitless "constitutional carry."

Even though permits were not needed in 1791, *Bruen* holds that shall-issue licensing is constitutional:

> To be clear, nothing in our analysis should be interpreted to suggest the unconstitutionality of the 43 States' "shall-issue" licensing regimes, under which "a general desire for self-defense is sufficient to obtain a [permit]." . . . Because these licensing regimes do not require applicants to show an atypical need for armed self-defense, they do not necessarily prevent "law-abiding, responsible citizens" from exercising their Second Amendment right to public carry.[67]

Shall-issue systems are based on narrow and objective criteria:

> [I]t appears that these shall-issue regimes, which often require applicants to undergo a background check or pass a firearms safety course, are designed to ensure only that those bearing arms in the jurisdiction are, in fact, "law-abiding, responsible citizens." And they likewise appear to contain only "narrow, objective, and definite standards" guiding licensing officials, rather than requiring the "appraisal of facts, the exercise of

[65] Open carry in the United States, Wikipedia https://bit.ly/3b8Pbu3 (last visited Aug. 1, 2022).

[66] Three of these 43 (Conn., R.I., and DE) have statutes that seemed to read like "may issue," but practice and judicial precedents made these three states functionally "shall issue." See Dwyer v. Farrell, 193 Conn. 7, 12 (1984) ("suitable person" denials are only for "individuals whose conduct has shown them to be lacking the essential character of temperament necessary to be entrusted with a weapon."); Gadomski v. Tavares, 113 A.3d 387, 392 (R.I. 2015) ("Demonstration of a proper showing of need" is not part of the licensing process); Eugene Volokh, 43 States to 6 States, Says the S. Ct. about Shall-Issue Concealed Carry Rules: What's the Missing State?, Volokh Conspiracy (June 25, 2022), https://bit.ly/3oIFB4v (concealed carry licenses are issued at a high rate in Delaware, and unlicensed open carry is lawful).

[67] Bruen, 142 S. Ct. at 2138 n.9 (citing Drake v. Filko, 724 F.3d 426, 442 (3d Cir. 2013) (Hardiman, J., dissenting); Heller, 554 U.S. at 635).

judgment, and the formation of an opinion"—features that typify proper-cause standards like New York's.[68]

The language about law-abiding "citizens" should not be taken hyperliterally. Post-*Heller* cases have long made it clear that states may not discriminate in carry permits against legal resident aliens.[69]

Narrow and objective criteria are not the only requisites of a constitutionally compliant permit system:

> [B]ecause any permitting scheme can be put toward abusive ends, we do not rule out constitutional challenges to shall-issue regimes where, for example, lengthy wait times in processing license applications or exorbitant fees deny ordinary citizens their right to public carry.[70]

Allegedly "exorbitant" fees will be litigated in the future. Georgetown law professor Randy Barnett described the $505 cost of obtaining a D.C. permit, and, thereafter $235 triennially for permit renewals. In Barnett's view, some of the mandatory training was essential information for students to know about D.C.'s rules about deadly force, sensitive places, and so on. But he considered the 18 hours of training to be excessive—and mainly for the purpose of erecting barriers to applicants. Unlike many jurisdictions, D.C. mandates that all the training must take place in person in classrooms. Many other states allow training online at one's own pace, plus in-person live fire training at a range. "I can afford all this, of course, though I cannot say the same for all other citizens of D.C.," Barnett concluded.[71]

F. Legal Tradition

By a wide margin, the New York attorney general and her amici allies failed to carry their burden of proving a tradition of prohibiting peaceable carry. Much of the supposed historical evidence was based on the imaginative but unreliable writings of Fordham history professor Saul Cornell.

---

[68] *Id.* (citations omitted).

[69] See, e.g., Fletcher v. Haas, 851 F. Supp. 2d 287 (D. Mass. 2012).

[70] Bruen, 142 S. Ct. at 2138 n.9.

[71] Randy Barnett, A Minor Impact on Gun Laws but a Potentially Momentous Shift in Constitutional Method, SCOTUSBlog (June 27, 2022), https://bit.ly/3ByF3Wc.

New York and others pointed to the 1328 English Statute of Northampton, which they claimed prohibited peaceable carry of all arms. But that statute was authoritatively interpreted in *Sir John Knight's Case* in 1686. Consistent with English practice in the 17th century, and in following centuries, the chief judge stated that the statute applied only to carrying *"malo animo"*—with evil intent.[72] Two colonial statutes copied some of the Northampton language to forbid carrying "Offensively"—again, a ban on misconduct only.[73]

For a few years in the late 17th century, the short-lived colony of East Jersey (separate from West Jersey) banned concealed carry and also forbade frontiersmen from carrying handguns at all, while allowing them to carry long guns. This "solitary" example, lasting "[a]t most eight years," was not enough to create a tradition.[74]

In the 19th century, statutes in nine states stated that someone whose carrying threatened to cause a breach of the peace could continue carrying only if he posted a bond for good behavior. But he could carry without need for a bond for self-defense against a specific threat or for militia duty. These laws presumed that people could carry; if a court found someone was behaving dangerously, he could be ordered to post a bond for peaceable behavior.[75] A study by George Mason law professor Robert Leider found that such surety statutes were enforced only against people engaged in other misconduct, except for a handful of possibly pretextual cases against black people.[76] To the arguable extent there was ambiguity about the above, the ambiguity did not meet New York's burden of proof.

After the Civil War, Texas enacted a statute that prohibited handgun carrying in most situations, while imposing no restriction on long gun carrying. The Texas Supreme Court upheld the statute in

---

[72] Rex v. Sir John Knight, 90 Eng. Rep. 330, 330 (K.B. 1686); Bruen, 142 S. Ct. at 2139–41.

[73] Bruen, 142 S. Ct. at 2142–43. The same was true for three post-Independence state statutes. *Id.* at 2144–45.

[74] *Id.* at 2143–44.

[75] *Id.* at 2148–50.

[76] *Id.* at 2149–50, citing Robert Leider, Constitutional Liquidation, Surety Laws, and the Right to Bear Arms, in New Histories of Gun Rights and Regulation: Essays on the Place of Guns in American Law and Society (Joseph Blocher, Jacob D. Charles & Darrell A.H. Miller eds., forthcoming). For a short overview, see Robert Leider, The Myth of the 'Massachusetts Model,' Duke Center for Firearms Law (June 16, 2022).

two cases.[77] In the latter 19th century, five of the western territories had statutes against handgun carrying in cities, but the territorial statutes were repudiated by the adoption of state constitutions guaranteeing the right to bear arms. Besides, "late-19th-century evidence cannot provide much insight into the meaning of the Second Amendment when it contradicts earlier evidence."[78] The "few late-19th-century outlier jurisdictions" were insufficient to prove that bearing arms for lawful defense was outside the American historical tradition.[79]

Broad state restrictions on peaceable carry did become more common in the 20th century, most famously with the 1911 New York "Sullivan Act" at issue in *Bruen*. But, "[a]s with their late-19th-century evidence, the 20th-century evidence presented by respondents and their amici does not provide insight into the meaning of the Second Amendment when it contradicts earlier evidence."[80]

G. Three Concurrences

While joining Justice Thomas's opinion in full, Justice Kavanaugh wrote a concurring opinion, joined by Chief Justice Roberts. They stated that "a mental health records check" could be part of a shall-issue system.[81] They also reiterated the continuing validity of two paragraphs from *Heller* and *McDonald* that had created a rebuttable presumption in favor of certain gun control laws: "longstanding prohibitions on the possession of firearms by felons and the mentally ill, or laws forbidding the carrying of firearms in sensitive places such as schools and government buildings, or laws imposing conditions and qualifications on the commercial sale of arms."[82] The concurrence repeated the *Heller* and *McDonald* language that the Second

[77] Bruen, 142 S. Ct. at 2153; English v. State, 35 Tex. 473, 480 (1872) (bemoaning "the early customs and habits of the people of this state," and tracing the problem to Spanish law and its Carthaginian, Visigoth, and Arab influences); State v. Duke, 42 Tex. 455 (1875). West Virginia enacted a similar statute in 1887, based on the defective theory that the right to bear arms did not include handguns. Bruen, 142 S. Ct. at 2153.

[78] *Id.* at 2154.

[79] *Id.* at 2147 n.22, 2153–55.

[80] *Id.* at 2154 n.28.

[81] *Id.* at 2162 (Kavanaugh, J., concurring).

[82] *Id.*

Amendment right is for arms "in common use," not "dangerous and unusual weapons."[83]

While also joining the *Bruen* opinion in full, Justice Alito concurred to respond to the dissent. As he pointed out,

> Our holding decides nothing about who may lawfully possess a firearm or the requirements that must be met to buy a gun. Nor does it decide anything about the kinds of weapons that people may possess. Nor have we disturbed anything that we said in *Heller* or *McDonald v. Chicago*, about restrictions that may be imposed on the possession or carrying of guns.[84]

The most "law and order" justice of the present Court, Justice Alito may be much less sympathetic than Justice Barrett to challenges to federal laws imposing lifetime gun bans for nonviolent crimes.[85]

Justice Alito criticized the dissent's laundry list of the harmful effects of gun misuse, such as mass shootings, domestic violence, or suicide, which had nothing to do with the law in question, that is, whether to grant carry licenses to adults who pass background checks and safety training. Alito asked of Justice Breyer's dissent: "Will a person bent on carrying out a mass shooting be stopped if he knows that it is illegal to carry a handgun outside the home? . . . Does the dissent think that a lot of people who possess guns in their homes will be stopped or deterred from shooting themselves if they cannot lawfully take them outside?"[86] Notwithstanding the dissent's cherry-picked statistics from gun control activists, the full body of social science data showed that shall-issue laws are either socially beneficial or not harmful.[87] As Alito summarized, "the real thrust of today's dissent is that guns are bad and that States and local jurisdictions should be free to restrict them essentially as they see fit."[88]

Also joining the majority opinion, Justice Barrett pointed out some unsettled issues about historical analysis. For example, "How long

---

[83] *Id.*

[84] *Id.* at 2157 (Alito, J., concurring).

[85] This perhaps is part of the reason why the Court denied two cert petitions challenging lifetime bans on nonviolent felons. Folajtar v. Garland, 141 S. Ct. 2511 (2021); Holloway v. Garland, 141 S. Ct. 2511 (2021).

[86] Bruen, 142 S. Ct. at 2157.

[87] *Id.* at 2158 n.1.

[88] *Id.* at 2160–61.

after ratification may subsequent practice illuminate original public meaning?" Should courts rely on original understanding as of 1791, when the Second Amendment was ratified, or also 1868, when the Fourteenth Amendment made the Second Amendment enforceable against the States? In Justice Barrett's view, "today's decision should not be understood to endorse freewheeling reliance on historical practice from the mid-to-late 19th century to establish the original meaning of the Bill of Rights. On the contrary, the Court is careful to caution 'against giving postenactment history more weight than it can rightly bear.'"[89]

H. Justice Breyer's Dissent

Joined by Justices Elena Kagan and Sonia Sotomayor, Justice Breyer argued in favor of the old two-part test because courts should be specially deferential to gun control laws since guns are dangerous.[90] As Justice Alito had pointed out in *McDonald*, and Justice Thomas reiterated in *Bruen*, the criminal procedure protections in the Bill of Rights can also be dangerous.[91] They set some dangerous, guilty criminals free, and some of those criminals later perpetrate more harm.

Whereas Justice Breyer's *Heller* dissent had carefully summarized the pro/con social science evidence about handguns, the *Bruen* dissent acknowledges none of the evidence from the briefs that handgun carry by responsible persons sometimes saves lives and stops crime.[92] The strongest part of the Breyer dissent in *Heller* was the criticism of the majority's ipse dixit (requoted by the Kavanaugh concurrence in *Bruen*) granting a safe harbor to certain types of modern gun control laws, even though some of those laws have a weak basis in pre-1900 history and tradition.[93] In this respect, Justice Breyer implicitly showed that living constitutionalism does influence even mostly originalist opinions. The same point could have been made about the *Bruen* majority's blessing of shall-issue

---

[89] *Id.* at 2162–63 (Barrett, J., concurring) (quoting Espinosa v. Mont. Dep't of Revenue, 140 S. Ct. 2246, 2136 (2020)).

[90] *Id.* at 2164 (Breyer, J., dissenting).

[91] *Id.* at 2126 n.3 (quoting McDonald, 561 U.S. at 783).

[92] Heller, 554 U.S. at 696–703 (Breyer, J., dissenting).

[93] Bruen, 142 S. Ct. at 2162 (reiterating the argument from Heller). For an extended critique of *Heller* on this issue, see Nelson Lund, The Second Amendment, Heller, and Originalist Jurisprudence, 56 UCLA L. Rev. 1343 (2009).

licensing laws. The first such law was Washington State in 1961.[94] The norm from the Jamestown settlement in 1607 to 1900 was permitless handgun carry, with the legislature having the authority to regulate the mode of carry.

A purely originalist *Bruen* decision would have told states to adopt permitless carry and, in a concession to postratification tradition, allowed states to choose whether that permitless carry would be open or concealed. Besides the six states directly affected by *Bruen*, such an originalist decision would have affected the laws of Minnesota, South Carolina, Connecticut, and Rhode Island (all of which require a shall-issue license for open or concealed carry), and Florida (shall issue for concealed carry, open carry forbidden).[95] As in *Heller*, originalism partly gave way to practicality.

IV. What Next for the Second Amendment?

A. Right to Bear Arms

After *Brown v. Board of Education*, some jurisdictions adhered to the rule of law, and some did not. Following the *Bruen* decision, Massachusetts, New Jersey, Maryland, and Hawaii seem to be following the law. Officials in those states have instructed licensing administrators to issue concealed carry permits under existing procedures, while omitting any requirement that the applicant prove some sort of special need.[96]

After *Brown*, a notable noncomplier was Mississippi Gov. Ross Barnett (1960–64). As his campaign song promised, "[h]e's not a moderate like some of the gents. He'll fight integration with forceful intent."[97] After *Bruen*, a notable noncomplier is New York Gov. Kathy Hochul. She also follows in the footsteps of her predecessor, Andrew Cuomo. Both passed their big gun control bills by sending a "message

---

[94] Wash. RCW 9.41.070.

[95] Open carry in the United States, Wikipedia https://bit.ly/3Q31kPV (last visited Aug. 1, 2022).

[96] Mass. Att'y Gen. and Exec. Off. of Pub. Safety, Joint Advisory Regarding the Massachusetts Firearms Licensing System after the Supreme Court's Decision in New York State Rifle & Pistol Association v. Bruen; Md. Att'y Gen., letter to Captain Andrew Rossignol, Commander of the Maryland State Police Licensing Division; N.J. Att'y Gen. Enforcement Directive No. 22-07; Haw. Att'y Gen., Op. No. 22-02 (July 7, 2022).

[97] Ross Barnett, Wikipedia https://bit.ly/3PW5f12 (last visited Aug. 1, 2022).

of necessity"—a maneuver to prevent legislative hearings and to deprive legislators of time to read a bill before they vote on it.

As the New York State Sheriffs' Association explained:

> The new firearms law language first saw the light of day on a Friday morning and was signed into law Friday afternoon. A parliamentary ruse was used to circumvent the requirement in our State Constitution that Legislators— and the public—must have three days to study and discuss proposed legislation before it can be taken up for a vote. The Legislature's leadership claimed, and the Governor agreed, that it was a "necessity" to pass the Bill immediately, without waiting the Constitutionally required three days, even though the law would not take effect for two full months.[98]

The Sheriffs' Association criticized "thoughtless, reactionary action, just to make a political statement," and "the burdensome, costly, and unworkable nature of many of the new law's provisions."[99] "We do not support punitive licensing requirements that aim only to restrain and punish law-abiding citizens who wish to exercise their Second Amendment rights."[100]

New York county clerks had no opinion on gun policy but focused instead on workability. As the Association of Clerks wrote to the governor, "[i]n haste to pass the new regulations as a reaction to the recent United States Supreme Court ruling, the process as it stands now will be riddled with complex, confusing and redundant barriers of compliance."[101]

---

[98] New York State Sheriffs' Association, "Statement Concerning New York's New Firearms Licensing Laws," July 6, 2022. The N.Y. Constitution states:

> No bill shall be passed or become a law unless it shall have been printed and upon the desks of the members, in its final form, at least three calendar legislative days prior to its final passage, unless the governor, or the acting governor, shall have certified, under his or her hand and the seal of the state, the facts which in his or her opinion necessitate an immediate vote thereon[.]

N.Y. Const., art. III, §14.

[99] Statement of Sheriffs' Association, *supra* note 98.

[100] *Id.*

[101] Wendy Wright, NY County Clerks Question Feasibility of Enacting Gun Permit Changes, SpectrumLocalNews (Rochester) (July 18, 2022), https://bit.ly/3zlXomJ.

But the governor was moving too fast to care about reality. A reporter asked her, "do you have the numbers to show that it's the concealed carry permit holders that are committing crimes?" She answered, "I don't need to have a data point to say this. I know that I have a responsibility of this state to sensible gun safety laws[.]"[102] Where will concealed carry permit holders be allowed to carry? "Probably some streets," she explained.[103] This directly contradicts *Bruen's* rule that "expanding the category of 'sensitive places' simply to all places of public congregation that are not isolated from law enforcement defines the category . . . far too broadly."[104]

Yet the first reason why the new New York law is unconstitutional has nothing to do with the right to *bear* arms. The law designates an enormous variety of places as "sensitive locations." Not only does the law prohibit concealed carry licensees from bringing their guns into these locations, the law makes felons of proprietors, owners, and employees who simply possess arms in the location.[105] Thus, a doctor who runs her own practice cannot have a handgun in a lock box in her office. A church cannot have volunteer security guards, such as the former police officer who thwarted a mass shooter at the New Life Church in Colorado Springs in 2007.[106] The same goes for every school of any level, government or independent, regardless of what the school wants.

Under the new law, licensed carry is also banned in all forms of public transportation, including in one's own car on a ferry. All these restrictions defy *Bruen's* rule that "*new*" (emphasis in original) types of "sensitive places" may be authorized by analogy to sensitive places from the 19th century and before. Ferries, churches, and doctors' offices are not "new," nor are restaurants with a liquor license that serve meals to customers who don't order drinks. Nor are

---

[102] Anne McCloy, Hochul Won't Allow NYS to Become "Wild West," Defends New Proposed Limits on Conceal-Carry, CBS6 (Albany) (June 29, 2022), https://bit.ly/3OYONfO.

[103] Luis Ferré-Sadurní & Grace Ashford, N.Y. Democrats to Pass New Gun Laws in Response to Supreme Court Ruling, N.Y. Times (June 30, 2022), https://nyti.ms/3OOZL71.

[104] Bruen, 142 S. Ct. at 2135.

[105] N.Y. Penal Law § 265.01-e.

[106] CNN, Security Guard Who Stopped Shooter Credits God (Dec. 10, 2007), https://cnn.it/3OMS15L; Judy Keen & Andrea Stone, This Month's Mass Killings a Reminder of Vulnerability, USA Today (Dec. 21, 2007); Jeanne Assam, God, The Gunman & Me (2010). New Life Church is a megachurch; there were thousands of worshippers present in the sanctuary when the killer entered.

entertainment facilities. Firearms possession is also forbidden at "any gathering of individuals to collectively express their constitutional rights to protest or assemble."[107] In other words, if two dozen members of the county branch of New York's Conservative Party gather anywhere (even in a private home) for a meeting, they may not protect themselves.

Beyond the enumerated list of sensitive locations, bringing a gun into *any* building is a felony unless the owner has posted a permission sign or granted express permission.[108] And permit applicants must submit "a list of former and current social media accounts of the applicant from the past three years."[109]

In California, S.B. 918, presently before the legislature, would expand no-carry areas in a manner similar to New York's. For the time being, California Attorney General Rob Bonta has urged county sheriffs to apply the statutory "good moral character" test on the model of the Riverside County Sheriff's Department: "Legal judgments of good moral character can include . . . absence of hatred and racism, fiscal stability[.]"[110] The attorney general added that "social media accounts" were fair game for inquiry. Further, denials could be based on "[a]ny arrest in the last five years, regardless of the disposition," or any conviction in the last seven.[111]

UCLA law professor Eugene Volokh suggests that it is plainly unconstitutional to deny the exercise of constitutional rights because of an arrest without a conviction. Likewise, under the First Amendment, "[t]he government can't restrict ordinary citizens' actions— much less their constitutionally protected actions—based on the viewpoints that they express."[112] For example, some people, such as followers of author Robin DiAngelo, believe that white people are inherently and irredeemably toxic. Other people, such as many

---

[107] N.Y. Penal Law § 265.01-e(s).

[108] *Id.* at § 265.01–d.

[109] *Id.* at § 400 1.

[110] Cal. Dep't of Justice, Off. of the Att'y Gen., "U.S. Supreme Court's Decision in New York State Rifle & Pistol Association v. Bruen, No. 20-843," OAG-2022-02, June 24, 2022.

[111] *Id.*

[112] Eugene Volokh, State Attorney General Suggests Considering Applicants' Ideological Viewpoints in Denying Carry Licenses, Volokh Conspiracy (June 26, 2022), https://bit.ly/3OFsbk3.

in Hollywood, express hatred of conservatives. Wrongful as these views might be, under the First Amendment they are not a lawful basis for government retaliation. Volokh is also skeptical about the denial of rights for "[l]ack of 'fiscal stability'—which may simply mean being very poor or insolvent."[113] Indeed, poor people are generally at greater risk of criminal attack than are wealthier people.

B. The Remanded Cases on Bans of Common Arms

As previously noted, after *Bruen*, the Supreme Court granted, vacated, and remanded several cases.[114] In the California magazine confiscation case, the Ninth Circuit shipped the case back to district court. Judge Patrick Bumatay dissented, preferring to hear what the parties had to say about whether the circuit should just redecide the case itself rather than sending to a lower court for eventual appeal.[115] In the New Jersey magazine confiscation case, the Third Circuit did ask for party briefs "addressing the proper disposition of this matter in light of" *Bruen*. The Fourth Circuit has not yet acted on the remand of the Maryland ban on common semiautomatic rifles.

In 2011, then-Judge Kavanaugh wrote a dissenting opinion concluding that bans like those above were unconstitutional under *Heller's* text, history, and tradition methodology.[116] In a 2015 dissent from denial of certiorari, Justice Thomas (joined by Justice Scalia) argued that bans on common firearms, such as AR platform semiautomatic rifles, plainly violated *Heller* and *McDonald*.[117] However, Justice Alito's *Bruen* concurrence expressly reserved the issue of "the kinds of weapons that people may possess."[118]

---

[113] *Id.*

[114] See *supra* note 1.

[115] Eugene Volokh, Ninth Circuit Panel Sends California 'Assault Weapons' Ban Challenge Back to District Court, Volokh Conspiracy (June 28, 2022), https://bit.ly/3PHQhMn.

[116] Heller v. District of Columbia (Heller II), 670 F.3d 1244, 1285–91 (D.C. Cir. 2011) (Kavanaugh, J., dissenting) (semiautomatic long gun ban unconstitutional under any test); *id* at 1296 n.20 (urging remand for "whether magazines with more than 10 rounds have traditionally been banned and are not in common use").

[117] Friedman v. City of Highland Park, 577 U.S. 1039 (2015) (Thomas, J., joined by Scalia, J., dissenting from denial of certiorari).

[118] Bruen, 142 S. Ct. at 2157.

In the remands, the lower courts will presumably examine the history of bans on particular types of arms, as well as ammunition capacity laws. Before 1900, there were no ammunition capacity limits. The first such laws were enacted by six states during Prohibition in the 1920s. All were later repealed, and all were less onerous than the California or New Jersey bans.[119]

The first American law against repeating firearms was enacted by Florida in 1893 after incidents in which armed black men had deterred lynch mobs. The new law required a license and an exorbitant bond to carry a "Winchester rifle or other repeating rifle." Handguns were added in 1901.[120] In 1941, a Florida Supreme Court justice wrote:

> The statute was never intended to be applied to the white population and in practice has never been so applied. . . . [T]here has never been, within my knowledge, any effort to enforce the provisions of this statute as to white people, because it has been generally conceded to be in contravention of the Constitution and nonenforceable if contested.[121]

The racist statute was repealed in 1987 by the same bill that created Florida's nationally influential shall-issue law for concealed carry licensing.[122]

Once "redeemed" white racist governments regained control over Tennessee and Arkansas after the end of Reconstruction, they banned concealable handguns, and the bans were upheld by state courts.[123] Given that *Bruen* affirms the right to carry a concealed handgun, these precedents are invalid.

V. Conclusion: Other Implications of *Bruen*

Between *Heller* in 2008 and *Bruen* in 2022, a very large number of lower court cases were decided under the now-defunct two-step test. Theoretically, the issues in every one of those cases are now

---

[119] David B. Kopel, The History of Firearms Magazines and of Magazine Prohibition, 78 Albany L. Rev. 849 (2015).

[120] Fla. Laws 1893, ch. 4147, § 1, amended by Fla. Laws 1901, ch. 4928, § 1. The 1893 statute had said "carry or own," but was narrowed to "carry" in 1901.

[121] Watson v. Stone, 4 So. 2d 700, 703 (Fla. 1941) (Buford, J., concurring) (agreeing with majority holding that statute does not apply to automobile carry).

[122] 1987 Fla. Laws ch. 24, § 4.

[123] State v. Wilburn, 66 Tenn. (7 Bax.) 57 (1872); Fife v. State, 31 Ark. 455 (1876).

open for relitigation under text, history, and tradition. These issues include:

Prohibited persons. Various people are prohibited from having a firearm, such as felons and people who have been convicted of a misdemeanor domestic violence offense. Challenges to these categories have little chance of success. Under the text, history, and tradition test, analogies can be drawn to historical laws disarming perceived dangerous persons, namely slaves, hostile Native Americans, and persons who support the enemy during wartime.[124]

Red flag laws. Red flag laws purport to identify potentially dangerous people (such as a possible mass shooter) and take away their guns. Proponents will argue that the surety of the peace statutes from the 19th century are historical analogues.[125] But modern red flag laws are much harsher, in that they confiscate arms rather than requiring the person to post a bond. Further, due process protections in red flag laws are much weaker than in the surety statutes.[126] Yet some courts might consider the surety laws a good enough analogy.

Special restrictions on 18–20 year-olds. During the colonial period, the most typical age for militia service (with militiamen required to bring their own arms to service) was 16–60. The minimum militia age was raised to 18 by the 1792 Militia Act, and many states followed suit. The first age-based restriction was an 1856 Alabama statute against giving handguns to male minors. By 1900, a significant minority of states had enacted some sort of limit on handgun sales to minors. There were few such laws for long guns.[127] In 2021, the Fourth Circuit held unconstitutional a federal statute barring young adults from buying handguns from licensed handgun stores, but the case was later vacated as moot after the plaintiffs turned 21.[128] This year, a three-judge panel of the Ninth Circuit ruled against a

---

[124] Joseph G.S. Greenlee, The Historical Justification for Prohibiting Dangerous Persons from Possessing Arms, 20 Wyo. L. Rev. 249 (2020).

[125] Discussed *supra*, Part III.F.

[126] David B. Kopel, Red Flag Laws: Proceed with Caution, 45 L. & Psychol. Rev. 39 (2021).

[127] David B. Kopel & Joseph G.S. Greenlee, The Second Amendment Rights of Young Adults, 43 S. Ill. U. L.J. 495 (2019).

[128] Hirschfeld v. Bureau of Alcohol, Tobacco, Firearms & Explosives, 5 F.4th 407 (4th Cir. 2021), vacated as moot, 14 F.4th 322.

California law banning young adults from acquiring centerfire semiautomatic rifles.[129]

Handgun bans. California and several other states have laws forbidding the sale of all handguns, except to those on a government roster. California's onerous subrules have banned hundreds of models of older guns (whose manufacturers are no longer in business to submit exemplars to the state), and all new semiautomatic pistol models since 2013 (by requiring manufacturers to make guns that double-microstamp cartridges, which is technically impossible). The Supreme Court denied certiorari on the microstamping question in 2020.[130] Under a straightforward application of *Heller*, the law should have speedily been held unconstitutional. There is no pre-1900 precedent for such a law, other than, arguably, the now-unconstitutional Tennessee and Arkansas bans on concealable handguns.

Whatever happens in future cases, *New York State Rifle & Pistol Association v. Bruen* has established a more level playing field. Going forward, the personal views of judges on gun policy will matter less. Instead, judicial decisions will be based on analysis of the historical facts of the American right to keep and bear arms.

When Justice Thomas joined the Court, many fields of constitutional law were overgrown with thickets of precedent that had obscured their original public meaning. A quarter century ago, Justice Thomas called attention to the long-neglected Second Amendment, for which the Court's precedent was thin. This year, the Supreme Court of the United States affirmed the third of the three essentials of the right to arms: the right to keep (*Heller*), the right to bear (*Bruen*), and the application to governments at all levels (*McDonald*).

When my Second Amendment work for the Cato Institute began in 1988, things did not look so sanguine. But judicial engagement with the Second Amendment has improved immensely since then. Some things do get better.

---

[129] Jones v. Bonta, 34 F.4th 704 (9th Cir. 2022).

[130] Pena v. Lindley, 898 F.3d 969 (9th Cir. 2018), cert denied sub nom. Pena v. Horan, 141 S. Ct. 108 (2020). Cf. Nat'l Shooting Sports Found., Inc. v. State, 5 Cal. 5th 428, 420 P.3d 870 (2018) (California statute that "The law never requires impossibilities" applies only when individual circumstances make an act impossible; it does not apply to acts that no one can perform).

Looking Ahead: October Term 2022

Ilya Shapiro*

Last term, the much-advertised, -expected, -feared, -longed-for con-servative Supreme Court majority coalesced. After many false starts, misfires, and disappointments—going back to Richard Nixon's pledge in the 1968 campaign to reverse the Warren Court's activism, or even Dwight Eisenhower's appointment of Earl Warren and Bill Brennan—conservatives will remember the term as the one when they finally, *finally*, had enough votes to overcome "defections."

Five years after Neil Gorsuch was confirmed, and in the sec-ond term with Amy Coney Barrett on the bench, the Republican-appointed majority asserted itself.

The statistics bear this out: of the term's 60 opinions in argued cases—a historically low number—14 involved a 6-3 "partisan" split, to which can be added ten 5-4 decisions, in all of which the three liberal justices stuck together. So 40 percent of cases were "ideologi-cal"—including the big ones on school choice, religion, guns, vaccine mandates, environmental regulation, and, of course, abortion—and only 25 percent (15 cases) were unanimous. These are striking num-bers—the former high, the latter low—and very different from any year since I became a Court watcher.

Moreover, when you look at those 5-4 cases, it wasn't a simple story about the cagey chief justice. Indeed, in all three 5-4 splits resulting in a conservative win, it was Gorsuch who joined the liberals. And in the seven liberal results, every conservative except Samuel Alito moved over, with John Roberts and Brett Kavanaugh doing so four times.

* Senior fellow and director of constitutional studies, Manhattan Institute; former vice president at the Cato Institute, director of Cato's Robert A. Levy Center for Consti-tutional Studies, and editor of 11 volumes of the *Cato Supreme Court Review* (2008–2018); author of *Supreme Disorder: Judicial Nominations and the Politics of America's Highest Court* (2020, updated paperback 2022). Thanks to Amy Howe for her invaluable write-ups of arguments and opinions at SCOTUSblog, as well as to that website generally for serv-ing as a clearinghouse for briefs, statistics, and media coverage.

What all of that numerology shows is that having a "margin of error" matters. There's just a lot of fluidity, showcasing the differing approaches to originalism and other text-, history-, and structure-focused interpretive methods on the right. It's intellectually fascinating, but in practice comes together to make for stability in the law. While some conservatives have made hay in recent years about the need for "common-good" constitutionalism, this year's return to *common-sense* constitutionalism has largely obviated that heterodoxy. While some liberals fear a reversal of the Warren Court's groovy civil rights gains of the 1960s, really what we're seeing is a stripping of Warren Burger's gaudy legal wallpaper of the 1970s.

These developments also mean that, to a large extent, this is much less the Roberts Court than it has been since Justice Anthony Kennedy retired. But even as Kavanaugh is still the median justice—he and Roberts were both in the majority 95 percent of the time—we can't really call it the Kavanaugh Court. Indeed, if anything this was the breakout term for Clarence Thomas, the senior associate justice, who wrote the majority opinion in the Second Amendment case (*N.Y. State Rifle & Pistol Association v. Bruen*) and assigned it to Justice Alito in the abortion case (*Dobbs v. Jackson Women's Health Organization*).

It's all the more remarkable when you realize that none of it would've happened without the following historical twists:

1. Democratic Senate Majority Leader Harry Reid nukes the filibuster for lower-court judges in 2013, which Republican Senate Minority Leader Mitch McConnell says Democrats will regret;

2. Justice Ruth Bader Ginsburg declines to retire under President Barack Obama;

3. Justice Antonin Scalia dies in February 2016, creating a rare election-year vacancy;

4. McConnell, now majority leader, pledges "no hearings, no votes" on a successor—and his caucus holds firm on that politically risky maneuver;

5. Donald Trump wins the Republican nomination with a plurality in a fractured field;

6. The open seat holds Republicans together, turning out cultural conservatives and populists, providing Trump winning margins in key states;

7. Trump empowers White House Counsel Don McGahn and his team to pick judges who will be originalist-textualist and have spines;

8. Senate Democrats, now led by Chuck Schumer, filibuster Gorsuch, leading McConnell to thermo nuke the filibuster for Supreme Court nominations;

9. The Trump White House stands with Kavanaugh when Democrats launch 11th-hour sexual assault allegations;

10. The Democrats' smear of Kavanaugh triggers Republican Senate gains in the 2018 elections;

11. Justice Ruth Bader Ginsburg dies on the eve of the 2020 presidential election;

12. Republicans push through the Barrett nomination.

Those unlikely events brought us to the point where the Constitution is now interpreted for what it says, not through alternative theories of outcome-oriented jurisprudence. On such hinges does history swing.

So where are we as we enter what promises to be another high-profile term? Well, the Court isn't backing off from controversy, as next term already has some blockbuster issues on the docket, including: the use of race in college admissions (*SFFA v. Harvard/UNC*); the proper test for determining whether wetlands are "waters of the United States" under the Clean Water Act (*Sackett v. EPA*); whether a graphic designer can be compelled to create a website for a same-sex wedding (*303 Creative v. Elenis*); the extraterritorial effects of pig-farming regulations (*National Pork Producers v. Ross*); and the "independent state legislature" doctrine (*Moore v. Harper*). Let's dive right in, in rough order of when the cases will be argued.

Environmental Regulation and Property Rights

The very first case of the term, to be argued at 10 a.m. on the first Monday in October, *Sackett v. EPA* involves an Idaho couple who have been prohibited from building a home because their lot allegedly contains wetlands that qualify as "navigable waters" regulated by the Clean Water Act. The justices will decide whether the U.S. Court of Appeals for the Ninth Circuit used the correct test to determine whether the wetlands are indeed "waters of the United States."

If that fact pattern sounds familiar, you have a good memory. The Supreme Court already ruled on the case *a decade ago*. In 2004, Mike and Chantell Sackett bought a vacant lot near Priest Lake, Idaho, and obtained local building permits. But when the Sacketts started the construction process, the Environmental Protection Agency (EPA) ordered them to stop work and sent a compliance order claiming the property contained a wetland. The EPA demanded costly restoration work and a three-year monitoring program, during which the property was to be left untouched. The agency also threatened the Sacketts with fines of up to $75,000 per day if they didn't obey the order. In 2012, the Supreme Court unanimously agreed that the Sacketts could challenge the administrative compliance order before the EPA began any enforcement action.[1]

For nearly a decade since, the Sacketts have been in court battling the EPA over the Clean Water Act, which protects the navigable waters of the United States from pollution. The definition of "navigable waters" has changed several times since the law went into effect in 1972. The Sacketts are asking the Court to revisit its fractured decision in *Rapanos v. United States* (2006), which held that the act doesn't regulate all wetlands but failed to produce a majority for any governing standard.[2] The EPA has since tried to sidestep that ruling by issuing new rules and guidance documents, each of which has been met with lawsuits and an uneven approach to *Rapanos*. The result is a confusing patchwork of regulations that are inconsistently applied across the country.

The Sacketts want the Court to adopt a test proposed by the four-justice conservative plurality in *Rapanos*, which would allow wetlands to be regulated only when they themselves have a continuous surface-water connection to regulated waters.[3] If I were a betting man, I'd bet that's exactly what the Court will do, in a ruling that, like *West Virginia v. EPA* last term, is likely to have the biggest jurisprudential and governance impact without necessarily drawing the most front-page headlines.[4]

---

[1] Sackett v. EPA, 566 U.S. 120 (2012).

[2] Rapanos v. United States, 547 U.S. 715 (2006).

[3] *Id.* at 732 (Scalia, J., joined by Roberts, C.J., and Thomas and Alito, JJ.).

[4] I was counsel of record on Cato's cert-stage brief in *Sackett*, and Cato went on to file on the merits as well.

Although the EPA withdrew its compliance order and its past threats of massive fines, it maintains that it has the power to regulate the Sacketts' property. But if that property can be regulated by the federal government, so too can the properties of other homeowners, farmers, and businesses that are engaging in non-harmful activities.

Civil Procedure

Civil procedure involves the rules regarding who can sue and be sued; how a lawsuit begins; what kind of service is required; the types of pleadings, motions, and orders allowed; the manner of discovery; the conduct of trials and post-trial procedures; and the process for judgments and available remedies. It's the backbone of litigation: what non-lawyers consider to be mind-numbing technicalities but mastery of which can mean the difference between great success and spectacular failure. It was also my best class the first year of law school, so I hope you'll indulge me in presenting a really important case in this area.

In *Mallory v. Norfolk Southern Railway Co.*, the justices take up the case of Robert Mallory, a longtime railroad employee who developed colon cancer. Mallory sued the railroad in Pennsylvania state court, seeking to hold the company liable for his exposure to asbestos and other toxic chemicals that he says caused his cancer. The state court dismissed his suit, agreeing with the railroad that it lacked jurisdiction over the company. The court rejected Mallory's contention that the company had agreed to be sued in Pennsylvania when it registered to do business in the state.

The Pennsylvania Supreme Court upheld that decision, holding that the Pennsylvania law requiring corporations to consent to suit to do business is unconstitutional. Noting that corporations frequently require consumers to enter into contracts that require them "to litigate disputes with businesses in often-distant tribunals," Mallory asked the U.S. Supreme Court to review that ruling. The specific issue is whether the Fourteenth Amendment's Due Process Clause stops a state from requiring a corporation to consent to "personal jurisdiction"—local-court authority—to do business in the state.

With this type of case, it's hard to be more specific without getting into the weeds very quickly. Suffice it to say, a change in the rules over where companies can be sued would quickly have a massive impact on how they conduct business—and the costs they pass onto consumers. Note, however, that "corporate personhood," an issue that riles progressive activists when it involves rights protections of the sort upheld in *Citizens United v. FEC* and *Hobby Lobby Stores v. Burwell*, isn't in dispute. The railroad is a person, but that doesn't answer the question of where it can be sued. State and lower federal courts are hopelessly split on that question, so it's high time that the Supreme Court resolved the confusion.

Pig Farming and the Dormant Commerce Clause

In 2018, California voters approved Proposition 12 (Prop 12), a far-reaching law designed "to prevent animal cruelty by phasing out extreme methods of farm animal confinement." The law requires that all pork, veal, and eggs sold in the state comply with new restrictions on how the animals can be confined. That means that pork producers in other states will have to comply with California law if they want to sell there.

In the wake of the law, lawsuits were filed by various agricultural entities arguing that the California law was unconstitutionally crossing state borders and regulating national markets. That's especially true for the pork industry, which has very little presence in the state—only about 0.2 percent of the country's breeding sows are in California. The pork industry is a highly integrated interstate market in which a pig farmer in North Carolina might sell his stock to a meatpacker in Illinois, who then distributes to California. It's near-impossible to trace a given cut of meat back to its source and verify that the farmer complied with a particular state's law.

The Ninth Circuit agreed with pork-producing plaintiffs that the law would "require pervasive changes to the pork production industry nationwide," but ruled that they had failed to make out a legally cognizable claim under what's known as the "dormant" Commerce Clause.

Because the Constitution gives Congress power over interstate commerce, it's possible for state laws that regulate extra-territorially to encroach on federal power. Claims of such encroachments invoke the dormant or "negative" Commerce Clause, and they have long been conceptually difficult for judges to evaluate. By no means a sleepy area of law, it also tends to cut across conventional ideological lines. Justices Thomas and Gorsuch, for example, tend to be skeptical of dormant Commerce Clause challenges, even as they apply robust limits to federal power through the "positive" Commerce Clause.

In *National Pork Producers Council v. Ross*, the Supreme Court will hopefully provide clarity, as well as give guidance to state legislatures that increasingly pass laws affecting their neighbors, sometimes intentionally so. Specifically, the justices will consider (1) whether allegations that a state law has dramatic economic effects largely outside of the state and requires pervasive changes to an integrated nationwide industry state a violation of the dormant Commerce Clause; and (2) whether such allegations, concerning a law that is based solely on preferences regarding out-of-state housing of farm animals, state a claim under *Pike v. Bruce Church, Inc.* (1970). *Pike* held that the power of states to pass laws interfering with interstate commerce is limited when those laws pose an "undue burden" on businesses. What's an undue burden? *Pike*'s half-century-old balancing test has allowed plenty of lawyers to bring home the bacon, but has failed to provide legislatures, lower courts, and businesses a clear answer.[5]

Not every law that burdens interstate commerce is necessarily unconstitutional, but Prop 12 will have Golden State agents travelling around the country to ensure that farmers in other states comply with California law. It will also raise the price of pork around the country. While laws that try to reduce animal cruelty are often admirable, the question here is not about the law's wisdom, but its scope.

Affirmative Action

The highest-profile case on the docket is undoubtedly the challenge to the use of racial preferences in university admissions. Given that the Court overturned *Roe v. Wade* and recognized the "abandonment" of *Lemon v. Kurtzman* last term, is *Regents of the University of California v. Bakke* the next 1970s precedent on the chopping block? *Bakke*, you'll recall, is the 1979 case in which one justice, Lewis Powell, planted the seed for the entire "diversity" conceit that now seems to be a bigger priority in higher education than the search for knowledge. Where four justices would've outlawed the consideration of race in admissions and four would've broadly allowed it to remedy past prejudice, Justice Powell voted to invalidate the racial

---

[5] I was counsel of record on Cato's cert-stage brief, which urged the Court to take the case due to the interstate nature of the pork industry and the unique burdens of Prop 12.

quotas at UC-Davis's medical school, but to allow the use of race as one of many factors to advance what he considered to be a compelling state interest in educational diversity. Twenty-four years later, in a pair of cases from the University of Michigan, the Court by a 5-4 majority endorsed that diversity rationale as part of a holistic race-conscious admissions program (*Grutter v. Bollinger*) while rejecting a mechanical system that assigned race a fixed number of points (*Gratz v. Bollinger*). The swing vote in those cases, Justice Sandra Day O'Connor, suggested that "25 years from now, the use of racial preferences will no longer be necessary to further the interest approved today."[6]

Well, here we are 19 years later and the trendlines aren't looking good for an organic sunsetting of the evaluation of college (and graduate/professional-school) applicants by the color of their skin. The composition of the Supreme Court has, of course, changed, with Justice O'Connor having been replaced by Justice Alito. Equally important, the author of the 2016 decision that upheld the University of Texas's consideration of race in undergraduate admissions—in an unusual 4-3 split after Justice Scalia's death and Justice Elena Kagan's recusal—Justice Kennedy, was replaced by Justice Kavanaugh. And that's not even mentioning the swap of Justice Barrett for Justice Ginsburg.

Enter an organization called Students for Fair Admissions (SFFA), a group of more than 20,000 students and parents working "to support and participate in litigation that will restore the original principles of our nation's civil rights movement: A student's race and ethnicity should not be factors that either harm or help that student to gain admission to a competitive university."[7] On November 17, 2014, SFFA sued the oldest private and public universities in the country, Harvard and the University of North Carolina (UNC), respectively, over their use of race in admissions. The case against Harvard focuses on Title VI of the Civil Rights Act, which bans racial discrimination by institutions that receive federal funding, while the case against UNC adds a Fourteenth Amendment equal protection claim.

The claims center on discrimination against Asian American applicants, who are much less likely to be admitted than similarly

---

[6] Grutter v. Bollinger, 539 U.S. 306, 343 (2003).

[7] Students for Fair Admissions, https://studentsforfairadmissions.org (last visited July 29, 2022).

qualified white, black, or Hispanic applicants. Both the district court and First Circuit upheld Harvard's policy—which SFFA likens to the Jewish quotas of a century before—prompting the group to file for cert back in February 2021. But the justices sat on that petition, and then in June asked for the solicitor general's views—a cynical maneuver to push the case past the 2021–2022 term, particularly given that there was no doubt as to what the Biden administration thinks. Indeed, in a brief filed last December that surprised no one, the Justice Department explained that it had "reexamined" and reversed the Trump administration's support for the lawsuit.

Meanwhile, the case against UNC got bogged down in procedural wrangling, with the district court finally ruling for the university in October 2021. SFFA then went straight to the top, asking the justices to consider the case alongside the one against Harvard even before the Fourth Circuit could rule on appeal. In January 2022, the Court did just that, granting cert in both *SFFA v. President & Fellows of Harvard College* and *SFFA v. UNC*, and consolidating them for argument.[8] Then in July, the Court un-consolidated the cases, which will allow the new Justice Ketanji Brown Jackson, who is recused from the Harvard case because she had served on the university's board of overseers, to participate in the UNC case.

The challengers can't be accused of hiding the ball or minimizing the significance of this litigation. The first question they present is the same in both cases: "Whether the Supreme Court should overrule *Grutter v. Bollinger* (2003) and hold that institutions of higher education cannot use race as a factor in admissions." The second in the Harvard case asks "whether Harvard College is violating Title VI of the Civil Rights Act by penalizing Asian American applicants, engaging in racial balancing, overemphasizing race and rejecting workable race-neutral alternatives." The second in the UNC case asks "whether a university can reject a race-neutral alternative because it would change the composition of the student body, without proving that the alternative would cause a dramatic sacrifice in academic quality or the educational benefits of overall

---

[8] I filed a cert-stage brief on Cato's behalf asking the Court to add the UNC case so a public institution would be in the mix, as it had been in all previous affirmative action cases. Later, I both signed and joined as co-amicus a brief filed by the Hamilton Lincoln Law Institute on the merits in the then-consolidated cases.

student-body diversity." In other words, the entirety of the racial-preferences-in-higher-education regime is at stake.

Nobody expects different results in the two cases, whether because of the public/private distinction or Justice Jackson's involvement in one but not the other. On the first point, a long line of cases has held the standards for evaluating the use of race under Title VI to be concomitant with those under the Fourteenth Amendment. There's no reason that it must be that way—we may think it worse when a public institution engages in racial discrimination—but there's no indication that the Court wants to reevaluate that aspect of affirmative-action jurisprudence here. On the second, if Harvard is likely to lose 6-2, then adding Jackson still gives UNC a 6-3 loss. Six votes for the challengers is indeed the most likely outcome, because the typically most "gettable" vote for progressives, Chief Justice John Roberts, has shown no sign of squishiness in race cases. He was in dissent in *Fisher v. UT-Austin II*, after all, and in a 2007 school busing case famously wrote, "The way to stop discrimination on the basis of race is to stop discriminating on the basis of race."[9]

Indeed, in his very first term on the Court, the new chief justice wrote, "It is a sordid business, this divvying us up by race."[10] So it would seem more likely than not that he'll follow his own logic and collapse the entire racialist edifice built on *Bakke's* shaky one-vote foundation rather than trying to engineer a patchwork compromise along the lines of his concurrence in *Dobbs*. That would mean that progressives' only hope for moderation, a "mend it, don't end it" compromise that pillories Harvard but salvages the "diversity" rationale for racialist shenanigans, lies with Justices Kavanaugh and Barrett. It's possible, but I wouldn't count on it.

Administrative Law

The term's big administrative-law case is different from most in recent years. Those often were about the level of deference that judges owe agency interpretations of their operative statutes or whether a generally phrased legal provision authorizes a novel but awesome

---

[9] Parents Involved in Cmty. Sch. v. Seattle Sch, District No. 1, 551 U.S. 701, 748 (2007) (Roberts, C.J., joined by Scalia, Thomas, and Alito, JJ.).

[10] League of United Latin Am. Citizens v. Perry, 548 U.S. 399, 511 (2006) (Roberts, C.J., concurring in part, concurring in the judgment in part, and dissenting in part).

grant of regulatory authority. The case doesn't even involve structural arguments about executive branch agencies, such as whether certain officers were properly appointed or whether they enjoy any removal protections. *Axon Enterprise, Inc. v. Federal Trade Commission* instead asks whether Congress can insulate the agencies it creates from constitutional challenge.

Axon, a body camera manufacturer, bought a competitor in 2018 and thereby incurred "antitrust concerns" at the Federal Trade Commission (FTC). After investigating for 18 months, the FTC threatened to initiate an in-house enforcement proceeding unless Axon agreed to onerous settlement terms. The company responded by suing in federal court, arguing that the FTC's in-house dispute-resolution processes are unconstitutionally stacked in favor of the government. Indeed, the agency hasn't lost on its home turf in more than a quarter century.

The district court sided with the government, holding that Axon could bring its constitutional challenges against the FTC's in-house court system only after the company first raised these arguments before the agency in the very proceedings that Axon challenges on constitutional grounds. The district court's holding makes little sense. Is it remotely plausible that the FTC would find itself unconstitutional? The district court's order seems to facially offend fundamental notions of fairness: should Axon have to suffer the crippling cost, business disruption, and adverse outcome of an FTC in-house proceeding before seeking judicial review of that proceeding's constitutional legitimacy?[11]

A divided Ninth Circuit panel upheld the district court, despite conceding that "it makes little sense to force a party to undergo a burdensome administrative proceeding to raise a constitutional challenge against the agency's structure before it can seek review from the court of appeals."[12] Ultimately, the majority felt bound by the Supreme Court, due to what many commentators feel is a misreading of that Court's precedent.

Axon asked the Supreme Court to weigh in on both whether the district court has the power to review constitutional challenges to

---

[11] Cato joined the Atlantic Legal Foundation on a cert-stage amicus brief that I signed, making this point.

[12] Axon Enter. v. FTC, 986 F.3d 1173, 1184 (9th Cir. 2021).

the FTC's structure and whether the FTC's structure violates the Constitution. The justices agreed to take up the first question, but not the second. The issue is framed as "whether Congress impliedly stripped federal district courts of jurisdiction over constitutional challenges to the FTC's structure, procedures, and existence by granting the courts of appeal jurisdiction to 'affirm, enforce, modify, or set aside' the Commission's cease-and-desist orders." It seems likely that a majority will say no, prompting further litigation that, given what we've seen in other recent challenges to agency structures,[13] augurs a return to the Court in a few years.

First Amendment

Five years ago, the blockbuster case was that of the baker who refused to bake a cake celebrating a same-sex wedding, in alleged contravention of Colorado anti-discrimination law. Was he a free-speech martyr or a half-baked bigot? Cato was the only organization in the entire country—and I'm proud to have been one of only three lawyers (the others are Thomas Berg and Douglas Laycock)—to have filed a brief supporting Masterpiece Cakeshop owner Jack Phillips after having filed in support of Jim Obergefell in the same-sex marriage cases a few years earlier.

Ultimately, the Supreme Court ruled 7-2 that the Colorado Civil Rights Commission expressed hostility to Phillips's Christian beliefs and thus violated his right to religious free exercise and reversed the commission's remedial order. In so ruling, the Court avoided considering the broader intersection of anti-discrimination laws and freedom of speech.

It also didn't rule on whether cake baking is an expressive activity protected by the First Amendment's Free Speech Clause, and later declined to take up a case that would've asked the same question, in the same context, with respect to floristry. Well, now we have a case where there's no question that the commercial activity at issue is protected speech. *303 Creative LLC v. Elenis* involves a graphic designer who has long wanted to expand her business to wedding websites but ran into the same Colorado law at issue in *Masterpiece Cakeshop*. Specifically, the state's law prohibits businesses that are open to the

---

[13] Jarkesy v. SEC, 34 F.4th 446 (5th Cir. 2022) (holding that the SEC's adjudication of fraud claims through its own administrative law judges violated the Seventh Amendment, the nondelegation doctrine, and the Take Care Clause).

public from discriminating against gay people or announcing their intent to do so.

Not waiting to be prosecuted, the designer, Lorie Smith, sought a ruling in federal court that Colorado could not enforce its public-accommodations law against her. The Tenth Circuit agreed that Smith's "creation of wedding websites is pure speech," and that Colorado law compels Smith to create speech that she would otherwise refuse. But the law survives constitutional scrutiny here, the court concluded, because it's narrowly tailored to the state's interest in ensuring that LGBTQ customers have access to the "custom and unique" product that Smith provides. The court characterized Smith as having "monopolistic" control over her specific designs. Refusing to provide her services would, definitionally then, result in some people being denied access to an entire "market." Same-sex couples might be able to have their wedding websites designed by someone else, but those customers "will never be able to obtain wedding-related services of the same quality and nature as those that" Smith offers.

That's a bizarre ruling, to say the least. It effectively says that every business is a monopoly unto itself and, indeed, that any artist or other expressive professional can be compelled to speak because that speech is, in every case, unique. In following and debating this type of litigation for many years now, I'd never before encountered this argument. If Smith ends up losing at the Supreme Court—which seems highly unlikely—it won't be under the Tenth Circuit's rationale.[14]

The Supreme Court will hear this case, but only on the issue of whether compelling someone to speak to comply with anti-discrimination law violates the Free Speech Clause. The justices declined to review two other questions that Smith raised in her cert petition: whether requiring Smith to create custom websites violates the Free Exercise Clause, and whether the Court should overrule *Employment Division v. Smith* (1990), which held that laws that infringe religious free exercise are constitutional so long as they apply to everyone equally. In other words, *Smith* tells people to seek religious accommodations in legislatures, not courts—which was the rule (and practice) before *Sherbert v. Verner* (1963) read implicit religious exemptions into generally applicable laws.

---

[14] I filed briefs, together with Professors Dale Carpenter and Eugene Volokh, through all stages of appeal. After my departure, Cato dropped out of this collective effort, declining to join our Supreme Court merits brief.

Will the Court in any event rule foursquare against speech compulsions, or again find some narrower path to avoid resolving the purported conflict between free speech and gay rights? It could perhaps vacate the lower court's self-monopoly ruling and remand for more conventional First Amendment analysis. Or it could adopt the more traditional monopoly analysis that was the basis for public-accommodations rules at common law: for example, that the only inn for miles around had to provide food and shelter to travelers but that competing merchants in a city owed no such obligation.

Indian Law

Back in February, the justices granted review in a quartet of cases challenging the constitutionality of a federal law intended to protect against the separation of Native American families. Supporters of the law contend that a ruling invalidating the law could have significant negative consequences for Native American children, while opponents argue the exact opposite.

Provisions of the Indian Child Welfare Act of 1978 (ICWA) dictate that in any custody proceeding "under State law" and involving an "Indian child," "preference shall be given" to placing the child with "(1) a member of the child's extended family; (2) other members of the Indian child's tribe; or (3) other Indian families" rather than with non-Indian adoptive parents. ICWA has long roused controversy, and these cases, coming out of Texas and consolidated under the name *Haaland v. Brackeen*, afford an opportunity for the Supreme Court to make clear that rights under family law cannot be made to depend on race. Of course, Indian law operates differently than normal considerations of race under the Fifth and Fourteenth Amendments, because it's based in ancestry connected to political sovereignty rather than skin color as such. Will that make a difference?

Last year, the Fifth Circuit declared some aspects of ICWA unconstitutional, but left other parts in place, creating confusion about how to comply with the law.[15]

---

[15] Cato joined the Goldwater Institute and Texas Public Policy Foundation on a cert-stage brief (which I signed) urging the Supreme Court to bring that confusion to an end by invalidating any provisions that treat kids and parents differently simply because of their biological ancestry and, ultimately, the color of their skin.

At the heart of this case is Andy, a young boy with foster parents who wanted to adopt him. Although Andy's birth parents agreed to that request, it was denied because Andy is part Navajo and part Cherokee, and tribal officials invoked ICWA to block the adoption.

If Andy were of any other ethnicity, his adoption would have been quickly approved, allowing him to stay with the family he has lived with for nearly his whole life. But ICWA says Texas must remove him from his foster parents and place him with "Indian" adults. Remarkably, ICWA applies to kids who are not members of tribes, who have no social or cultural connection to a tribe, and who have never lived on a reservation or in Indian country, simply because a tribe's own rules designate them as biologically "eligible" for tribal membership.

When states are required to impose differing outcomes in family law depending on race, many people lose rights: birth parents, adoptive parents, and the children themselves. To make matters worse, the law in practice has tended to prevent many abused or neglected children from finding safe and loving permanent homes, in cases that occasionally make national news.

ICWA is also in conflict with an area of law—family law—that has almost universally been the preserve of the states. Indeed, the Fifth Circuit ruled that certain provisions violate, among other things, the Tenth Amendment because they "commandeer" the states.

Securities Law

In April 2016, the Securities and Exchange Commission (SEC) began an enforcement action against Michelle Cochran, a Texas-based accountant, for alleged violations of federal accounting regulations. The SEC brought this action internally, where the agency acts as both prosecutor and judge. From the start, Ms. Cochran has denied the government's allegations, but she also challenges the constitutionality of the agency's in-house courts.

An administrative law judge (ALJ) agreed that Cochran had violated federal law, fined her over $20,000, and banned her from practicing before the SEC for five years. After the Supreme Court's 2018 decision in *Lucia v. SEC*, which held that the appointments of SEC ALJs violated the Constitution because they were made by the SEC's staff rather than the commission itself, the SEC sent Cochran's case back for a new hearing in front of a different ALJ.

Cochran went instead to a federal district court in Texas, seeking to block the administrative proceedings entirely. She argued, among other things, that restrictions on the SEC's power to remove ALJs—who can only be terminated "for cause"—violate the Take Care Clause, which requires the president to ensure that the laws are "faithfully executed."

The district court dismissed Cochran's case, reasoning that she must first exhaust the (interminable) administrative trial process before she can get an Article III judge to weigh her constitutional arguments, which, again, challenge the very legitimacy of that administrative process. A split three-judge panel on the Fifth Circuit affirmed, but the en banc Fifth Circuit reversed, siding with Cochran and allowing her constitutional challenge to proceed.

The SEC filed a cert petition but asked the Supreme Court to hold it until the Court decides *Axon Enterprise v. FTC*, a somewhat similar structural challenge that seeks a judicial off-ramp from internal agency adjudication (see above). But Cochran urged the justices to grant review now, arguing that doing so is the only way to eliminate both the conflict among the lower courts and "the otherwise inevitable and unnecessary spin-off litigation that would accompany an FTC-specific decision in Axon." On the merits, the government seeks to have Cochran restart the administrative process at step one.

The SEC's sluggishness forced Cochran into a Catch-22: either she bets the farm on her constitutional claims by defaulting on the underlying allegations—and thereby "wins" her day in federal court—or she continues to litigate in the agency proceeding, which has lasted for more than six years with no plausible end in sight. As Cato's brief puts it, that's "a choice worthy of Camus or Kafka, not America."[16]

Election Law

The Supreme Court is finally taking up an issue that recurs with increasing frequency—and acrimony—at election time: whether there's a federal constitutional violation or remedy when a state court rewrites the electoral rules devised by the state legislature. Pointing to the Elections Clause (Article I, Section 4), proponents of

---

[16] Cato filed briefs throughout this litigation, which I signed, and went on to file a brief on the merits as well, highlighting the SEC's backlog of cases, which have been languishing for an average of six years.

cutting back state judicial authority frame the issue in stark terms: "Whether a state's judicial branch may nullify the regulations governing the 'Manner of holding Elections for Senators and Representatives . . . prescribed . . . by the Legislature thereof,' and replace them with regulations of the state courts' own devising, based on vague state constitutional provisions purportedly vesting the state judiciary with power to prescribe whatever rules it deems appropriate to ensure a 'fair' or 'free' election."

Those "vague constitutional provisions" regarding "fair or free elections" come from the North Carolina Constitution, such that the specific dispute at issue arises from the Tarheel State's redistricting after the 2020 census. In *Moore v. Harper*, the state supreme court set aside the legislatively devised congressional maps as being too gerrymandered.

Those challenging those invalidations invoke the "independent state legislature" theory, which holds that only the legislature has the power to regulate federal elections, without interference from state courts. Chief Justice William Rehnquist was an early proponent of the theory, outlining it in a concurring opinion in *Bush v. Gore* (2000) that Justices Scalia and Thomas joined. There, Rehnquist argued, the recount ordered by the Florida supreme court conflicted with election deadlines set by the state legislature.

The issue returned to the Supreme Court in 2020, when the justices both before and after that hotly contested election declined to review a Pennsylvania supreme court ruling that extended the deadline for receipt of mail-in ballots and changed the standard for their validity. In an opinion accompanying the court's order, Justice Alito (joined by Justices Thomas and Gorsuch) suggested that the state court's decision likely violated the Constitution.

A year later, a group of Democratic voters and activist groups challenged the new congressional map devised by the Republican-controlled North Carolina legislature. These plaintiffs alleged that allowing Republicans to gain as many as 10 of the state's 14 seats violated the state constitution. In February 2022, the North Carolina supreme court agreed and ordered the trial court to either approve or adopt a new map before the end of the month. The trial court adopted a new map, drawn by three experts appointed by the court.

Republican legislators then asked the U.S. Supreme Court to stay the state ruling and reinstate the original map at least for the primaries, which took place May 17. The Court turned down that emergency request, again over a dissent by Justice Alito that was joined by Justices Thomas and Gorsuch. Justice Kavanaugh wrote a concurring opinion, however, that agreed with the dissent that the Court would have to consider the independent state legislature theory "sooner or later."

Well, that time is now—but it's hard to predict what the Court will do, perhaps harder than in any other major case yet on the docket. The Court closed the door on federal constitutional challenges of partisan gerrymanders in 2019 for want of an administrable standard, which is why *Moore v. Harper* was brought under state constitutional law. Will a majority of justices now be able to decide when a state court's otherwise legitimate interpretation of state law crosses the line into depriving the legislature of its role in regulating elections?

I should also mention another election law case, to be argued in the Court's first sitting in October. *Merrill v. Milligan* considers whether Alabama's redistricting plan for its seven seats in the House of Representatives violates Section 2 of the Voting Rights Act, which prohibits racial discrimination in voting. This is the first Section 2 case since 2021's *Brnovich v. Democratic National Committee* set out a heightened standard—plaintiffs now essentially have to prove actual racial discrimination, as in most civil rights laws—for making such claims.

Criminal Law

The biggest criminal law case on the docket so far is *Percoco v. United States*, which asks whether a private citizen who holds no government office or employment—but has informal influence over governmental decisionmaking—owes a fiduciary duty to the public such that he can be convicted of honest-services fraud. The question arises in the case of Joseph Percoco, who served as the manager for New York Governor Andrew Cuomo's re-election campaign. A developer, Steven Aiello, paid Percoco $35,000 to lobby a state agency to allow Aiello's company to receive state funding without entering into an agreement with a local union. Percoco was convicted and sentenced to six years in prison. Aiello was separately convicted of bribery, but his cert petition is still pending, most likely awaiting the outcome of Percoco's case.

The Court has taken up several honest-services-fraud cases in the last decade, as well as considering other broadly worded criminal statutes that leave it to prosecutorial whim whether to prosecute behavior that might be "shady" but not technically illegal. After all, when a private citizen accepts money to convince the government to do something, we call that person a lobbyist—and it's unclear why a private citizen's close relationship to a government official (even the governor!) transforms that transaction into a bribe. Public officials hold a fiduciary obligation to act in the best interests of the public, while private citizens—even political consultants—do not.

That basic dichotomy lies at the heart of our representative democracy: Citizens are entitled to petition the government in service of their own interests, while public officials and employees are entrusted with making final decisions based on the public good as a whole. The Second Circuit's rule here made it a jury question whether a private person exercises enough de facto influence over government decisionmaking that he can be convicted of public corruption.

On the other hand, the facts of this particular case muddy the waters of those lofty principles. Percoco had served as executive deputy secretary in the governor's office and only temporarily left that state job to manage Cuomo's campaign. Despite formally leaving state employment, however, Percoco used his executive-office desk and phone, and made representations that he would return to the Cuomo administration after the election. Indeed, after Cuomo was reelected and Percoco signed his state reinstatement forms, but a few days before he officially returned to his old job, Percoco called a state official from his official desk and directed him to waive the required labor-peace agreement for Aiello's project. And Percoco continued doing other favors for Aiello, though not ones explicitly tied to the $35,000 payment.

I honestly don't know how this one will end, but pop some popcorn ahead of what could be an entertaining oral argument—though perhaps less entertaining without a two-minute hypothetical from Justice Stephen Breyer.

Immigration Law

As of this writing, the last case the Court added to its docket is one reviewing executive authority over immigration policy. Given Congress's inability to legislate in this important area, immigration is perhaps the preeminent example of "pen and phone" governance, so this is by no means the first—and won't be the last—time the justices will grapple with a claim that a president is violating the law by acting or not acting in a certain way in this context. The case also involves four controversial procedural mechanisms that seem to be on the upswing: (1) "shopping" for favorable district judges who will enter (2) nationwide injunctions, which are appealed on (3) the Supreme Court's emergency (or "shadow") docket by (4) a solicitor general seeking "cert before judgment" (without waiting for a federal circuit court to review the merits of a case).

In *United States v. Texas*, Texas and Louisiana, supported by 19 other states, allege that a Biden administration policy that sets priorities for the arrest and deportation of illegal aliens is both contrary to the Immigration and Naturalization Act (INA) and violates the Administrative Procedure Act (APA). The policy stems from a September 2021 memorandum by Department of Homeland Security (DHS) Secretary Alejandro Mayorkas—all these disputes seem to start with a memo—explaining that DHS doesn't have the resources to apprehend and deport all illegal aliens and thus instructing immigration officials to prioritize the apprehension of three groups: suspected terrorists, people who have committed serious crimes, and those caught at the border.

U.S. District Judge Drew Tipton vacated the policy on June 10, 2022, but there's disagreement between the parties whether that vacatur effectively represents a nationwide injunction against reliance on the priority-setting memo. The Fifth Circuit then rejected the Biden administration's emergency request to stay that ruling pending appeal, as did the Supreme Court, in a 5-4 vote that represented the first recorded official act by Justice Jackson, who joined the court on June 30.[17] That vote also featured a novel alignment that won't necessarily become too common, with all the male justices in the majority and all the female justices in dissent—meaning that Justice Barrett joined the progressives. Regardless of the decision to deny a stay, the Court granted the solicitor general's request to treat the filing as a petition for cert before judgment, setting the case for argument in November.

The government argues that states don't even have standing to challenge the policy because otherwise they could "challenge

---

[17] In a separate case, Arizona, Montana, and Ohio also challenged the policy in a federal district court in Ohio. The court there also ruled against the Biden administration, but the Sixth Circuit reversed that ruling.

virtually any federal policy by leveraging even a dollar's worth of incidental, indirect effect on state expenditures into a nationwide vacatur or injunction."[18] Moreover, it asserts, Judge Tipton's ruling impermissibly compels the executive branch to exercise policy discretion in a certain way, thereby disrupting DHS operations and violating the separation of powers.

The states reply that they have a right to sue over direct financial harms from a federal policy, such as certain aliens' remaining in state prisons for longer than they otherwise would. Moreover, they claim that the Mayorkas memo conflicts with Congress's specific statutory instructions regarding INA enforcement and that DHS didn't jump through the proper hoops in setting its policy (which was a stumbling block for President Trump's attempt to rescind DACA).

Those are indeed the issues the Supreme Court will be resolving: whether the states can bring the lawsuit; whether the policy is consistent with the INA and APA; and whether Tipton had the power to set aside the policy. Interestingly, the decision to hear *United States v. Texas* came less than a month after the Court ruled 5-4 in the Biden administration's favor regarding its desire to end the "remain in Mexico" policy for people seeking asylum at the southern border, which was another case brought by Texas's active office of attorney general.

Conclusion

If you get your legal news from social media, with occasional links to reporting by actual media, you'd think that the Supreme Court has made an extreme right turn in the law and is pushing ahead full steam in that direction. On this reading, its rulings on last term's big cases represent an ideological hijacking of our Constitution. What's more, because the six justices in the majority of each of those cases were appointed by Republican presidents, these radical decisions were all just partisanship disguised as law.

That take, which unfortunately comes not just from Twitter trolls and Facebook lawyers but from highly regarded law professors and journalists in all the top print and broadcast media, is disingenuous at best. To use the technical legal term, it's hogwash.

---

[18] Reply in Support of Application for Stay at 2, United States v. Texas (2022) (No. 22A17), https://bit.ly/3zByTTZ.

I don't mean that reasonable people, legally trained or otherwise, can't disagree on these cases, or that anyone who contradicts my analysis is stupid or politically motivated. To the contrary, it's those attacking the Court's legitimacy and calling the justices partisan hacks who seem to believe that the only way to reach the results we've seen is to act in bad faith. That sort of attitude isn't healthy for our republic, particularly at a time when institutional trust is already low and political tribalism increasingly prevents either side from accepting electoral outcomes.

Although I don't have any magic fixes for our national discord, there's a way to understand what's going on at the Court as a very deep and serious legal dispute that nevertheless easily fits within the parameters of the rule of law. All one has to do is take at face value the originalism and textualism that the Court's majority applies. It's perfectly fine to disagree with that methodology or its application, but there's no more evidence that Justices Roberts, Thomas, Alito, Gorsuch, Kavanaugh, and Barrett are results-oriented than that Justices Breyer, Sotomayor, and Kagan are.

To be sure, some on the right accuse the latter three of acting on their policy preferences, but there's no reason to question their good faith either. They simply have a different way of looking at the law, especially in the politically sensitive cases with ideological salience. Perhaps many of the Court's critics who align with the liberal justices think that all jurists are results-oriented and vote their values— *which is illegitimate when going in a conservative direction.* I'm not versed enough in psychology to know if that kind of "projection" is at play, but it's really no way to run a popsicle stand.

In no sane world are the legal rules announced in last term's big cases, or those proposed in the high-profile cases I analyze above, radical. People (and lawyers) can debate them in good faith, but there's simply nothing extreme about them. The policy consequences may or may not be significant, but that's not the constitutional question. And with abortion, the issue that's gotten the most attention, it's healthier for us to fight democratically. That's what most countries have done—Europe generally settled at restrictions after 12 or 14 weeks, which is more conservative than the Mississippi law that the Supreme Court upheld—and what would've happened in the United States had *Roe v. Wade* not short-circuited that process nearly 50 years ago.

As the *Wall Street Journal* put it, "The fury of the left's reaction isn't merely about guns and abortion. It reflects their grief at having lost the Court as the vehicle for achieving policy goals they can't get through legislatures."[19] It's an understandable impulse but not one that fairly impugns the highest court in the land.

I for one am here for a further unraveling of the Burger Court.

---

[19] The Justices Don't Lie to the Senate, Wall St. J., June 26, 2022, https://on.wsj. com/3ozon9G.

Contributors

Jonathan H. Adler is the inaugural Johan Verheij Memorial Professor of Law and the founding director of the Coleman P. Burke Center for Environmental Law at the Case Western Reserve University School of Law, where he teaches courses in environmental, administrative, and constitutional law. He is the author or editor of seven books, including *Marijuana Federalism: Uncle Sam and Mary Jane* (2020), *Business and the Roberts Court* (2016), and *Rebuilding the Ark: New Perspectives on Endangered Species Act Reform* (2011). His articles have appeared in publications ranging from the *Harvard Environmental Law Review* and *Yale Journal on Regulation* to the *Wall Street Journal* and *New York Times*. He has testified before Congress a dozen times, and his work has been cited in the U.S. Supreme Court. A 2021 study identified Adler as the fifth most cited legal academic in administrative and environmental law from 2016 to 2020. In 2004, he received the Paul M. Bator Award, given annually by the Federalist Society for Law and Policy Studies to an academic under 40 for excellence in teaching, scholarship, and commitment to students. Prior to joining the faculty at Case Western Reserve, Adler clerked for the Honorable David B. Sentelle on the U.S. Court of Appeals for the D.C. Circuit. From 1991 to 2000, Adler worked at the Competitive Enterprise Institute, a free-market research and advocacy group in Washington, D.C., where he directed CEI's environmental studies program. He holds a B.A. *magna cum laude* from Yale University and a J.D. *summa cum laude* from the George Mason University School of Law.

Enrique Armijo is a professor of law at Elon University School of Law and a faculty affiliate of the Yale Law School Information Society Project and the UNC-Chapel Hill Center for Information, Technology, and Public Life. He teaches and researches in the areas of the First Amendment, constitutional law, torts, administrative law, media and internet law, and international freedom of expression. His current scholarship addresses the interaction between new technologies and free speech. His scholarly work has recently appeared in the *Boston University Law Review*, the *Florida Law Review*, the *Boston College Law Review*, the *Washington & Lee Law Review*, the *North Carolina Law Review*, the peer-reviewed *Communication Law and Policy and Political Science Quarterly*, and other journals. His work has been cited by the Federal Communications Commission, the Federal Election Commission, and other agencies, and in testimony before the U.S. Senate Committee on Governmental Affairs. He also has provided advice on media and internet law reform to governments, stakeholders and NGOs located around the world, including in Africa, Asia, and the Middle East. Most recently, he has worked on media and communications reform projects in Myanmar (Burma) for the U.S. Department of State with Annenberg's Center for Global Communications Studies at the University of Pennsylvania. Prior to joining Elon Law, Armijo practiced with Covington & Burling LLP in Washington, D.C., where he advised journalists, news organizations and trade associations on media law-related issues. Armijo clerked for the Honorable Karen LeCraft Henderson at the U.S. Court of Appeals for the D.C. Circuit after law school. He earned a J.D. from the University of North Carolina, where he was editor-in-chief of the *North Carolina Law Review*.

Rachel E. Barkow is the vice dean, Charles Seligson Professor of Law, and faculty director of the Peter L. Zimroth Center on the Administration of Criminal Law at New York University School of Law. Her scholarship focuses on applying the lessons and theory of administrative and constitutional law to the administration of criminal justice. She has written more than 20 articles, is co-author of one of the country's leading criminal law casebooks, and is recognized as one of the country's leading experts on criminal law and policy. Her book, *Prisoners of Politics: Breaking the Cycle of Mass Incarceration* (2019), demonstrates the ways in which our current criminal justice policies undermine public safety and explains how we can get better outcomes by relying less on a flawed political process and instead making institutional changes that allow data and evidence to guide our choices while respecting important constitutional limits. She received the NYU Distinguished Teaching Award in 2013 and the law school's Podell Distinguished Teaching Award in 2007. In June 2013, the U.S. Senate confirmed her as a member of the United States

Sentencing Commission. She has been a member of the Manhattan District Attorney's Office Conviction Integrity Policy Advisory Panel since 2010. In 2015, she co-founded a clemency resource center that obtained sentencing commutations for 96 people as part of President Barack Obama's clemency initiative. For her work on clemency with NYU students, she received the NYU Making a Difference Award, given to those who have made a profound and lasting impact for the better on the city, region, nation, or globe. After graduating from Northwestern University, Barkow attended Harvard Law School, where she won the Sears Prize. She served as a law clerk to Judge Laurence H. Silberman of the U.S. Court of Appeals for the D.C. Circuit and Justice Antonin Scalia of the U.S. Supreme Court. Barkow was an associate at Kellogg, Huber, Hansen, Todd, Evans & Figel in Washington, D.C., before joining the NYU Law faculty.

Evan D. Bernick is an assistant professor of law at Northern Illinois University College of Law where he teaches courses in constitutional law, criminal law, criminal procedure, administrative law, and legislation. From 2020 to 2021, he was a visiting professor at the Georgetown University Law Center and the executive director of the Georgetown Center for the Constitution. Before that, he served as a clerk to Judge Diane S. Sykes of the U.S. Court of Appeals for the Seventh Circuit. From April 2017 to April 2019, he was a visiting lecturer at Georgetown and a resident fellow of the Center for the Constitution. His scholarship covers a range of topics, from constitutional law, to philosophy of law, to social movements, to law enforcement. He has published with the *Georgetown Law Journal*, the *Notre Dame Law Review*, the *William and Mary Law Review* and the *George Mason Law Review*, among other journals. With Professor Randy E. Barnett, he co-authored *The Original Meaning of the Fourteenth Amendment: Its Letter and Spirit* (2021), published by Harvard University Press. Bernick received his bachelor's degree in 2008 from the University of Chicago, where he studied philosophy and graduated with honors. He received his J.D. in 2011 from the University of Chicago Law School.

Thomas A. Berry is a research fellow in the Cato Institute's Robert A. Levy Center for Constitutional Studies and managing editor of the *Cato Supreme Court Review*. Before joining Cato, he was an attorney at Pacific Legal Foundation and clerked for Judge E. Grady Jolly of the

U.S. Court of Appeals for the Fifth Circuit. His academic work has appeared in *NYU Journal of Law and Liberty, Washington and Lee Law Review Online, Federalist Society Review,* and the *Cato Supreme Court Review.* His popular writing has appeared in the *Wall Street Journal, National Law Journal, Investor's Business Daily, Reason,* CNN, *National Review Online, Lawfare,* and *The Hill.* He has testified before the U.S. Senate Subcommittee on Federal Spending Oversight and Emergency Management, and his work has been cited by the U.S. District Court for the District of Columbia. Berry holds a J.D. from Stanford Law School, where he was a senior editor on the *Stanford Law and Policy Review* and a Bradley Student Fellow in the Stanford Constitutional Law Center. He graduated with a B.A. in liberal arts from St. John's College, Santa Fe.

Michael Bindas is a senior attorney with the Institute for Justice (IJ) and leads IJ's educational-choice team. In this role, he oversees a talented group of IJ attorneys who help policymakers design constitutionally defensible educational-choice programs and who defend those programs in courtrooms nationwide. He argued on behalf of petitioners before the U.S. Supreme Court in *Carson v. Makin* and was part of the litigation team in *Espinoza v. Montana Department of Revenue,* two landmark cases concerning educational-choice programs. Michael led IJ's defense of the Choice Scholarship Program for elementary and secondary students in Douglas County, Colorado, and he successfully challenged Washington's denial of special education services to children in religious schools, as well as the state's exclusion of sectarian options from its state work-study program. Prior to leading IJ's educational-choice team, he litigated extensively to secure economic liberty, property rights, and freedom of speech throughout the nation. Prior to joining IJ, he spent three years as an attorney with Perkins Coie LLP. He is a former law clerk to Judge Rhesa Hawkins Barksdale of the U.S. Court of Appeals for the Fifth Circuit and served as an engineer officer in the United States Army and Pennsylvania Army National Guard before beginning his legal career. Bindas received his law degree *cum laude* from the University of Pennsylvania Law School in 2001, where he served as articles editor for the *Journal of Constitutional Law* and was elected to the Order of the Coif. He received his undergraduate degree from the United States Military Academy at West Point in 1995.

Trevor Burrus is a research fellow in the Cato Institute's Robert A. Levy Center for Constitutional Studies and editor-in-chief of the *Cato Supreme Court Review*. His research interests include constitutional law, civil and criminal law, legal and political philosophy, legal history, and the interface between science and public policy. His academic work has appeared in journals such as the *Harvard Journal of Law & Public Policy*, *NYU Journal of Law & Liberty*, *NYU Annual Survey of American Law*, *Syracuse Law Review*, and many others. His popular writing has appeared in the *Washington Post*, *New York Times* (online), *USA Today*, *Forbes*, *Huffington Post*, and others. Burrus lectures regularly on behalf of the Federalist Society, the Institute for Humane Studies, the Foundation for Economics Education, and other organizations, and he frequently appears on major media outlets. He is the co-host of "Free Thoughts," a weekly podcast that covers topics in libertarian theory, history, and philosophy. He is the editor of *A Conspiracy against Obamacare* (2013) and *Deep Commitments: The Past, Present, and Future of Religious Liberty* (2017). Burrus holds a B.A. in philosophy from the University of Colorado at Boulder and a J.D. from the University of Denver Sturm College of Law.

Kelly K. Dineen Gillespie is an associate professor of law and the director of the health law program at Creighton University School of Law, where she teaches health care law, bioethics, torts, and public health law seminars that have focused on pandemic ethics or drug policy. She has a secondary appointment as a professor of medical humanities at the Creighton University School of Medicine. She holds a Ph.D, with distinction, in health care ethics from Saint Louis University, as well as a J.D., with a concentration in health care law. Before attending law school, she worked as a nurse in neurosurgery and transplant ICUs, clinical research, as well as with functional neurosurgeons caring for people with chronic persistent pain and movement disorders with implanted programmable medical devices. After law school, Gillespie practiced in the health law practice group at Husch Blackwell and later held academic and administrative roles at Saint Louis University. She is an expert on health law, ethics, and policy, and she researches and writes on issues related to public health policy, drug use and controlled substances prescribing, pandemic ethics, and health inequities and discrimination. Her work is highly interdisciplinary, and her recent work has focused on the impact of harm-inducing laws and biased decision-making by health care providers on people with substance use disorders, chronic pain, and in other stigmatized and minoritized populations. Gillespie has served by invitation for both the American Bar Association and the American Health Lawyers Association on working groups on the opioid related crises. She is the co-chair of the American Bar Association's Opioid Crisis Task Force, for which she organized the first ever meeting on the overdose crisis co-sponsored by the American Bar Association, the American Medical Association, and the American Society of Addiction Medicine in 2021. Recently, she co-authored two amici briefs on behalf of U.S. professors of health law and policy before the United States Supreme Court in *Ruan v. United States*. Her work has been published in law and interdisciplinary journals including *Arizona State Law Review, Kansas Law Review, American Journal of Bioethics, Journal of Addiction Medicine, Journal of Law, Medicine & Ethics, Hasting Center Reports*, and others. She is the co-editor and author of several chapters in *Prescription Drug Diversion and Pain: History, Policy, and Treatment* (2018), published by Oxford University Press. She has been interviewed by many media outlets.

Elizabeth Goitein is senior director of the Brennan Center for Justice's Liberty and National Security Program. She is a nationally recognized expert on presidential emergency powers, government surveillance, and government secrecy. Her writing has been featured in major newspapers and magazines including the *New York Times, Washington Post, Wall Street Journal, USA Today, Los Angeles Times, The Atlantic,* and *The New Republic,* and she has appeared frequently in major media outlets. She has testified on several occasions before the Senate and House Judiciary Committees. Before coming to the Brennan Center, Goitein served as counsel to Senator Russ Feingold, chairman of the Constitution Subcommittee of the Senate Judiciary Committee, and as a trial attorney in the Federal Programs Branch of the Civil Division of the Department of Justice. Goitein graduated from Yale Law School and clerked for Judge Michael Daly Hawkins on the U.S. Court of Appeals for the Ninth Circuit. In 2021–2022, she was a member of the inaugural class of Senior Practitioner Fellows at the University of Chicago's Center for Effective Government.

David B. Kopel is an adjunct professor at the University of Denver Strum College of Law, an adjunct scholar with the Cato Institute, and research director of the Independence Institute, a public policy research organization in Denver, Colorado. He is also vice-chair of the Colorado State Advisory Committee to the U.S. Commission on Civil Rights, and a trustee of the Anne S.K. Brown Military History Collection at the Brown University Library. Kopel is one of several contributors to the *Volokh Conspiracy*. He has written hundreds of opinion articles for periodicals such as the *Wall Street Journal*, *New York Times*, *Los Angeles Times*, and *Denver Post*. He is the author of 17 books, and over 100 scholarly articles published in journals from Harvard, Yale, the University of Michigan, University of Pennsylvania, Johns Hopkins, Brown University, and others. His topics include constitutional law, international law, criminal justice, technology, antitrust, media issues, and environmental policy. He has contributed entries to 13 academic encyclopedias and served on the board of editors for one. His research has been cited by 22 state court appellate opinions, 15 federal circuit court of appeals opinions (including opinions by Judges Kavanaugh and Gorsuch), and over 700 law review articles. In 2008, he appeared before the United States Supreme Court as part of the team presenting the oral argument in *District of Columbia v. Heller*. His *Heller* amicus brief for a coalition of law enforcement organizations and district attorneys was cited four times in the Court's opinions. His brief in *McDonald v. Chicago* was cited by Justice Alito's plurality opinion, and twice by Justice Stevens's dissent. He has testified numerous times before Congress and state legislatures, including before the U.S. Senate Judiciary Committee on the Supreme Court nominations of Elena Kagan and Sonia Sotomayor. Before joining the Independence Institute, he served as an assistant attorney general for the state of Colorado, dealing with enforcement of hazardous waste, Superfund, and other environmental laws. In 1998–1999, he served as an adjunct professor of law at New York University. From 2001 to 2009 he was a media columnist for the *Rocky Mountain News*.

Jennifer L. Mascott is an assistant professor of law and co-executive director of the C. Boyden Gray Center for the Study of the Administrative State at the Antonin Scalia Law School. She writes in the areas of administrative law, constitutional law, and the separation of powers.

Her scholarship has been cited extensively by the Supreme Court and has been published in the *Stanford Law Review,* the *Supreme Court Review* by the University of Chicago Press, the *George Washington Law Review,* the *BYU Law Review,* and the *George Mason Law Review,* among other journals. In 2022 she joined as co-author of *Administrative Law: Cases and Materials* for the 2022 annual supplement and is a permanent commentator at the *Yale Journal on Regulation's Notice and Comment* blog. Mascott serves as a public member of the Administrative Conference of the United States and as a vice chair of the Constitutional Law and Separation of Powers Committee within the ABA's Section of Administrative Law and Regulatory Practice. She has testified in the U.S. Senate and U.S. House on topics ranging from executive privilege to regulatory reform to Supreme Court jurisdiction and has testified during the confirmation hearings for two U.S. Supreme Court justices. She is the founder of the Separation of Powers Clinic at the Scalia Law School and developed the congressional education program, Article I Venture, through the law school's Gray Center, where she holds educational seminars for U.S. Senate and House policy and legal staff on structural constitutional doctrines. She regularly provides commentary related to her academic expertise in the national media and trade press. She has published in the *Wall Street Journal* and *Washington Post* and has been quoted or cited in many print outlets. Separate from her formal responsibilities in those two roles, Mascott assisted with aspects of Justice Amy Coney Barrett's confirmation process and argued cases in federal appellate and trial courts during her government service. Mascott is a former law clerk to Supreme Court Justice Clarence Thomas and to then-Judge Brett M. Kavanaugh, formerly of the U.S. Court of Appeals for the D.C. Circuit. She graduated *summa cum laude* from the George Washington University Law School, where she earned the highest cumulative graduating GPA on record at the law school.

R. Trent McCotter is a partner with Boyden Gray & Associates. He previously served as deputy associate attorney general of the United States and as an assistant U.S. attorney, where he oversaw the DOJ's Civil Appellate and Federal Programs branches, which are responsible for defending nearly all major litigation against the federal government. He formulated litigation strategy for high-profile administrative and constitutional matters and personally argued eleven federal appeals. McCotter has authored and submitted nearly 50 briefs to the U.S. Supreme Court, raising issues of sovereignty, constitutional rights, due process, and criminal law. During his time with the Department of Justice, he assisted with the confirmations of two Supreme Court justices and over a dozen lower-court justices. McCotter served as an inaugural clerk to Judge Steven J. Menashi on the U.S. Court of Appeals for the Second Circuit and also clerked for Judge R. Lanier Anderson III on the U.S. Court of Appeals for the Eleventh Circuit. He graduated *summa cum laude* from the University of North Carolina at Chapel Hill, with a degree in economics, and graduated *magna cum laude* from the University of North Carolina School of Law, where he received eight book awards for the highest grade in a class and served as an articles editor on the *North Carolina Law Review*.

Ilya Shapiro is a senior fellow and director of constitutional studies at the Manhattan Institute. Previously he was executive director and senior lecturer at the Georgetown Center for the Constitution, and before that a vice president of the Cato Institute, director of Cato's Robert A. Levy Center for Constitutional Studies, and publisher of the Cato Supreme Court Review. Shapiro is the author of *Supreme Disorder: Judicial Nominations and the Politics of America's Highest Court* (2020), coauthor of *Religious Liberties for Corporations? Hobby Lobby, the Affordable Care Act, and the Constitution* (2014), and editor of 11 volumes of the *Cato Supreme Court Review*. He has contributed to a variety of academic, popular, and professional publications, including the *Wall Street Journal*, the *Harvard Journal of Law & Public Policy*, *Washington Post*, *Los Angeles Times*, *USA Today*, *National Review*, and *Newsweek*. Shapiro has testified many times before Congress and state legislatures and has filed more than 500 amicus curiae "friend of the court" briefs in the Supreme Court. He lectures regularly on behalf of the Federalist Society, is a member of the board of fellows of the Jewish Policy Center, was an inaugural Washington Fellow at the National Review Institute, and has been an adjunct law professor at the George Washington University and University of Mississippi. He is also the chairman of the board of advisers of the Mississippi Justice Institute, a barrister in the Edward Coke Appellate Inn of Court, and a member of the Virginia Advisory Committee to the U.S. Commission on Civil Rights. Earlier in his career, Shapiro was a special assistant/adviser to the Multi-National Force in Iraq on rule-of-law issues and practiced at Patton Boggs and Cleary Gottlieb. Before entering private practice, he clerked for Judge E. Grady Jolly of the U.S. Court of Appeals for the Fifth Circuit. He holds an A.B. from Princeton University, an MSc from the London School of Economics, and a J.D. from the University of Chicago Law School.

Ilya Somin is a professor of law at George Mason University. His research focuses on constitutional law, property law, democratic theory, federalism, and migration rights. He is the author of *Free to Move: Foot Voting, Migration, and Political Freedom* (2020), *Democracy and Political Ignorance: Why Smaller Government is Smarter* (2nd ed. 2016), and *The Grasping Hand: Kelo v. City of New London and the Limits of Eminent Domain* (2015). His work has appeared in numerous scholarly journals, including the *Yale Law Journal, Stanford Law Review, Northwestern University Law Review, Georgetown Law Journal, Critical Review,* and others. He has also published articles in a variety of popular press outlets, including the *New York Times, Washington Post, Wall Street Journal, Los Angeles Times, CNN, The Atlantic, USA Today,* and others. His writings have been cited in decisions by the United States Supreme Court, multiple state supreme courts and lower federal courts, and the Supreme Court of Israel. He has testified on the use of drones for targeted killing in the War on Terror before the U.S. Senate Judiciary Subcommittee on the Constitution, Civil Rights, and Human Rights. In 2009, he testified on property rights issues at the U.S. Senate Judiciary Committee confirmation hearings for Supreme Court Justice Sonia Sotomayor. He writes regularly for the popular *Volokh Conspiracy* law and politics blog.

William Yeatman is a research fellow in the Cato Institute's Robert A. Levy Center for Constitutional Studies, where he works on administrative law, constitutional structure, and regulatory reform. He has testified many times before Congress and state legislatures, and he is a frequent contributor to major media outlets. His scholarly work has appeared in academic journals like the *Georgetown Law Journal* and *Appalachian Natural Resources Law Journal,* and his popular writing has appeared in the *Wall Street Journal, Foreign Policy, Bloomberg,* and elsewhere. Before joining Cato, he specialized in environmental policy at the Competitive Enterprise Institute. From 2004 to 2006, he served as a Peace Corps volunteer in the Kyrgyz Republic. Yeatman holds a B.A. in environmental sciences from the University of Virginia, an M.A. in international studies from the Denver University Graduate School of International Studies, and a J.D. from the Georgetown University Law Center.